THE EXCLUSION OF WOMEN FROM THE PRIESTHOOD:
Divine Law or Sex Discrimination?

*A historical investigation of the Juridical
and doctrinal foundations of the Code of
Canon Law, canon 968, §1*

by

IDA RAMING

translated by

NORMAN R. ADAMS

with a preface by
Arlene & Leonard Swidler

The Scarecrow Press, Inc.
Metuchen, N.J.   1976

Library of Congress Cataloging in Publication Data

Raming, Ida.
    The exclusion of women from the priesthood.

    Translation of Der Ausschluss der Frau vom priester-
lichen Amt.
    Bibliography: p.
    Includes index.
    1. Women--Legal status, laws, etc. (Canon law)
2. Clergy (Canon law) I. Title.
Law   262'.14   76-23322
ISBN 0-8108-0957-5

Manufactured in the United States of America

TRANSLATOR'S ACKNOWLEDGMENTS

I wish to acknowledge the abundant help I have received in translating Dr. Raming's book from Dr. Rudolf Herrig, of Westminster College, and Dr. James Biechler, of La Salle College, both of whom gave generously of their time and expertise. Dr. Raming herself also made suggestions. I am of course responsible for any mistakes that may still remain. Thanks are due to Arlene and Leonard Swidler for writing the preface and for other advice and assistance during the preparation of the volume. I am also grateful to Dr. John Van Hook, of Siena College, and to the library and staff of St. Anthony-on-Hudson, who went beyond the call of duty in assisting me. Finally, my wife, Edna, not only helped with the index and the proof, but was throughout a source of encouragement.

Norman R. Adams
Norton Hill, N.Y.
December, 1975

CONTENTS

Translator's Acknowledgments   iii

Preface   (Arlene and Leonard Swidler)   vii

Introduction   1

Part I.   CANON LAW BACKGROUND   5
       Foundation of the Code of Canon Law, Canon 968,
       § 1, in the Corpus Iuris Canonici

1.   Gratian's Decretum as Source for Sex
     Discrimination in the Priesthood   7

     a.   Gratian's Sources   7
     b.   Gratian's Opinion   26
     c.   Source of Discrimination: Denigration of
        Women   28
     d.   Influence of the Church Fathers   33
     e.   Gratian's Use of Roman Law   38

2.   Survey of the Position of Women According to
     Roman Law   40

     a.   Roman Family Law   40
     b.   General Civil Law   41
     c.   Influence on Gratian   43

3.   Subsequent Influence of Gratian's Decretum on
     the Place of Women in the Church   45

     a.   Its Authority   45
     b.   The Decretists   47

4.   Decretals as Source for Sex Discrimination in
     the Priesthood   70

     a.   The Decretals of Gregory IX   70
     b.   The Decretalists   78

5. Summary of the Most Significant Conclusions   94

6. Exegetical Excursus on the (Patristic) Scriptural
   Proof for the Subordination of Women   98

Part II.   DOCTRINE   117

7. The Traditional Conception of the Priesthood--
   An Argument for the Exclusion of Women   117

   a. Traditional Understanding of Ecclesiastical
       Office   117
   b. A Critique   120

8. Equal Rights for Women in the Church Today--
   A Requirement of Justice and the Condition for
   Their Full Development and Cooperation   130

Chapter Notes   135

Bibliography of Sources   255

Index   259

PREFACE

The study of canon law is something anyone interested in the renewal of the Catholic Church cannot afford to neglect. All institutions of any longevity naturally develop a body of law, though with varying degrees of formality. Since the Roman Catholic Church has the great legal traditions of both Judaism and the Roman Empire as part of its heritage, the place of law in its life should be expected to be substantial. As in all human affairs, this is not something in itself to be regretted. In modern civil society we express the desire to be governed not by people but by law, hopefully choosing thereby order rather than caprice. Law is seen as an essential instrument, an indispensable means, to a successful society. To be effective, however, the law must always remain alive, growing, responsive to the needs of the people it governs and thereby serves. But to be made responsive, the law must first be studied and understood. This is also true when the question addressed is how women, one-half the People of God, can exercise their full talents in and through the Church, including all its clerical offices. It is to an essential part of this task of research and understanding that Dr. Ida Raming has devoted herself in this book.

Dr. Raming's research uncovers the disturbing fact that the ecclesiastical law which restricts Holy Orders to baptized males (canon 968, § 1) is largely based on forgeries, mistaken identities, and suppressions. The patriarch of canon law, Gratian, laid the foundation of the science of canon law with his massive work of codification, the Decretum, in the 12th century (1140). In this work Gratian formulated a number of laws restrictive to women on the assumption that women as such were inferior human beings. Among the legal sources for these laws and this assumption, he cited as authoritative the Pseudo-Isidorian Decretals, which he did not know were largely forgeries. Another "authoritative" source used against women by Gratian were the decrees of the Council of Carthage (A.D. 389) as he found them in the Statuta Ecclesiae Antiqua. We now know that the Statuta were composed by Gennadius of Marseille between 476 and 485, and the quotations Gratian used are not at all from a (non-existent) Council of Carthage in A.D. 389, or any other Council--the legal basis of Gratian's restrictive law (and of course all subsequent canon law on this matter) is thus undermined.

Gratian also based some of his restrictive laws against women on laws of the Roman Empire. His references are authentic enough, but what is depressing is his habit of choosing only those Roman laws which supported the subordination of women and ignoring those which supported the equality of women. He tended, moreover, to pick out the earlier Roman laws, more restrictive of women, rather than the later ones, which tended to liberate women. A similar predisposition was also exhibited in Gratian's use of the decree from the Ecumenical Council of Chalcedon (A.D. 451). This authentic decree stated, "Deaconesses may not be ordained (ordinari) before forty years of age ..." and went on to speak about their remaining celibate after ordination. Gratian did record the decree, but only as evidence that "those who take the vow of celibacy may not marry." The fact of the ordination of women as deaconesses was ignored by him here, and downgraded to a non-clerical vow elsewhere, even though the original Greek of the Council decree used the proper technical term, cheirontonia, for ordaining deaconesses.

Indeed, in the ancient Byzantine liturgy the ordination of the deaconess, which took place between that of the deacon and the sub-deacon, exactly paralleled the deacon's: "The archbishop likewise having placed his hands on the head of the (woman) to be ordained prayed thus (homoiōs ho archiepiskopos tēn cheira epi tēn kephalēn cheirotonoumenēs epeuchetai koutōs): Lord and Ruler ... grant the grace of your Holy Spirit to your handmaid ... and fill (her) with the grace of the diaconate (kai tēn tēs diakonias apoplērōsai charin)--as you gave the grace of the diaconate to your Phoebe--whom you called to the work of this public divine service (hēn ekalesas eis to ergon tēs leitourgias)." The deaconess was then invested with the stole (stolam diaconicam in the Latin translation), received the holy chalice (to hagion potērion) and placed it on the "holy table," altar (apotithetai en tē hagia trapedzē).

But all this clear documentation of the full ordination

of women as deaconesses is overlooked by Gratian and most of his Latin successors. Perhaps the single most important exception is to be found in the writing of Joannes Teutonicus, whose work early in the 13th century became the Glossa Ordinaria commentary on Gratian's Decretum. There Joannes Teutonicus records the opinion of canonists who disagree with him and insist that women can be ordained because anyone who has been baptized can be ordained (post baptismum quilibet potest ordinari). Again it is depressing to learn from Dr. Raming's research that the collection of canon law, Corpus Juris Canonici, which served as a source book for the 1917 Code of Canon Law now in force, records only the anti-woman opinion of Joannes Teutonicus and neglects entirely any reference to this opposite opinion recorded by him.

Ultimately, Dr. Raming finds, all the arguments against the ordination of women are founded on the assumption that women are inferior to men and that consequently they ought to--and in fact do--live in a state of subjection (in statu subjectionis) to men. This assumption surfaces again and again in the writings of canonists, theologians, Fathers of the Church, and even biblical writers. Even to a late 20th-century thinker such an assumption would not seem strange. But what might be surprising to her or him is the fact that these earlier Christian writers expressed that assumption with absolutely no embarrassment. To them it was as perfectly clear that women were inferior to men as, say, that the sun rose in the East and set in the West. With extremely rare exceptions, it is only after the Enlightenment and the subsequent feminist movement in the 19th century that some Christian, as well as other, writers began to be discomfited and attempted to argue that far from treating women in an inferior manner, Christianity had in fact raised the status of women.

To develop this argument Christian scholars usually described the status of women in the Greco-Roman world into which Christianity was born as extremely low and depraved. This was a difficult feat to accomplish for it was clear from an abundance of documents that many women in the Hellenistic and Imperial Roman world were quite unrestricted in many facets of private, social, economic and religious life: they could marry or divorce as they decided, mix freely in society, own and inherit property as a man did, take leading, indeed, priestly, roles in religion. But this difficulty was usually overcome by modern Christian

scholars with a double attack: On the one hand the Greco-
Roman freedom for women was depicted not as something
good, or even as a mixed value, but as an essentially evil
kind of licentiousness that was leading women, and men and
the world, to perdition. For such a view the writings of
the Fathers of the Church (is it strange that there are no
Mothers of the Church? In parallel fashion, one reads almost solely of the Desert Fathers, although there were already 20,000 Desert Mothers when St. Pachomius first began
to gather his male followers) provided a storehouse of rail-
liery against both the immoral license of pagan Roman society and woman's central role in it.

On the other hand these modern Christian scholars
almost inevitably, and paradoxically, also brought forth documentation to show how restricted and unfree a status women
had in the Greco-Roman world. Unfortunately, for their argument, all of this documentation concerns the Rome of two
or three hundred years before Christ and the Greece of four
or five hundred years B.C. The historical facts are that
an ever-growing women's liberation movement in the Greek
world from around 300 B.C. onward continued to deepen and
broaden almost until the demise of the Roman empire in the
West--that is, until the public triumph of Christianity; the
status of women went into severe decline thereafter. Thus,
in reality, Christianity (but not Jesus) heralded not a raising
but a lowering of the status of women, and in many ways
significantly contributed to that decline.

A modern Christian of course can, without too much
difficulty, admit that there have been errors committed in
the name of Christianity and the Church, even horrors such
as conversions by the sword, and the Inquisition. The difficulty becomes more acute, however, when the problem is
moved back into the New Testament. What does the believing Christian do with St. Paul's statement: "The women
should keep silence in the churches" (1 Cor. 14:34)? Or,
"A man ... is the image of God and reflects God's glory;
but woman is the reflection of man's glory" (1 Cor. 11:7--
a reference to Gen. 1:27, "God created man in his own
image")? Especially when the same St. Paul, speaking of
how men and women should conduct themselves at services,
refers to a "woman who prays or prophesies with her head
unveiled ..." (1 Cor. 11:5), clearly assuming women do
rightfully pray or prophesy aloud in church. Or again,
"there is neither Jew nor Greek, there is neither slave nor
free, there is neither male nor female; for you are all one
in Christ Jesus" (Gal. 3:28).

Dr. Raming carefully analyzes these and other pertinent passages, applying two basic accepted modern exegetical principles. First, a careful distinction has to be made
between the central religious message of a passage and the
contingent cultural vehicle, including scientific, social and
moral assumptions of the New Testament author's time and
place--thus Paul's silencing of women is seen not as part of
the Gospel, but of Paul's contingent moral values, like his
acceptance of slavery. Second, if an earlier Scripture statement or story is used by a later Scripture author, the original passage still must properly be understood within the context of its own time--thus modern exegesis understands that
Gen. 1:27 was originally an egalitarian statement ("God
created humanity (ha adam) in his own image ... male and
female he created them") and Paul's use of it in 1 Cor. 11:7
in a superior/inferior fashion is a reflection of the contingent use of Scripture of his time and culture, namely, that
of a Pharisaic Jew living in an "apocalyptic" era.

Dr. Raming finds, again rather depressingly, that
Catholic exegetes, even with the approval of Vatican documents, have long been able and willing to make the distinction called for by the first principle in such areas as slavery, but not in the question of the status of women. The
metaphorical rather than the literal understanding of Genesis,
demanded by the second principle, has become acceptable in
many areas, to Catholic scholars, and even to the Roman
Biblical Commission, but in considering the creation of woman and man there is still among them a clinging to the assumption of an historical, literal understanding of the story
of Adam and Eve, with the implication of man's superiority
over woman. Again, as so often throughout history, a sort
of second standard is applied to women.

The Christian subordination of women on a biblical,
especially New Testament, basis is particularly puzzling in
light of Jesus' attitude toward women. In a religious and
social culture that forbade men to speak to women, even
wives, in public, in effect prohibited women from studying
Scripture, refused to allow any legal standing to the testimony of women, made women ritually unclean and untouch-
able during their menses, and encouraged men to pray daily,
"Praised be God for not having made me a woman," Jesus
never said or did anything that indicated he thought of women as inferior to men. Instead he often went out of his
way to breach the misogynist customs of his time. Jesus
frequently spoke to women in public (cf. John 4:1ff.), per-

mitted women of ill-repute to touch him (Luke 7:36-50), had
women disciples (Luke 8:1-3), rejected the blood taboo (Mark
5:24-34; Matthew 9:18-26; Luke 8:40-56), insisted women had
a vocation to the intellectual life as a rabbinical disciple
(Luke 10:38-42), first revealed himself to women as the
Messiah (Luke 1:40-42) and as the Resurrection (John 11:25),
appeared as the Risen One first to women (Matthew 28:9),
and sent women to give testimony, to be "evangelists," of
the most important event of his life, his resurrection (Matthew 28:10; John 20:17).

In comparing Jesus' attitude toward women with that
found in the Pauline writings, and the first epistle attributed
to Peter, one finds a dramatic contrast. Jesus' attitude is
totally positive, even aggressively so, whereas the attitude
expressed in the Pauline, and Petrine, epistles is ambivalent,
and at times clearly subordinationist, apparently flowing for
the most part from Paul's rabbinic Jewish background. What
is puzzling here is that, although a strong anti-Jewish and
pro-Greek trend quickly developed in Christianity as it spread
throughout the gentile world, unfortunately leading to a rejection of much of Jesus' and Christianity's Jewish heritage,
on the subject of women it was the Hellenic stance which was
rejected. Why, with such a clear difference in attitude expressed by Jesus and by some of the Pauline writings, did
Christianity's choice go not to Jesus but to the Pauline writings? Apparently the rigid patriarchal system, which Jesus
did his best to dismantle (cf. Matthew 10:37f.; Luke 14:26),
was so pervasive in the lives of the majority of Christians
that they were blind to this choice; they automatically gravi-
tated toward the most restrictive, subordinationist passages
of the New Testament.

Perhaps the most depressing revelation of Dr. Raming's book is that this restrictive attitude did not simply
overcome the liberationist thrust of Jesus' life and "Good
News" and then stabilize itself on a sort of plateau. Rather,
the restrictiveness grew. For Jesus, Mary Magdalene was
an apostle to the apostles ("Go to the brethren and tell
them...," John 20:17; Matthew 28;9). For Paul, Phoebe
was a woman deacon, not a deaconess (diakonon, not diakonissa, Rom. 16:2) and a ruler (prostatis--nowhere in Greek
literature does this word mean anything like "helper," as it
usually is translated here) over many, and even Paul himself
(Rom. 16:2; see the Greek rather than translations). After
the third century women could be deaconesses (diakonissa),
a Holy Order lesser in status than that of the male deacon.

By the early middle ages even this Holy Order was lost to women in the West. In the 12th century Gratian, as we have seen, codified and "legalized" the restrictive views prevalent up to then. The Decretals of Pope Gregory IX (1234) took from abbesses their right of public preaching and reading of the Gospel and of hearing the confessions of their nuns. Slowly through the rest of the late middle ages the significant quasi-episcopal jurisdiction of abbesses (consult Joan Morris, The Lady Was a Bishop, New York, 1973) was eroded, especially by the Council of Trent, which in several ways forced most convents under the jurisdiction of bishops. The few exceptional cases where the decrees of Trent did not bind were wiped out by the French Revolution and its aftermath, except for the convent of Las Huelgas of Burgos, Spain, and its twelve dependent abbeys. Then in 1873 Pope Pius IX suppressed this last vestige of quasi-episcopal jurisdiction of an abbess; the irony was that Pius IX, as persistent and violent an opponent of democracy as the papacy has ever seen, gave as his reason for the suppression that with the change in contemporary society it was inopportune, even harmful, for such a power to be wielded by an abbess.

Thus it can be argued that today women stand at the lowest point legally in the Church that they have ever occupied in the history of Christianity.

Canon 968, § 1, which decrees that only a male is proper subject for ordination, is merely one of a substantial number of canons which distinguish between men and women to the detriment of the latter. It is, of course, the most important, for even in these days when papal statements encourage women to contribute creatively to the world's culture, all canon law, including that relating solely to women, is formulated by male clerics. When women are consulted, it is solely on matters which are considered of special interest to them, with the rest of ecclesiastical reality remaining a clerical, male preserve. The Commission that has been re-writing canon law these past few years is entirely male. Clearly women cannot expect to have their ideas represented in ecclesiastical legislation until some of their sex are ordained to the priesthood and episcopacy.

At the same time the admission of women to Holy Orders--or even the admission that there are no impediments besides social attitudes within the Church--would be such a dramatic statement of women's equality that all lesser restrictions would soon disappear. Here is the dual reason for

the focus on the priesthood question: the exclusion of women
is both symbol and cause of their state of subjection within
the Church.

A look at the legal context within which Canon 968 appears is worthwhile. Even those canons which have tradi-
tionally been interpreted as favoring women take on new color
in the light of contemporary feminist thought. Canon 1067,
§ 1, which permits a "man" to marry at 16 and a "woman"
at 14, does indeed recognize that women mature earlier, but
the maturity is strictly physical. At the same time the
canon adds its support to the common assumption that a wife
ought to be younger--and hence more inexperienced and less
educated--than her husband, and thus dependent upon him and
his judgment. It also assumes a woman has little need to
prepare herself for a productive adulthood.

Again, Canon 98, § 4, which makes it a simple matter
for a married woman to change to the rite of her husband at
marriage and then back to her original rite at the death of
her husband, all without having to get specific permission--
though the husband had no parallel freedom--is no longer seen
as a kindness to the woman. It merely assumes that the rite
of the husband is more important, and thus suggests that a
woman's membership in her parish is subordinate to that of
her husband. The stipulation in Canon 756, § 2, that when
the parents are of two different rites, the child takes the
rite of the father, confirms the inferiority of the wife.

Even canons which have been seen as fairly trivial
in the past play important roles in forming the image and
self-image of women. The fact that women may not initiate
a cause for canonization of saints (Canon 2004, § 1), for example, means that all the ecclesiastical role models for
women are installed by males according to standards set up
by males for what they would like their women to be. The
limitation of membership on seminary boards of governors
to clerics (Canon 1359, § 2) means that women are denied
that voice in determining the education of the men who will
later lead and teach them and their daughters.

From the above it can be seen that the canons discriminating against women are varied. Some are specifically
directed against women, some merely against the laity (juri-
dically all women, including sisters, are laity). Some deal
with participation in church and liturgy, some with marriage;
a goodly number deal with restrictions placed on religious

women. The following are typical. (Translations of the canons are taken from John A. Abbo and Jerome D. Hannan, The Sacred Canons [St. Louis: B. Herder, 1957].)

Canon 506, § 2 and § 4. "In monasteries of nuns, assemblies convoked for the election of the superiores shall be held under the presidency, without his entering the cloister, of the local ordinary or his delegate, with two priests as tellers, if the nuns are subject to the local ordinary; if not subject to him, under the presidency of the regular superior; but even in this case the local ordinary shall be duly informed of the day and the hour of the election, that he may assist at it, either personally or through a delegate, along with the regular superior, and by assisting preside over it.

"In congregations of women, the election of the mother general shall be held under the presidency, either in person or by delegate, of the ordinary of the place in which the election is held; and in the case of a congregation of diocesan approval, the local ordinary has the right to confirm or rescind the election as his conscience may dictate. "

Canon 607. "Superioresses and local ordinaries shall be vigilant to prevent religious women from going out alone without necessity. "

Canon 742, § 2. "(Non-solemn baptism can be administered by anyone ....)" "But if a priest is present, he should be preferred to a deacon; a deacon, to a subdeacon; a cleric to a layman; and a man to a woman, unless in the interest of modesty it is more becoming that a woman rather than a man should baptize or unless a woman is better acquainted with the form and the method required in baptizing. "

Canon 813, § 2. "The Mass server shall not be a woman unless a sound reason justifies it when a man is not available, and in that case the woman must recite the responses from a distance and she must not for any reason approach the altar. "

Canon 1264, § 2. "Women religious may sing in their own church or oratory, if they are permitted to do so by their constitutions and by the laws of the liturgy and if they have the permission of the local ordinary, but they must do so in a place in which they cannot be seen by the people. "

Canon 1312, § 1. "One who legitimately exercises dominative power over the will of the person who made a vow may validly and also, for a justifying reason, lawfully annul it in such a way that its obligation never subsequently revives."

Commenting on this last law, the 1957 edition of Abbo-Hannan, perhaps the most distinguished canon law textbook in the United States, says "There is a sharp division of opinion in regard to the authority of a husband to act directly on a vow of his wife; his right to do so is supported by no convincing arguments, but authors of high repute affirm that he possesses it, and their contention enjoys the tacit approbation of the Church."

*   *   *

As this book was in press, a good deal of attention was focusing on the Ordination Conference, "Women in Future Priesthood Now," held in Detroit, November 28-30, 1975. Over 1200 people attended to share experiences and hear major talks by S. Elizabeth Carroll, a former college president and former president of the Leadership Conference of Women Religious (LCWR); S. Anne Carr, assistant dean of the University of Chicago Divinity School; S. Margaret Farley, associate professor of ethics at Yale Divinity School; S. Marie Augusta Neal, professor of sociology at Emmanuel College; S. Mary Daniel Turner, executive director of the LCWR; and S. Marjorie Tuite of the Jesuit School of Theology in Chicago. The official respondents included such lay people as Rosemary Ruether, Elisabeth Fiorenza, Arlene Swidler and Leonard Swidler, and such priests as George Tavard and William Callahan. (Callahan is the founder and executive secretary of "Priests for Equality," a group supporting the ordination of women; started in July 1975, it had grown to 660 members at the time of the Conference.)

The success of the Conference, first as a convening of women either hoping for ordination themselves or sympathetic to the cause, and secondly as a model and impetus of further action around the country, is occasionally cited as an indication that the emphasis on the question of ordination for women is somehow a peculiarly American phenomenon. The earlier excitement over the illegal ordinations of women within the American Episcopal Church simply confirmed this attitude in some minds.

This book, of course, is one piece of evidence to the contrary, but there are many more.

The earliest positive analyses of this ordination question are apparently two works by Jesuit priests--Dutch Father Haye van der Meer's doctoral thesis written under Karl Rahner in Innsbruck in 1962 (now available in English as Women Priests in the Catholic Church? trans. by Arlene and Leonard Swidler, Philadelphia, 1973), and Peruvian Father Jose Idigoras' booklet La Mujer dentro del Orden Sagrado (Lima, 1963), the following year. The subject first came to broad public attention with the petition to the Second Vatican Council of a Swiss attorney, Gertrud Heinzelmann. St. Joan's International Alliance, a group with a largely European membership, then presented the first of what were to be annual petitions to the Vatican in 1963:

> St. Joan's International Alliance re-affirms its loyalty and filial devotion and expresses its conviction that should the Church in her wisdom and in her good time decide to extend to women the dignity of the priesthood, women would be willing and eager to respond.

Thus, American contribution to the movement for women priests in the Catholic Church has been relatively recent. However, it has now clearly attained considerable momentum in America, both in the spheres of research and activism. The publication and translation into English of Dr. Raming's fundamental research in the juridical area of this question could not, therefore, have come at a more opportune time; it is certain to significantly accelerate that momentum. Hence, profound thanks are due to Dr. Raming, and also to Prof. Norman Adams for his painstakingly precise and timely translation, as well as the Scarecrow Press for making publication possible.

Leonard and Arlene Swidler

INTRODUCTION

Among the questions and challenges which spontaneously arose during Vatican II were those that concerned the contemporary place of women in the church. For the first time, the complete absence of women in the Council, which had been originally constituted as an assembly of men only, created an unfavorable impression and was considered a defect. In addition several Council speeches and interventions dealt with the need for the reform of women's place in society and in the church, and offered guidelines and suggestions for improvement.[1]* Also, outside the Council meetings the value and position of women in the church were critically investigated and recommendations for changes were brought forward in various Council petitions and pronouncements.[2] Following the Council the quest for reform of the situation of women in the church has by no means subsided: on the contrary, it is increasing in importance and relevance.[3]

Various factors have brought about this critical questioning. On the basis of the political rights of women already achieved in many state constitutions, which have given women an independent vocational existence in the secular realm and which have made possible the development of their personalities, the discrepancy between the ecclesiastical and the secular orders of society has become obvious to many women who have "come of age" in the modern world. They have been increasingly offended by the fact that in the church they are not respected as equal to men.

Nevertheless the demand women make for a position appropriate to the times in which we live--expressed concretely in the demand for ecclesiastical office[4]--does not arise simply out of a comparison between the secular and ecclesiastical structures of society or from the contrast between legal rights in the Catholic church and in the Protestant

---

*Footnotes for the Introduction and Chapters 1-8 begin on page 135.

church, in many branches of which women already have a
share of official positions. [5] More deeply understood, the issue is a religious one, since in it the wish is expressed for
women to obey their call to the priestly vocation. Of course
it is true that this struggle is against an almost two thousand
year tradition of church teaching and canonical practice, which
has kept women, just because they are women, from becoming priests, and which allegedly rests on divine law, [6] according to widespread theological opinion, and therefore cannot
be changed. This tradition, however, as well as the ecclesiastical regulations based on it, severely limits the religious
freedom of human beings because it denies women in principle
yet solely on the basis of sex the practice of a priestly vocation, which is obviously so important to the redemptive activity of the church. Obviously such a tradition ought to be
theologically incontestable and able to defend itself against
any cross-questioning if it is to uphold the claim to have divine origin and therefore be unchangeable. [7] Nevertheless this
very presupposition is not established by the arguments so
long advanced by Catholic theology. It can be shown by several lines of theological investigation that the traditional exegetical and dogmatic arguments for the exclusion of women
from priestly office are not valid[8] and therefore cannot justify this exclusion.

It is hoped that the present work, which is developed
from the standpoint of the history of canon law, will help to
clarify the problem. The basis for the regulation in the official ecclesiastical law book (canon 968, § 1, Code), according
to which only the (baptized) male can be validly ordained--
implying that women are incapable of ordination--will be carefully investigated. [9] The major emphasis will be a consideration and critical analysis of the supporting evidence for the
above canon in the Corpus Iuris Canonici, which is the most
important of the sources for the ecclesiastical law book presently in force. These sources will be investigated not only
from the aspect of their relationship to canon 968, § 1, and
other canons closely related to it, but also according to the
conception of women which lies at their basis. Actually, an
examination of these components is necessary if we are to
form an objective opinion about prohibitions and legal limitations relating to women. We shall also make an investigation of the works of the canonists of the Middle Ages, where
they are available. These are informative in the interpretation and evaluation of sources contained in the Corpus Iuris
Canonici and therefore important in the development of church
law.

In an exegetical excursus adjoined to the historical part of the present work, the validity of patristic scriptural evidence used in the Corpus Iuris Canonici and especially in Gratian's Decretum to support the position of female subordination will be examined by the use of historical-critical exegesis. The reason for this study is that patristic interpretations of particular biblical passages (Gen. 2:18-24; 3; 1 Cor. 11:3-9, 14:34f.; Eph. 5:22-33, and others) comprise an essential support for the inferior position of women in church law.

In the dogmatic part of the book a critical analysis of the traditional understanding of office and representation is intended as a supplement to the exegetical-dogmatical investigations already undertaken.[10] Arguments are made, on the basis of this traditional understanding, against permitting women to be ordained, and it does not seem to me that enough is being written in current literature concerning such argumentation.

Finally, drawing our conclusions together it will be indicated that in excluding women from ordination and thus from ecclesiastical office because of her sex, a limitation of freedom results which means an injury to the personal dignity of women and a rejection of responsibility to God. The removal of such limitation is demanded in the name of justice, in order that the gifts with which women are endowed may develop without hindrance in the church.

Part I

CANON LAW BACKGROUND
(Foundation of the Code of Canon Law,
canon 968, §1, in the Corpus Iuris Canonici)

       The current Code of Canon Law preserves to a great
extent the connection with the traditional church law largely
set forth in the Corpus Iuris Canonici. [1] The Code appro-
priated the massive legal materials in the Corpus, in so far
as they belonged to "vigens ecclesiae disciplina" at the time
it was drawn up, and reduced them to a succinct form. [2]
Thus the normal "agreement" of previous law with that of the
Code[3] holds also for canon 968, §1 (Code), [4] according to
which only the baptized man can be validly ordained, and a
woman, including one baptized, is thereby excluded from the
reception of ordination. It is true that in the quotations from
the Corpus Iuris Canonici cited by Cardinal Gasparri[5] for this
regulation it is not obvious that the male requirement for
ordination has its basis in the old law, since the reference
here is exclusively related to the baptismal requirement for
valid ordination. [6] It is quite possible that this lack of reference to sex may be due to the fact that the further requirement of masculinity was simply taken for granted, so that
Gasparri felt that a quotation to this effect would be superfluous. In any case we cannot draw the conclusion that the
masculine requirement has no support in classical canon law,
even though, we should note, it does not appeal to a ius
divinum. [7] Actually we discover just the opposite, if we look
through the Corpus Iuris Canonici for relevant evidence:
numerous stipulations in the Corpus Iuris concerning the ecclesiastical position of women--statements which become, at
least in part, the basis for other canons of the Code consistent with canon 968, §1, and which are in fact based upon
it--make clear that this canonical requirement (sacram ordinationem valide recipit solus vir baptizatus) goes back to classical canon law--not, to be sure, in form but certainly in
direction and content. In this respect the Code clearly up-
holds the legal tradition.

       Beyond this, the relevant sources of the Corpus Iuris

Canonici (and the texts used to explain them) provide an insight into the evaluation of women[8] that is basic to these sources and do so more clearly than the succinctly formulated canons of the Code, which to a certain extent only present an extract of the sources. This insight is indispensable for the interpretation and critique of the legal sources as well as of canon 968, §1 of the Code that derives from them. Only when the evaluation of women is understood can the reasons for the regulations concerning women be uncovered and explained.

Chapter 1

GRATIAN'S DECRETUM AS SOURCE FOR SEX DISCRIMINATION IN THE PRIESTHOOD

a. Gratian's Sources

Gratian's Decretum[1], the Concordia Discordantium Canonum, contains important source material for our question.[2] In large part taken from older collections and systematically reworked[3], a great mass of source materials is to be found in this textbook of church law, which was composed in scholastic form about the middle of the 12th century (perhaps around 1140)[4] by the Camaldolese monk and teacher, Gratian of Bologna. In the course of time, already toward the end of the twelfth century, people forgot the private "character of the Decree and considered it to be 'Corpus iuris canonici' from ancient times to Gratian's day."[5]

The following references in this collection are relevant to our inquiry: (1) chapter 25 of distinctio 23, containing the prohibition of women from carrying out certain ceremonial functions, namely touching the consecrated vessels and cloths and incensing the altar; (2) chapters 41 and 42 of distinctio 1 de consecratione, which reserve to ordained men any handling of these objects, and thus, indirectly if not specifically, exclude women from such action; (3) the explicit prohibition in chapter 29 of distinctio 2 de cons. which forbids women to take communion to the sick; (4) the prohibition against teaching by women, contained in chapter 29 of distinctio 23 and in chapter 20 of distinctio 4 de cons., in the latter case mixed with a baptismal prohibition; and (5) finally, regulation dist. 32 c. 19, according to which no so-called presbyterae may be established in the church. (6) Besides these chapters, which contain exclusively prohibitions of liturgical and cultic activity of women, we must take account of other sources which mention deaconesses, especially chapter 23 in quaestio 1 of causa 27, then also chapters 38, C. 11, q. 1 and 30, C. 27, q. 1.

The first passage to be discussed here, dist. 23 c. 25, is arranged in a context that is noteworthy in regard to our question and therefore deserves our attention. In accordance with the introductory paragraph,[6] distinctio 23 describes the ordination of various clerics from the highest level to the lowest. The ordination regulations for each clerical grade, including those of the so-called minor orders, presuppose only male ordinands. This fact is a clear indication that canon law in the time of Gratian is aware of an exclusively male priesthood; the deaconess is nowhere mentioned.[7] Except for the regulation of chapter 24, which concerns the dress of a nun (sanctimonialis virgo) at the time of her consecration, distinctio 23 contains nothing but prohibition for a woman. It is clear from the structure of this distinctio[8] that it has to do with legal prescriptions binding in the time of Gratian. Gratian's paragraphus to chapter 25 presents additional support for this conclusion: "Women who are consecrated to God are forbidden [prohibentur] to touch the sacred vessels and altar cloths and to carry incense around the altar."[9] Gratian's words, according to the rubric to chapter 25,[10] are based on an excerpt from a letter written by Pope Soter to the Italian bishops, which reads as follows:

> It has been brought to the attention of the apostolic see that women dedicated to God, or nuns, touch the sacred vessels or altar cloths and carry incense around the altar. No truly sensible person will doubt that such practices deserve to be censured and eliminated. Therefore on the authority of our holy office we direct you to eliminate them as quickly as possible. And in order that this pestilence does not spread into other areas we demand that it be stopped immediately.[11]

Actually this quotation, which Gratian cites as papal authority, is a part of the (second) Pseudo-Isidorian epistola decretalis of Soter[12] and thus a forgery. It was, however, like the whole Pseudo-Isidorian collection, considered genuine by Gratian, in agreement with the dominant opinion of the Middle Ages.[13] Haye van der Meer[14] has already pointed out the fact of forgery in this text and in other decretals similar in content although not included in the Corpus Iuris Canonici, and he has rightly objected to the uncritical use of such materials as traditional proofs for the exclusion of women from the priesthood.[15]

Yet aside from the unquestionably spurious nature of

this so-called epistola Sotheri, there still remains the question of its historical worth. As a source for this excerpt from the decretal, which Gratian numbers chapter 25 in distinctio 23, Hinschius[16], followed by Friedberg[17], points to chapter 2 in the Vita Sotheri of the Liber Pontificalis, according to which Soter decrees that no monk (nullus monachus) may touch the sacred altar cloths or incense the church. [18] Duchesne has suggested why this chapter could serve as the source for the decretal excerpt, despite the nullus monachus instead of the expected nulla monacha:

> This decree reappears in the notice of Boniface I[19] but applied to nuns. Here the very words 'no monk' (nullus monachus) have been changed in many ms. to 'no nun' (nulla monacha).... The author of L. P. is a cleric, so also the copiers; their principle is always, monks for prayer, clerics for serving at the altar. [20]

Thus in many ms. nullus monachus has been changed to nulla monacha, doubtless because of a contempt for women widespread at that time, especially in clerical circles. Besides, as Duchesne points out, the Liber Pontificalis, product of a (Roman) cleric, is itself not free from a biased presentation, which of course damages its historical validity. Its first part, entries up to the year 496, is considered to be generally unreliable--not, to be sure, for all items but probably for those concerning discipline and liturgy--and therefore must be used carefully. [21]

     In conclusion, it is clear that the excerpt from the Pseudo-Isidorian decretal of Soter, which Gratian in dist. 23, c. 25 takes as authority, has no convincing historical basis and therefore cannot be used uncritically, i. e., without considering this fact as a traditional proof for the exclusion of women from liturgical functions. Furthermore it is clear from the contents and style of the epistola that a derogatory conception of women is the basis for the prohibition. Although in earlier times and in various churches deaconesses were permitted to enter the chancel and to incense for the mass--it was even possible to go beyond what was forbidden in the decretal, for instance to distribute the Holy Communion--[22] all this is now sharply condemned as censurable behavior (quae omnia vituperatione et reprehensione plena esse). The bishops who receive the letter must put a complete end to such repulsive pestilence (pestis) as quickly as possible. [23] This ruthless action against the service of women in the chancel is explained--in the context of the decretal immediately

following the passage cited above (p. 8), although omitted by
Gratian--as follows:

> ... the Apostle says:[24] "I have betrothed you to one
> man, in order to present you as pure virgin to Christ."
> That is to say, the virgin is virgin Church, bride of
> the one man Christ, a bride who will not permit her-
> self to be besmirched by any kind of error or dis-
> honorable fault, so that she might everywhere pre-
> serve for us the single entirety of the one pure fel-
> lowship. [25]

The basis of such an argument is obviously the concept that
the chastity and purity of the virgo ecclesia would suffer
great injury from a cultic-liturgical activity of women, a concept which can only be explained by saying that women are
impure creatures--in the sense of the Old Testament laws
about impurity (cf. Lev. 12:1ff.; 15:19ff.)[26]--or by devaluing
them as temptation for men.

The same situation is apparent in chapters 41 and 42
of distinctio 1 de cons. [27] in the third section of the Decretum.
Here too are excerpts from the Pseudo-Isidorian decretals,
thus forgeries. Like chapter 25 of distinctio 23, they contain regulations, although only by implication, prohibiting
women from touching consecrated vessels and altar linens.
According to the summaria (brief headlines) of the chapters, [28] it would seem that the only ground for the prohibition
is the insacratum esse, the unordained status, but the content (and context) of chapter 41 makes it clear that ordination is simply an additional requirement for the cultic function, while the basic presupposition is that the functioner be
a male. The text of chapter 41 is as follows:

> The Holy See decrees that the consecrated vessels
> may be handled only by holy men [hominibus] ordained
> to the Lord's service and by no others, in order that
> the Lord in his anger may not punish his people with
> calamity, in which those who have not sinned [against
> this commandment] may be also destroyed, since it
> often happens that the righteous suffer for the ungod-
> ly. [29]

Gratian omits the passage in the Pseudo-Isidorian decretal
which immediately follows the word hominibus, although it
appears in the so-called Editio Romana[30] of Gratian's Decretum. What it says is: "For it is highly improper that any

holy vessels of the Lord should serve human purposes or be
touched by other than men [viris] who stand in the service of
the Lord and are ordained for him. "[31] There can be no
doubt that the word homines, according to usage at that
time, [32] refers to the male sex. In a similar regulation of
chapter 42, which permits only the sacrati homines to touch
the sacred altar linen, [33] homines is also clearly limited to
the male gender.

Even if these texts may not be valued as authentic evidences of tradition--we are dealing here as above with for-
geries--they are nevertheless, if considered in the context of
chapter 25 of distinctio 23, very instructive concerning the
evaluation of women in the ecclesiastical realm. For while
in the case of men some form of consecratio[34] is everywhere
recognized as sufficient qualification for the cultic functions
we have been considering--it is of course characteristic of
the thinking of that age, that baptism as such is not sufficient, although in conjunction with faith it lays the basis for
Christian existence[35]--the case is not the same for women.
A "woman consecrated to God" (sacrata Deo femina, cf.
p. 8) stands on the same level with "non-consecrated men"
(viri insacrati): for her as well as for them admission to
the chancel and touching of consecrated objects is forbidden.
From this it follows that the basic requirement for cultic
practice is not the religious quality of being dedicated to God,
but rather just being a male, which is actually in itself a
religiously irrelevant fact. Contrary to a man, a woman is
considered to be burdened with such a grave defect that no
kind of religious act of consecration can eradicate it. This
conception is essentially conditioned by the continuing influence
of Old Testament prescriptions for ceremonial purity, which
hold the Christian service of worship in captivity to Old Testament laws and which together with other causes have deprived women of admittance to cultic function. [36]

Although the two texts we have discussed--chapter 25
of distinctio 23 and chapters 41 and 42 of distinctio 1 de
cons.--are a clear expression of devaluation of women and
in addition are forgeries, they have nevertheless been used
as sources for the law of the Code. [37]

If according to the texts we have so far discussed,
women are considered unworthy to handle holy cloths and
vessels, it is quite certain, as we discover from chapter 29
of dist. 2 de cons., that they are not entrusted with the Body
of the Lord, even if only to take it to the sick. The strongly

binding character of the prohibition is emphasized by the
severity of its restrictions:

> It has been learned that certain priests have shown
> disrespect for the divine mysteries by giving the holy
> Body of the Lord to a lay person or a woman, in
> order that they may take it to the sick. In this way
> people who are forbidden to enter the sanctuary and
> approach the altar are entrusted with the Holy of
> Holies. All God fearing people know that this practice
> is shocking and detestable. Therefore the Synod most
> strongly forbids it, so that such irresponsible and
> illegal behavior may never happen again. In every
> case the priest must himself take the communion to
> the sick. Anyone who does otherwise runs the danger
> of being degraded. [38]

According to the rubric, this chapter concerns canon
2 of a synod at Reims. (This may be the synod which
Hefele-Leclerq places between the years 624 and 625.)[39] It
is true that one does not find the above cited regulation among
the 25 canons of this synod that are listed in the history of
the councils. However, according to Hefele-Leclercq,[40]
other canons were attributed to the Synod of Reims by Burchard of Worms and Ivo of Chartres, upon whose collections
of source materials Gratian depends,[41] and the above canon
belongs to these.[42] Admittedly Friedberg gives no indication of the source of the canon, but he does refer to a resolution of the Synod of Rouen, A. D. 650,[43] which has a similar content: women and laity shall by no means be given the
holy eucharist in the hand, but only in the mouth. Violation
of this prohibition will be considered as contempt for God
and appropriately punished.[44] Likewise, dist. 2 de cons.
c. 29 declares that it is rude disrespect of the divine mys-
teries for (male) laity and women to be given the Body of
the Lord in order to take it to the sick. As those who are
forbidden to approach the altar,[45] they are not considered
worthy to hold the sancta sanctorum in their hands. Now of
course we must not overlook the fact that the prohibition applies to the laicus, as to women. But when besides the
laity, women are specifically named, we see in the unnecessary differentiation, which also appears in other texts,[46]
a conscious formulation which intends to express the
fact that the (male) layperson qua laicus may not take communion to the sick because of his low position in the church,
as any layperson was considered to be in a low position at
that time, but that women may not take communion to the

sick not because they are laity but qua femina, because, that
is to say, of their disrespected sex. [47] The Glossa Ordinaria
at this place proves that this interpretation is not misguided,
as may be mentioned here, somewhat in anticipation: for
the case in which the priest is prevented from taking communion to the sick, which he himself is stringently required
to do, the gloss provides for the following solution, that besides a deacon a laicus catholicus may represent the priest. [48]
Without doubt this means only a male layperson, for according to the understanding of some decretists even a puer
catholicus, a boy, could take over the task of the hindered
priest. [49] A woman, however, even one consecrated to God,
is not considered worthy to perform this service, even in an
emergency. [50] It is thus clear that church discipline in the
Middle Ages did not actually and exclusively classify woman
under the rubric of laity, but rather because of her sex she
was given a special and prejudicial treatment. She was assigned a status below the level of the male laity. Here is
the reason for the fact that the higher evaluation of the laity,
which took place in the course of time, was mainly limited
to the male laity (for instance, admission to sacristan and
lector positions).

The rule in chapter 29 of dist. 2 de cons. creates
the basis for canon 845 of the Code, according to which the
administration of Holy Communion by laypersons is forbidden. [51] Some easing of the prohibition took place in the post
Vatican II period, but, characteristically, this applied first
only to male laity or in special cases to nuns, [52] and only
later to female laity. [53]

Two more prohibitions, found in chapter 29 of dist.
23 and in chapter 20 of dist. 4 de cons., have the same
goal as the regulations we have already noticed, to exclude
women from any official religious activity, including any
liturgical function. (Since one of the prohibitions, that concerning teaching, is common to both chapters, it seems best
to treat the texts together.) The wording is as follows:
"Even if a woman is educated and saintly, she still should
not presume to instruct men in a [congregational] assembly.
A [male] layperson, however, should not presume to instruct
in the presence of the clergy, unless he is asked by them
to do so. "[54] "Even if a woman is learned and saintly, she
still must not presume to baptize or to instruct men in a
[congregational] assembly. "[55] According to the respective
rubrics both chapters are decrees of a council of Carthage.[56]
But actually what we have in each case is a composite of

two canons of the "Statuta Ecclesiae Antiqua, "[57] a collection of 102 chapters on church discipline, which are given in the Collectio Hispana (Isidoriana)[58]--which was for a long time the only source of our knowledge of the Statuta--under the title of a council of Carthage (the fourth) in the year 389. [59] As canons of this council the two prohibitions next became parts of the Pseudo-Isidorian collection[60]--by way of the Hispana Gallica Augustodunensis--which in turn served as source for medieval canon law collections, especially Gratian's Decretum, including the canons we are now considering. [61] In this way the Statuta became widely known and, what is more decisive, were for a long time considered to be regulations of the fourth Council of Carthage. [62] The Editio Romana (1582) of Gratian's Decretum also assigns the canons of the Statuta accepted by Gratian to this Council. [63] However the results of research long ago[64] proved that the Statuta cannot be attributed to the fourth Council of Carthage --supposedly held in A.D. 398, although there is no evidence that it ever took place[65]--nor to a later (A.D. 418) Council of Carthage. [66] The source of the Statuta has really nothing to do with any council. They are rather the work of an anonymous author, or compiler, and in fact, as Munier has been able to show, he is the Presbyter Gennadius of Marseille. [67] The collection was brought together between 476 and 485. [68]

We are here mainly interested in the kind of materials and sources Gennadius may have utilized for his compilation. Munier's investigations give us information about this too. [69] They show that the Statuta in the composition of its different parts is derived from many source materials. The Statuta's regulations about discipline, to which the chapters from Gratian's Decretum which we have been discussing (p. 13) belong, are mainly dependent upon the so-called Apostolic Constitutions, [70] the most important of the pseudo-apostolic collections containing church law and liturgy from the fourth century. [71] The connection between the Statuta and the Constitutions, in the case of chapters 37 and 41 concerning women, which Gratian has taken from the Statuta, is quite obvious. [72] The prohibition against teaching (c. 37, p. 13) is based on the corresponding detailed regulation of the Apostolic Constitutions (III, 6) and reduces it to a concise formula. It is true that the special tendency of the prohibition, that women must not presume to teach men in an assembly (viros in conventu docere), does not derive directly from the Constitutions nor from the Syriac Didascalia, which lies behind the Constitutions. (The Didascalia is itself a pseudo-apostolic writing from the first decades of the third century.)[73] It is possible that such a precise prohibition is intended to serve as a protection of the celibacy of the clergy (or monks), especially since further chapters of the Statuta support this objective. [74]

Concerning the question we are discussing we may draw the conclusion that the prohibition against women's religious-cultic activity is closely connected to measures taken to protect celibacy, as will often become clear in the course of our continuing investigation. We should more probably assume, however, that the prohibition against the practice of public teaching by women in a congregational gathering[75] consisting mostly of men is intended to circumvent the suspected desire of women to rule over men, a contradiction of the "order of creation."[76] At any rate this aspect of the question is clearly the intent of the text of c. 37 of the Statuta taken over by Gratian, the prohibition in the Apostolic Constitutions against teaching, which reads as follows:

> We do not permit women to practice the office of teaching in the church; instead they should pray and listen to teachers. For our Teacher and Lord, Jesus himself, sent only us Twelve to instruct the people [Israel] and the heathen, but he never sent women, although women were not lacking: with us was the mother of the Lord and her sisters, and also Mary Magdalene and Mary, the mother of James, and Martha and Mary, the sisters of Lazarus, Salome and some others. Thus if it had been suitable for women to proclaim the teachings of Jesus, he would himself have called them from the beginning to undertake with us the instruction of the people. For if the man is the head of the woman, it is not proper that the rest of the body should rule the head. So the widow should always remember that she is the "sacrificial altar"[77] of God, and she should remain at home and under no pretext enter the homes of believers, in order to get something, for the altar of God does not wander about but rather remains fixed in a definite place. [78]

The sentence of the Constitutions, "For if the man is the head of the woman ..." paraphrases the so-called order of creation. The author clearly relies on 1 Cor. 11:3 and Eph. 5:23, 28f. [79] The other reference used as justification for the prohibition of teaching--which some are still fond of today[80]--that Jesus commissioned no women to proclaim the Gospel, is refuted by the Didascalia itself, the forerunner of the Constitutions. For, immediately before the teaching prohibition, Did. III, 5, we read:

> [the widow] should send those who want to be instructed to the heads of the community.... But no widow or layman is obliged to speak about the destruction of idols, about the fact that God is one, about the kingdom of the name of Christ and about his leadership. For in so far as they speak without knowledge of the teaching, they bring contempt upon the Word. For if educated heathen hear the Word of God but it is not proclaimed to them in an orderly and suitable fashion for the production of eternal life, especially because it is a woman who is telling them how the Lord assumed a body and how he suffered, they will laugh and mock instead of praising the teachings. In such fashion a woman brings guilt upon herself in the great Day of Judgment. [81]

Here we find expressed, though doubtless unintentionally, such a strongly pronounced bias of society against women in the early third century, when the Didascalia appeared, that women clearly had no opportunity at all to be teachers in public life. Because of their despised sex and also because of their lack of culture, their word was from the first not accepted and taken seriously. Since the Syriac Didascalia is considered a valuable historical source, [82] as far as its description of congregational relationships is concerned, it may be assumed that the social evaluation and the position of women set forth in Did. III, 5, correctly characterizes the circumstances of that time. Now we are also well informed about the situation of women in the time of Jesus, [83] and it was in no way more favorable. Jesus did what could be done for women in his time: his example and his teaching give impressive witness to that fact. [84] In his recognition of women as directly called and blessed by God, he created the internal impulse for and the basis of her emancipation from the position of inferiority to men, a fact which was, to be sure, overlooked by the early church, imprisoned by rabbinical ways of thinking. [85] Still, Jesus could not send women out as apostles, that is, as official witnesses of the Gospel, since that was forbidden by the conditions of the time. This is also, rightly, the opinion of René Metz: "... If he had wished, Christ could not really have acted in any other manner. It would have been asking too much of his companions, whose feelings about this he could not offend: a female apostle was inconceivable in the Jewish milieu at that time."[86] But out of this silence of Jesus--clearly understandable from the situation--the Didascalia, and following it the Apostolic Constitutions, construct a prohibition. (This is a methodology used even today.)[87]

The prohibition against teaching in the Didascalia and the Apostolic Constitutions, which served as model for that in the Statuta, takes up a tradition based on the statements of 1 Cor. 14:34f. and 1 Tim. 2:11f., themselves in turn influenced by rabbinical regulations and conceptions.[88] (The partial word-by-word dependence on these texts cannot be overlooked.)[89] Thus we trace back to its origin, through its developmental stages in the Apostolic Constitutions and the Didascalia, the teaching prohibition of the Statuta which Gratian considered binding. We get back to the basic understanding of women as essentially and ethically inferior, clearly evident in the motivation of the teaching prohibition of 1 Tim. 2: "I do not permit a woman to teach.... For Adam was created first and then Eve. And Adam was not deceived but the woman allowed herself to be deceived and became a transgressor" (1 Tim. 2:12-14).

The textual source of the Statuta's prohibition of baptizing (Mulier baptizare non praesumat, c. 41), which Gratian places with the prohibition of teaching in chapter 20 in dist. 4 de cons. (see p. 13, is to be found, according to Munier,[90] in the Apostolic Constitutions III, 9. Both prohibitions are universal, and in the Constitutions the intention is so basically a matter of principle that the regulation can hardly be interpreted in the sense that it forbids women to baptize officially in public worship but does not forbid them to do so in cases of emergency.[91] Besides, an exception in such cases was apparently made first by Pope Urban II (1088-1099).[92] The baptizing prohibition of the Constitutions is quite informative, especially in the reasons given, in the matter of evaluation of women. The following text can be seen as the context and background of the concise formulation of chapter 41 of the Statuta:

> About baptizing by women we want you to know that those who presume to baptize bring themselves into no small danger. So we do not advise it, for it is dangerous, yes, even forbidden and godless. That is to say, if man is the head of woman and he is promoted to the priesthood, it militates against divine

justice to disturb the arrangement of the Creator by
degrading man from the preeminence granted to him
to the lowest place. For woman is the body of man,
has come from his rib and is placed in subjection to
him, for which reason also she has been chosen to
bear children. The Lord says, 'He will rule over
her.' Man has lordship over the woman, since he is
also her head. But if we have already forbidden wom-
en to preach, how would anyone want to permit them
to enter the priesthood? It would be unnatural. For
women to be priests is an error of heathen godless-
ness but not of Christ's way. But if women are permitted to baptize, then Christ would surely have been
baptized by his mother and not by John and he would
have sent women with us to baptize also, when he
sent us out to baptize. But now the Lord never made
any such arrangements nor left us with any such
scriptural admonition, since he as creator of nature
and founder of its order knew the gradations of nature
and what is proper. [93]

The evidence in this text is undeniable, that the baptizing
prohibition and the exclusion of women from priestly office
connected with it rests on a pronounced contempt for woman
("the lowest member [$\tau\grave{o}\ \check{\epsilon}\sigma\chi\alpha\tau o\nu\ \sigma\tilde{\omega}\mu\alpha$] ... of the body of
man, ... from his rib and subject to him") and on her clas-
sification as biological and sexual: "chosen to bear children."
The author of the Constitutions sees in woman's participation
in the priestly office a disturbance of "the order of the creator." He is very zealous to maintain this order, but surely
his questionable motive is clear: this order assures to man
the position of superiority and authority over woman. As
support for his argument he interprets, and misinterprets, a
similar scriptural passage, Genesis 3:16 ("but he will rule
over her") as divine sanction for the predominance of man. [94]
Because of his manner of thinking, characterized by a thoroughly patriarchal environment, the author of the Constitutions
cannot imagine a community of men and women together in
the priestly office and service. The clear-cut desire to
"rule," which betrays itself in the repeated use of this word
and which completely misunderstands the teaching office (cf.
the teaching prohibition, p. 15) and the priestly office as a
form of ruling and exercise of power, completely excludes
the possibility of such a community of men and women. The
additional argument taken up by the Constitutions from the
Didascalia, that Jesus was not baptized by Mary but by John,
witnesses to an immature theological mentality conditioned

by its time and therefore equally untenable. On the contrary, it should be noted that John was the one at that time called by God to baptize for repentance, and he was the one by whom Jesus wished to be baptized in solidarity with sinful humanity, whose guilt he vicariously took upon himself. Baptism by Mary would have had no meaning or relationship to salvation history. [95]

The baptizing prohibition as well as the teaching prohibition is specifically directed against the church widow. Apparently she had previously baptized on the basis of charismatic qualifications. [96] In any case the prohibition itself suggests that she had carried out this function. [97] According to Achelis-Flemming, the erosion of the widow's ecclesiastical rights and activities has its origin in the movement to strengthen the monarchical episcopate, which the author of the Didascalia strongly advocates. [98] In place of the charismatic institution of churchly widows which is henceforth limited to quiet prayer and at most also the care of the sick, [99] the Didascalia substitutes the female office of the diaconate as a pliable organ in the hand of the bishop with a firm place in ecclesiastical hierarchy. [100] Some functions that the widow had carried out are now taken over by the deaconess. [101] But of the former baptismal functions of the widow there remain for the deaconess only certain acts of assistance in the baptism of women by immersion, such as anointing the body --which seems proper for women to do--while the anointing of the head and the baptismal act itself are reserved for the bishop, then in his place the presbyter and the deacon--exclusively male clergy. [102] The development initiated in the Syriac Didascalia concerning the position of widows and the office of deaconesses reached its conclusion in the Apostolic Constitutions about 100 years later. [103]

Concerning the prohibition of baptizing in the Statuta, it seems to be directed toward the churchly widow and the nun, especially since according to chapter 100 of the Statuta[104] the preparation of women catechumens for baptism and their instruction in the basics of Christian living are given over to them. It is clear that the reference is not to the deaconess because the Statuta never even mentions this office, which is not surprising since the office of the female diaconate had nearly disappeared in Gaul in the second half of the fifth century, when the Statuta was composed. [105] But also the church widow, though still in existence, is no longer included in the ecclesiastical hierarchy according to the Statuta. [106] The Apostolic Constitutions had already decreed that the widow, in contrast to the deaconess, should receive no ordination with laying on of hands. She was to be installed in her position only through taking the vow--like the virgo sacrata. [107] The conclusion of this development is found in the Statuta: here too we find the common treatment of widows and nuns (cf. ch. 100) as in the Constitutions, the direction of the widow to prayer (cf. ch. 102), [108] her exclusion from the official teaching function (ch. 37) and from baptizing (ch. 41).

Gratian weakens the prohibition of baptizing in the Statuta insofar as he does not consider it to be binding in cases of emergency. [109] He refers in this to the already mentioned (p. 17) decretal of Urban II, Super Quibus (C. 30, q. 3, ch. 4), according to which emergency baptisms may be performed by women and their validity recognized.

Both regulations, the prohibitions of teaching and baptism in the Decretum, influenced the presently operative law of the church: can. 1342, §2 of the Code, forbids all laypersons, including the religious, to preach in the church; [110] among other legal sources, dist. 4 de cons., ch. 20, is cited. [111] It is true that the canon concerns laity in general, but it especially has practical consequences for women. Thus although the regulation was limited by article 35, number 4, of the Constitution on the Sacred Liturgy [112] of Vatican II--so that leadership of a "service of the word," which should at the most include a talk, [113] may be turned over by the bishop to a commissioned layperson--this possibility is not as yet granted to women, except in actual distressed areas of the church, for instance in Latin America. [114] Furthermore, several male laypersons were permitted to lecture in the Council lecture hall, but not a single woman. [115] Even the office of lector was at first sternly denied to women in the post conciliar period; [116] it was finally permitted, but only hesitantly and with limitations, on the basis of new decrees. [117]

It is true that the baptismal prohibition (in ch. 20, dist. 4 de cons.) does not appear among the fontes of the Code's regulations about baptizers, but it certainly influenced the content of the Code, canon 742, §2. Although §1 had said that anyone can baptize in case of emergency, preference is given in §2 to a cleric if present, but if he is not present, preference is given among laypersons to a man rather than a woman. [118] Among other sources for this relegation of women to the last place in the "hierarchy" of possible baptizers, Hinschius [119] sees a dependence on the Apostolic Constitutions III, 9, and c. 41 of the Statuta, in other words a

dependence on the baptizing prohibitions discussed above.
Moreover the gradations of canon 742, §2 of the Code remind
us clearly of 1 Cor. 11:3, where the woman is to receive
less honor than the man and an immediate subordination to
Christ is denied her. (On this cf. chapter 6, Exegetical
Excursus.)

The so-called presbytera is the subject of a prohibition presented in ch. 19 of dist. 32. It has to do with canon
11 of the Synod of Laodicea.[120] The canon appears in Gratian according to the version of the Hispana,[121] which differs
somewhat from the Greek original,[122] and reads as follows:
"Those women who are called presbytides [presbyterae] by
the Greeks but by us are called widows, senior women,
univirae and matricuriae, may not be installed in the church
as ordained persons."[123] Gratian's introductory paragraph
(Presbiteram vero quam debeamus accipere, Laudicense Concilium ostendit, dicens), as well as the summarium to the
chapter (Viduae vel seniores presbiterae appellantur),[124] in-
form us that the chapter in the context of the distinctio has
only the function of more carefully explaining and defining the
concept presbitera, which has appeared in the immediately
preceding chapter (18), where it means the wife of a presbyter
(uxor presbiteri). But this use of auctoritas by Gratian does
not remove the prohibition. For the basic principle remains,
that each item of source material in the Decretum has that
applicability and authority "which belongs to it itself, quite
apart from its acceptance in the Decretum."[125] So the question is what the canon actually forbids. As Hefele shows,[126]
the decree has experienced various interpretations, which
came about because the meaning of πρεσβύτιδες (presbytides)
and προκαθημέναι (female directors) on the one hand, and of
ἐν Ἐκκλησίᾳ καθίστασθαι (being installed in the church) on the
other hand, is not clear and simple. On the basis of the
treatise by Epiphanius against the Collyridian women,[127]
Hefele comes to the conclusion that the presbytides were the
oldest of the deaconesses,[128] possibly the directors (προ=
καθημέναι) of the other deaconesses. According to this,
the canon may be understood to mean that in the future no
more such "Archdeaconesses" or presbytides should be installed.[129]

Another explanation[130] has it that the πρεσβύτιδες
were the ordinary deaconnesses; their characterization as
directors refers to their oversight over the women in the
Christian community, whereas the characterization presbytides comes from the repeated directive to accept only older

women into the diaconate.   The phrase $\mu\grave{\eta}$ $\delta\epsilon\tilde{\iota}\nu$ ... $\acute{\epsilon}\nu$ $\tau\tilde{\eta}$
$'E\kappa\kappa\lambda\eta\sigma\acute{\iota}\alpha$ $\kappa\alpha\theta\acute{\iota}\sigma\tau\alpha\sigma\theta\alpha\iota$ would mean that no more deaconesses
were to be ceremonially ordained in the church.   But against
this Hefele points out that while it is true that some later
Synods[131] did stop the older practice of ordaining deaconesses,
ordination--a $\chi\epsilon\iota\rho o\tau o\nu\epsilon\acute{\iota}\sigma\theta\alpha\iota$ of deaconesses--was still taking
place in the Greek church at least at the time of the Trullian
Synod (A. D. 692; see canon 14).   Besides, he notes, the
canon says nothing about ceremonial consecration nor any-
thing at all about ordination, but only about a $\kappa\alpha\theta\iota\sigma\tau\alpha\sigma\theta\alpha\iota$.

A third and final explanation[132] is that the presbytides
are not "archdeaconesses" but older women from the people
who had been given oversight of the women in the church.
This arrangement was then, according to this theory, set
aside by the Synod of Laodicea.   The Correctores Romani[133]
allied themselves to this interpretation of the canon. [134]
The version of the canon which Gratian accepted (cf. p. 21)
seems to point to another, peculiar manner of understanding: it substitutes a long list of (Latin) designations (viduae,
seniores, univirae and matricuriae) for the concept of the
Greek version.   (From this we may conclude that the office
of $\pi\rho\epsilon\sigma\beta\tilde{\upsilon}\tau\iota s$ was not known in the Latin church or that it
had a different definition.)   Gratian's version also under-
stands $\kappa\alpha\theta\acute{\iota}\sigma\tau\alpha\sigma\theta\alpha\iota$ in the sense of ordination (in ecclesia
tamquam ordinatas constitui non debere). [135]

Although the exact meaning of the canon can hardly
be determined, as the various interpretations may have
shown, it is nevertheless certain that by the regulation a
specific and still extant functional area--an office, so to
speak--was closed to women.   We still cannot say why it
happened.   However since the Synod of Laodicea in its regulations about discipline exhibits a strong ascetic orientation
in regard to sexual relations, [136] and since it shows itself
concerned about "more strictness with regard to the hierarchical order, "[137] we can rightly assume that here, and
especially in the first factor named, lies the basis for the
elimination of women's ecclesiastical office by means of
canon 11.   So motivated, this in effect anti-feminist action
also shows itself especially clearly in canon 44 of the same
Synod, since this canon for the first time presents a general
exclusion of women from the chancel area, [138] and in so doing created a situation, operative through the centuries until
today, in which discrimination against women in the church
is a most obvious fact.

The regulations we have been discussing, which effectively excluded women from any official function in the church and which, as we have shown, have continued to influence operative church law as a result of its strong ties to classic canonical law, brought to an end a development that tended toward the active participation of women in ecclesiastical affairs. Besides two unimportant texts, there is in Gratian a regulation about deaconesses that is a direct reference to an earlier more favorable position of women in the church, a position we can only infer from the above prohibitions. The way in which Gratian utilizes this source, by the way, shows that in contrast to the prohibitions we have discussed, it no longer had anything to do with a determination of the law operative at that time. This is no doubt the reason why it did not have any influence on the present Code of Canon Law.

This regulation about deaconesses, a resolution of the Council of Chalcedon in 451, is placed by Gratian in ch. 23 of C. 27, q. 1--i. e., in the section of his collection of sources given over to marital law--and reads as follows:

No woman shall be consecrated as deaconess before she is 40 years old, and then only after careful examination. But if, after receiving this consecration and fulfilling her office for a period of time, she should marry, thus disdaining the grace of God, let her be anathema along with him who entered marriage with her. [139]

The canon is used as evidence for the paragraph which introduces quaestio 1: "Those who take the vow [of celibacy] may not marry."[140] This shows that although the first part of the canon, the regulation about the age limit of forty years for admission of women to the diaconate consecration, [141] is in itself important, it was thought by Gratian to be quite unimportant. He considered that only the second part, concerning the celibacy obligation of deaconesses, justified acceptance of the canon, which would also explain the fact that the regulation does not appear in distinctio 23, in which the requirements for all ecclesiastical offices are found. [142] While Gratian in accordance with the introductory paragraph seems to consider the deaconess' ordinatio regulated by the canon as a vow, comparable to or identical with that of the widow or the God-consecrated virgin, [143] it is in actuality a matter of clerical ordination. The original form of the canon used here the technical term $\chi\epsilon\iota\rho o\theta\epsilon\sigma\acute{\iota}\alpha$ or $\chi\epsilon\iota\rho o\tau o\nu\acute{\iota}\alpha$. [144] The consecration formulation[145] which has come down to us proves

that the consecration of the deaconess in Byzantine Asia Minor
was conducted in a form parallel to that of the deacon: the deaconess like the deacon was ordained by the laying on of hands
by the bishop. The first part of the consecration prayer goes
back to the one recorded in the Apostolic Constitutions
(VIII, 20), [146] where it forms, along with the χειροτονία of
the bishop, the consecration rite of the deaconess, which is
placed between that of the deacon and that of the sub-deacon. [147] In the text of the prayer of the Byzantine consecration formula, which goes beyond its models in the Constitutions, it is said that the deaconess is accepted into the ordo
ministrorum by the grace of God. God is implored to grant
the ordinand the spiritual gifts of the diaconate (ministerii
diaconici gratia), which he has also granted to the deaconess
Phoebe (cf. Rom. 16:1). [148] The consecration takes place in
conjunction with the liturgy of the mass. At the conclusion
of the consecration the deaconess was invested with the stole
and presented the chalice, which she herself then returned to
the altar.

After observing such a well-developed rite of consecra-
tion--there is good evidence that it was by no means limited
to the Byzantine deaconess but was used in similar form for
this office in other lands[149]--some authors have declared that
the clerical character of the deaconess consecration cannot
be denied; some place it among the lower clerical rites[150]
while others count it among the higher. [151] It is of course
true that there are some who represent the opposite opinion,
considering the deaconess ordination as simply a benediction. [152] In part they base this opinion on the smaller authority
granted to the deaconess in comparison to the powers of the
deacon. [153] Although there is not in every respect an equalization of the deaconess with the deacon, [154] this is doubtless
due to the fact that women as such were considered inferior,
and not to any lesser quality of her consecration. Discrimination against women is surely the reason why the office was
not uncontested even during the time of its existence and why
finally it was condemned to perish. [155] In my opinion it is
because of a lack of knowledge or consideration of these in-
terrelations that some have much too hastily concluded that
the deaconess consecration is not really a clerical consecration. The strict celibacy obligation in the above canon (C.
27, q. 1, c. 23), which results from ordination for the deaconess as well as for the clergy, [156] implies the clerical
character of the consecration. Any disloyalty to this law of
celibacy is, according to the chapter, an affront to the grace
of God (iniuriam faciens gratiae Dei); this could indirectly

constitute additional evidence of clerical consecration as means of grace.

As this canon further tells us, the deaconess was given an ecclesiastical office (ministerium; the original text uses λειτουργία). In Byzantine Asia Minor this consisted more than anything else in assistance at baptism. [157] There is evidence of this deaconess function, as well as of that of instructing baptized women in Christian living, in other areas of the East, and in many places there was in addition the distribution of the Holy Communion to women and children, as well as non-liturgical activity such as caring for the sick. [158] According to the report of Theodor Balsamon, the famous canonist of the Orthodox Church of the 12th century[159] (who used a vivid imagination, though marked by tradition, in his account of the deaconess in Byzantium), deaconesses as well as deacons shared in altar functions. When asked about the office of deaconesses, he gives the following instructive answer--which also contains information about the cause of the dissolution of the office:

> Formerly the order of deaconesses was recognized as in accordance with ecclesiastical law. They themselves had access to the altar. But because of their monthly defilement their office was removed from the cultic sphere and from the holy altar. It is true that deaconesses are [still] being chosen in the venerable church at Constantinople, although they are no [longer] admitted to altar [duties]. In several places they have convents and direct there a community of women according to church regulation. [160]

Thus in the 12th century there was nothing left of the former ministerium liturgicum. By that time deaconesses had only the direction of communities of women, a task they earlier had in part, in addition to ecclesiastical service. [161] So the deaconess was restricted to convent life and in this way excluded from the service of the congregation. This happened not only in the Byzantine area but also otherwhere in the Orient as in the West, and it is traceable to the victorious advance of monasticism. [162] Also Balsamon's commentary on the Chalcedonian canon 15 about the deaconess, which appears in Gratian, shows that the regulation was no longer in effect in his (Balsamon's) day, because an antithetical canon debarred women from the altar. [163]

Two further sources used by Gratian that mention the

deaconess are taken from imperial laws. They characterize the deaconess as an ecclesiastical official who enjoys the special privileges recognized by public law and receives official protection. In a letter of Pope Gregory the Great to a certain Defensor Johannes--the first part of which is found in Gratian, ch. 38, in C. 11, q. 1--the Prooemium of c. 21 of Novel 123[164] is quoted word for word: it grants to the deaconess, along with other ecclesiastical persons, the privilegium fori, and says that she is under the authority of the bishop. [165] According to C. 27, q. 1, c. 30, taken from Julian's Epitome Novellarum, Const. 115, c. 67,[166] the deaconess, and also the female ascetic[167] and the nun, are protected by imperial law against robbery, abduction and rape.

Now it is true that these final capitula from Gratian do not say much for the membership of the deaconess in the clergy, since the nun is also granted the same privileges. But other texts, not used by Gratian, from the imperial legislation of the eastern Roman Empire provide evidence for the ordination as well as for the clerical position of the deaconess. [168]

b.   Gratian's Opinion

Because Gratian's Decretum is of interest to us not only as a collection of sources, but also as a textbook, [169] the question arises what Magister Gratian himself thought of the possibility of ordination of women. [170]   As a matter of fact, the sources which he collected (treated in the preceding section of this book) point in a definite direction.   For the choice of these legal texts and the manner of their arrangement in the Decretum are doubtless conditioned by his opinion about this question.   So his one utterance on the subject does not at all surprise us: "Women can attain neither to the priesthood nor even to the diaconate ... "[171]   (C. 15, q. 3, princ.).   It is not clear, to be sure, whether Gratian understands the non posse provehi, the fact that women cannot be admitted to the diaconate and the priesthood, as being the result of ecclesiastical law alone--in which case it is difficult to understand why he did not deal with all clerical levels--or whether he understands it as being the result of a divine and therefore unchangeable apostolic decree.   Several observations in the larger context of the treatment seem to point to the second explanation. [172]

Since Gratian knows and uses legal sources that refer

to the female office of the diaconate, especially canon 15 of the Council of Chalcedon, it is astonishing that he as decisively denies the possibility of the admission of women to the diaconate as to the presbyterate. This contradiction may be explained, on the one hand, by the fact that in the time of Gratian (12th century) there were no more deaconesses in the Western Church. It is true that several 11th-century papal decretals,[173] as well as the <u>Ordines Romani,</u>[174] refer to a consecration of the deaconess reserved to the bishop, which took place by a laying on of hands and which was considered to be a part of the consecration of the higher clergy.[175] But these regulations were limited to the city of Rome.[176] In other areas of the Western Church the female office of the diaconate disappeared more quickly. Several synods in Gaul from the fourth to the sixth centuries expressly forbade the ordination of deaconesses.[177] In the Western Church[178] there is no evidence for such wide extent and such relative permanence of the office of deaconesses as in the Eastern Church, where, for instance in Byzantium, it is still traceable in the 11th century.[179] According to an extant tenth-century Western source, only unclear conceptions of the female diaconate prevailed at that time.[180] The sporadically early disappearance of the office in the Latin church as well as its relatively weak beginnings there and perhaps also its different complexion there,[181] could be the source of Gratian's denial of ordination of women to the diaconate. Some decretists also find similar reasons for Gratian's statement: they suggest that Gratian specifically mentions the diaconate because entrance of women to this order seemed possible, since there were deaconesses earlier, whereas in his time this office no longer existed in the church.[182]

On the other hand the statement of Gratian may have another source: the Magister may have doubted that the early Christian female diaconate was a true diaconate order in the strictest sense of the word.[183] At any rate this is the position of several decretists who had themselves no knowledge of the historical source materials concerning the consecration of deaconesses and the office joined to it.[184] They support their position by reference to a text of Ambrosiaster falsely attributed to Ambrose, according to which the ordination of deaconesses is described as contrary to the authoritative (apostolic) decree and therefore inadmissible.[185] It must be assumed that Gratian was familiar with this patristic authority directed against the deaconess, especially since he had a high opinion of the teachings of the fathers and on many issues finds a place for them in his collection of sources.

c. Source of Discrimination: Denigration of Women

An objective evaluation of the sources we have studied, as well as of Gratian's own opinion about the exclusion of women from office in the church, necessarily requires a more exhaustive investigation of the question, What conception of women is implied or presupposed?[186] Clear understanding about the justification or lack of justification of legal regulations will result from a knowledge of how and in what manner women are esteemed. It might already be concluded that the evaluation of women as inferior underlies their exclusion from cultic-liturgical activity. Such evaluation of inferiority is shown with full clarity by other texts in Gratian's Decretum, texts which in part go beyond our special interests here. Statements of condescension directed toward women are found in great numbers in the Decretum and they stand in causal relationship to the legal limitations and prohibitions which women suffer and which also concern other areas of life.

Depending upon a long tradition, the author of the Decretum is guided and influenced[187] in his presentation of the legal status of women by a very low evaluation of women. This evaluation is explicit at various places in the book, as it is also in the dictum[188]--which introduces the third quaestio in C. 15 (i.e., in the context of the statement of Gratian already mentioned)--that women should have access neither to the priesthood nor to the diaconate. Gratian is here dealing with the question, whether a woman may go to court as plaintiff against a priest (an mulier sacerdotem accusare valeat). Gratian observes that according to canon law, this would seem to be completely excluded, for there is a general decree in a decretal of Pope Fabian (C. 2, q. 7, c. 6)[189] that neither complaint nor testimony may be raised against the priests of the Lord by those who sui ordinis non sunt, nec esse possunt, that is, those who do not have (or cannot have) an equal status with them. Gratian applies this generalized regulation to women, as follows: "Women cannot, however, achieve the priesthood or even the diaconate and for this reason they may not raise a complaint or give testimony against priests in court."[190] To sustain his argument Gratian appeals, however, not only to canonical law (sacri canones) but also to the leges, that is, to Roman law.[191] In Roman law, too, Gratian says, a woman is forbidden to bring a complaint before a court, and the reason is the necessity for feminine modesty (ob verecundiam sui sexus), unless she wishes to prosecute an injustice done to

her or to a member of her family.[192] From this it might be
concluded, Gratian continues, that a woman for whom the exception is not applicable may not be permitted to register a
judicial complaint against a priest.

But Gratian, in a kind of dialectical procedure, raises
an objection to this preliminary conclusion, supported as it
is by ecclesiastical and secular law. First, he points out
that anyone who can be a judge may not be prevented from
becoming a plaintiff in court. But women became judges in
the Old Covenant, as the Book of Judges clearly shows.
(Here obviously reference is made to Deborah, a judge with
prophetic talents, as the fourth chapter of the Book of Judges
relates.) So it may be said that those cannot be excluded
from the role of plaintiff who have often fulfilled the role of
judge and who are not forbidden by any word of Scripture to
act as plaintiff. The solution of this problem, which doesn't
seem to be a difficult one for Gratian, shows clearly that he
is limited by the bias of an ideology that is marked by rabbinical, Pauline concepts and that suppresses the freedom of
women. Thus he argues as follows[193]:

In the Old Covenant much was permitted which today
[i.e., in the New Covenant] is abolished, through the
perfection of grace. So if [in the Old Covenant] wom-
en were permitted to judge the people, today because
of sin, which woman brought into the world, women
are admonished by the Apostle to be careful to practice a modest restraint, to be subject to men and to
veil themselves as a sign of subjugation....

Thus Gratian perceived the Old Covenant practice of allowing
women to be judges to be basically an unauthorized concession, an imperfection that was overcome by means of the
New Covenant, whose perfectio gratiae manifests itself, in
the case of woman, in her punishment because of original
sin, for the entrance of which into human history she and
she alone is responsible. This punishment takes the form
of both her losing the freedom of an independent human being
and her status of subjection to man.

The conception of woman as a being continuously sub-
ordinated by the stain of guilt and punishment was for the
most part adopted by Gratian, presumably by way of patristic
texts,[194] from 1 Tim. 2:12-14, ascribed to the Apostle Paul,
a passage manifestly exhibiting rabbinic ways of thinking.[195]
Beyond this he was able to support his position about the

subordination required of women by reference to Eph. 5:22, 24; Col. 3:18; 1 Cor. 11:7-10 and 14:34f. The status su-biectionis of women justified further legal limitations, accord-ing to Gratian: their exclusion from being judges and from the right of complaint in a court room (likewise established in Roman law), as follows from dictum C. 15, q. 3 princ. The exclusion of women, mentioned in the same context, from the diaconate and the presbyteriate, is doubtless no ex-ception, since it is likewise based on the situation of sub-ordination inflicted on women.

The conviction of Gratian about the ethical inferiority of women, which led him in dictum C. 15, q. 3 princ. to depict woman as the author of sin, is expressed very clearly in another connection and nuance, in the dictum added to ch. 18 in C. 32, q. 7. Here Gratian is critical of the comments on 1 Cor. 7:10f., which appear in the commentary of the so-called Ambrosiaster[196] (mistakenly attributed to Ambrose) and which Gratian uses in ch. 17. Discussing the Corinthian passage, Ambrosiaster says that a woman who has separated from an adulterous husband must either remain unmarried or become reconciled to her husband, whereas a husband is per-mitted in the case of an adulterous wife to remarry.[197] The Magister does not doubt that this conception, giving such freedom to a husband during the lifetime of his wife, is con-trary to the official church teaching and tradition. Yet he refers to a contemporary interpretation, which in order not to question the authority of Ambrose tries to bring his meaning into line with church teaching by insisting that the statement is limited to a very particular case, that of adul-tery with blood-relations. This interpretation is taken over by Gratian and corrected by him to conform with church teachings.[198] In this way, it is true, a certain assimilation of patristic doctrine to the ecclesiastical viewpoint on mar-riage was achieved, but meanwhile the possibility existed that a man might protest that he is not being allowed more free-dom in marital legality than a woman in a similar situation. Gratian anticipates such a possible protest by a man, and does so in a way quite characteristic of his concept of wom-en: the man should realize that the designation vir (man) is, according to Ambrose, not derived from the sex but rather from virtus animi (moral strength, perfection), and that the designation mulier (woman) on the contrary derives from mollities mentis, that is, from weakness and softness of character.[199] The feeling of superiority and higher worth-fulness because of being male asserts itself here in crass form, exhibiting at the same time a contemptuous condescension toward the "weak sex," whose characteristic is, according to Gratian, the mollities mentis and for whom the opposite of mollities, [200] the virtus animi of the man, is hardly attainable. For Gratian, who doubtless adopts for himself the prevailing viewpoint of his time, the concept mulier is so closely associated with low morality that mulier can be used as appropriate designation for lack of chastity and for adultery in the case of both sexes because of their wicked depravity: "[prostitute or fornicator], each of whom ... is called a woman by reason of the corruption of lust."[201] Thus, far from being a value-neutral concept, mulier (or, femina), according to a centuries-old understanding that Gratian takes up and mediates to the future, implies a serious stain and inferiority, while vir indicates according to the same traditional way of thinking a human being in ideal form, and is thus likewise an ethically qualified term.[202]

Of course Gratian agreed with the church tradition of monogamy and unbroken marriage.[203] On the one hand this limited the greater sexual freedom man had come to demand as his natural right, since he was obligated to be faithful in sexual matters to the same degree that had always been expected from the woman. On the other hand, the man was granted, as a kind of recompense for his "sacrifices," unlimited dominion over the woman.[204] Here too Gratian was not breaking with tradition, as we may see from his remarks added to ch. 11 and 20 in C. 33, q. 5. According to the dictum p.c. 11,[205] which is supported by various authorities, the dominion of man over woman is limited only in the area of intimate relationship, where husband and wife seem to be given equal rights (in debito coniugii eque mulier habet potestatem viri, sicut et vir mulieris). So for instance one partner may not take a vow of sexual abstention (votum continentiae) without the agreement of the other (quod continentiae vota nec mulier sine viri consensu, nec vir sine mulieris consensu Deo reddere potest). But in all other areas of life, as Gratian emphasizes, the relationship of superiority and inferiority obtains between man and wife. Quia vero in ceteris vir est caput mulieris, et mulier corpus viri. (It is however obvious that this duty of subordination on the part of the wife could only reflect negatively on her rights involving intimate relationship, where her equality was recognized.)[206]

The rulership of the man is implied, Gratian thinks, by the idea that man is the "head," a conception taken from Paul (especially from Eph. 5.22f. and 1 Cor. 11:3) and

from patristic texts.[207] The idea that woman is the "body,"
on the other hand, implies her subordination to man. The
characterization of woman as "body of man" is likewise bor-
rowed by Gratian from Pauline terminology. It appears in
similar form in Eph. 5:28f., in a somewhat different context,
however, since it serves there in the first place as a description of the harmony of husband and wife.[208] Paul's
usage, followed by Gratian, of the concepts "head" and "body"
for husband and wife in their relationship to each other derives in the final analysis from a literal rabbinic understanding of the Yahwistic creation narrative, according to which
woman was formed from the body of man.[209] Such a usage
of "head" and "body" results from the concept of the inferiority of woman from the very creation. The obvious consequence of this type of thinking, as well as of the above-
mentioned concept of the ethical inferiority of woman, is her
status of subjection and the concrete legal limitations which
accompany such a status. These limitations, according to
the dictum p. c. 11, include the prohibition without the approval of her husband to take a vow of self-denial (fasting,
etc.) for religious reasons. (This so-called votum abstinentiae is clearly separated by Gratian from the votum
continentiae, which aims at sexual abstinence.) In this way
Gratian makes the wife so subject to the dominion of her
husband that she cannot fulfill a vow made with his approval
if he afterwards retracts his consent. "And the reason for
this is the position of servile submission (propter conditionem
servitutis) of the wife, on the basis of which she must in
everything be subject to her husband."[210] Gratian has no
difficulty finding support, incontestable in those days, for the
conditio servitutis assigned to women. He quotes ten passages (genuine and spurious) from church fathers, which deduce woman's status subiectionis from her ostensible inferiority, both creaturely and morally.[211] On the basis of this
authority he formulates the following (p. c. 20) as conclusive
result, which harmonizes with the previous dictum (p. c. 11):

> It is completely obvious that the husband is so thor-
> oughly the head of the wife that without his permis-
> sion she may take no vow of abstinence or religious
> way of living before God. Even if such a promise is
> made with the approval of her husband, she may not
> fulfill it, if he revokes permission.[212]

The degradation and insult of such "order" lies not least in
the fact that it takes from woman control over even the most
personal affairs of her life and thus she is denied the inde-

pendent activity of an unmediated relationship with God. Her relation to God is regulated by and through the husband so that she herself is demoted to an inferior being like a minor. The Old Testament has the same regulation. [213] It is therefore clear that Gratian has to a large degree preserved the Old Covenant order of law which resulted from extreme patriarchal thinking. According to this legal order the wife is the property and possession of the husband, [214] and this was true despite the fact that the New Covenant had been in existence for hundreds of years. If we may presume that today no one would seriously question the immediacy of woman's relationship to God, the Old Testament legality is still not overcome, insofar as women still find themselves dependent upon men in their relationship to God. The reason is that only men are the official preachers of the Word of God and administrators of the eucharist and of penance, sacraments definitive of Christian existence. [215]

All legal limitations and every kind of legal deprivation of women may be traced back to the status subiectionis laid upon women because of their alleged inferiority, as René Metz rightly emphasizes: "All the juridical incapacities of which she may be the object are explained by her status of subjection: 'Because of the condition of servitude, which [the woman] owes to man in all things, she submits.'"[216] Herein is also the cause of the exclusion of women from ordination. [217]

Gratian's judgment of women, which is not only personal but reflects also the thinking of his age, [218] is decisively marked by several factors: besides those Pauline statements about women we have already discussed there is, first, the viewpoint of the Church Fathers and, secondly, the viewpoint of Roman law. These two bases of Gratian's thinking are extensively treated in the Decretum and therefore deserve special consideration.

d. Influence of the Church Fathers

The authority of the Church Fathers was held in high esteem during the Middle Ages. Their statements were considered as genuine legal evidence[219] and as such had the same standing as decisions of councils and papal dispensations. [220] But it was particularly in the area of scriptural interpretation that the Fathers had unrivaled primacy. Thought to be inspired by the Holy Spirit, they were con-

sidered as authoritative commentators and exegetes.221 Gratian makes use of their scriptural exegesis in his quaestio
5 of causa 33--which is especially interesting at this point--
in order to establish and legitimize the assigned place of
women as "servile subjugation, on the basis of which they
must be in all things subject to men" (dictum p.c. 11). The
passages from the Fathers that Gratian uses fulfill this objective in a manner which could hardly be more literal or
uncritical in its interpretation of the Bible.222 There are
statements in various texts concerning a female inferiority
already set forth in the creation and the consequence is that
the imago dei is expressly denied to women. Here the extent of derogation is especially visible, as in Gratian's ch.
13--taken from Quaestiones Veteris et Novi Testamenti--at-
tributed to Augustine:

> This is the likeness of God in man [the male], that
> he is created as the only being, from whom the others
> have come, and that he possesses, as it were, the
> dominion of God as His representative, since he bears
> in himself the image of the one God. So woman is
> not created in the image of God; that is what [scrip-
> ture] says: 'And God created man [the male], accord-
> ing to the image of God he created him'; and there-
> fore the Apostle also says: 'Man certainly must not
> cover his head, because he is image and reflection of
> God, but woman must cover her head because she is
> neither the reflection nor the image of God.'223

That woman is not the image of God is likewise asserted in
the passage of ch. 19 attributed to Ambrose in explanation
of 1 Cor. 11:3ff.: "A woman must cover her head because
she is not the likeness of God; in order that she may appear
submissive ... she must wear this sign...."224 It is true
that the texts do not come from Augustine and Ambrose, as
Gratian supposes, but rather from Pseudo-Augustine and
Pseudo-Ambrose;225 their attribution by Gratian to the great
Church Fathers agreed with prevailing opinion in the Middle
Ages.226 Today it can be taken as certain that the commentary to the 13 Pauline letters, from which the text of ch.
19 is taken, and the questionable Quaestiones, are products
of the same author, in other words that Pseudo-Augustine
and Pseudo-Ambrose are the same person.227 The identity
of the author, so-called Ambrosiaster, is not yet clear.228
From his writings we conclude that he was schooled in Roman law.229

The scriptural proof for the contention of Ambrosiaster
that woman is not in the image of God is derived in ch. 13
from the Yahwistic creation narrative (Gen. 2), then from
Gen. 1:27 (taken over almost word for word), and from 1
Cor. 11:6f. (with an addition not found in Paul[230]).   From
this last passage is also derived in ch. 19 the not-in-God's-
image status of women.   The genuine Ambrose in his Liber
de Paradyso also derives the pre-eminence and primacy of
the male and the secondary position of the female from the
Yahwistic creation narrative.   The relevant passage is placed
by Gratian in ch. 20 (ibid.):

> It is not without significance that woman was not
> formed from the same earth as Adam, but rather
> was created from a rib of this Adam....   So at the
> beginning [of the creation] it was not two who were
> created, man and woman, nor two men nor two wom-
> en, but first the man and after him the woman out of
> him.... 231

Jerome in his Titus commentary (to Tit. 2:5) refers to 1
Cor. 11:3 (likewise derived from Gen. 2[232]), the passage
about the man being "head" of the woman, in order to give
a religious basis to the requirement that women be subordinate to men--thus giving this requirement the needed emphasis.   The text appears in Gratian as ch. 15 (ibid.): "Since
the man is the head of the woman, while the head of the
man is Christ, any wife who does not subordinate herself to
her husband as her head is as guilty as a man who does not
subordinate himself to Christ."[233]

In connection with the so-called order of creation
Jerome also introduces natural law (lex naturae) in support
of an inferior position for women. [234]   Augustine likewise
makes use of this category in his commentary on Genesis
(q. 153; c. 12 in Gratian, ibid.) in order to legitimate the
servant relationship of women to men: it corresponds to nature's just ways that the lesser should serve the higher.[235]
René Metz has rightly noted that the concept ordo naturalis
as used by Augustine simply characterizes the actual situa-
tion--understood of course as unchangeable and determined
by nature--in which women were placed, in state and in
church, at that time: "From a factual situation St. Augustine
deduces a condition of right; he infers from it the inferiority
of woman vis-à-vis man."[236]   From Augustine's standpoint
the Old Testament regulations about the subordination of wom-
en contain nothing foreign or offensive.   The Church Father

sees in them only a manifestation of the order of nature, as
well as a recognition of divine law.   An illustration is the
stipulation of Num. 30:7ff, according to which a wife is
completely dependent upon the will of her husband in taking
a vow.   (Gratian gives this Augustinian commentary as cc.
11 and 16 in C. 33, q. 5.)   Another illustration is the regulation of Dt. 22: 13-21, where a wife--accused by her husband of unchastity before their marriage--was to be stoned
if the evidence of the husband proved to be true.   However
the same punishment of stoning did not apply to a false witness, although in other cases in Israel the basic ius talionis
was in effect--that is, the false witness was punished in the
same fashion as the accused person in the case of truthful
evidence.   (The Augustinian commentary on this passage appears in Gratian as ch. 14, ibid.)   This Augustinian type of
reasoning, to deduce norms of natural law from the factual,
is by no means unique in the history of natural law.   Similarly, for instance, the actual existence of slavery was ra-
tionalized as natural necessity, which in turn led to the fundamental permission to hold slaves:237   they were considered
as "by nature not free" and so by nature "intended for servitude. "238   This unhistorical, superficial and shortsighted type
of judging, in which the actual subordination of women is
understood as determined by natural law--went further in the
case of Augustine.   It led him to understand the lack of development of the character of women (their ignorance and
lack of education), hindered as it was by profound injustice,
as if it was a psychic weakness and inferiority determined by
nature.   For it is said, in the Augustinian text mentioned
above (p. 35) and given by Gratian (c. 12, ibid.), "that the
lesser should serve the higher, " or more clearly in the original text, "that the person with weaker mentality should serve
the one with stronger. "   Likewise the next sentence (not used
by Gratian) reads as follows: "Thus true justice is found in
the relationship of masters and slaves, that those who are
outstanding because of their higher mental powers should
assume the place of dominion. "239   Pseudo-Augustine (Ambrosiaster) even goes so far as to derive women's not-in-
the-image-of-God status from the fact that women exercise
no public, legal functions.   He holds it absurd to think that
women as well as men are distinguished by the imago dei
and thus intended for dominion.   He rejects applicability of
the imago dei to women by pointing to their immaturity and
lack of business skills in public affairs.   He asks, "How
can anyone maintain that woman is the likeness of God when
she is demonstrably subject to the dominion of man and has
no kind of authority?   For she can neither teach nor be a

witness in a court nor exercise citizenship nor be a judge--
then certainly not exercise dominion" like a man![240] Gratian
uses the text in somewhat shorter form[241] and attributes it
to Ambrose.

The legal situation of women exhibited in chapter 12
is clearly recognizable as one imposed on women by Roman
law. In the latter they may not serve as witnesses,[242] they
may not be active as citizen and judge, they are completely
excluded from all public office.[243] But Ambrosiaster is in
no way critical, from his Christian point of view, of this
severe oppression of women by secular law. On the contrary he tries to show the agreement of Roman law, well
known to him and also highly valued by him,[244] with the
"order of creation." He tries to derive the inferiority of
women as created and her not-in-the-image-of-God status
from Roman legal regulations--that is, to confirm the former
by the latter.[245] Since women, because of their exclusion
from all official church functions, are no better off by ecclesiastical law than by Roman law, Ambrosiaster certainly
did not need to feel his opinion about women was any contradiction of ecclesiastical understanding.

The statements of Augustine and of Ambrosiaster have
not lost relevance even to the present day. Their
prejudicial and hasty manner of judging women is by
no means overcome today: because women hold practically no church office, because of the canon law
which forbids it, it is concluded that they are not
capable of holding such office. It is today forgotten
but not therefore less true that women were as long
as the law permitted considered incapable of profiting
from any education, and there were no available
means for education,[246] until finally experience dis-
posed of this pre-judgment. Furthermore from wom-
en's present situation and behavior one infers forth-
with an unchangeable, inferior feminine nature, without at all taking account of the fact that the long-ex-
isting suppression of women did not fail to make an
impression on them, that their personalities were not
a little stunted and undeveloped, which often in fact
makes them seem inferior and worthy of contempt.
It was precisely the failure to take account of these
components of historical development which determined
the mistaken judgment, namely the depreciation of
women (cf. Ambrosiaster).[247] This devaluation, although seldom pronounced openly today, nevertheless

expresses itself clearly in the present situation of women.

Besides the secondary creation of women (after and out of Adam), from which their not-in-the-image-of-God status is concluded, and besides the "order of nature" argument, the Fathers bring up the question of original sin, for which women are said to bear the principal guilt or even the only guilt. This contention becomes another way to establish and sanction their status subiectionis, and it determines the line of thought in Gratian's chapters 18 and 19. According to ch. 18, which is taken from the Hexaemeron of Ambrose but which also depends on 1 Tim. 2:14, Eve--and with her, womankind--receives the blame for man's being seduced into sin. Man, the victim of her seduction, should to a certain extent act in the place of God to see to her punishment by bringing her under his dominion. It is implied that an attitude of constant mistrust toward women seems advisable.[248] Similarly ch. 19,[249] which is taken from the Ambrosiaster commentary,[250] shifts original guilt and the punishment of mankind onto women alone, and as the text makes clear, not without a certain psychological intent: in this way women are induced to keep their essential and ethical inferiority in mind. Thus intimidated and submissive, they will adapt themselves as meekly as possible to a strictly hierarchical and patriarchically structured system:

> Women must cover their heads because they are not the image of God. They must do this as a sign of their subjection to authority and because sin came into the world through them. Their heads must be covered in church in order to honor the bishop. In like manner they have no authority to speak because the bishop is the embodiment of Christ. They must thus act before the bishop as before Christ, the judge, since the bishop is the representative of the Lord. Because of original sin they must show themselves submissive.[251]

e. Gratian's Use of Roman Law

Besides the writings of the Fathers (which in turn rely on Genesis and the Pauline letters), Gratian makes use of the regulations of Roman law, in order to support his opinion of the worth and place of women in the affairs of the church. Since Gratian was a teacher in Bologna, it was easy for him to utilize Roman law, the scholarly study of

which had reached a time of flowering in the famous Bologna
law school of the 11th and 12th centuries and won for Roman
law the rank of world law. [252]   But for the monk Gratian,
the more decisive reason for utilizing Roman law was, probably the fact that the church had always such a high esteem
for the lex romana. Ecclesia vivit sub lege Romana[253] was
an uncontested axiom in the lands of the Western Church.
The church constitution as well as the canonical discipline
were to a large extent influenced by Roman institutions and
Roman principles. [254]

     Roman law was already accepted in the collections of
law made before the time of Gratian. But Gratian's Decretum contains, besides the texts that appear in these collections, further Roman legal sources, which imply a direct
knowledge and usage of the Justinian compilations. [255] Gratian discusses the relation between secular and ecclesiastic
law in distinctio 10 of the first section of his Concordia.
To a certain extent he postulates here the theory that is basic
to his usage of secular law in his collection. He begins by
explaining (dist. 10 princ.) that legal regulations of secular
rulers do not take precedence over ecclesiastical laws but
rather are subordinate to them. [256] He supports this principle by reference to various papal dispensations (cc. 1-6)
and them completes it with a further principle, at the beginning of the second section of the distinctio (dictum ante
c. 7, sentence 2): "If they [secular laws] do not contradict
the basic principles of the Gospel and the regulations of
canon law, they must be considered worthy of observance in
every respect."[257] Next Gratian cites various authorities
as proof, specifically emphasizing the duty to recognize Roman law and to obey it. [258] Thus Roman law, when it agrees
with church law, always has a subsidiary function in relation
to it. It serves as a supplementary source of law[259] and is
as such dignified with every recognition and respect (omni
reverentia). Undoubtedly this principle of the relation existing between ecclesiastical and Roman law is important for
the question at issue: since Roman law was prejudicial to
women in the same way as church law, [260] it was used by
Gratian exclusively as subsidiary authority. As a result it
gave considerable emphasis to the Pauline and patristic
statements about the inferiority and status subiectionis of
women, which we have already discussed. The regulations
from Roman law that Gratian accepted should be understood
as part of the larger pattern presented in the following chapter, summarizing the situation of women according to Roman
law, and which became one of the factors determining the legal status of women in the church.

Chapter 2

SURVEY OF THE POSITION OF WOMEN
ACCORDING TO ROMAN LAW

a.   Roman Family Law

In old Roman (patrician) times Roman family law is
decisively marked by the patria potestas, the paternal authority over the agnate family, i.e., the association naturally
formed by blood relationship on the father's side (per virilem
sexum) or artificially formed on the strength of legal trans-
actions (by adoption or in manum conventio).   So this association, by blood and law or else by law alone, stands under
a common pater familias. [1]   The "Roman-patrician agnate
principle," or the institution of patria potestas, is based on
the theory of male procreation, according to which the male
is exclusively the procreator of posterity and is, so to speak,
its "most logical continuation." [2]   The contribution of women
to the production of new life (partnership in procreation,
giving birth) is so thoroughly ignored in the old Roman agnate
family and the so-called manus marriage that the wife has a
sort of child relationship to her husband and consequently a
sort of sister relationship to her own children.   Together
with her children she is subject to the household authority
(patria potestas). [3]   It is clear from the formation of the old
Roman manus marriage (coemptio, confarreatio, usus--that
is, possession of manus), [4] and especially from the general
rights of husbands over wives--rights which are connected
with the manus authority over wives and which are identical
with those which come from the patria potestas [5]--that a wife
is the possession of her husband and is completely subject
to his control.   In regard to her he has the authority of life
and death (ius vitae ac necis), and he is permitted any kind
of punishment of her. [5]   A wife caught in such a degree of
arbitrary power and violence had recourse for some protection only to the court set up for difficult family problems. [7]
A wife in manu also remains on the level of a child in matters of property law.   She has no rights of possession: everything which she and her children acquire belongs to the
master of the house, including the inheritance which the wife
brings to the marriage. [8]

In the course of time, however, the manus marriage
with its strict patriarchalism could not last; by the end of the
Republic it is more and more superseded by the so-called
free marriage. [9] Already the law of the Twelve Tables (450
B. C.) knows both forms. [10] Nevertheless the manus marriage
did not fully disappear until the empire. In the legislation
of Justinian, free marriage, which takes place by mutual
agreement, is the only form recognized. [11] It is true that
in free marriage the wife no longer stands under the patria
potestas of her husband--both father and mother are legally
head of the family--but still the husband has the legal authority (although it is less strict than the patria potestas) "to be
the final arbiter in all questions of married life."[12] He de-
cides the place of residence, which the wife has to share
with him, he determines what is to be the education of the
children, to him alone is formally granted the right to live
together with his wife, [13] from which follows that violation of
marital fidelity by him remains largely unpunished. [14] While
adultery by a wife is legitimate grounds for divorce in every
stage of development of Roman law, it is only in the late
empire that adultery of the husband is recognized--through
the influence of Christianity--as grounds for divorce. [15] On
the other hand, in free marriage the wife gains a basic independence and considerable equality with the husband in regard
to the laws of property, because separation of property laws
are then in force. [16]

b. General Civil Law

Corresponding to her subordinate position in the Roman
family, a Roman woman as a female is also disadvantaged
as civis Romanus, [17] that is to say, in the area of general
civil law. This is true in regard to her legal competence
as well as her commercial rights (Dig. 1, 5, 9: In multis
iuris nostris articulis deterior est condicio feminarum quam
masculorum). [18] The limitation of her legal rights is clear
from her exclusion from all public office and legal proceed-
ings. [19] Absolute impediments to eligibility for office are:
female sex and physical or mental illness. [20] Besides passive franchise, active franchise is also denied her. [21] In
civil cases she has no rights pro aliis, that is, to go to
court for another person, [22] or to be a juror. [23] In criminal
cases also she only very exceptionally has the right of plain-
tiff--actually only "as plaintiff in an offense against her or
against her family."[24] Further, a woman is denied the
right to be a guardian (Dig. 26, 1, 16 and 18: tutela virile

officium est);[25] only in Justinian's law have mother and
grandmother the right of guardianship over child and grand-
child, provided they do not marry again.[26] In drawing up a
will, a woman cannot function as witness (Institutiones Justi-
nians 2, 10, 6),[27] and she has no legal competence for "sol-
lenity" testimony, i.e., "the use of witnesses in legal affairs."[28] The denigration of women in Roman law[29] is also
obvious from the fact of their being listed along with minors,
slaves, deaf mutes and men deprived of civil rights, as legal
incompetents.[30]

Besides age and health, sex is one of the factors in
Roman law which influence commercial rights: the limitations
of women in this area prevent their undertaking certain acts
of civil law without a guardian (tutor).[31] Even under classical law an adult woman, if she is not under the authority
of her father (in patria potestate) nor that of her husband
(in manu mariti), comes under legal guardianship (tutela legitima) of the closest agnate (i.e., the closest male relative
of her father or her deceased husband). Only the Vestals
were free from this guardianship. The reason for the requirement of guardianship is again very characteristic of the
estimation of women: they need a guardian because of the
weakness of their sex (propter sexus infirmitatem) and because of their ignorance of public affairs.[32] By means of
the lex Julia (A.D. 4) and Papia (A.D. 9) women were ex-
cused from the agnate tutela if they had the ius liberorum
(in the case of three children of a free-born woman or four
of an emancipated). Childless women were also granted the
privilege of ius liberorum.[33] Claudius rescinded the tutela
legitima of the agnate and thus its practical significance was
lost,[34] but the tutela mulieris disappeared altogether only in
the fifth century.[35]

The privileges granted to women by Roman law because of their sex (privilegia favorabilia) hardly improve their
disadvantaged legal situation, especially in the old Roman
and early classic period. These privileges are rather the
result of that disadvantaged situation, and express the fact
that women are not accepted as of age, as responsible persons. An illustration is regulation Dig. 22, 6, 9 pr., to the
effect that women are to be forgiven legal errors (ignorantia
iuris) "because of the weakness of their sex" (propter sexus
infirmitatem). This privilegium holds for minors, soldiers
and others who are ignorant of business (rustici).[36]

Although it is true that because of the influence of

humanitarian ideas on Roman law, the situation of women began to improve--they became more independent legally and in business[37]--still "the Roman basic principle" remained that women "belong in the home," despite the "humanitarian demands of legal equality for the sexes." The regulation which resulted from this basic principle--"Women are excluded from all political or public office ..." (Dig. 50, 17, 2)--continued to be binding for the whole Roman law and thus for the legal standard characterizing the evaluation and the status of women.[38]

c. Influence on Gratian

In the legal aspects of marriage and in the matter of lawsuits, we see in Gratian the negative influence of Roman law on the place of women in classic canon law. It should be noted that the more favorable situation of women in late Roman marital law was ignored by Gratian.

In discussing the question (C. 32, q. 1) whether a man may marry a prostitute (meretrix)--an licite meretrix ducatur in uxorem--in which term Gratian includes an adulteress, Gratian rests his case on a Roman legal decree which requires a man to prosecute and separate from his adulterous wife.[39] If he does not do so, he is a "protector of immorality" (patronus turpitudinis) and is guilty of pandering (dictum p. c. 10). Gratian expressly says that on the other hand a wife does not have the same responsibility in the case of an adulterous husband. She is in fact not permitted to accuse her husband of adultery, as Gratian proves by reference to a Roman law.[40] Gratian has not one word of disapproval for this crass "double standard" of Roman law, involving as it does a "double morality," strictly requiring wives to remain true but allowing husbands to go unpunished for unfaithfulness to the extent of adultery.[41] It is true that at the end of the dictum Gratian insists: "Married couples must preserve the faithfulness and indissolubility of the marriage bond; if these are lacking, they are not married partners but marriage breakers."[42] This statement implies the obligation of husbands to marriage fidelity, but on the other hand the one-sided faithfulness of wives is so strongly emphasized, by means of ecclesiastical and Roman legal auctoritates, that the above quotation from Gratian does not restore the balance, and thus the message of Christ concerning the complete equality of marriage partners (cf. Mt. 19:3-9) does not become productive.[43] Since Gratian in granting a husband (specifically a cleric) the right to punish his unfaithful wife appeals to a council decree[44] that was influenced by Roman law, it is clear how little church law was able to distance itself from the conceptions of old Roman law, according to which women were the possession of men and therefore subject to their disposal. In only one respect does Gratian (in dependence on cc. 5-9 in C. 33, q. 2) deviate from Roman law: he rejects the death penalty for wives. He goes no farther in opposing the objection of Christian conscience to the inhumanity of secular law: "If their wives have failed, the clerics are permitted to keep them in custody--without too much severity--and to force them to fast, but nevertheless not to mortally wound them."[45] Gratian never speaks of such punishment for an unfaithful husband.

The negative evaluation of the female sex that is characteristic of Roman law, considerably limiting the legal and commercial capability of this sex, has influenced not only marital law but also the decrees of classical canon law concerning litigation.[46] Simply because of her sex (propter sexum) a woman is forbidden by canon law to accuse someone in court--there are a few exceptions (cf. C. 15, q. 3)[47]-- to be a witness in cases involving punishment and in matters relating to wills (C. 4, q. 2/3 c.1[48] and c.3, § 22),[49] to postulate for someone (C. 3, q. 7 c. 2, § 2, and C. 15, q. 3 princ.). Likewise she is excluded from the office of judge and from all functions connected with judgeship[50] (such as procurare, advocare, postulare). (Cf. C. 3, q. 7, dict. p. c. 1., c. 2, § 2.) The determining factor in the possession or non-possession of these important rights and functions and in the admission or non-admission of persons to them, both in Roman law and in canon law, is before anything else the sex of the persons in consideration. Only in the second place is their spiritual and ethical condition of importance, as it is unmistakably clear in the decree about witnesses in wills[51] which Gratian took over from Roman law, according to which a hermaphrodite's legal capability is determined only by which sex predominates. The ecclesiastical use of this kind of irrelevant principle--to make one's sex the standardizing criterion--determined, together with the Pauline and patristic statements we have noted, the inferior legal status of women in the church and certified its tenacity. Thus even today we witness the continuing exclusion of women from public liturgical-cultic functions, especially those of the diaconate and the presbyterate.[52]

Chapter 3

SUBSEQUENT INFLUENCE OF GRATIAN'S DECRETUM
ON THE PLACE OF WOMEN IN THE CHURCH

a. Its Authority

In addition to the discussion of the texts of Gratian's
Decretum which concern our subject, the question of the
authority of the book, and its influence on the subsequent development of law, presents itself. Students of the history of
law assign great significance to this work, both for the subject of canon law itself--founded by Gratian as an independent
branch of theology[1]--as also for the formation and development of canon law. [2] As a collection of the older law[3] and
in serving the purpose of "bringing conformity into church
law"--which had existed as a parallel of old and new, general
and particular regulations, with resulting contradictions[4]--
Gratian's Concordia soon (by the end of the 12th century)
displaced all older law collections. [5] It became the essential
collection of sources of canon law. [6] This great respect was
in large part the result of the reception of the work by the
school for canonists founded in Bologna by Gratian. [7] In this
school the Decretum formed the basis and the subject of
teaching and of scholarly study. [8] Of course as a whole it
never achieved the status of law, since it was actually the
work of a private person, and the individual sources in it
have that authority "which belongs to them in and for themselves, "[9] apart from their acceptance by Gratian. Even
when popes Pius IV and V arranged for an official text of
the Decretum Gratiani (Editio Romana), its non-official character remained. The purpose of this edition was simply to
prepare a reliable text for the widespread use of the work
in school and court. [10] This text of the Editio Romana was
declared authentic by the constitutions of Gregory XIII, Cum
pro Munere (A. D. 1580) and Emendationem Decretorum
(A. D. 1582), and any alteration was forbidden. Yet that
act did not lend the Decretum more authoritative legal status. [11] On the other hand the unassailed valuation and the
great respect accorded it as source of ecclesiastical law are
attested by the fact that Gregory XIII made it the first part
of the Corpus Iuris Canonici. [12]

On the basis of its own authority the Decretum exercised a significant influence on ecclesiastical practice and on the further development of law. The evidence shows that besides its use in the "school," it was used in the papal chancery and thus in the legislative work of the curia. [13] It was cited at various times by ecumenical councils[14] and it influenced numerous synodal decrees. [15] Out of some regulations in Gratian's Decretum, which were themselves of the nature of particular law, universal law developed. [16] Likewise common law statements were abstracted from papal decretals (issued for individual cases) which Gratian embodied in the Corpus as auctoritates. [17] Even the dicta of Gratian, the authority of which was only "doctrinal" although "important,"[18] have had influence in many directions on scholarly work and practice, so that prescriptive laws have grown from them. [19] The Decretum, and thus the opinions of the Magister, created the real basis for the absolute legislative power of popes, which came to full strength immediately after Gratian. [20] In view of these facts and of the general importance of the Decretum, it is highly significant that Gratian accepted the Pseudo-Isidorian decretals as papal authority for his source book, without recognizing them as forgeries but simply going along with the judgment of his time, which attributed them to Isidore of Seville. [21] Thus it was an unavoidable consequence of the great respect shown to Gratian's Decretum that the forged legal materials were widely taken over into church practice and influenced the development of church law. [22] This was especially unfortunate since the Correctores Romani, who arranged for the Editio Romana[23] of the Decretum, maintained the genuineness of the Pseudo-Isidorian decretals as late as A.D. 1580, [24] although repeated doubt had been expressed about their authenticity and the proof of the forgery had already been advanced by the Magdeburg Centuriators. [25]

It is clear from the application of this discussion to the problem before us that the Decretum had a negative influence on the evaluation and the position of women in the church. The ritual regulations for women, which consist exclusively of prohibitions--including the Pseudo-Isidorian decretals and texts (Statuta Ecclesiae Antiqua) falsely attached to an important council--have established or at least confirmed a status of legal deprivation and inferiority for women in the ecclesiastical sphere. (Assisting in the process were genuine and non-genuine patristic citations, which were used in the Middle Ages as legal sources, [26] and the accepted opinions of Magister Gratian.) This status became a generally accepted and permanent condition, which is still determinative[27] for the law of the Codex Iuris Canonici. [28]

b. The Decretists

The Decretum formed "the basis of the whole instruction in canon law" in the new school of Bologna "up to the last decade of the 12th century. "[29] The so-called decretists thoroughly explained and commented on the work in lectures and writings. [30] Especially important for canon law, the result of these writings is the extensive literature on the Decretum, consisting of glosses, [31] apparatus and Summas. [32] The literature of the decretists exercised a great influence on the further development of canon law in the period between Gratian and Pope Gregory IX (1227-1241), [33] for the papal decretals, which formed the primary foundation of church law, originated in close connection with the school and the works which issued from it. "The most famous law-givers of the 12th and 13th centuries" (Alexander III, Innocent III, Gregory IX, Innocent IV) were themselves "educated in the schools of the glossators. "[34] "Everything set down in the writings [of the canonists], in the nature of new ideas, explanation of sources and hints for living, was used in the decretals, "[35] which since the time of Alexander III were normative for the legal affairs of the church. For the doctrines of the canonists "claimed to work in practice, to be usable in legal affairs, in lawsuits 'quoad causarum tractatum,' in a word, to be 'Ius'. "[36]

The writings of the decretists on the texts of Gratian's Decretum discussed above are thus not simply of interest for the subject before us, but must be taken into account for the investigation of the development of the legal history of this problem up to the "decretals of Gregory IX. "

* * * * *

The Summa of Gratian's pupil Paucapalea, which appeared between 1140 and 1148, [37] was the first work of the Bologna school on the Decretum, but it does not contribute much to our question, because it is only "in a minor way an independent exegetical work"[38] and often simply repeats the wording of Magister Gratian's dicta. [39] Paucapalea ignores the prohibition of liturgical-ecclesiastical activity for women which we have studied, and he ignores the question

of deaconesses. He merely explains the concept presbytera,
from chapters 18 and 19 in dist. 32, and presents two mean-
ings for it: she is either the wife of a priest whom he had
married in minor orders--which would correspond to the
wording of c. 18--or a cloistered nun (conversa ecclesiae),
who was also called matricuria because she took care of
those things mothers usually take care of (washing altar
cloths, baking bread and preparing food).40 But this explanation cannot in any way be applied to the original Greek
form of canon 11 of Laodicea, given by Gratian as chapter
19 in dist. 32. For although the import of the concepts
πρεσβύτιδες and προκαθημέναι in this canon are debatable, 41
there can be no doubt that they connote an ecclesiastical function, an office. The meaning given by Paucapalea is thus
incorrect. The designation matricuria for presbytera is taken
by Paucapalea from the Latin version (the Hispana) of canon
11 of Laodicea which Gratian had used. Apparently the concept presbytera in the Latin church had a different and more
varied form than in the Greek church. This is indicated by
the majority of the designations for presbyterae in the Latin
version: viduae, seniores, univirae and matricuriae.

When Paucapalea comes to the question of dist. 5--
whether a woman may come to church during menstruation
and after a birth--to which Gratian depending on a decretal
of Gregory the Great (cc. 2, 3) had given a positive answer,42
he equivocates. He seems to give credence, more than Gratian does, to the completely unchallenged superstitious and
unenlightened attitudes of the age regarding sexual behavior,
particularly of women, which contributed significantly to the
exclusion of women from the cultic sphere. Following Isidore
of Seville, 43 Paucapalea describes in detail the allegedly
devastating effect of menstruation blood: "... only women
are menstruating creatures; by touching their blood, fruits
will not ripen, wine will sour, grass will die and trees lose
their fruit. Iron rusts and air gets dark; when dogs drink
it, they develop rabies."44 Opposing Gratian's acceptance
(in c. 2) of the authoritative statement of Gregory, according
to which a woman may enter the church immediately after
giving birth, Paucapalea refers to a contrary opinion in the
Penitential of Bishop Theodore of Canterbury (born in 690). 45
However, Paucapalea is able to harmonize the mutually contradictory statements only by an interpretation of Theodore
which misuses the sources: he says that in contrast to
Gregory, Theodore is speaking of a woman who does not
come into the church to pray (non causa orationis) but happens to enter it for some other reason. 46 This solution of

the problem makes it quite clear that the idea that menstruation and giving birth lay a burden of stain on women has not
been overcome.[47] For according to Paucapalea and his times,
only an attitude of humility can be somewhat compensatory:
Sic et menstrua orationis causa non prohibetur ecclesia ingredi.[48]

Paucapalea fully accepts the viewpoint of Gratian that
women must be subordinate to men in marriage and in the
other areas of life. In his discussion of C. 33, q. 5, he
uses word for word the dictum Gratiani, p. c. 11, which
makes a woman as "the body of the man" subject to the man
as her "head," "because of her situation of servile subjugation."[49] The only exception is in the sexual relationship.
The legal consequence of this status in the public sphere is
characterized by Paucapalea in the following manner: "She
is thus not able to teach, to be a witness, to act as a citizen, to be a judge."[50] In this declaration he takes over
from Ambrosiaster, almost word for word, a statement
strongly marked by the regulations of Roman law for women.
(Cf. C. 33, q. 5, c. 17.)

* * * * *

Rolandus Bandinelli, the later Pope Alexander III
(1159-1181), remarks in his Stroma to C. 27, q. 1, c. 23
(=canon 15 of the Council of Chalcedon), which he composed
before 1148[51] in Bologna, that in ancient times (antiquitus)
it was doubtless customary to ordain deaconesses in the
churches, though only after age 40, who were then sternly
forbidden to marry.[52] Roland defines the deaconess as
evangeliorum lectrix, that is, as lector, a person commissioned with the reading of the Gospel. But there is very
little evidence that the deaconess had exercised this function.[53] As we have already noted (p. 25), other tasks in
community worship were usually assigned to the female
diaconate, especially assistance in immersion baptisms, instruction of female catechumens, the job of door keeper, and
also, in part, the distribution of Holy Communion to women
and children. So Kalsbach[54] assumes that Roland
came to the idea of identification of diaconissae and evangeliorum lectrices because of the similarity of the names, deacon and deaconess. On the other hand, Freisen sees in
Roland's remark only a "conjecture thrown out at random."[55]
In any case such a definition shows that by the time of Roland
there was no longer any clear perception of the deaconess

and her tasks, because the institution especially in the Latin
church belongs to the past. From the same confused understanding comes also, perhaps, the identification of deaconesses
and abbesses[56] that often occurred in the early Middle Ages
and later and also in the works of decretists we shall soon
study. It is possible that an identification of deaconesses and
abbesses lies behind Roland's characterization of deaconesses
as _evangeliorum_ _lectrices_, since abbesses of the Carthusian
order, which had received a consecration ritually similar to
that of the subdiaconate, sang the Epistle or Gospel at high
mass, during the Middle Ages. [57] Nevertheless the very
vague conception of the deaconess--completely inadequate for
an evaluation of the office, its characteristics and the functions assigned to it[58]--seems to have led Roland to a certain
reserve in his statement about the incapacity of women to
fill clerical offices. Thus while Gratian (C. 15, q. 3 _princ._)
objects to the entrance of women to the office of the priesthood as well as to the diaconate, though without giving reasons (_Mulieres autem non solum ad sacerdotium, sed nec_
etiam ad diaconatum provehi possunt), Roland limits women's
incapability to the priestly office, or at least he does not
specifically mention the diaconate in this connection. [59] But
otherwise Roland's judgment of women and their legal position in other areas is exactly the same as that of Gratian.
At the end of the explanation of C. 15, q. 3 _princ._, which
we have just mentioned, he emphatically stresses the exclusion of women from accusation and witnessing, with the exception of cases like simony, heresy, and lèse-majesté--
as provided in Roman law--as well as cases having to do
with marriage. [60] Because of the patristic authorities whom
Gratian cites, Roland thinks that the Magister's belief that
wives must be fully subject to their husbands, even in their
relation to God (_dictum_ p. c. 11 in C. 33, q. 5), is sufficiently and definitively supported. [61] He also offers no objection
to the authority granted to husbands (i. e., to clerics) to
punish their wives (cf. C. 33, q. 2, c. 10). [62]

* * * * *

More thoroughly than Roland, Rufinus in his extensive
Summa decretorum, written between 1157 and 1159, [63] a work
that became normative[64] for the subsequent decretists literature, analyzes the problem of the ordination of women, as
in his discussion of C. 27, q. 1, c. 23 on canon 15 of Chalcedon. He expresses his surprise that the Council could
direct that women under 40 should not be ordained as dea-

conesses, since according to Ambrose any deaconess ordination was contrary to an authoritative regulation. Ambrose
in his commentary on 1 Tim. 3:11 had appealed to (apostolic)
authority against the Cataphrygians (Montanists), who derived
from this biblical passage the right and duty to ordain deaconesses. [65] The allegedly Ambrosian commentary quoted by
Rufinus is in reality the Glossa Ordinaria[66] to 1 Tim. 3:11;
the gloss in turn is a short summary of the Ambrosiaster
commentary[67] on the passage. [68] This explains the attribution of the text of the gloss to Ambrose, who in the Middle
Ages was considered to be the author of the Ambrosiaster
commentary. [69] In solving the problem of the conflict between
the Chalcedonian regulation and the (earlier) statement of
"Ambrose," Rufinus sees the latter, as auctoritas patrum,
to be determinative. He makes a distinction between sacramental ordination, which relates to services at the altar, and
an ordination (better, benediction) for some other ecclesiastical service. As sacramental, the diaconate ordination for
women would be contrary to the authoritative prohibition, and
canon 15 of Chalcedon is understood to permit only the second
form, the non-sacramental ordination. But even the deaconesses consecrated in this way are no longer in existence in
the church and it may be, Rufinus thinks, that abbesses were
ordained in their place. [70]

But the deaconess ordination of canon 15 of Chalcedon
is hardly only an ordination "for some other ecclesiastical
duties" in the sense of a simple benediction, as Rufinus
maintains. For as we have already determined in the discussion of canons (p. 23f.), the technical term used for clerical
consecration is χειροτονεῖν and the consecration (χειροτονία)
of deaconesses in Byzantium, together with the ceremonies
accompanying it, is structured parallel to that for deacons. [71]
The presentation of stole and chalice indicates the liturgical
character of the office. In addition, the deaconess, on the
basis of her consecration--like the clergy of higher orders--
was obligated to remain celibate, as the regulation of Chalcedon clearly shows. It is thus rash and unfounded to characterize the ordination of the deaconess, administered according to the canon mentioned, as a non-sacramental consecration, [72] a characterization to which Rufinus has apparently been led by the Ambrosiaster commentary (to 1 Tim.
3:11) and by ignorance of the sources about the deaconess.
Besides, this commentary and the Glossa Ordinaria supported
by it by no means present an exegesis faithful to the text.
I Tim. 3:11 is not referring to woman in general, as Ambrosiaster supposes, when it says: "Women must likewise

be honorable, not slandering, sober, true in all things." The context of v. 11 in the midst of regulations about deacons (1 Tim. 3:8-13) undoubtedly forbids such an interpretation. Also the γυναῖκες named in v. 11 cannot be the wives of the διάκονοι in vv. 8-10, 12f., for the expected αὐτῶν is lacking and furthermore the family relationships of the deacons are treated separately in v. 12.[73] It would indeed be surprising if an admonition like that of v. 11 applied only to wives of the deacons and not at all to those of the bishops (cf. 1 Tim. 3:2),[74] whose prominent position in the community would rather lead us to expect the admonition for them, and to feel that they might need it more.

Accordingly, v. 11 of 1 Tim. 3 must be interpreted as, among others, Kalsbach does[75] (taking account of the context):

> This parallel [in language and content] to v. 8,[76] together with the subject of the whole section 3:1-13, which has to do only with ecclesiastical offices, compels us to explain the 'women' of v. 11 as follows: the Apostle is finding a place for women in the congregation to conform to that of the male diaconate.

So v. 11 has to do with guidelines for the deaconess in the early church, just as they are given for the deacon in v. 8. (Of course no further information is given in v. 11 and likewise in v. 8ff. about the type of consecration or the extent of authority of the office.) Thus we have shown that the supposedly erroneous exegesis of the Cataphyrgians, which derived their call for deaconess ordination from 1 Tim. 3:11, is in fact a very good interpretation of v. 11, while the exegesis of Ambrosiaster, who tried to counter that argument by noting that (in Acts 6) only seven male deacons were chosen, is not valid. Ambrosiaster does not understand that the action of the apostles (Acts 6) was conditioned by the circumstances of the time and its cultural relationships, and as a result he arbitrarily raises that action to a timeless principle, misusing the text of 1 Tim. 3:11. Actually underlying this text is a more developed understanding of office than that of Acts 6, an understanding which includes women in the role of ecclesiastical officeholder, despite all the remaining reservations towards women inspired by rabbinic unspirituality (1 Tim. 2:11ff.). These reservations challenged the office of deaconess from the outset and in later times. It was especially because of this anti-feminist manner of thinking,[77] but probably also because of his ignorance of the

Eastern deaconess office, that Ambrosiaster in his commentary on 1 Tim. 3:11 argues against the female diaconate, though accurate exegesis would have supported it. For Rufinus the high authority of Ambrose was simply determinative and apparently it did not seem necessary to him to undertake an investigation of the validity of the Ambrosiaster commentary. At the end of his discussion of C. 27, q. 1, c. 23, Rufinus draws a parallel between deaconess and abbess which often appears in decretist literature and which presumably is dependent upon a regulation of Gregory the Great: the regulation derives the age limitation from the so-called deaconess law (1 Tim. 5:9) and sets it also as the norm for the virgin abbess. [78] Rufinus' parallel is also dependent upon the fact that the structure of the consecration of the canoness-abbess was analogous to that of the diaconate. [79] Thus simply on the basis of the age limitation (age 40) of the Council of Chalcedon, Rufinus thinks he sees in C. 20, q. 1, c. 13, a directive for the deaconess, [80] although the wording of the capitulum[81] gives no occasion to do so. This interpretation, according to which "nun" (sanctimonialis) is equated with diaconissa and "veiling" with "ordination," obviously betrays a lack of clarity about the deaconess office that we have already observed in Roland.

Concerning the distribution of communion to the sick, which is limited to priests in dist. 2 de cons. c. 29, Rufinus foresees the possibility of distribution by a puer, [82] in case the priest himself is detained by sickness. Thus a (still under-aged) boy is trusted with such a duty but not an (adult) woman, who--whether a lay person or a nun--is not even considered by Rufinus for this task. The complete exclusion of women from ritual functions is not surprising in view of the fact that Rufinus, even more than Paucapalea, is prejudiced by Old Testament ideas about purity and the denigrating judgment of sexual actions accompanying them. Following Julius Solinus, [83] he speaks of "execrable and defiling menstruation blood" and he develops in detail a conception of its effects[84] which for modern enlightened thinking is strange and even absurd. In contrast to Gratian and Paucapalea Rufinus nullifies the permission of women to enter church immediately after giving birth, a permission granted by Gregory the Great (cf. dist. 5, c. 2) but which Rufinus rejects on the basis of contrary custom and especially on the basis of the regulation in Theodore's Penitential. [85]

Appealing to the statement of Ambrosiaster (C. 33, q. 5, c. 17), according to which a woman may not be a

witness, Rufinus denies the competence of women as complainant or witness in criminal cases but not civil cases, except in matters relating to wills. [86]   Although in Roman law
women may perhaps act as witness in secular criminal cases
--this relates to exceptional cases provided for in Roman law
(cf. C. 15, q. 3, c. 1)--canon law on the contrary refuses
to accept their witness in ecclesiastical criminal cases. [87]
Rufinus is here more strict than Roland, who permits a woman to be a complainant in the so-called crimina excepta and
in marital cases. (On C. 15, q. 3, cf. p. 50.)

* * * * *

Stephan of Tournay, whose Summa, [88] written in the
1160's, depends largely on Rufinus' Summa and Roland's
Stroma, follows their lead in general, in his conception of
the female diaconate and in fact of any acceptance of women
in the clergy. Concerning C. 27, q. 1, c. 23 ad v. Diaconissam, Stephan writes that deaconesses were at one time
ordained in the church and given the task of reading the
Gospels, but that now since we do not find them in the
church any longer, we may assume that they are today called
abbesses, who may not be ordained until 40 years of age. [89]
The identification of deaconesses with lectors is taken from
Roland[90] and the parallel of diaconissa and abbatissa goes
back to Rufinus. [91] Stephan gives a similar definition of deaconess on C. 11, q. 1, c. 38: in the early church certain
nuns who were called deaconesses were permitted to read
the Gospel, which now no longer happens. [92] The identification of nuns and deaconesses clearly reveals an insufficient
knowledge of the female diaconate. The latter disappeared
exactly because of the advances of ascetic monasticism, so
that the deaconess was brought into the convent and in this
way completely excluded from congregational service. [93]
This parallel of nuns and deaconesses (like the parallel mentioned above between diaconissa and abbatissa) should probably be explained by an attempt to replace a lesser-known
concept by a well-known, modern one. [94] In contrast to
Rufinus, Stephan does not comment on the character of the
deaconess ordination--that is, whether it should be understood as sacramental or non-sacramental. Clearly his idea
on this point is not to be taken from his interpretation of
the dictum Gratiani C. 15, q. 3 princ. (women cannot become priests or deaconesses), although here the status of a
clerical order is recognized for the early church female
diaconate. That is to say, Stephan remarks about the pas-

sage ad v. nec ad diaconatum, that the same thing could be
said about any lower order--that women have no admission
to it--but that Gratian names the diaconate because this order
seemed to be a possibility for women since there were deaconesses earlier; but it no longer exists. [95]   Thus it is admitted that early church law in contrast to medieval law recognized the membership of women in the clergy.   This
means, then, that a change in church discipline to the dis-
advantage of women had taken place.   So Stephan's observation, that women have no place in the diaconate nor anywhere
else in the clergy, may have been meant and should be understood not in the sense of a fundamental incapacity of wom-
en, but rather in the sense of an exclusion of women from
the clergy simply because it is so prescribed in the statute
law of the church.

The commentary to dist. 2 de cons. c. 29 is taken
literally from Rufinus. [96]   No woman but in cases of necessity a boy may bring communion to the sick.   The only task
remaining for women--and it does not have a close connection with the liturgical service--is, according to Stephan's
comment on dist. 1 de cons., c. 40, § 1--the washing and
mending of palls and linens used in the services and also the
preparation of hosts for the sacrifice of the mass.   This
was the activity, for instance, of the so-called Veglonisses,
nuns (religiosae mulieres) of the Milan church.   But that is
not compatible with the prescription contained in the relevant
chapter, which assigns the washing of palls and cloths within
the sanctuary to the deacons and subordinate helpers. [97]   But,
Stephan notes, [98] this regulation has been rescinded by general custom.   Furthermore, Stephan finds nothing inappropriate or unfitting in giving to nuns the task of preparing
objects required for the liturgical celebration and keeping
them clean, but--and there is no real change in this today--
that is the extent of women's activity in the ritual-liturgical
sphere.

* * * * *

Another product of the Bologna school is the Summa
of Joannes Faventinus, [99] a compilation of the works of
Rufinus and Stephan of Tournay. [100]   So also is his commentary to the passages of Gratian's Decretum which concern us at this point.   He takes over literally Stephan's
treatment of the dictum Gratiani C. 15, q. 3 pr. ad v. nec
ad diaconatum, [101] and he uses Rufinus as a model in his

discussion of C. 27, q. 1, c. 23 ad v. Diaconissam. [102]
Likewise he depends on Rufinus in his interpretation of C.
20, q. 1, c. 13, in relating the chapter to the deaconess,
although the chapter is really about nuns (sanctimoniales).
Joannes thinks that the consecration rite consisted of the
presentation of the veil to the deaconess. [103] But according
to the sources, the essential characteristics of the deaconess
consecration were the imposition of hands by the bishop in
connection with a special prayer of consecration during the
holy mass and the presentation of the stole and in some areas
of the chalice. [104] Nevertheless knowledge of the actual ordination rites of the deaconess had already disappeared from
the knowledge of the times, as shown by the identification of
ordination and veiling as equivalent, which Joannes also
adopted from Rufinus.

Among all the Bologna Summas before Huguccio, the
Summa of Joannes Faventinus was the most widely known.
It more and more supplanted the Rufinus and Stephan models
upon which it was based because it was found to be a handy
compilation of the teachings of its precedents. [105] In relation to our problem, the great influence of the Summa of
Joannes Faventinus brought with it this consequence, that
through it the doctrinal opinions of Rufinus about the prohibition of the sacramental ordination of deaconesses--a prohibition supported by the authority of Ambrose--and about the
non-sacramental deaconess consecration supposedly decreed
by Chalcedon, were effectively disseminated, as can be
proven by the later decretists (especially Huguccio).

* * * * *

The Summas of the French school of decretists, which
were in part contemporary with those we have studied and in
part somewhat later, and which exhibit an internal relationship to the works of the Bologna school, [106] contain some,
but not many, productive discussions.

The Summa Parisiensis, [107] which is dependent on the
Bologna decretists Paucapalea and Roland Bandinelli, [108]
gives no reason for their comment on dist. 32, c. 19:[109]
"Women may not be ordained like the clergy." Apparently
the operative legal norm is simply accepted as if it contained no problems. According to the author, the dictum
Gratiani about the exclusion of women from the priesthood
and from the diaconate (C. 15, q. 3 princ.) indicates

(innuitur) that there are no longer any deaconesses as there
were in the early church. [110] However the Summa contains
no further consideration of this early church office. The
author understands by presbytera dist. 32, c. 18) either a
nun who lives by an ecclesiastical benefice, or the former
wife of a priest. [111] When in dist. 23, c. 24, reference is
made to the consecration of women, one must not conclude
from that, he declares, that they were for this reason permitted to touch the holy vessels and altar cloths; this was
granted them only for the purpose of cleaning the cloths and
getting them ready for use and of decorating the altar. [112]
When the author watches over women in such a petty fashion,
to be sure they do not overstep the bounds set up for them,
the inconsistency and logical deficiency of his statements apparently completely escape him: when it is a question of
cleaning and caring for the altar and liturgic utensils, the
prohibitions set up for official church services suddenly become inoperative! As in the ritual-liturgical activity of wom-
en, public teaching by women--perhaps of men in a congregational assembly--is without exception an error which must
be removed, according to the author in agreement with Gratian. Such instruction in spiritual matters by a woman, for
example an abbess, can only be given to members of her
own sex. [113]

The Summa Parisiensis agrees entirely with the teaching of Gratian about the subordination of women (dist. p. c.
11 in C. 33, q. 5) and with the authority of the Church
Fathers which serves as support for the teaching of Gratian. [114] However the author seems to limit the statement of
Ambrosiaster (c. 17, ibid.), that women may not be witnesses, to the case of drawing up a will:[115] the reason for
the rejection of women as witnesses is said to be that they
could have had no experience with wills. No account is
taken of the fact that women's lack of knowledge and education, thus unmistakably brought to light, is determined by
their inferior position. In other (contract) agreements, on
the other hand, women are said to be competent as witnesses,
even though they are excluded from public office "because of
the weakness of their sex. "[116] Following this principle of
Roman law, the author justifies the exclusion of women from
judgeship, despite Old Testament evidence for the execution
of this office by women (cf. Judges 4). He thinks, with
Gratian, [117] that this Old Testament tradition--although its
historicity can hardly be denied[118]--is simply an astounding
miracle with no real significance. [119] Thus a legitimate conclusion is not drawn from this tradition--in contrast to the

Yahwistic narration (Gen. 2:21 ff.), which has a mythic background without any historical nucleus.

* * * * *

The Summa Monacensis, written between 1175 and
1178[120] and also a product of the French school, differentiates, as does Joannes Faventinus, several kinds of veils.[121]
The velamen ordinis is said to have been at one time presented to deaconesses (who have now however disappeared
from the scene) though not before their fortieth year.[122]
Once again, in dependence on Joannes and thus on Rufinus,
the deaconess ordination is mistakenly called a veiling. Moreover, since the author of the Summa differentiates several
kinds of laying-on of hands (manus impositio)--he calls the
manus impositio consecratoria religionis given to God-dedicated virgins a sacrament, just like the manus impositio
consecratoria ordinis for priests and deacons (deaconess
consecration is not mentioned!) and the manus impositio
consecratoria dignitatis for bishops[123]--it becomes clear that
the concept of sacrament was not well defined at the time
and not exclusively reserved to the sacred signs today regarded as sacraments. We notice here also a difference between the Summa Monacensis and the viewpoint of Rufinus,
who had already made a distinction between sacramental and
non-sacramental ordination, in order to have a category for
the consecration of deaconesses.[124]

* * * * *

One of the most important works of the French school
is the Summa Decretorum of Sicardus of Cremona,[125] which
appeared between 1179 and 1181[126] and which exhibits a certain amount of dependence on the Summa Monacensis as well
as an influence from the older decretists. More than some
of the writings we have studied, this one has a typical Summa
character: there is considerable "lack of commentary and
gloss."[127] Material is treated in part in generalizing formu-
lations, so that we find only succinct observations relating to
our problem.

In discussing the question (C. 15, q. 3) whether a
woman can go to court against a priest, Sicardus, depending
on Gratian, makes the counter-argument: "Those who cannot be priests cannot raise a complaint against priests nor

be a witness against them. "[128] No reason is given for the supposed incapability of women to be priests--their exclusion from the diaconate (as in Gratian) is not even mentioned. But his further counter-arguments, which bear the imprint of a patristic manner of thinking, show clearly a denigrating opinion of women. It can only be concluded that Sicardus, constrained like his predecessors by that kind of bias, sees the practice of ecclesiastical office as incompatible with the position and character of women. For example, in dependence on the statement of Ambrosiaster (C. 33, q. 5, cc. 17, 19), he remarks: "A woman must cover her head for two reasons--because of original sin and in order to honor the bishop. She is not permitted to speak in the presence of the bishop; she may not teach, etc. "[129] Clearly influenced by Old Testament conceptions of ritual purity, [130] Sicardus says in another place (on dist. 1 de cons.) that women (including nuns) may not touch the consecrated ceremonial vessels because of the respect due to them (reverentia utensilium). Only "consecrated men" are worthy enough to do so. [131] It is hardly surprising that Sicardus, burdened with such a heavily prejudicial view of women, thinks an actual ordination of a woman would be ineffectual, [132] which means that women are on the same level as the unbaptized.

As in the ecclesiastical sphere so in the marital: Sicardus places women in a substantially subordinate position. He sets up a hierarchical model for marriage, in which man is the principle and the origin of woman[133]--a conception later undergirded philosophically and then expanded by Thomas. [134] In working out this creaturely dependence, which was undoubtedly derived from Gen. 2:21ff., woman is so subjugated to man, according to Sicardus, that she must accommodate herself unresistingly to his will, yes even to his caprice. Like a straw in the wind she must give way before him and humble herself. [135] Only a ruthless will to oppress, which seeks self-affirmation in mastery and power over woman, can make such a demand, despising as it does the personal worth of woman. It thoroughly prevents woman from attaining the liberty of personal decision and control, since it places her under the authority of another human, and therefore imperfect, being.

It remains to note that Sicardus goes along with the Summa Monacensis completely in his understanding of the different kinds of veils (among others the velamen ordinationis, which is not presented until age forty). [136] The same is true for his understanding of the sacramental character of the

laying-on of hands granted to the God-dedicated virgins (manus
impositio consecratoria religionis). [137]

* * * * *

The Bologna pupil of Gratian, Simon de Bisiniano, produced a Summa perhaps between the years of 1177 and 1179, [138]
shortly before Sicardus's work, which is dependent upon it.
It itself depends in many ways on Joannes Faventinus in its
treatment of our subject. [139] To solve the problem of the
contradictions arising from the inconsistent dates used in
chapters 12-14 in C. 20, q. 1, Simon points to the different
kinds of veils. Thus like Joannes and Sicardus he refers
mistakenly to the deaconess, understanding her ordination as
a veiling. [140] He seems to answer in the negative the question of the possibility of ordination of women, in agreement
with dist. 32, c. 19. [141]

Besides his Summa and even before writing it, Simon
was active in glossing. [142] His gloss on chapter 12 in C. 20,
q. 1, mentioned above, is important for our question and at
the same time characteristic of the theological thinking of
that time. He refers to the regulation in the chapter, which
says that an abbess, but not a bishop, must be virginal. The
justification for this is, he says, that the abbess represents
the virgin church and the bishop represents Christ; but at the
same time, it is as though Christ has had two wives [143]:
first, the church that has come from the Jewish people and
then the church that has come from the pagans. [144] Here
the questionable manner by which Simon seeks to justify the
differing presuppositions for the assumption of the office of
bishop and the office of abbess does not concern us as much
as the symbols he uses. The bishop is the embodiment of
Christ and the abbess--that is, the female--is the representative of the church, a symbolization based on an interpretation of Eph. 5:22-23. The result has been a decisive imprint
on Catholic thinking about ecclesiastical office, [145] creating a
foundation for opposition to the admission of women to church
office. [146] Of course an objective exegesis of Eph. 5 will
not yield any such symbolization. [147] Besides it needs to be
pointed out that in the New Testament the relationship between
the bishop (or office-holder) to the Christian congregation is
never described in terms of bridegroom-bride. That is a
relationship obtaining only between Christ and Church. [148]
In the scriptural passage used in the gloss, 2 Cor. 11:2, [149]
Paul does not see himself as the bridegroom of the congrega-

tion but rather at most as the one who brings the bride to
the bridegroom, thus as the one who leads the congregation
to Christ, [150] a function which by its very nature is not reserved to the male sex.

* * * * *

The Summa of Huguccio, which was not finished before
1188, [151] is considered to be the most important work of the
Bologna school, because of its extensiveness, its detailed
treatment--never before achieved--of the Decretum, and its
critical evaluation of the older decretists. [152] As one might
expect, it is more thorough than its predecessors in discussing the question of women and church office, although it is
still to a large extent dependent on them.

In his exposition of chapter 23 in C. 27, q. 1, concerning canon 15 of the Council of Chalcedon, which gives
rules for the deaconess ordination, Huguccio--like Rufinus--
favors instead the statement of "Ambrose" that the deaconess
ordination is contrary to authority. [153] This statement, it is
particularly emphasized, preceded the Council decree. In
solving the contradiction, the contrarietas canonum, Huguccio
too accepts the Ambrosiaster passage as normative: the
ordination of deaconesses consisted simply in the fact that
they were chosen and appointed in a certain ceremonial form
for any services that belonged to the deacons. Perhaps what
they did was to sing the gospel and recite prayers during
matins and this function was characterized as diaconal. [154]
Like the earlier decretists, Huguccio takes the duty of the
abbess as criterion for the female diaconate, which he himself expresses as the practice of abbesses (described above)
in many communities. Deaconesses of this kind, he continues,
no longer exist, unless one could say that the abbesses take
their place, and that is the sort of ordination the Council of
Chalcedon is referring to, while Ambrose on the contrary
refers to ordination for the various levels of Holy Orders[155]
--i.e., to sacramental ordination. This or a similar understanding of diaconissa is expressed in other passages of the
Summa, where the deaconess is often simply identified with
the nun (monacha, monialis), who is ordained "only for a
special function, not with regard to the order (of the diaconate)"--for instance, to recite the Gospel during matins. [156]
It is worthy of note here that besides the conception of the
nature and tasks of the female diaconate already described,
there was another though not so common conception, so

Huguccio tells us. According to it, married women were
ordained up to the diaconate; later, during the time of Ambrose, this ordination was forbidden; still later, at the time
of the Council of Chalcedon, women were again ordained,
which now of course, says Huguccio, no longer happens. [157]

Thus the deaconess ordination of the early Christian
age and of Chalcedon was even in the Middle Ages not regarded as simple benediction. The prevailing opinion, which
however thinks of it as such, rests for proof on the Ambrosiaster passage and thus on an untenable foundation.

Huguccio's attitude to the whole question of ordination
of women agrees with his conception of the female diaconate.
In the context mentioned, to C. 27, q. 1, c. 23, he declares
that women are incapable of ordination and he brings forward
a justification for this contention that is new in decretist literature. The incapacity of women for ordination, he says,
rests on an ecclesiastical decree pronounced on account of
their sex. A factual ordination would therefore have no
spiritual validity. For this reason and in conjunction with
a reference to the Pseudo-Isidorian decretal dist. 23, c. 25,
Huguccio says that women are also forbidden to exercise the
related functions of office (officia ordinum). [158] In accordance
with Huguccio's interpretation, male sex is thus the most
important presupposition not only for the validity of ordination but also for the practice of church office in medieval
canon law. The unlimited acceptance of this principle becomes particularly clear in the treatment and arrangement
of a special case, that of the hermaphrodite: if in the
hermaphrodite the male sex predominates, he may in theory
be ordained, although in actuality he cannot be because of his
deformity. So the ordination would be valid, though not permitted. But if the female sex predominates, the hermaphrodite would not be ordained even if a factual ordination takes
place. That would be true also in case neither sex predominates. As Huguccio remarks, Roman legal regulations for
hermaphrodites (in matters connected with wills) were normative for the formation of canon marital law on this issue. [159]
This clearly pronounced dependence of canon law on Roman
law continued to be determinative, even during the subsequent
period down to the law in force today. (Cf. canon 968,
§ 1.)[160]

The viewpoint represented by Huguccio and his epigones,
that male sex is the conditio sine qua non for the validity and
effectiveness of ordination as well as for the exercise of the

functions of clerical office, is based in the first place on a
fundamental misunderstanding of ordination. As official commissioning and spiritual preparation for ecclesiastical service,
ordination can never have sex as essential presupposition for
its validity and operation: it is always directed toward a
human being. In the second place and especially, Huguccio's
viewpoint is based on disrespect for woman, her baptism,
and her personal and religious worth, all of which qualify her
as well as man for receiving ordination and for the exercise
of the functions of clerical office. Therefore it must be
emphatically emphasized that the church opposes the ethos of
the Christian message in an essential point, as long as it
preserves this viewpoint and elevates it to a legal norm.

Huguccio himself furnishes ample proof that the constitutio ecclesiae facta propter sexum--the regulation which
he says excludes women from ordination because of their
sex--is the consequence of a massive denigration of women.
Using the text of Ambrosiaster, which Gratian takes over as
Ch. 13 in C. 33, q. 5--the text in turn finds support in the
Yahwistic creation narrative of Gen. 2--Huguccio affirms in
agreement with the prevailing opinion of his time the dependence of woman on man and her subjugation to his authority.
The subjugation is a matter of essence and finds its basis
therefore in the creation. The result is that she partakes
of the dignity of the imago dei in far less measure than man.
In three respects it is claimed that man but not woman is
the image of God and Christ: just as all life has its source
in God, so all those who follow the first man (i. e., male)
have their source in him; just as out of the side of the cru-
cified Christ the church has come forth under the sign of
water and blood, so out of the side of sleeping Adam his
bride Eve was formed; finally, just as Christ administers
the church and leads it, so the husband rules and leads his
wife. For this reason a man must not--like a woman--bear
a sign of subordination, but rather a sign of freedom and
authority. Only for one reason could a woman also be considered as in the image of God: if as a being endowed with
spiritual understanding and reason she had access to knowledge of the being of God. [161] Analogically Huguccio sees the
glory and honor of God embodied only in man: by making
man, God has shown himself more powerful and more glori-
ous, for only man has come immediately and originally from
the hand of God, while woman on the contrary is formed
from man. Only man glorifies God principally and directly,
while woman on the contrary only does so through the mediation of man, if she is first directed and taught by him to
praise God. [162]

The woman as a derived being, who has her origin in
man and therefore depends upon him and remains subject to
him, who lacks direct access to God in her being and her
religious life and is thus deprived of full independent person-
hood--that is the view of women we get from Huguccio and
his times, mainly as the final consequence of the Yahwistic
Creation account and of certain passages from the New Testament (1 Cor. 11; 1 Tim. 2: 11ff.). This view, together with
the prejudicial conception of women that lies at the basis of
Roman law, brought about their exclusion from orders. It
would certainly be a mistake to suppose that the decree of
law in effect today (can. 968, § 1) rests on other presuppositions and foundations, since the continuity between the old
and the new law was in this respect definitely maintained. [163]

It is difficult to overestimate the influence of Huguccio
on the canonists of later time and thus on the later development of law. [164] As the most complete commentary to Gratian's Decretum, his Summa became the essential foundation
of the great gloss apparatus of Laurentius and also that of
Joannes Teutonicus. [165] "The following age needed only to
use it as source, not much more had to be done."[166] Consequently its sharply formulated thesis about the incapacity
of women for ordination because of their disdained sex had
a strong influence on subsequent canonical theory and practice.

* * * * *

Although Robert of Flamesbury's Poenitentiale represents a "special category only bordering on genuine canonistics,"[167] it should be considered because already there is
a clear dependence on Huguccio. [168] There is the same unconditional presupposition of the necessity of male sex for
ordination. It is, according to Robert, the first factor of
the substantia ordinis, i.e., it sets forth the essential requirement for the validity of ordination. Baptism is named
only in second place, followed by further prerequisites. [169]
In accordance with this premise, Robert declares definitively:
"Woman [in principle] are only blessed, they are not ordained." It is not prejudicial to this premise, he says, that
deaconesses once existed, for the designation diaconissa had
another meaning than the designation diaconus in his (Robert's) time. A woman never had the office that the deacon
now holds. [170] Huguccio had judged just as sharply the early
church office of the deaconess. Compared to Roland and

Stephan--less so to Rufinus--a strengthening of the tendency
to deny woman any capacity for ordination is apparent.

* * * * *

At the end of the decretist literature stands the Apparatus ad Decreta by Joannes Teutonicus, published soon
after the fourth Lateran Council (1215).[171] It became the
Glossa Ordinaria of the Decretum. Besides the work of the
previous decretists, especially Huguccio, the more recent
legislation of popes (especially Alexander III)[172] is assimilated into the Joannine gloss. In the following age it becomes
the real foundation for the study and usage of the Decretum
and is evaluated as almost itself the fountainhead of law.[173]
This explains its great significance. Its definitive revision
was made by Bartholomaeus Brixiensis in the 1240's,[174] and
in this revised form it became the basis for subsequent research.[175]

The statements of the Apparatus on C. 27, q. 1, c.
23 are especially important for our question. First of all,
the diaconissa of canon 15 of Chalcedon is interpreted as
abbatissa without further explanation--which not only misses
the meaning of the canon but also disregards the degree of
uncertainty that still clung to the judgment of the decretists
before Huguccio about equating deaconess and abbess. Over
against the Council's decree on ordination Joannes--clearly
following Huguccio (cf. p. 103, above)--places the earlier
statement of "Ambrose," which opposes deaconess ordination.[176] This statement seems to be determinative for the position of Joannes himself, agreeing as it does almost verbatim
with Huguccio's statement: "Women cannot receive the [sac-
ramental] character [of orders] because both their sex and
church regulation prevent it."[177] Joannes draws two conclusions from this alleged incapability of women to receive
ordination. (1) Women can exercise no function that requires
a consecration (officium ordinum); the Pseudo-Isidorian
decretal (dist. 23, c. 25) is added as proof. (2) The deaconess ordination of Chalcedon was not a sacramental ordination but only a benediction, on the basis of which some special kind of duty was assigned, perhaps the reading of homilies or of the Gospel at Divine Office, which was not permitted to other (nuns).[178] When it deals with the relevant
chapters from Gratian, the gloss emphasizes the exclusion
of women from the officia ordinum or from the duties connected with them. Joannes justifies the prohibition of

teaching in dist. 23, c. 29, by pointing out that teaching is
the responsibility of the priesthood; besides, C. 33, q. 5,
c. 17 (Ambrosiaster!) rejects any possible teaching right of
women because of their subordination to men. [179] Baptizing
by women (dist. 4 de cons. c. 20) is regularly prohibited,
according to Joannes--agreeing with Gratian--but in cases of
necessity an exception is permitted. [180] The gloss on dist.
2 de cons., c. 29, allows for distribution of communion to
the sick, if the priest is prevented, by a deacon or a laicus
catholicus. [181] (Of course this means a male lay person, as
already mentioned, pp. 12f., above; however the gloss, in contrast to Rufinus and Stephan, does not specifically mention
the possibility that a boy could also act as deputy for the
priest.)

The reason for the exclusion of women from the functions just mentioned--especially from orders that according
to contemporary opinion alone make these functions possible--
lies, for Joannes (as we have noted) in the sex of women
(impediente sexu), which means it lies in their inferiority.
Many passages in the gloss are quite candid about this. We
have already shown that such a denigrating opinion of women
goes back in part to the considerable influence of Roman law
on medieval canonistics, a fact clearly discernible in Joannes
Teutonicus. Whether a hermaphrodite can be a witness in a
will or before a court (in iudicio), whether he can be ordained, depends entirely, according to the gloss, on the predominance of the male sex. [182] Like Gratian the gloss accepts uncritically the rigid role differentiation that Roman
law prescribes for the sexes: it grants a free and honorable
position to the male but requires an oppressive dependency
relationship for the female. For Joannes, too, all public
offices and functions (officia civilia vel publica)[183] are considered male positions (officia virilia). The spiritual office
and the duties relating to it stand on the same level with
these public offices and functions, [184] which results in the
exclusion of women not only from ecclesiastical offices but
also from the practice of judgeship, [185] from being witnesses
in wills and in criminal cases, [186] and from being plaintiffs
(except in cases involving judicial punishment for injustice
against them or their families). [187] Instead of these, the
principal duty of women (praecipuum officium mulieris), according to the gloss in agreement with Roman law and with
Ambrose (cf. C. 32, q. 2, c. 1), is the preservation and
propagation of the species: to be childless is a disgrace for
(married) women. [188] This narrow definition of existence
[Daseinsbestimmung] gives woman an exclusively biological

reality; it does not value her as a person and individual. In
addition, it necessarily prevents her development to full humanity. According to the view of Joannes--which is informed
by old Roman, extremely patriarchal family law and the
teaching of the Fathers[189]--a (married) woman is denied independent existence to such a degree that a slave-like position
is expected of her as a matter of course. She is obligated
to serve her husband--her lord and master--in two ways:
she must be sexually compliant and she must also serve him
in the home.[190] If she fails this obligation, or if she should
even be faithless to her marriage vows, the husband as "head
of the wife" is empowered to pass judgment on her and rep-
rimand her. Joannes says he may also punish her but not
strike her too hard. The law gives him the opportunity to
treat her as the master treats his slaves or day laborers.[191]
From such classification of women it of course follows necessarily that they are unfit to receive ordination and to carry
out ecclesiastical offices.

It is true that the viewpoint of Joannes Teutonicus,
that women are unfit for ordination because of their sex, did
not remain completely uncontested, although it was doubtless
the prevailing opinion of his time. We may gather this from
his concluding discussion of C. 27, q. 1, c. 23: Alii (i.e.,
those who don't agree with him) dicunt, quod si Monialis
ordinetur, bene recipit characterem (ordinis): quia ordinari
(quaestio) facti est et post baptismum quilibet potest ordinari.[192] The indispensable presupposition for valid ordination,
according to this variant (from traditional thinking) conception, is not male sex but only baptism: if ordination is
granted on the basis of being baptized, then the validity of
ordination is acknowledged eo ipso with its factuality (post
baptismum quilibet--i.e., everyone, man or woman, potest
ordinari). The proof offered here is a decretal of Innocent
III (X 3. 43. 3), which says that an unbaptized person cannot be ordained and, if he is factually ordained, he does not
actually receive the character of ordination. Thus the question of the conditions requisite for valid ordination is ob-
jectively if not quite fully[193] answered: the only foundation,
or the necessary presupposition, for the validity and efficacy
of ordination, as well as for the exercise of ecclesiastical
office, is the baptized and believing person (to which may be
added, a person with a particular qualification, i.e., charisma for his vocation). The sex of the ordinand is irrelevant.[194]

* * * * *

The Rosarium Super Decreto, written between 1296 and 1300[195] by Guido de Baysio, who was already one of the decretalists, takes account of materials not used in the Glossa Ordinaria and of literature written after Joannes and is thus a kind of supplement to the gloss.[196] It presents a clear confirmation of the fact we have already noted in discussing the major works of the decretists, that the conviction that women are unfit for ordination rests on a belief in their inferiority. In his treatment of the chapter (C. 27, q. 1, c. 23) that regulates the ordination of deaconesses, Guido shows his agreement with the view of Joannes Teutonicus, that women are unfit for the sacramental character of ordination, by arguing as follows: "... Ordination is reserved for perfect members of the church, since it is given for the distribution of grace to other men. But women are not perfect members of the church, only men are."[197] The imperfection here attributed to women is understood by Guido as substantial, in accordance with creation. For in agreement with Huguccio[198] he says that woman in contrast to man is not gloria dei, because she did not come into existence immediately from the hand of God, but rather was formed from man and has a relationship to God only through man. Guido, supported by some of the patristic texts (C. 33, q. 5, cc. 18, 19) discussed above (p. 38), finds further reasons for the exclusion of women from ordination in their alleged moral inferiority: as the principle of sinfulness and the tempter of Adam, woman has become the effective cause of damnation; accordingly she cannot also be, by virtue of the grace-mediating power of ordination, the effective cause of salvation.[199] Thus Guido derives the exclusive fitness of men for the priesthood--for the "bestowal of grace to other men" (collatio gratiae in altero)--from the substantial and ethical perfection ostensibly characterizing only the male. This kind of justification betrays not only a considerable amount of hubris and arrogance, but also makes clear to what extent the truth has disappeared from view--the truth that the ministry of the church is based on the priesthood of Christ and permanently remains in relationship to it alone, and that therefore a purely creaturely perfection or any kind of "merit" on the part of human beings can never serve as a sufficient prerequisite for the priesthood. Just as untenable is the opinion of Guido that woman's alleged stain of having been the "efficient cause of damnation" cannot be eradicated even by the redemption offered by Christ. Guido says that the extent of Eve's guilt cannot be balanced even by the fact that

Mary is the Mother of God, since Mary was only the "material cause of salvation." Because woman was created from man, Guido allows the female sex in general only the ability to be the material cause of salvation, [200] though, paradoxically, she can be the only efficient causation for sin, according to Guido. The method of the whole abstruse argumentation makes it especially clear that the negative understanding of women, based on certain scriptural passages and considerably strengthened and shored up by patristic and pseudo-patristic exegesis and scholastic speculation, fully repressed the statement in Gal. 3:28 about the fundamental parity of male and female in Christ. This negative judgment became, consequently, the sole determination of the value and place of women in the church.

Guido comments about dist. 32, c. 18 ad v. presbyteram that one must not conclude that this word [presbytera] has to do with a female priest, for if a woman should be ordained she would still not receive the (sacramental) character of ordination "because of her sex and because of the rules of the church which do not permit it" (here Guido takes over the formulation of the Glossa Ordinaria). He admits that some of the rules are contradictory to this--referring to the objection to the traditional point of view mentioned by Joannes Teutonicus (p. 67). Presbytera, according to Guido, means rather the wife of an ordained man. [201]

Following Joannes, Guido maintains that by diaconissa we must understand an abbess, or perhaps it was once the designation for a woman who served the priest as acolyte. But this form of female diaconate no longer exists in the church. [202]

Chapter 4

DECRETALS AS SOURCE FOR SEX DISCRIMINATION
IN THE PRIESTHOOD

a. The Decretals of Gregory IX

Gratian's establishment of universal papal legislative
authority resulted in the promulgation of a large number of
papal decretals, especially by Alexander III and Innocent III,
which claimed universal recognition. [1] These so-called
decretales extravagantes--i. e. , they circulated outside the
Decretum--were brought together in separate collections, five
of which, the Quinque Compilationes Antiquae, were everywhere accepted in the schools. [2] In 1230 Pope Gregory IX
(1227-1241) commissioned his chaplain and confessor, the
Dominican monk Raymond of Pennaforte, to complete the
compilations of decretals with new additions, to eliminate
both the inconsistencies between texts and also some material that would prove to be extraneous, and to create a unified composition. [3] Raymond's methodology was hardly scientific: he eliminated inconsistencies by suppressing decretals
or changing them and he often shortened them by eliminating
some of the evidences (the so-called pars decisa). Conse-
sequently the decretals do not appear in anything like their
original form. [4] Gregory published the Compilatio Nova (the
so-called Liber Extra) on September 5, 1234, and sent them
to the universities of Bologna and Paris with the mandate to
use only this collection of decretals in the ecclesiastical
courts and schools. "In this way the collection became an
official, authentic, consistent, universal, and (vis-á-vis the
Compilationes Antiquae but not the Decretum) exclusive book
of law. "[5] The result is that all chapters of the compilation
have legal authority in the form in which they appear, without regard to the original wording. [6]

Only a few of the large number of decretals that
Gregory's compilation contains deal specifically with our
problem, which is perhaps evidence that the subordinate position of women in the church had hardened considerably[7]--not
the least reason for which was the antecedent collection of

Gratian's. Of particular importance is the decretal of Innocent III, Nova Quaedam[8] (X 5. 38. 10), which was sent in
1210 to the bishops of Burgos and Palencia (Spain) and also
to the abbot of a Cistercian monastery. It sharply condemns
the practice of certain abbesses in these dioceses of giving
ecclesiastical, and thus priestly, blessing to nuns under
them,[9] of hearing their confessions,[10] of reading the Gospel
and preaching publicly. The practice of these abbesses obviously aroused the ire and the disapproval of the Pope, for
he calls it intolerable and absurd, thus showing unmistakably
that such practice is thoroughly incompatible with his narrow
view of women. Here too, then, the motivation of the prohibition is the pejorative view of women as conditioned by the
times. Moreover--of course not without inner connection
with this traditional motivation, which was already evident in
Gratian's Decretum--a "theological" reason appears now for
the first time: reference to Mary who in contrast to the
apostles did not receive the power of the keys.[11] This argument, which some even today like to raise against the admission of women to ecclesiastical position,[12] calls to mind the
objection of Epiphanius of Salamis (died 403)[13] to the priestly
office of women: God did not even give Mary the authority
to baptize--Jesus did not have himself baptized by her but by
John--not to mention the office of the priesthood. The kind
of theological thinking which underlies such argumentation is
of course completely untenable, but it is nonetheless accepted
by many today, and therefore we cannot entirely avoid a discussion of it.

Obviously we cannot go deeply into the question of the
priesthood of Mary in the framework of the present investigation. This would require a separate Mariological study, and
we must content ourselves with a few hints and observations.
First of all, in regard to the objection that Mary never received priestly ordination and the "power of the keys" (potestas clavium) established by it, H. Van der Meer[14] has already noted recent publications on this issue and has emphasized that the question of the priesthood of the Mother of
God is far from solved--even if one does not misunderstand
this priesthood as parallel to the priesthood of Christ and
independent of it. It is true that Mary is granted priesthood
in a certain sense by theological writers but not the priesthood of office (sacerdotium ministeriale)--which is mistakenly
understood as priesthood in the full sense. The reason for
this rejection, as R. Laurentin has shown,[15] is that Mary
was not fit to receive the sacrament of ordination, according
to these theologians, because she was a woman. This kind

of reasoning certainly raises questions and leads to the conclusion that the denigration of the female sex on the one hand,
and the over-emphasis on the sacramental priestly office on
the other, could have brought about a falsification and distor-
tion of Mariology in this respect.   H. Van der Meer[16] rightly points out that the argument--Mary was not a priest because a woman cannot be a priest--can no longer be used as
proof for the thesis that a woman may not be a priest.   For
this unproved thesis is being used as basis for the statement
that Mary is not a priest: one cannot at the same time
prove the first by the second and the second by the first.

But beyond this, other criticism can be made of the
traditional assumption that rejects the priesthood of Mary.
There is not the slightest reason to confine to the so-called
lay aspect of the church the predicate applied to Mary by
tradition, and also by the Constitution on the Church of Vatican II,[17] that she is the archetype of the church.   Such a
conception, represented for instance by O. Semmelroth and
R. Laurentin,[18] suggests a truncated understanding of the
function of Mary in salvation history, as well as a remark-
ably exaggerated understanding of priestly office--which does
not conceive ministry in terms of the whole church and its
charismatic essence but rather as isolated from them.[19]
Mary is not only the image of the receiving and believing
church--loving as a bride[20]--she is also, and for this very
reason, just as much the image of the church proclaiming
the Gospel and conferring the grace of salvation in sacramental signs.   This is, in traditional terms, the church of
priestly office and Mary is the one who bestows upon the
world the gift of the eternal Word of the Father, the redeemer and the source of salvation, after she had conceived
him in free consent.   It is not legitimate to sever the two
aspects of the church--on the one hand receptive attitude
toward God and his grace and on the other hand active extension of salvation as deputy of Christ--nor is it legitimate to
identify these two aspects with the church of the laity, on
the one hand, and with the church of priestly office, on the
other.   The church's (active) work of salvation in the name
of Christ and at his behest inevitably presupposes the ("passive") reception and assimilation of the grace of salvation.

Insofar as Mary can rightly be called model of the
church her priestliness cannot be taken from her.   Of course
her priesthood must not be understood as a limitation of the
one, highest, only-effective priesthood of Christ.   It is rather
a participation in his priesthood--by grace and at the same

time the result of her free decision--just as the priesthood of the whole church (in the sense of 1 Peter 2:9; Rev. 1:6; 5:10) does not infringe or obscure the independence and the sole effectiveness of Christ's redemptive act. Such a misunderstanding is completely excluded--if one thinks of the ministry as charged with the duties of universal priesthood for the "upbuilding of the body of Christ" (Eph. 4:11f.)[21]-- when it is remembered that the New Testament avoids using the concept ἱερεύς for office-holders and simply characterizes their activity as διακονία.[22] From the fact that Mary is not numbered among the 12 apostles and was not given the power of the keys we must not conclude that she is not a priest. Her priesthood is realized in the acceptance and birth of the Son of God and in the complete giving of herself in participation in his passion and death. This brings her into God's redeeming act itself and links her most closely to the priesthood of Christ. Just as the priesthood of Christ did not come about through an act of ordination and yet ecclesiastical office was only made possible and legitimized by it, so the priesthood of Mary did not require establishment by a sacramental ordination or by apostolic office, since it had its source in the immediate election and calling by God.

Considering then the place of Mary in the salvation activity of God, it seems clear that the Mariological argument of the Nova quaedam decretal has little merit. Therefore the prohibition of blessing, hearing confessions, and preaching cannot be justified by reference to Mary and her position. On the contrary it is weakened by such reference.

The medieval abbess was not only forbidden these liturgical and pastoral functions, which are partly dependent on ordination, but also the potestas iurisdictionis[23] linked to her office was limited, so that, although it is true that in this sphere she had considerable authority, one cannot speak of any equal authority with the abbot in regard to jurisdiction. Again the reason is certainly to be found in her exclusion from the sacrament of ordination.

This situation is evident in the decretal Dilecta[24] written in 1222 by Pope Honorius III (X 1.33.12) to the abbot of Michelstein (Halberstadt diocese).[25] The Pope refers to a request he has received from the abbess of Quedlinburg, relating that she had suspended from office and benefice a number of canonesses and clergy (canonicas suas et clericos suae iurisdictioni subiectos) because of disobedience and certain offenses, but that since she could not excommunicate

them they ignored the suspension. The Pope accordingly commissions the abbot to force the canonesses and clergy, if
necessary by an ecclesiastical censure, to obey the regulations
and show proper deference to authority.

From this decretal it is quite clear that the Pope recognizes and confirms the authority of the abbess of the Quedlinburg foundation over the canonesses and clergy who belong
to it. In general the abbess of a foundation of canonesses[26]
had considerable official authority; she had charge of all
foundation property; she distributed prebends, benefices,
churches and offices in the churches.[27] Beyond this, she
was especially responsible for the care of the canonesses and
their moral education.[28] All who lived in the convent owed
her obedience. The foundation clergy, too--canons who had
charge of the services in the foundation's churches and were
responsible for pastoral care--had to take an oath of obedience when they were received into the foundation chapter.[29]
On the basis of her position the abbess exercised a certain
amount of discipline over the canonesses and foundation clergy. She could admonish, suspend, demote and even dismiss
them for carelessness or infraction of rules.[30]

Now, according to the decretal the Pope does not indeed dispute this authority, but nevertheless he does limit
it. The abbess, in contrast to the abbot, is not empowered
to impose ecclesiastical censure--specifically mentioned is
excommunication[31] as the most severe censure--in order to
lend greater emphasis to her disciplinary measures. Because of this fact, that the right to use censure as punishment is reserved to the abbot, it is clear that the abbess'
suspension of duties and incomes (suspensio ab officio et
beneficio) should not be understood as censure[32]--which per
se it could be except in case of vindictive punishment[33]--but
rather as a disciplinary measure (without the punishment
aspect)[34] permitted to the abbess on grounds of her administrative powers.

In harmony with the fact that the abbess does not
have the authority to inflict ecclesiastical censure, the so-
called "bowing" punishment, she does not have the right to
absolve from such a punishment. We learn of this from the
decretal of Innocent III, De Monialibus[35] (X 5.39.33), in
A.D. 1202, in which it is decreed that nuns may be absolved
by the local bishop, if they have been excommunicated because of a violent act (involving physical injuries) against a
fellow sister, lay brother or lay sister or against clerics

commissioned for pastoral care in their cloister. Such authority is not given to their immediate superior, the abbess.

As in the decretal we have just discussed (X 1.33.12), the failure of her subordinate clerics to recognize the superior position of the abbess forms the background and occasion for the decretal Dilecta of Honorius III (X 5.31.14), directed to the prior (? praepositus) and archdeacon of the city of Soissons. Although only the abbess as presiding officer of the foundation chapter and as representative of the whole foundation had the right to use her seal[36] in certification of foundation documents, the clerics of an abbey church in the diocese of Meaux demanded the right to use their own seal. This demand was contrary to regulations--they were a part of the cloister chapter and so did not constitute an independent collegium--and they were acting against the will of their superior. The Pope empowers the prior and the archdeacon of Soisson to forbid these clergy the right to prepare and use their own seal under threat of censure. Here is explicit recognition of the abbess' position as caput et patrona of the clergy involved. [37]

The outstanding position of the abbess (or also of the secular female ruler)--outstanding at least in comparison with the general situation of women in that time--brought with it the attendant result that the normal hindrances which women experienced in law suits were sometimes breached. We learn from the decretal of Innocent III, Quum Dilecta (X 2.30.4), of the year 1206, that the abbess of Gandersheim,[38] contrary to canon law derived from Roman law,[39] was appointed by the Pope to be procurator--i.e., plaintiff in a case at law. She was to represent him (vice nostra) in defending the rights of her cloister before the dean of Paderborn who was acting as judge.[40] (Her abbey had been given exemption privileges by Innocent III's predecessors, which were however being disputed as superannuated by canons of the Hildesheim bishopric.)

In another case a principle of canon law that also agrees with Roman law--a woman cannot function as referee in a court of arbitration--is breached by customary legal practice: the judicial decision of a Frankish queen is accepted as valid in the decretal Dilecti Filii of Innocent III (X 1.43.4), in A.D. 1202. (It concerned the usage of a piece of forest territory disputed by the Cistercian convent of Eschailly[41] and the Hospitalers[42] of the Sens diocese in France.) In considering the fact that the Hospitalers contested the decision of the Queen, the Pope points out that female rulers in Gaul--in contrast to general secular law which excludes women from such public office and from any judicial function--are permitted normal jurisdictional authority over their subordinates in accordance with recognized custom. So he orders the Hospitalers to submit to the Queen's decision, especially since it was strengthened by the presence and advice of bishops. [43]

We may conclude from a number of the decretals discussed that a limited jurisdictional authority of women is recognized and protected by the official church, but it is also clear how much this authority needs such protection since it is often seriously contested and endangered by limitations of right and freedom that burden women in the secular as well as the ecclesiastic sphere. Not least injurious for women is the prejudice against them as inferior by reason of sex, a prejudice that more than any other factor conditions the legal limitations of women. The decretals of Gregory IX are not free from it. According to X 5.40.10, an excerpt from the Etymologies of Isidore of Seville, in judging the qualifications of a witness one must be sure that the witness is of the male sex. [44] The reservations applied to the testimony of a woman result from the idea that her statements are always contradictory and unreliable. [45] As absurd and contrary to Christian thinking as such an understanding is, that a person should have a higher credibility because he belongs to the male sex, it still was bound to work a great hardship on women especially in an unfriendly environment and historical period, when they tried to carry out any official office they may have had.

Although decretal law allows important women, such as abbesses or regents, a certain amount of independence and responsibility in the jurisdictional sphere--except for authority in punishment and in absolution--comparable opportunities in the ritual-liturgical sphere are denied (even to the abbess). This is proved--besides the decisive decretal Nova Quaedam we have discussed on p. 71, which forbids the abbess essential functions despite her office--by canon 3 (used in expanded form as X 3.2.1.) of the Synod of Nantes in A.D. 658 (A.D. 895 is also a possible date). [46] This canon makes general judgments against women and excludes them entirely from the chancel during mass. The wording of this chapter presents no difficulty in understanding the motive that lies at the basis of the prohibition. First of all, a priest is firmly forbidden to live in the same house with a woman not closely related by blood. But in order to prevent any possible incestuous relationship, even the mother, sister, or aunt of the priest is prohibited from living in the same house with him, although disciplinary council decrees in general permit this. Similar to these regulations is the liturgical prohibition: added to the immediately preceding, it appealed to the authority of the canons[47] with increasing insistence in the following words--including a part of a sentence omitted by Raymond of Pennaforte: "In accordance with the binding regulations of the canons, no woman may presume to approach the altar to serve the priest or even to stand or sit within the chancel."[48] The basis for this strict ruling is again to keep a woman away from the priest in order to prevent any possible illicit relationship.[49] The prohibition thus serves to protect celibacy, like the preceding regulations about living arrangements. The forceful denial of liturgical function to women within the area of the altar, as it was ordered in the cited capitulum, shows, however, to what degree priestly celibacy--zealously promoted and finally required by law in the medieval church--was enacted at the expense of women; through what degradation and legal deprivation of women it was purchased and supported. A law which requires such coercive means to keep it in operation only brings upon itself the suspicion it deserves and finally a fundamental doubt of its reasonableness.

Particularly mentioned in the capitulum as a generally forbidden liturgical function of women at the altar is that of acolyte, which according to decretal law[50] even male children may perform. It is thus clear that religious aptitude does not count as the determinative criterion for this duty, nor does appropriate age, but merely sex. This regulation discriminating against women is still in effect. The chapter mentioned (X 3.2.1) supports canon 813, § 2, of the Code of Canon Law,[51] which decrees that a woman may not be an acolyte, except when a man--or else a boy--is not available and there is a legitimate reason. Even in this case she must give the responses from a distance and in no case approach the altar.[52]

The official post-conciliar church still holds in principle to the traditional discipline. In a circular of the post-conciliar Liturgy Commission, dated January 25, 1966, the practice of sometimes using girls and women as acolytes in the Netherlands and in the United States was characterized as a serious offense against church discipline and strictly forbidden.[53] (The practice had been introduced in accordance

with art. 14 of the Constitution on the Sacred Liturgy, [54]
which encouraged all members of the people of God toward
conscious and active participation in liturgical celebration and,
in fact, said that they were obligated to participate.) Even
quite recently, November 5, 1970, the prohibition was again
expressly enjoined by the Third Instruction concerning the
orderly implementation of the Constitution on the Liturgy. [55]
Although, to be sure, this kind of regulation is likely to lead
to the gradual formation of its very opposite in prescriptive
law, nevertheless the fact that official church regulations declare a woman to be "such an unworthy being" that "every
service near the altar must be forbidden" to her, [56] is a
scandal. As long as such regulations belong to operative
ecclesiastical law, the statement of the Constitution on the
Church of Vatican II (art. 32)[57] that there is no inequality
in the church based on sex, remains an untrue affirmation.

b. The Decretalists

A great many canonists, the "decretalists," made a
thorough study of the Gregorian collection of decretals, so
that one can speak of a blossoming-time of canon law in this
period. [58] The canonical works of the first period--from
Gratian to Gregory IX--consisting of the summas and glosses
of the decretists, were exploited by the new generation of
decretalists and in this way were gradually pushed into the
background. [59] In treating the decretals that concern the object of the present study, the decretalists also follow to a
great extent the writings of the decretists.

Raymond of Pennaforte (see p. 70) takes a negative
attitude to the ordination of women, in his Summa de Poenitentia which appeared[60] before the promulgation of the decretals of Gregory IX, i.e., before A.D. 1234. [61] He depends
mostly on Huguccio, which means on the Glossa Ordinaria of
Joannes Teutonicus on the Decretum, but he also partly includes the more recent decretal legislation and affirms, with
reference to the Ambrosiaster passage rejecting ordination
of women, that women cannot receive the sacred character
of any clerical order because their sex is against it and also
the directives of the church are against it (impediente sexu
et constitutione ecclesiae). For this reason in his opinion
even abbesses cannot preach, [62] bless, excommunicate, [63]
absolve, assign penance, judge, [64] nor exercise any office
connected with any order, no matter how learned, saintly or
religious they may be. Several of the texts of the Decretum

treated above are used as proof-texts for this position, plus
the Mariological argument which Raymond takes from the
decretal Nova Quaedam. [65] (We have already given this argument, pp. 71ff.) In concluding his own position on the question, Raymond rejects the opinion of those who accept the fitness of women for ordination both in reference to the diaconate and the presbyteriate, and who support their opinion, he
says, by reference to C. 27, q. 1, cc. 23 and 30 for the
diaconate, and by dist. 32, c. 18 for the presbyterate. Raymond is hasty and without justification in accusing the representatives of this position of lying; he places them on the
same level with Montanists. He seeks to minimize their
evidences--which at least for the female diaconate are con-
siderable--as did Huguccio and Joannes Teutonicus, by interpreting the diaconate ordination as a simple benediction which
qualifies for special duty, for instance reading the homily[66]
in matins or something similar. (As already mentioned, such
an understanding of the female diaconate cannot be harmonized
with our sources; the uncritical copying of previous writers
ensures the continuation of error and mistaken interpretation.)
Raymond understands presbytera to be the wife of a priest,
which accords with the content of dist. 32, c. 18, or rather
one of the persons named in dist. 32, c. 19 (see p. 21)--a
widow, or the so-called matricuria. This of course does
not agree with the meaning of presbytera in canon 11 of the
Council of Laodicea, by which the (female) bearer of an ecclesiastical office is designated.

* * * * *

Goffredus de Trani, in his Summa super Titulos
Decretalium, written between 1241 and 1243,[67] produces an
almost literal excerpt from Raymond's Summa. Like the
latter, he affirms that women called deaconesses had no
diaconal orders but that they apparently simply had the privilege of reading the homilies during matins. [68]

* * * * *

In his important Apparatus in Quinque Libros Decreta-
lium--completed[69] immediately after the first Council of
Lyon, in 1245--Pope Innocent IV, formerly Sinibald Fieschi,
presents, in contrast to Raymond and Goffredus, no more
exact reason for the Nova Quaedam (X 5.38.10) prohibition
of liturgical participation by abbesses. He simply adds to
functions already prohibited in the decretal (of preaching,
reading the Gospel, blessing and hearing confessions) the

declaration of absolution (from ecclesiastical censures), teaching, acting as judge and the giving of the veil to nuns by the abbess.[70] All of these, says Innocent, are also precluded by canon law. Among other supports, these prohibitions are supported by those texts of the Decretum that clearly express the conception of the inferiority of women and of the status subiectionis which must consequently be required of them--which shows that Innocent could not harmonize these ecclesiastical functions with the ideas of women he had absorbed from his age. Thus Innocent's reason for the regulation (X 5. 39. 33) that nuns cannot be absolved from a censure by their abbess but only by the local bishop is that "that kind of behavior is not seemly for a woman."[71] This is a reason that could apply to a prohibition of all pastoral and liturgical functions. The only liturgical activity Innocent considers to be congruous with the nature of women is the reading of the Gospel, or the homily, during the Divine Office.[72] The reference in this connection to C. 27, q. 1, c. 23 (Diaconissam) shows clearly that Innocent understands the deaconess--exactly as Raymond, Goffredus and previously the decretists did--as nuns. That fact is also apparent in his discussion of the decretal Presbyter (X 3. 41. 1): he remarks that cultured women of orders like priests have the right and even the duty to pray the officium, because they too, it might be said, receive through benediction a kind of orders, and this is the reason some of them are deaconesses--again referring to C. 27, q. 1, c. 23, which is canon 15 of Chalcedon. However, he says, even if this ordination should extend to saying the office, it still doesn't belong to the seven ecclesiastical orders.[73]

Innocent takes from the decretal Dilecta (X 1. 33. 12) the fact that the abbess may suspend the clerics under her from office and from their benefices. He understands the reason to be that she has official jurisdictional power through customary right. Innocent however emphasizes specifically, referring to a Roman legal regulation, that this is an exception from ordinary law (ius commune),[74] and he doesn't forget that the abbess had no right to excommunicate, to interdict, or to absolve.[75]

* * * * *

Bernard of Botone's Apparatus ad Decretales Gregorii IX, written in 1245,[76] presents a more detailed treatment of our problem than the commentary of Innocent IV. Because

of its completeness, its thorough treatment of the material
and its consideration of previous literature, it was soon accepted as the Glossa Ordinaria to the Liber Extra. [77] Not
surprisingly it retains the traditional doctrine on our question; viewpoints already expressed appear, expanded by new
viewpoints taken from decretal law.

Concerning the decretal Nova Quaedam (X 5. 38. 10),
which should be especially noted here, Bernard like Innocent
remarks that perhaps abbesses had been permitted to read
the Gospel during matins and for this reason were also called
deaconesses. [78] Again, incorrectly and contrary to the
sources, C. 27, q. 1, c. 23 is cited as evidence. Thus in
the judgment of medieval canonists the office and tasks of
the deaconess shrink to this one scanty liturgical function.
Joined to the preaching prohibition of the decretal, which is
applicable to the abbess and to women in general, the gloss
lists a whole catalogue of liturgical functions and other offices from which women are excluded because of their sex--
e. g. , touching sacred vessels, teaching activity, judgeship,
acting as arbitrator, being a plaintiff in a law suit, and performing as counsel in court. For this Bernard refers in
part to the already recognized texts of Gratian's Decretum
and in part to the new decretal law. He describes the legal
situation of women in its dependence on Roman law and concludes that in principle women are forbidden the practice of
every official function (viri officium) that is intended for the
male. [79] Bernard himself brings up the question whether an
abbess may install and suspend in office--e. g. , clerics--and
this leads him to the decretal Dilecta (X 1. 33. 12), where
this problem (ad v. iurisdictioni) is especially treated. [80]
In dependence on the wording of the decretal, in which the
pope gives the abbess jurisdictional authority over the clerics
under her, the gloss here accepts that authority--despite contrary legal norms which forbid women to judge or to hold
any official office. But at the same time the gloss adds a
not inconsiderable limitation: in contrast to the male person
(abbot) the abbess possesses only an incomplete jurisdictional
authority. It is true that in cases of disobedience she can
suspend from office and from benefice her nuns and the clergy
under her--in accordance with the content of the decretal--
since she is responsible for management of temporal and
spiritual things (habet enim administrationem temporalium et
spiritualium). Also because of her administrative authority
she has, like the abbot, the right to assign churches and
benefices and to install clerics in the churches of her cloister
(instituere clericos). But she does not have the authority to

excommunicate and to absolve (from an ecclesiastical censure). One could also say that she cannot punish by suspension[81] and by interdiction, since these also belong to the
power of the keys; but they are not assigned anyhow to the
female but only to the male sex. (Here the gloss repeats
the argumentation of the decretal Nova Quaedam word for
word.) For even if the Blessed Virgin Mary were more exalted than all the apostles, the Lord did not nevertheless
give to her but to them the keys of the kingdom.

    In other respects woman may not have such great
authority because she is not created in the image of God[82]
--only man is the image and reflection of God. The woman
must rather be subject to the man and be at his service as
a maid, since the man is head of the wife and not the contrary. The foregoing gloss expresses most clearly the causal
relationship between the serious denigration of women as
human beings (denial of their image-of-God status) and their
exclusion from the power of the keys by their lack of ordination. The argument is supported by Gratian's capitulum 13
(Haec Imago) and capitulum 15 (Cum Caput) in C. 33, q. 5,
which themselves depend on Pauline statements informed by
the rabbinic spirit. Other passages indicating a denigration
of the feminine sex, mixed with untenable theological argument, show clearly that such contempt is the only reason for
denying women access to orders and the liturgical and jurisdictional functions connected with them. For example, just
as in the gloss, Bernard in explaining the decretal De Monialibus (X 5. 39. 33) remarks that feminine sex must be understood
as the main reason for the fact that the abbess cannot absolve the nuns under her, that furthermore she cannot hear
their confessions, give them her blessing or expound the
Gospel. All this, which the decretal itself indicates, results
from women's not receiving the power of the keys (claves
ecclesiae). [83]

    With similar bias the gloss finds a basis for the status
of women's inferiority in areas beyond the liturgical and
jurisdictional. Thus the extent of disdain and contempt of
women--in an environment which made them vulnerable to
inhumane situations and stunted their personal development--
is clear from a blatant commentary on the reason for the
classic canon law which excluded women from the function of
witness in criminal cases and cases of wills and testaments.[84]
The commentary is as follows: "What is lighter than smoke?
Wind. What is lighter than wind? Air. What is lighter
than air? Woman. What is lighter than woman? Nothing!"[85]

A similar tendency to masculine arrogance is expressed in the gloss to the decretal Duo Pueri (X 4.2.12), which says that because the man has the "headship," as in C. 33, q. 5, c. 15, he should be believed before a woman. [86] This absurd principle of canon law--to bind credibility to the masculine sex--is contrary to human experience and to the Christian spirit, yet it is uncritically taken over and even supported by the gloss.

* * * * *

Henricus de Segusio, who later became cardinal-bishop of Ostia and was therefore called (Cardinalis) Hostiensis, was one of the most important canonists of his time[87] because of his thorough comprehension of both [Roman and church] laws. In his Summa super Titulis Decretalium (Summa Aurea), which was probably written between 1250 and 1253, [88] he takes up the question of the particular requirements for valid ordination, one of which is masculine sex of the ordinand. [89] Depending closely on Raymond and Goffredus, he declares that, following the comments of Ambrose (Ambrosiaster) on 1 Tim. 3:11, rites of consecration are only for men (homini!), not for women. For women could not be tonsured and their hair could not be cut. [90] Besides they could not exercise the power of the keys (potestas clavium) and also could not serve at the altar--a large number of texts we have already considered are added to prove the latter. Like Innocent IV and Bernard of Botone, Hostiensis also names the reading of the Gospel at matins as the only liturgical activity possible for women, and like them he mistakenly refers to C. 27, q. 1, c. 23, as support. It is true, writes Hostiensis, that some others understand the deaconess mentioned in this canon as abbess and understand the concept ordinari to mean the bestowing of the veil (velari). [91] But Hostiensis sees no argument against his thesis that women cannot be ordained, either in the legal sources which speak of the deaconess, or in capitula 18 and 19 of distinctio 32 which mention presbytera and which he interprets exactly as his authorities Raymond and Goffredus.

In another important work, Commentaria in Quinque Decretalium Libros, completed after 1268, [92] Hostiensis, referring to the relevant decretals--and here more in the form of commentary and gloss--gives his opinion about the legal status of women in the church, often clearly depending on the Glossa Ordinaria of Bernard of Botone. Like Bernard,

Hostiensis (ad v. et legentes evangelium) remarks about the
decretal Nova Quaedam (X 5. 38. 10) that the prohibition of the
abbess' reading the Gospel probably concerns high mass; she
could perhaps read it during Divine Office, for which reason
she is also called deaconess (once again reference is made
to C. 27, q. 1, c. 23). Hostiensis thinks the purely private
instruction of nuns concerning the rules of their order, etc.,
is compatible with the prohibition of public activity on the
part of abbesses. [93] Besides the activity of preaching, he
also, ad v. praedicare, sets forth other functions that are
forbidden to women: teaching, and touching liturgical ves-
sels--not even masculine lay persons are permitted that.
(It is surely in keeping with Hostiensis' manner of speaking
to add--then certainly not women!) He justifies the fact that
the decretal characterizes the practice of such activities by
women as intolerable and absurd by insisting that such activities apply to public functions and therefore--according to
the viewpoint of that age--are exclusively masculine functions
(quae officia virilia censentur a quibus mulieres regulariter
sunt exclusae). It is clear from the assertion of the Roman
legal source Dig. 50, 17, 2--that women are to be kept from
all public offices--that this very principle of Roman law was
applied without reservation to canon law and so barred wom-
en's entrance to all ecclesiastical official functions. Because
of this legal principle, Hostiensis maintains, an abbess cannot bestow the veil on her nuns or absolve them--in addition
to the already mentioned prohibitions. She cannot act as
judge nor arbitrator, unless she has this office by succession
or custom. Likewise she cannot appoint or suspend clerics. [94]
Hostiensis is more strict about the latter than Innocent IV
(see p. 80) and even more strict than the Glossa Ordinaria. [95] This is clear from his discussion of the decretal
Dilecta (X 1. 33. 12) which treats the place of the abbess in
jurisdictional matters. Ad v. suae iurisdictioni[96] he accepts
in essential points the justification of the gloss for the exclusion of the abbess from the so-called power of the keys
and from the functions that depend upon it: not to Mary but
to the apostles were the keys of the kingdom given; besides,
woman in contrast to man is not made in the image and
likeness of God and so she stands in a sort of servant relationship to man, her head. Because of the modest reserve
required of her, a woman may not interfere in the affairs
of men--a viewpoint which Hostiensis takes from Roman law.
The abbess, he thinks, is simply in possession of an administratio spiritualium et temporalium, on the basis of which
she may grant benefices but which do not give her the right
to suspend.

This contention, that the abbess does not have power to suspend, differentiates Hostiensis (ad v. observent)[97] from other canonists. His reasoning is that suspension is to a certain extent the consequence of the power of the keys and, together with excommunication and interdiction, comes under the rubric of ecclesiastical censure, a means of punishment not granted to the abbess according to the decretal. It is not necessary to consider what actually happens--the suspension of clerics by the abbess as mentioned in the decretal-- but only what may rightly happen. Above all, since this kind of function is generally forbidden to women, it is always forbidden, if not expressly declared. And since the law contains no express declaration that a woman can suspend de jure, Hostiensis says, one may not conclude it from the opinion expressed above. Her office allows the abbess only to admonish and to hand out assignments, but not to punish. [98]

In his discussion of X 1.43.4, Hostiensis presents a thorough and comprehensive description of the legal situation of women according to classic canonical and secular law. He comes to this by the decretal's reference to Roman law, according to which women are excluded from public office. He finds 18 points in which a woman is legally disadvantaged in comparison to a man and thus demonstrates the authority of the Roman legal maxim (Dig. 1, 5, 9), [99] which says that the position of women is in many ways worse than that of men, and this includes the sphere of the church. (Of the many examples, which in each case are documented by the corresponding ecclesiastical or Roman legal sources, only the most important can be given here.)[100] The inferior status of women, according to Hostiensis, is expressed for example in the fact that teaching and preaching as well as the functions resulting from the power of the keys are forbidden her, and that she may not be ordained--which would give basis for the other functions. (For the last named point the Pseudo-Isidorian decretal dist. 23, c. 25 is used as evidence, although in fact it has no historical source value.) Hostiensis refers to the contradictory canon C. 27, q. 1, c. 23, and solves the contrarietas canonum, as Raymond of Pennaforte does: either the concept diaconissa is used in the canon only in an inexact way or else it is considered as a deaconess ordination to indicate not that the deaconess is ordained like the deacon and receives the character of Orders, but simply so that she may read the Gospel during matins, not, to be sure, in a solemn form but as a simple recitation. Some of the further examples which

Hostiensis uses of the disadvantageous situation of women in
the ecclesiastical as well as the secular realm are: their
exclusion from judgeship and from arbitration functions, and
from the right to present a case and enter complaints in
courts (postulare, accusare) and to act as counsel or, in
wills and testaments, as witness. Finally in point 18,
Hostiensis refers to the neglect of women which to a certain
extent constitutes the basis for all the particular legal limitations: their status subiectionis under men and their alleged
inferiority (not made in the image of God), reinforced by the
three already discussed chapters of Gratian's Decretum, C.
33, q. 5, cc. 13, 15, 17.

As contrast to the many examples of women's disadvantages, Hostiensis presents three examples of the advan-
tages which he says women have, all of them taken from
Roman law. One point concerns a concession to women, that
of ignorance of the right and of laws in specific cases.[101]
But when one realizes that this privilege is granted to wom-
en, according to the relevant Roman legal regulation (Dig.
22, 6, 9) "because of the weakness of their sex" and, as
Hostiensis remarks in another place, "not only because of
their lack of knowledge but also because of their naivete and
intellectual limitations,"[102] then it is apparent that a deep
contempt for women lies behind such ostensibly preferential
treatment.

* * * * *

If Hostiensis suggests the method for demonstrating
the position of women consisting of balancing their legal limitations with their so-called privileges, one of the following
canonists, Aegidius de Bellamera, develops the method in
almost exaggerated form. In his Praelectiones in Libros
Decretalium[103] he presents 31 examples of the disadvantages
of women in comparison with men. As in the case of
Hostiensis, there is the exclusion of women from public
teaching and preaching, from jurisdictional authority and
from orders, also denial of their entrance into the altar area,
their supposed lack of the image-of-God and their subordination to men.[104] In so far as these many disadvantages do
not contain in themselves the viewpoint that women are inferior, they are explained in a manner unmistakably implying a contempt for women. For instance, women cannot be
entrusted with the office of judgeship because they are "fickle
and weak in character;" besides, they do not possess the

required intelligence and education. [105]   Concerning 16 alleged
privileges of women suggested by Aegidius, R. Chabanne has
already noted[106] that they are hardly recognizable as such.
Like the legal limitations, they are deduced from the supposed ontic and ethical inferiority of women.   For example,
Guido explains the earlier physical development of women,
on the basis of which they attain maturity earlier than men,
by noting that weeds are known to grow rapidly. [107]   He also
thinks that the fact that in certain cases women receive
easier treatment in court is justified by their "weakness and
instability" as well as by the fact that "nature has endowed
them with less strength of character and good judgment. "[108]

The manner in which Hostiensis and, following him,
Bellamera characterize the position of women is especially
instructive and important for our problem because it shows
clearly that the exclusion of women from orders and from
the consequent functions of teaching, preaching, pastoral
care--as well as the status of subordination of women in
general--is an unfortunate and unfavorable legal situation.
On the contrary, today--since the question of admission of
women to church office is conditioned by social evolution--
we often find the opinion expressed that the exclusion of wom-
en from the office of the priesthood and the functions connected with it are neither disadvantageous nor any kind of
discrimination. [109]   This kind of argument, however, reflects
a lack of knowledge or a failure to observe the historical
sources and developmental interrelationships upon which ecclesiastical church law for women is based.   For it is exactly these sources and relationships which prove that the
position of women in the church--despite asseverations of
equivalence with men--is today in main features still identical
with their status in medieval canon law, a status described
by Hostiensis and other canonists as "a worse situation than
that of men" (conditio deterior quam virorum).   It is nothing
other than the direct consequence of a contempt for women,
of their alleged exclusion from the image-of-God status.

* * * * *

The important commentary by Joannes Andreae, his
Novella in Decretales Gregorii IX, completed in 1338, [110] in
large part makes use of the canonical literature at hand, including that of Hostiensis.   In doing so Joannes has the intention of supplementing by use of various works available
to him the Glossa Ordinaria of Bernard of Botone. [111]   With

this goal in mind we would expect that Joannes would continue the direction taken in regard to the present question by
his predecessors, if necessary adding a few new viewpoints
to strengthen it.

Supplementing the Glossa Ordinaria treatment of the
decretal Nova Quaedam--which contains the prohibition of
blessing, preaching and hearing confessions by the abbess--
Joannes refers to the argumentation of several decretalists
against the ordination of women. Thus he alludes to the
view of Goffredus Tranensis who (in reference to the decretal
mentioned as well as to dist. 23, c. 29 and C. 33, q. 5, c.
17) goes back to the formulation of Huguccio and of Joannes
Teutonicus[112] in declaring that a woman may not receive
the (sacramental) character of ordination because of her sex
and because of the regulations of the church against it. In
refutation of the chapter about the deaconess and the presbytera which contradicts that position, Joannes points to Joannes
Teutonicus' comments on the chapter, not omitting 'Ambrose's'
statement against ordination of deaconesses[113] with which
Raymond of Pennaforte had supported his argument. But in
addition to these well-known viewpoints he adds a new argument against the ordination of women, which reveals an influence of scholastic theology on sacraments and may have
been taken from Thomas Aquinas: because of the subjection
of woman to man, she does not have the capability to mark
out for herself a prominent position (praeeminentia gradus),
and thus she lacks the adequate and necessary presupposition
for the reception of the sacrament of orders, which involves
such a prominent position.[114] Thus it is from the subordination of woman--which Joannes Andreae grounds in the Genesis
passage, 3:16, and the rabbinically influenced passage, 1
Tim. 2:11ff.--that he concludes the unfitness of women for
ordination. The lack of verisimilitude in the argumentation
reveals itself especially in the fact that the Bible passages
used as support are not convincing.[115] But apart from that,
a viewpoint about ordination is apparent in the discussion
that is characteristically exaggerated and marked by scholastic understanding of sacrament. It tends toward a misunderstanding of the priestly office as a kind of domination.
Joannes Andreae's concluding argument also implies such
a distorted understanding of office: "Clerics must wear a
[hair] crown [i.e., tonsure], which is not permitted for a
woman."[116] Here Joannes refers not only to 1 Cor. 11 but
also to dist. 30, c. 2, which says: "God gave her [woman]
hair as a veil, as a sign for remembering her subjection to
man."[117] Of course the unfitness of women for ordination

established in this way draws with it the consequence, according to the viewpoint of Joannes Andreae, that no woman may minister in the sanctuary. [118]

In interpreting the decretal Dilecta (X 1. 33. 12), which has to do with the extent of the jurisdictional authority of the abbess, Joannes Andreae for the most part follows Hostiensis. Like him, he denies the abbess' authority to suspend the clerics under her from their office, because the use of censure as means of punishment--which includes suspension along with excommunication and interdiction--is not permitted her. [119] He mentions in this connection (ad v. ab officio suspendere) the teaching of a certain Vincentius, according to which while the abbess does not have the right to inflict suspension, in the sense of a canonical punishment--in which the celebrant or the father confessor brings upon himself an irregularity (ex delicto) because of a violation of suspension [120]--she does have the right to forbid clerics to celebrate mass and the right to cut off their income. [121]   This differentiating interpretation may more accurately reflect the true state of affairs than the all too one-sided viewpoint of Hostiensis (see pp. 84f.).

Explaining Bernard's reasons for female exclusion from full jurisdictional powers--it is due, he had said, to the fact that woman is not made in the image of God--Joannes Andreae refers to the Old Testament narrative about the creation of the woman from Adam (Gen. 2:21f.), misunderstanding it in the way Ambrosiaster did (C. 33, q. 5, c. 13) as historical account and expounding it as proof of the inferiority of woman as a human being. [122]

* * * * *

The Commentaria in Decretales by Peter of Ancharano (1330-1416) is a comprehensive work that widely uses the preceding literature [123] and depends especially on Hostiensis and Joannes Andreae, in dealing with the object of our study.

Repeating the argumentation of Joannes Andreae-- which had been influenced by Huguccio, Joannes Teutonicus and then by Thomas Aquinas--Peter gives a negative answer to the question raised by the decretal Nova Quaedam (X 5. 38. 10) concerning women's fitness for ordination. [124]   Concerning the decretal's prohibition of blessing, hearing confessions, preaching, etc. , Peter, like Hostiensis, soberly considers that a woman is not as well adapted to these functions as a man. [125] He thinks that the alleged unfitness of women to receive ordination is the reason for the regulation of the decretal X 3. 2. 1, that no woman may approach the altar as acolyte. [126] Actually this interpretation, which agrees with that of Joannes Andreae, does not accord with the tendency of the decretal (cf. pp. 76ff.).

From the decretal Dilecta (X 1. 33. 12) Peter draws the following conclusions concerning the position of the abbess:[127] 1. The clerics, the canonesses and all persons belonging to the convent are obliged to obey the abbess; thus a woman can be in charge of churches (procuratrix ecclesiarum), but only as abbess--because of the honor of her position (ratione dignitatis) she is granted management rights (administratio)--but not simply as a woman (simplex femina). Peter notes that in this way the situation of a woman is less fortunate, since she cannot be a judge, an advocate, or manager--in the sense of one who engages in business (procuratrix). 2. The abbess has jurisdictional authority, but it does not extend to punishment by ecclesiastical censure for disobedience on the part of those under her. This is the obvious result of the fact that the pope has commissioned someone else, the abbot, with that authority. From the decretal it is not possible to decide surely, Peter thinks, whether the abbess has authority to suspend from office. He refers to the opinion of Vincentius on this problem (cf. p. 89), already expressed by Joannes Andreae, and then goes on to agree with Hostiensis' view that a woman cannot rightly inflict the punishment of suspension from office--in the form of an ecclesiastical censure. The circumscribed jurisdictional authority of the abbess is also the object of the discussion of the decretal De Monialibus (X 5. 39. 33). Peter notes that in contrast to the abbot the abbess is not empowered to absolve her nuns from a censure, since she is unable to use the power of the keys, which of course has not been transmitted to the female sex. [128]

Peter also sees a secondary position of the abbess in contrast to the abbot, in the difference between the consecration of the abbot and abbess, from which authority arises. Although the abbess receives the same benediction as the abbot, it does not have the same effectiveness: in contrast to the abbess the ordained abbot has the capability of bestowing the ecclesiastical blessing and the minor orders on the monks under him. [129] The reason given for the limitation of these functions to the abbot--that they are, without any qualification, male functions--is again typical of the narrow viewpoint about women which one has come to expect from those times.

* * * * *

The extensive commentary on the decretals of Gregory IX by Antonius de Butrio (1338-1408) exhibits, like that of Peter of Ancharano, a strong dependence on the earlier decretalist literature. [130] This is true of the treatment of decretals we will now discuss. In an almost word-for-word copy of Joannes Andreae, Antonius answers the question of the fitness of women for ordination (Quaero, an mulier recipit characterem ordinis) that had been asked in connection with the decretal Nova Quaedam (X 5. 38. 10). [131] Depending on the Glossa Ordinaria of Bernard of Botone and referring to the Pseudo-Isidorian decretal dist. 23, c. 25, he finds reason for the decretal's explicit prohibition of preaching in the argument that the function of preaching is incompatible with the nature of women. [132] It is true that such a judgment reflects the outlook of the times, but on a more profound level it also reflects the extent of women's lack of freedom, for the boundaries of their activity possibilities are laid down, without regard to their own wishes and capabilities, by the arbitrary determination of men, to the detriment of any development beyond these narrow boundaries.

Antonius handles the question raised especially by the decretal Dilecta (X 1. 33. 12), the question of the jurisdictional authority of the abbess, mainly in the form of a detailed discussion of what the gloss has to say on the subject. Expanding the gloss' position--that in contrast to men, women do not have full authority--he remarks that a woman as private person and as an individual cannot act as judge nor in any way carry out male functions, but as a person in a high position (ratione dignitatis) she can do these things. For, in this case, it is not she herself who carries out these functions but rather the dignity of her office, so to speak, is doing them. [133] This point of view again documents very clearly the fact that female sex in itself was considered as fundamental disqualification for the exercise of public office. According to the outlook of the times, such disqualification could apparently receive some alleviation in a high position. Naturally with such a narrowing and denigrating view of women Antonius denies their capability of possessing and using the power of the keys just because of their sex. He finds the reason given by the gloss--Mary in contrast to the apostles was not given the "keys to the kingdom of heaven" and women could not have such authority because they are not created in the image of God and because they are in subjection to men--quite binding and sufficient. Influenced by Hostiensis and other decretalists as well as by the gloss, he maintains that the abbess has no right to excommunicate or to suspend from office--both rights come under that of censure and both depend on the power of the keys. However he allows the abbess the right to suspend from benefice, since this is an administrative authority. 134

Similarly to the exclusion of women from the exercise of ecclesiastical disciplinary authority, Antonius also explains the fact--decreed in the decretal De Monialibus (X 5. 39. 33)-- that the abbess is not authorized to absolve her nuns from a censure. He declares that the basis for these and other relevant limitations of rights (prohibition of hearing confession, giving blessing and reading the Gospel) consists likewise in the supposed incapacity of women for stewardship of the power of the keys because of their sex. 135

* * * * *

Finally we must consider the Lectura in Decretales of Nicolaus de Tudeschis (1386-1445 or 1453), 136 who is accounted one of the most important canonists of the Middle Ages. He utilizes the previous decretalist literature but supplements it, as far as that was possible after the writings of Joannes Andreae, on which he depends. Von Schulte says that later canonists did not go beyond him but simply exploited his materials. 137

Writing about the prohibitions contained in the decretal Nova Quaedam (X 5. 38. 10)--mainly prohibitions of hearing confessions--Nicolaus agrees that an abbess or another woman in high position may have jurisdictional authority as special right in foro contentioso, i. e. , in the realm of law suits; proof texts for this are given, among other sources, in the two decretals (X 1. 43. 4 and X 5. 31. 14) we have considered above. But, he declares, this authority does not apply in forum poenitentiale, for the jurisdiction in this realm is a consequence of the power of the keys and the power of ordination, for the possession of which a woman is completely unfit (totaliter est incapax). This is so true that even in the case of a factual ordination a woman would not receive the character of orders, according to general opinion, which, indeed, represents the Glossa Ordinaria (of Joannes Teutonicus) to C. 27, q. 1, c. 23.[138] This sharp judgment is also apparent in Nicolaus' view of the nature of women. It is a narrow and negative view consistent with the outlook of his times. Thus in considering the fact that the decretal characterizes blessing, hearing confessions and public preaching[139] on the part of abbesses as intolerable and absurd (absonum et absurdum) and consequently condemns them, Nicolaus agrees, noting that in order to oppose any opinion or action it is sufficient to indicate the resulting absurdity, the argument ab absurdo.[140] On this theme he remarks in another place--in explaining the requirement of X 5. 40. 10 that witnesses be male--that when women are permitted to be witnesses they are not as credible or trustworthy as men and therefore the testimony of men must be preferred when two men and two women disagree as witnesses. The concept mulier is not derived, he claims, from the female sex but from the softness and weakness of feminine character. The concept vir, on the other hand, is also not a denotation of sex but is derived from the constancy and virtue of man.[141] (There is internal evidence that this judgment of women has been taken from the dictum Gratiani C. 32, q. 7, p. c. 18, discussed on pp. 30f.)

Following the decretal Dilecta (X 1. 33. 12), Nicolaus describes and circumscribes the abbess' area of competence in jurisdictional matters--including the power to punish--in the same fashion as his predecessors. The abbess does have the authority to grant benefices and so she possesses the ius conferendi et instituendi which belongs to iurisdictio spiritualis but not to iurisdictio ordinis. As woman she is excluded from all rights and authorities which depend upon the power of the keys--itself connected with orders. For this reason an abbess cannot grant her nuns absolution from sins, nor can she excommunicate, although she is a persona religiosa. Nicolaus notes that the canonists do not generally grant the abbess the right, in the strict sense of the word, to interdict and to suspend ab ordine--i. e., to forbid the exercise of the power of orders bestowed in the rite of ordination--so that a violation of the suspension brings upon itself an irregularity (ex delicto). So he too denies the abbess this authority, following the reasoning of his predecessors.[142]

Chapter 5

SUMMARY OF THE MOST SIGNIFICANT CONCLUSIONS

The fixed status of subordination of women in operative ecclesiastical law--more particularly their exclusion from office and from every official pastoral and liturgical function connected with it--has its foundation in the corresponding decrees of classical canon law contained in the Corpus Iuris Canonici. The decisive bases of the contemporary legal situation of women in the church were already set forth in the source-collection of Gratian about the middle of the 12th century. It contains various stipulations taken from older law collections, which prevent women from the exercise of every cultic-liturgical function within the altar area, the taking of communion to the sick, public teaching as well as baptizing. (Cf. p. 7.) The theme of these prohibitions --which come partly from excerpts of the Pseudo-Isidorian decretals and partly from Council decrees or texts mistakenly attributed to Council decrees (Statuta Ecclesiae Antiqua)-- clearly reveals a pejorative conception of women because of their sex, a conception strongly conditioned by the continuing influence of Old Testament ideas about cleanness as well as by exaggerated sacralization of the cult connected with this influence. (Cf. pp. 10f., 12f.) As an addition to the regulations mentioned, Gratian's understanding of the substantial and ethical inferiority of women and the status subiectionis deduced from it provide a negative reinforcement. This inferiority is derived from particular Pauline passages or passages attributed to Paul (1 Cor. 11:3ff; 1 Tim. 2:11ff.) that were influenced by a rabbinical type of thinking, but especially from patristic and pseudo-patristic texts as well as Roman legal regulations for women. (Cf. pp. 28ff., 43 ff.) Although the doctrine of Gratian achieved no legal but only doctrinal authority, it nevertheless achieved considerable importance for the further development of law.

In their scholarly studies of the texts of the Decretum of Gratian, the decretists for the most part adopted his doctrines. However, while Gratian simply states concerning the question of the ordination of women that they can never

attain the diaconate nor the presbyterate (p. 26)--he fails to
give any reasons and ignores the early church office of deaconess, apparently thinking, one gathers from his arrangement of texts about the deaconess, that this office has no
great importance--some decretists present a more detailed
treatment of the office of deaconess as well as of the question of ordination of women in general. Yet it must be clearly noted that although these scholars are familiar with the
existence of this early church office, they are not clear about
just what it was and they have some mistaken impressions
about it. They place the deaconess parallel to the abbess or
identify her with an ordinary nun. They think her office consisted merely in reading the Gospel or a homily during matins, and they understand the deaconess ordination as bestowing of the veil. (Cf. pp. 53, 54, 61.) This contra-histor-
ical judgment about office and ordination of the deaconess,
in connection with the increasingly clear tendency--especially
since Rufinus--to deny women any ordination qualifications,
may be traced back to a statement of Ambrosiaster mistakenly attributed to Ambrose, as well as to a lack of knowledge
of historical evidence. This statement of Ambrosiaster, as
the result of a mistaken interpretation of 1 Tim. 3:11, sharply condemns the ordination of deaconesses. (Cf. pp. 50ff.)
Under the weight of this auctoritas patrum, Rufinus, and then
the important decretists who followed him (Joannes Faventinus,
Huguccio, Joannes Teutonicus) interpret as simple benediction
the deaconess ordination of canon 15 of the Council of Chalcedon (C. 27, q. 1, c. 23.). The benediction supposedly authorized the function mentioned above. The result of this
interpretation is the exclusion of women from sacramental
ordination.

However, an actual rationalization of the exclusion of
women from clerical orders is made for the first time in
decretist literature, by Huguccio. He contends that women's
unfitness for ordination is determined by church decree and
by feminine sex--or, more exactly, by church decree drawn
up because of feminine sex. (See p. 62.) This explanation
is accepted by the Glossa Ordinaria of Joannes Teutonicus and
later also by several decretalists. As shown by the formulation itself (constitutio ecclesiae facta propter sexum), the
reasoning presupposes an inferiority of women, which has its
foundation in patristic and pseudo-patristic exegesis of particular Bible passages (cf. pp. 63f.) and beyond this in
Roman law. Thus in approximation to the regulation of Roman law, according to which women must be kept from all
offices and public functions, women in the church are denied

competence for official activity. (Cf. pp. 62, 66.) The application of this principle of Roman law to canonical ordination law remains, especially since Huguccio, a determinative feature of decretist and decretalist literature.

There is evidence in the Glossa Ordinaria of Joannes Teutonicus that some decretists, [1] finding support in the above mentioned Chalcedonian canon (C. 27, q. 1, c. 23), opposed the prevailing opinion and recognized the fitness of women as well as men for ordination on the basis of their baptism (cf. p. 67). But this position was not strong enough to maintain itself. That it did appear so early in history, however--a correctly established theological position opposing a prevailing tradition based on untenable arguments--is noteworthy.

The decretals of Gregory IX (cf. p. 70) supplement the basic precepts, already given in Gratian's Decretum, for the ecclesiastical position of women in the Code of Canon Law, by adding a few more. Thus the decretal Nova Quaedam (X 5.38.10) of Innocent III is especially significant in its strict prohibition of public preaching or Gospel reading by an abbess, of her giving the (ecclesiastical) blessing to her nuns or hearing their confessions. (Cf. p. 71.) Further, the decree of a Synod of Nantes, recorded as X 3.2.1, in general forbids women to enter the sanctuary during divine services and act as acolyte for the priest. (Cf. pp. 76f.) The indication that not Mary but the apostles were given the "keys to the kingdom of heaven" serves as basis for the prohibitions of the decretal Nova Quaedam--an argument without validity, to be sure, in light of its inadequate understanding of the position of Mary in the story of redemption. (Cf. pp. 71ff.) In contrast to the cultic-liturgical realm, a woman--as abbess or regent--is granted in the jurisdictional realm certain powers over persons under her, in recognition of the authority belonging to her office. Nevertheless the position of the abbess is in no way comparable to that of the abbot, since, as the decretals Dilecta (X 1.33.12) and De Monialibus (X 5.39.33) indicate, she has no authority to inflict specific ecclesiastical punishments and to absolve from them, because of her exclusion from orders. (Cf. pp. 73f.)

The treatment of the Gregorian material by the decretalists follows closely the teaching of the decretists, especially the Glossa Ordinaria of Joannes Teutonicus and thus the writings of Huguccio. Substantial support for the prevailing viewpoint that women are not qualified for ordination, and therefore must be excluded from the liturgical and jurisdictional functions dependent on ordination, is provided for the decretalists by the statement of Ambrosiaster (see p. 95), which has the consequence that the deaconess ordination is interpreted as simple benediction and the office of deaconess simply as the privilege of reading the homily during matins. With this argument the decretalists commonly suggest the additional argument of the decretal Nova Quaedam, that the power of the keys was not extended to Mary--and thus not to the feminine sex. As the evidence of many sources would show, the judgment of the decretalists in this question, like that of the decretists, rests on a narrow and negative conception of the nature of women. In keeping with the outlook of the times in which they lived, they reserve liturgical and jurisdictional functions in principle and exclusively to men (virilia officia), considering the inferior nature of women to be inconsistent with the exercise of such functions. (Cf. pp. 84, 93.) The statement of the Glossa Ordinaria of Bernard of Botone--woman does not have the power of the keys because she is not in the image of God and must serve man in full subordination--is often repeated by subsequent decretalists and is to a certain extent symptomatic of the causal relationship between the denigration of women and their exclusion from church office. This causal relationship is also determinative for the relevant regulations of the Corpus Iuris Canonici and the current law built upon them.

Chapter 6

EXEGETICAL EXCURSUS ON THE (PATRISTIC)
SCRIPTURAL PROOF FOR THE SUBORDINATION
OF WOMEN

In consideration of the fact that the Church Fathers
(and in agreement with them, Gratian--and, following him,
the great majority of decretists and decretalists) derive from
particular scriptural passages of the Old and New Testaments
the inferiority of women and as consequence their distinct
limitations of freedom and law, an investigation of the validity of the scriptural proofs given is necessary. The question
also rises how binding are the passages used as proof, especially since the patristic authorities in Gratian's Decretum
constitute an essential source for the law currently in effect[1]
and have placed their mark on the regulations for women in
that law.[2]

The scriptural proof given by Gratian (cc. 13 and 19,
C. 33, q. 5 in his Decretum) for the statement of Ambrosias-
ter--that women are not in the image of God--is Gen. 1:27
(also Gen. 2:7-24) and 1 Cor. 11:6f.[3] Let us first of all in-
vestigate the dependability of the Old Testament proof. Gen.
1:27a is quoted almost literally in c. 13;[4] since Ambrosiaster
explains the expression homo exclusively in the sense of vir,
Gratian derives from v. 27a the Godlikeness of man alone.
But is it permissible to understand the Hebraic concept ādām
in this way--since it is necessary of course to go back to
the Hebrew--and thus to limit it exclusively to man? According to the present position of exegesis, the question must
be answered in the negative. Investigations of the concept
ādām have shown that a collective meaning of the word is the
original,[5] and that this meaning is present in Gen. 1:26f.[6]
Accordingly it is the judgment of the commentators that Godlikeness of woman is likewise asserted, since precisely the
species "mankind"--to which, as expressly emphasized in
v. 27b ("he created them as male and female"), both sexes
belong--is created as God's image.[7]

It is true that J. Boehmer[8] notes the alternation be-

tween singular and plural object in the text of Gen. 1:27,
which reads: וַיִּבְרָא אֱלֹהִים אֶת־הָאָדָם בְּצַלְמוֹ בְּצֶלֶם אֱלֹהִים בָּרָא אֹתוֹ זָכָר וּנְקֵבָה בָּרָא אֹתָם
("And God created man (ādām) in his image, in the image of
God he created him; as male and female he created them."
From this alternation Boehmer concludes that hā ādām in v.
27a should be limited to man--i.e., to the male sex--and
thus that it is about him alone that Godlikeness is affirmed:
"According to the image of God 'man' κατ᾽ ἐξοχήν (=the man)
is created, not the woman (cf. 1 Cor. 11:7): he is the one
indicated as he in אֹתוֹ. As a secondary element it is added
that mankind is divided in a male and a female part: this
duality is expressed in אֹתָם and it is exactly in this plural
form that the illusion is prevented, that man and woman
might share an equal status. Thus אֹתָם refers to the male
and female halves of humanity." The restriction of Godlikeness to the male follows, according to Boehmer, from the
circumstance that the Old Testament narrator could not be
expected to attribute to woman as to man the analogous lordship over the animal world (c. v. 26), which is an expression
and consequence of Godlikeness. For this the Old Testament
with its view of women is evidence:

> A religion whose adherents still pray:
> ברוך אתה יי אלהינו מלך העולם שלא עשני אשה 9 (Sachs, Gebetbuch
> der Israeliten, p. 6), and in this point resemble
> Plato's deathbed prayer; a religion whose cult sign is
> circumcision and in which woman is rated one way or
> another like animals as 'helpmates' for man, in ac-
> cordance with Gen. 2:18ff--to mention only a few
> characteristics; which has branches running into the
> New Testament, e.g., 1 Cor. 7 and 11:7-10: for
> such a religion the idea that woman is in the image
> of God and shares in the lordship of the world is ab-
> solutely impossible. Anyone who thinks otherwise,
> in fact all those who consider women to have a rather
> high place in the Old Testament, are caught in the
> bonds of a traditional Christian-idealizing exposition
> of Gen. 1 and 2, especially in the explanation of Jesus
> in Mt. 19:4-6 and similar passages. After every
> ירדו 10 ["Let them have dominion," Gen. 1:26], the
> narrator refers to אדם, i.e., to a group of men, to
> all men--many or few--existing at that time. The
> totality of the then contemporary male world is called
> to lordship over animals and plants, and that is at-
> tributed in Gen. 1:26 to the original will of God. 11

In a monograph that takes account of the latest research,

W. H. Schmidt criticizes Boehmer's position.[12] First, he
agrees with Boehmer that according to Gen. 1:26 humanity is
created, not a human pair (as in Gen. 2:7, 21f.).[13] He says,

> While אדם in the Yahwistic creation narrative of Gen.
> 2-3 and in the priestly Toledot book (Gen. 5:1a, 3-5)
> refers to an individual, the meaning in Gen. 1 is ob-
> viously a plural--'the human race.' This is indicated
> by the plural of the verb in v. 26b ('in order that they
> may have dominion') and the introduction of the bene-
> diction of v. 28. Also in Accadian creation narratives
> it is likewise 'humanity' which is created....[14]

The pluralistic meaning as "humanity" is implied, he thinks,
despite the use of the article with ādām in v. 27 (diverging
from v. 26).[15] Perhaps the article is used in v. 27 because
the word has already been used in v. 26.[16] The אתו (him)
of v. 27a, Schmidt continues, refers to הָאָדָם, "the man" of
v. 27a, which is to be understood as collective; the plural
אתָם (they) in the (secondarily added) part of the verse, 27b,
refers to the duality of the sexes and thus the two singular
and plural suffixes are not inconsistent with each other.[17]
Schmidt thinks that v. 27b ("as male and female he created
them") seems unnecessary, since "man" in Gen. 1:26f.
stands for mankind collectively and thus already contains
the plural indicated in v. 27b. The type of language, style
and meter of v. 27b proves that this part of the verse is in
fact a secondary addition. As the priestly document, having
in mind cultic prescriptions, adds to the reference to plants
and animals "each according to its kind" (Gen. 1:11f., 21,
24f.), so it inserts in the reference to mankind the sentence,
"He created them as male and female." (Cultic laws required this differentiation.)[18] Thus it is stated, according
to Schmidt, that humanity consists "from creation on, of
both sexes."[19]

Thus in contrast to Boehmer, Schmidt sees in v. 27
(creation of mankind according to the image of God) a statement of the priestly narrator which includes women. It is
true that he adds the limitation that in v. 27b ("male and
female he created them") it is not a question "of an equalization of man and woman through creation;" and although v. 28
refers to both--i.e., blessing and dominion[20] are promised
to mankind, not only to man--v. 27b names man before woman. Thus Schmidt thinks that although the preeminence of
man is by no means so sharply emphasized in the priestly
document as in the Yahwist document (Gen. 2:7, 18-25), it

is nevertheless not absent there (in this connection he also refers to Num. 1; 3:15ff.). [21]

Besides what Schmidt says about Boehmer's exposition of Gen. 1:26f., the following critical comments may be made. It seems to me that Boehmer, in finding reference only to man in the Godlikeness and dominion rights of Gen. 1:26f., entirely overlooks the fact that woman is included in the dominion mandate and privilege repeated in v. 28. For immediately preceding, in v. 27b, the sexual differentiation of mankind is indicated: "as man and woman he created them," from which follows in v. 28: "God blessed them and said to them: 'Be fruitful and multiply and fill the earth and make it submissive to you and have dominion over the fish of the sea ... and over every creature....'" Very probably the Old Testament narrator wants the charge of procreation to be understood as directed to both sexes, [22] especially since the sexual differentiation of the human species has just been mentioned. The further imperative, "bring the earth in subjection to you," and "have dominion," follows then immediately and speaks of the same subject: "mankind," consisting of men and women. But now since the lordship over non-human creation is the consequence of Godlikeness (cf. Gen. 1:26), [23] the statement about the creation of ādām as image of God (1:26f) must be applied to woman also. [24] Of course, it still remains true that the priestly document as well as the Old Testament in general undoubtedly sees in man the more valuable human being[25] and therefore recognizes in him preeminently the dignity of the image of God. In indicating this situation Boehmer has touched upon a decisive point--with which Schmidt agrees, although he does not formulate it so sharply--that has been given too little attention up to now in both Old Testament and New Testament exegesis, insofar as the latter, especially in the apostolic letters, is based on the Old Testament point of view regarding women. The position which the Old Testament accords to women in the social and cultic realms must be appreciated and taken into account as the context for special statements about women. Thus a brief discussion of this position is needed. [26]

Since earliest times the patriarchal large family was the exclusive societal form in Israel. [27] It must be assumed that the Israelites brought the patriarchate with them when they entered the Promised Land, especially since they came from a nomadic life. [28] The consequence for women was that they were inferior to men in social and religious relationships. In marriage, which often had a polygamous structure, a woman was legally considered the property of her husband,[29] who as her "baal" ruled over her[30] and to whom she was obligated to be obedient. Only the husband had the right of divorce (cf. Deut. 24:1). Her task as wife consisted mainly in the exercise of sexual and procreative functions. The Old Testament genealogies[31] show clearly that in accordance with the outlook of the times her role in reproduction was considered to be a purely passive one: she "received" the "seed" of her husband and "bore" him children.[32] The real begetter of new life was thought to be only the man. Male progeny was particularly desired and valued.[33] The denigration of women articulated in these facts is further evident in the estimated value of women in Leviticus 27:1-7, which is about half that of men.

The social position of women in Israel, which was marked by the laws and customs of the ancient Orient, was matched by their religious-cultic position. The oldest cult law[34] had to do with men only and demanded of them alone an appearance in the sanctuary, three times a year. Women were not obliged to share in pilgrimages or in the Passover meal. They were in principle excluded from priestly function, i.e., from serving in the sacrifices and in the temple.[35] Although women had a closer relationship to religion in early Israel--as charismatic prophets and judges[36]--they were increasingly forced out of official cultic activity by the progressive strengthening of the priesthood and the development of legal emphasis in religion. A not unimportant aspect of this process must have been the laws of purification (Lev. 12; 15:19ff.). Thus the official practice of religion and the fulfillment of the law were essentially the prerogative and duty of the free Israelite male, who bearing the sign of the covenant, circumcision, was, in contrast to the female, the only "fully authorized member" of the covenant people.[37]

It is in the context of this given situation, especially of the position given the Israelite woman of Old Testament times in the social sphere, that the Yahwistic creation narrative (Gen. 2:7-24) must be understood and judged: in the patristic and pseudo-patristic statements accepted by Gratian the inferiority of woman as not God's image (Ambrosiaster) is derived from this narrative, as well as from other sources.[38] The so-called biblicistic understanding of Gen. 2 clearly underlies these patristic maxims and indicates the untenability of their reasoning.[39] The Fathers considered it an historical fact that the man "Adam" was the first-

created human being, in whom all others have their origin--
in the first place, woman.[40] In keeping with this historical
interpretation, the consequence drawn by the Fathers from
Gen. 2:22ff. is a thoroughly real consequence, which has defined the life of woman: the status subiectionis to man.
Modern theology has not yet divorced itself completely from
this patristic exegesis--which is supported by Pauline inter-
pretation--and patristic evaluation of the Yahwistic creation
narrative. Even today, Gen. 2:21ff. is considered to some
extent the locus classicus for the subjection of woman to man,
supposedly set forth and founded on the order of Creation.[41]
Strengthened by the Pauline statements (1 Cor. 11:3ff.; 1
Tim. 2:11ff., among others) that go back to it, this passage
from Genesis has become authoritative for the position of
women in current church law. The decree of the Bible Commission of June 30, 1909, "On the Historical Character of
the First Three Chapters of Genesis" (Denz. 2121-2128),
strengthened the almost literal understanding of Gen. 2:21ff.
Paragraph 3 of this decree sets forth the exegetical principle
that where the Genesis chapters have to do with "facts which
touch upon the fundamentals of the Christian religion," there
must be no questioning of "the literal historical sense."[42]
In this context a few examples are given which are to be
understood as facts connected with doctrine, among others
"the formation of the first woman from the first man" (Denz.
2123). H. Renckens, who thinks that the Bible Commission
was unfortunate in the treatment of paragraph 3, describes
the influence of the decree on the exegesis of Gen. 2:21ff.
in the following manner: "Without apparent motivation the
unanimous but contrived conclusion was thus reached that the
rib belongs to the symbolic wording of the report but that
the physical derivation of woman from man is taught as historical fact."[43] Even after the relaxation of the decree by
a letter from the secretary of the Commission to Cardinal
Suhard in 1948,[44] and even after and despite the statement
of the Commission itself that its earlier decrees are to be
understood as conditioned by the times,[45] Catholic exegesis
retained in large part the traditional explanation of Gen. 2:
21ff. Yet in relation to other aspects of the Yahwistic creation narrative, Catholic exegesis very easily shed its liter-
alism. Thus in more recent publications of Catholic writers
--from the 1950s and the 1960s--the doctrine of evolution is
by no means rejected, although a literal interpretation of
Gen. 2:7ff. would exclude it. At the same time they follow
the Bible Commission in finding woman's origin in man.[46]
The conclusion of natural science that woman cannot be derived from man[47] demands, however, a decisive break with

a biblicistic interpretation of the text. [48] The latest exegesis
is today largely ready for this break, since it ascribes only
symbolic and etiological significance to the Yahwistic description of the creation of woman. But once again the result of
this exegesis is often the deduction from the alleged allegorical form of the text, that subordination of woman to man is
the divine order of creation[49]--completely ignoring the long-
standing patriarchal milieu of the author.

Renckens reasonably suggests that the Bible Commission had its eye on the New Testament texts 1 Cor. 11:7-12,
1 Tim. 2:31 and Eph. 5:28-30, in explaining the "formation
of the first woman from the first man" as an historical fact
consistent with doctrine. For these texts refer to Gen. 2:
21ff. (creation of woman from man) as factual event. [50] Further explanation for the position of the Bible Commission,
Renckens thinks, may be found in the place Gen. 2:21ff. has
in church tradition, which wanted to see in the creation of
Eve a model for the birth of the church from the side of
Christ. [51] In addition Renckens has the following comment
on the reasons for the Commission's decree:

> No matter how important a New Testament fact that
> has a typological relation with an event of the Old
> Testament may be, and no matter how urgent the ref-
> erence to the Old Testament may be, one cannot
> therefore conclude that the Old Testament event is
> an historical fact. A literary fact is obviously suf-
> ficient.... The Old Testament is for them [i.e., the
> New Testament writers, especially Paul] a store-
> house from which they unhesitatingly take whatever
> meets their needs, sometimes whatever happens to
> come to mind.... Thus, where Holy Scripture so
> often quotes itself, comments on and reinterprets it-
> self, we seem to be led to the exegetical principle--
> in seeking to answer the question, what has happened
> objectively--that the oldest scriptural passage, which
> became the source of a whole series of quotations and
> allusions, has a certain primacy before the whole
> tradition which resulted from it.... In other words,
> the later data, which in dependence upon Genesis speak
> about the appearance of the first woman, are of such
> a nature that our conclusion could be: Genesis must
> have the last word. [52]

Thus we are left with the text itself, for the objective understanding of which reference to the time of writing of the

Yahwistic creation narrative--in contrast to the priestly narrative some 500 years later--may be helpful: the Yahwist
probably lived after David's death, i. e., in the tenth to ninth
century B. C., and presumably in the neighborhood of Solo-
mon's residence. [53]

From a literary standpoint, Genesis 2 and 3 were put
together into a unified whole by the Yahwist who had at his
disposal two originally independent documentary themes. It
has been called a "well constructed anthropological aitologume-
non" because it answers the question, "How did empirical-
historical mankind come to its present miseria conditionis
humanae status?"[54] Thus the fall of man is the real theme
of Gen. 2:4b--3:24. [55] Into this central theme of the narrative various peripheral themes--etiological myths in literary
form--are woven, one of which is the creation of woman in
Gen. 2:21ff. [56] Haag convincingly suggests the likelihood that
the account of the creation of man (Gen. 2:7--ādām) originally
included both sexes, but that as the author worked a folk tale
of the creation of woman into the story, he decided to limit
the first account to the creation of the male, [57] who was thus
placed alone at the beginning of the human race. Thus it
is in accordance with the strongly monogenetic thinking of
the Yahwist--which means of his Israelite ancestors--that he
not only appoints a particular progenitor for each tribe[58] but
also traces back the whole of mankind to one beginning and
source, concretized in one single man (ādām). This is the
way he explains the unity of mankind. [59] It is incontestable
that this person, who "as the absolute beginning point is
carrier of the fullness of everything human,"[60] could only
be, and must be--in the conceptual world of the Yahwist as
of the Old Testament in general--a male. According to J,
the originators of various peoples (Israel, Edom, Moab, Am-
mon, etc.) are not tribal parents but tribal fathers, which
corresponds to the general position of the Old Testament,
that only the male can beget offspring. [61] Following this
understanding of reproduction--specifically, monogenetic
thinking about ancestors which was conditioned by his understanding of reproduction--the first woman must come from
the Adam-man, [62] the Yahwist believes, in order that all
men may originate from him. The Yahwist could explain
this event only by an unmediated intervention of God, since
a normal reproduction was of course excluded.

In this connection it is worth noting that the idea of
a derivation of woman from man is not found only in the Old
Testament: there are similar myths in other patriarchal

cultures. [63] The Old Testament narrative (Gen. 2:21ff.)
should be read in the framework of this mythic viewpoint:
it adopts a very old tradition with strongly marked characteristics. [64] Of course the Yahwist utilizes this available
motif about the origin of woman from man not only to trace
the whole of humanity--not excluding the woman--back to one
ultimate origin and ancestor, but also, surely, in order to
explain why man finds in woman, and not in animals, a being
profoundly close to him (v. 23a), [65] and especially why love
binds the two sexes to "become one flesh."[66] But the narrow horizon of patriarchal thinking is clearly shown by the
use of the mythic derivation of woman as explanation of love
between man and woman. Love thus goes back to the original
unity of the sexes, yet the author finds the unity embodied
only in man (v. 21). The primacy of the male according to
J is also expressed by the fact that the man alone is the
name-giver, not only for animals (v. 19f.) but also for woman (v. 23; Gen. 3:20). [67] Many exegetes find further confirmation of the secondary significance and position of woman in contrast to man (according to J in Jahweh's formation
of woman from the rib[68] of man in order to provide him "a
helper fit for him" (v. 18). This is the line of approach
taken by Gunkel: the myth does not mean "that woman originally is 'coordinated' with man, that she is 'under him,'"
but rather that woman is only a "help" for man and man (the
male) is "the human being" per se. The myth does not present the ideal, according to Gunkel; it intends to explain
facts. [69] Opposing this interpretation, other expositors lay
more weight on the phrase כְּנֶגְדּוֹ, which more carefully defines
the concept 'help' and from which they conclude that man,
according to J, finds in woman "his opposite number, his
complement, "[70] an equal partner, [71] and thus, in this view,
any derogation of woman is excluded. [72] Taking into account
the conceptual horizon of the Yahwist, Renckens paraphrases
the content of the concept 'help' in the following way: "The
hagiograph refers to the social phenomenon of the family in
general; one misunderstands the universal import of the account if one is thinking here only of the sexual act. At the
same time it is even less possible to exclude it. The passage itself makes that fact abundantly clear. "[73]

In conclusion, it may be said about Gen. 2:21-24 that
it should be understood <u>not as historical fact,</u> [74] but, as
Renckens says, as an etiological explanation and interpretation of the following empirical phenomena: "1. the absolute
unity of the human species; 2. the relationship between man
and woman [as the Yahwist views it]; 3. the Hebraic expres-

sion for blood relationship: 'to be of someone's flesh and bones'; 4. the Hebrew words for man and woman: <u>isch</u> and <u>isschah</u>. "75 But the etiological character of the Yahwistic creation narrative, into which mythic materials are clearly assimilated, forbids us to draw any dogmatical or legal consequences to the effect that woman is not made in the image of God, that she is inferior in accordance with the order of creation and therefore that she is rightly subordinate to man. 76 An exegesis that does not avoid drawing such conclusions from Gen. 2 completely ignores the time-conditioned horizon of the biblical writer--a practice inadmissible in every respect. 77 Or such exegesis may actually be based upon the same or similar sociological structure as that of the biblical writer, and thus lack any critical objectivity toward him--as in the case of the Church Fathers (cf. the discussion of the Gratian chapter, pp. 33ff.). But in any case a misunderstanding results and false conclusions are drawn about the right classification and evaluation of women. It may be added that the priestly account of Genesis 1 supplies a kind of correction and relativization for the Yahwistic creation narrative which is often wrongly taken in an absolute sense78 or as if it were a more exact explanation of Genesis 179--a process that is bound to work out to the detriment of a true view of women. The relationship between the two accounts is rather the following: "The second chapter [i.e., of Genesis] is ... older than the first and adds no historical detail to it. The relationship is the reverse of the biblical order. That is, Genesis 1 is later, presents a further stage of development and is therefore theologically more cautious: <u>Gen. 1</u> directs the <u>anthropological pictures of chapter 2 to their root, to its doctrinal content</u>. The same thing is true concerning the origin and equivalence of the two sexes ... (Gen. 1:27; cf. 5:1f.). "80

Favorable to this evaluation of Genesis 1--with its more timeless and thus more valid formulation, in comparison with Genesis 2--is the fact that Jesus specifically, in Mt. 19:4-6, refers to the priestly account and only uses chapter 2 in the reference to man and wife "becoming one body." Jesus says nothing about the origin of woman in man nor about any derived, inferior existence of women. On the contrary he rejects as illegitimate, and as inconsistent with the divine order of marriage, any one-sided right of divorce for the husband resulting from such a view of women and from hardness of heart (Mt. 19:3-9). Thus it becomes very clear that Jesus wants women to be regarded as independent, free, and equal persons having a claim on equal rights81

and thus neither possessions of men nor in any way subject
to their domination.

Besides using the two creation narratives, especially
the Yahwistic, the Church Fathers, followed by Gratian--who,
however, is even more dependent on Paul--make use of the
story of the Fall (Genesis 3) as support for the status subiectionis of women. They see in Eve, and thus in woman in
general, the originator of sin, who as such must remain under the dominion of man. (Cf. C. 33, q. 5, cc. 18 and 19
as well as the dictum Gratiani, C. 15, q. 3 princ.) A
principle objection to such an interpretation of Genesis 3 and
the conclusion drawn from it is that the Fall narrative should
not be taken as an historical account. [82] It should be understood as etiology that makes use of mythic representation to
answer the question about the origin of evil and suffering in
the world. The answer it gives is: "They do not come from
God but rather solely from the sin of man.... In this way
sin is defined as man's disregard for the will and order of
God. If that is true, it is quite irrelevant what the concrete
form of sin was."[83] The writer worked various materials
together that tell in several differing forms of the original
sin of man. [84] According to J. Begrich, the so-called Paradise or Fall narrative is a composite of two differing sources.
The one dealt with the offence of a primeval man, which he
committed in the Garden of Eden and for which he was punished by being driven by God out of the Garden. The other
source tells of the woman and the serpent (Gen. 3:1-6a): the
woman was punished for the transgression of a particular
prohibition and the serpent for tempting to the transgression. [85] The story of primitive man was reduced because of
its strongly mythological coloring, according to Begrich: he
thinks that combining the two sources of traditional materials
resulted in the elimination of the cause of the anathema
against primeval man, in place of which the redactor has the
man (ādām) share in the offence of the woman[86] (cf. Gen.
3:6).

The temptation story (Gen. 3:1-7), in the middle of
which we find the serpent and the woman, is of Canaanite
origin and contains an emphasized polemic against the Baal
cult of the serpent for which Palestinian archeology has provided evidence. [87] The actual theme is fertility:

The figure that looms behind the serpent in Gen. 3
is the Canaanitic Baal, appearing in the guise most
tempting to Israel, that of a serpent. For in this

particular shape he was the life-giver, the life-renewer, the phallus. As such he belonged especially to the Canaanitic autumn and New Year feast, with its sexual excitement and frenzy. But to the prophets and their circles this 'renewal of life' was simply and solely immorality and sensuality (cf. Hos. 4:12b-14)."[88]

The conception that the woman succumbs first to the temptation of the serpent and then tempts the man is found in similar form in several Fall myths in patriarchal cultures: the woman is blamed for transgressing a prohibition and for the loss of life and paradise in connection with that act.[89] The writer's willingness to accept such mythic explanation and to use it in the setting of Israelite milieu and history may have been the result of the common Old Testament experience: Israelite women felt themselves drawn to the neighboring foreign cults--not least because of the purely masculine character of the Yahweh cult--and thus threatened the latter.[90] The idea in Gen. 3 is not that the woman led the man astray and therefore is the one more easily tempted--thus proving, as so often happens, her ethical inferiority[91]--but rather that because she is excluded from the Yahweh cult, and thus lacks possibilities for sufficient religious development, she herself is led astray into a surrogate religion.[92] According to the text of Gen. 3:8-19, Yahweh's penal sentence does not distinguish which of the two human beings first fell into sin-- no matter how the role of woman may be described by the narrator for the reasons mentioned above. Both are personally and directly addressed by God, brought to judgment and punished.[93]

In content the punishment gives religious meaning to concrete empirical reality as the Yahwist understands it-- reality burdened by the many sufferings and troubles of both women and men. The hagiograph traces this distress in human life back to an anathema, to a divine punishment meted out to mankind as consequence of an original sin.[94] It is clear from the threat of divine vengeance, which is directed against the woman, that the Yahwist sees her as being ruled by man as a consequence of her sin (Gen. 3:16), in addition to the grievances of pregnancy and the pains of child-birth, while the punishment for the man is carried out in the area of his life and work as the Yahwist portrays this area--curse of the field, toil of earning a living (Gen. 3:17ff.). The Palestinian coloring is sharply reflected in the sentences meted out.[95] The sentence, "... He [the man] shall rule over you" וְהוּא יִמְשָׁל־בָּךְ (Gen. 3:16), has long been understood as divine command in the sense of a decree. This interpretation seems to be present in the New Testament[96] and some of the passages from the Church Fathers quoted by Gratian appear to understand Gen. 3:16 as divine decree.[97] But the passage cannot legitimately be taken in this way (as one could gather from the context): "... The words 'he shall rule over you' are not a commandment but a threatening announcement of the consequences of human disobedience.... Here the position of women as it really was in the ancient Near East-- in contrast to the will of the creator--is conceptualized: no order is proclaimed."[98] The author of Gen. 3 was obviously a witness to the rulership of men over women and it seemed to him like the misfortune of destiny, so that he was moved to seek the cause and explanation--as for the other plagues which afflict mankind--in an original sin. But if we ignore this clearly etiological character of the story--which also characterizes the myths of the Fall among primitive people[99] --then we do arrive at the misguided interpretation of Gen. 3:16 as divine command or punishment which is not supposed to be annulled. Besides its untenability, such an interpretation, which even today has legal consequences in the church, demonstrates a no less heartless and inconsiderate position than that of the ultra-conservative Calvinists which "on the basis of Gen. 3:16 rejects modern, painless 'natural child-birth' and on the basis of Gen. 3:17-19a refuses to permit innoculation against disease, even for animals!"[100]

The New Testament, especially the Pauline, passages presented--in patristic statements used by Gratian--as proof for the status subiectionis of women, are dependent upon the Old Testament passages we have just considered. In chapter 13 of C. 33, q. 5, which is dependent upon Ps. Augustine (Ambrosiaster), 1 Cor. 11:7a is cited (along with Gen. 1:27) as scriptural proof for woman's supposed lack of the image of God: "Therefore the apostle says: 'For a man ought not to cover his head, since he is the image and glory of God'"; Ambrosiaster continues: "A woman, however, must cover her head, because she is neither the reflection nor the image of God (mulier ideo uelat, quia non est gloria aut imago Dei)."[101] If the scriptural text does not itself draw this conclusion, it must still be granted that the sentence added by Ambrosiaster corresponds at least to the sense of the Apostle's words. It does say in 1 Cor. 11:7b that "woman is the glory of man." It is clear from this and from the whole context that for Paul the image of God status is limited to man, as will be shown in more detail below. This consequence is also drawn from 1 Cor. 11 in chapter 19 in

C. 33, q. 5, which is taken from the Corinthian commentary of Ambrosiaster. [102] For Paul the limitation to man of the image of God status also implies man's position of rulership over woman (cf. 1 Cor. 11:3; Eph. 5:23) and her subordination to him (cf. Eph. 5:22, 24), as also discussed in some patristic statements used by Gratian (cf. cc. 15 and 19 in C. 33, q. 5). Paul presents the following justification of the preferential position of man: "For man is not made from woman but woman from man. Neither was man created for woman but woman for man" (1 Cor. 11:8f.; [cf. 1 Tim. 2: 13: "For Adam was created first, then Eve"]). Obviously reference is made here to the Yahwistic creation narrative (especially to Gen. 2:21-24), which Paul understands as an account of a factual event. [103] 1 Cor. 11:8f. also shows that Paul views the Yahwistic creation narrative as interpretation of the priestly narrative: in 1 Cor. 11:7a he assigns the narrow meaning "man" to the collective concept אָדָם (ādām) in Gen. 1:26f.--which leads to the limitation of the image-of-God concept to man (male): "for it is the man who need not cover his head because he is the image and reflection of God."

In order to understand 1 Cor. 11, one must observe that Paul stands entirely within the Jewish-rabbinical tradition of Genesis interpretation, as exegesis research has proved incontestably. [104] Following this tradition he accepts Genesis 2:21ff. as completely historical and thus arrives at the position that a "difference of essence,"[105] a difference in hierarchal classification, exists between the two sexes, since man appeared first and without mediation from the hand of God but woman was formed later and in fact from the man. Such thinking is clearly marked by the rabbinical and generally Oriental conception, "Everything good comes first" (or "The older is the more valuable"). [106] The earlier and unmediated creation of Adam by God implies, according to late Jewish conceptualization, that he alone is the reflection of God;[107] woman is a "derived, secondary being" and therefore is denied participation in this evaluation: "Eve is not created according to the image of God but her existence is derived from Adam."[108] When Paul in 1 Cor. 11:7b characterizes woman as δόξα ἀνδρός "reflection of man"--in contrast to his characterization of man in rabbinical language[109] as εἰκὼν καὶ δόξα θεοῦ --he is saying that the relation of woman to man is like the dependent relationship between a reflection and the (real) picture. The real picture is man [Bild], the reflection [Abbild] is woman. [110] Here too Paul stands within the framework of rabbinic tradition. [111] Without doubt, it is not woman but man alone who is the true image of God, according to Paul, although there is doubt about the nature of a Godlikeness that is established in creation and limited to the male. (Jervelle[112] notes that late Jewish conceptualization emphasizes the dominion status of man, especially his religious prerogatives.) In any case, from the limitation of Godlikeness to man--i.e., from his primary creation--late Judaism, and Paul following it, derives man's position as "head" vis-à-vis woman, as 1 Cor. 11:3 says. What Paul is doing here--in dependence on rabbinic tradition[113]--is setting forth a descending classification: God--Christ--man--woman, in which each preceding member of the series is "head" ($\kappa\epsilon\phi\alpha\lambda\dot{\eta}$), in the sense of "master," or the establishing beginning or source (=$\dot{\alpha}\rho\chi\dot{\eta}$), [114] of the following member. Johannes Weiss comments on this:[115] "The climax: God (Christ), man, woman assigns to woman a status not only underneath man but also distant from Christ and God.... We must admit that v. 3 [of 1 Cor. 11:3] remains below the level of Gal. 3:28 in typical Jewish-rabbinic derogation of woman." By the argumentation of 1 Cor. 11:3ff. Paul attempts to establish theologically the custom taken over into the Christian community from Judaism, requiring women to wear a veil in congregational assembly, at prayer and in prophesying. For Paul this custom has the signification of indicating the inferior position of women in accordance with the "order of creation."[116] Closely related is the further signification that Paul (v. 10) gives to the veil: it serves as protective device against demons. The explanation is as follows: late Judaism thought of Godlikeness as present in the head or perhaps even more in the face ($\pi\rho\dot{o}\sigma\omega\pi\sigma\nu$) of the male[117] and that this constituted a protection against attacks and temptations from the demons. [118] The reason for this was that dominion status was connected with Godlikeness: possession of $\dot{\epsilon}\xi\sigma\upsilon\sigma\dot{\iota}\alpha$ over animals, demons and the other creatures. [119] Now since woman as only $\delta\dot{o}\xi\alpha$ of man is helpless before the demons, she must wear $\delta\iota\dot{\alpha}$ $\tau\sigma\dot{\upsilon}\varsigma$ $\dot{\alpha}\gamma\gamma\dot{\epsilon}\lambda\sigma\upsilon\varsigma$, [120] (v. 10) a substitute protection, a sign of power ($\dot{\epsilon}\xi\sigma\upsilon\sigma\dot{\iota}\alpha$) in the form of a head covering. [121] As Jervell rightly remarks, [122] this obligation excludes the possibility that Paul grants woman Godlikeness, even if it be only secondary, for in this case the veiling would be superfluous. It is, according to Paul, not only the fact that women are not created in the image of God that requires her to wear an $\dot{\epsilon}\xi\sigma\upsilon\sigma\dot{\iota}\alpha$, a sign of power, on her head, but also the fact of her "weakness," her "religious-ethical inferiority."[123] This point of view goes back to a late Jewish exposition of the origins narrative (Gen. 3), according to which only Eve, not Adam,

sinned.[124] The serpent was not able to touch Adam; the
power of Satan came through the woman.[125] Evidence of
this tradition, besides 1 Cor. 11:10, is found especially in
2 Cor. 11:1-4[126] and 1 Tim. 2:14,[127] which expressly states:
"and Adam was not deceived but the woman was deceived and
became a transgressor." (This line of thought becomes, as
in 1 Tim. 2:11ff, the justification for the subordination of
woman in the patristic passages used by Gratian: cf. cc. 18
and 19 in C. 33, q. 5.) In 1 Cor. 11:10 the rabbinic interpretation of Gen. 3 is combined with Jewish speculation about
Gen. 6:1ff. (intercourse of the sons of God[128] with the daughters of men). J. Weiss interprets the allusion of Paul to
this passage in 1 Cor. 11:10 as follows:

> As according to Gen. 6:1ff. the sons of God, charmed
> by the beauty of the daughters of men, seduced them...,
> so the danger is always present that the lust of angels
> (i.e., spirits, demons) will be aroused when a woman
> in prayer approaches the heavenly realms. This is
> why she must cover herself, in order by wearing the
> veil to hold off the attacks of angels, which could not
> happen to a man,[129]

since according to Paul he alone is the image of God. As
evidenced in rabbinic sources, the veil serves in general to
keep woman in subordination to man,[130] which is also the
significance of the veil for Gratian.[131] Jervelle explains the
connection between the two functions involved in covering the
head--on the one hand it is a means of protection against
demons, on the other hand it is symbol of subordination--as
follows:

> ... One may understand ... the $\dot{\epsilon}\xi o u \sigma i \alpha$ (cf. 1 Cor.
> 11:10) as a kind of head covering which, exactly be-
> cause it represents the secondary position of woman
> in subordination to man, also serves as protection
> against demons or apostate angels. By covering her
> head she shares in the protection against demons which
> man has because of his image-of-God status. Since
> she is not Godlike, she must have a head covering.[132]

In one way Paul weakens his statement (1 Cor. 11:
3ff.) concerning female inferiority in terms of Creation--using
this inferiority to justify wearing the veil--by explaining in
v. 11f.: "Nevertheless, in the Lord man is not independent
of woman nor woman of man; for as woman was made from
man, so man is now born of woman. And all things are

from God." This could mean that man and woman are bound together "in the Lord"[133] and that neither of the sexes receives any preferential status before God.[134] Yet the statement must not be read as abrogating previous statements that have placed women in essence below men.[135]

A passage in Ephesians, chapter 5:22-33, is clearly influenced by the Yahwistic creation narrative about the creation of women (Gen. 2:21ff.) and the Jewish-rabbinic interpretations of it. Depending on patristic authority, which he cites (e.g., in C. 33, q. 5, c. 15), Gratian (dictum p. c. 11 in C. 33, q. 5) takes from this Ephesians passage the statement about woman as "body of man" (corpus viri) and the statement about man as "head of woman" (caput mulieris). (In connection with 1 Cor. 11:3 we have already discussed the characterization of man as "head of woman" and traced it back to Gen. 2:21ff. See pp. 110f.)

Paul makes use of a common Jewish formula in calling woman σῶμα or σάρξ of man in Eph. 5:28, 29.[136] This formula goes back to the Yahwistic narrative about the generation of woman from the body of men,[137] which is itself to be taken as an etiological explanation for the presumably existing formula "to be someone's flesh and bones" (cf. Gen. 2:23)--indicating blood relationship--and for the formula for the sexes "to become one flesh" (cf. Gen. 2:24).[138] Since Paul in Eph. 5:31 quotes Gen. 2:24 word for word, many exegetes conclude that Paul's characterization of the wife as σάρξ of the husband has come from this verse.[139] Yet in the Yahwistic narrative both events, the formation of woman from man and the sexes becoming one body, stand in correlation to each other, so that it is sufficient to take Gen. 2:21-24 in general as the source of the concept "body" or "flesh" applied to woman in Eph. 5.

More important for us is the fact that in using this concept Paul characterizes woman less as an independent, self-responsible person than as the possession and property of man, as a being subordinate to him, who for direction is referred to him as her "head."[140] Now of course it must not be forgotten that the word σῶμα "always means for Paul the whole person, not a part of the person;" it indicates the person "vis-à-vis God or another person."[141] Thus it practically means "person." However, it is noteworthy that σῶμα (or σάρξ) is never used for man in his relationship to woman--which should also be possible in view of the sexes "becoming one flesh"[142]--but in Paul the man is always the

"head" of the woman and never (or never also) her "body."[143]
He is given the power-of-command over her (Eph. 5:22) because he is "head."[144]   But beyond this position, man is
called upon to love his wife--indeed "as his own body,"[145]
since the marriage relationship of man and wife stands parallel to the relationship between Christ and the church.   Contrariwise the wife must subordinate herself to the husband
"in everything" ($\dot{\epsilon}\nu$ $\pi\alpha\nu\tau\acute{\iota}$), v. 24; in fact, she must fear him,
v. 33.   From this classification of higher and lower--man
and wife, "head" and "body"--and from the differentiation in
the demands made on each in relation to the other, it is
clear that strictly speaking Paul considers only the male human being to be a free, independent person.   (As already
mentioned, the reason for this evaluation is the Pauline concept that the male is the source of existence for the female,
the origin of her being--in accordance with the literal interpretation of the Yahwistic narrative in Gen. 2:21ff.)[146]   This
leaves the woman in a dependent, relative and subordinate
position.[147]   Thus it must be affirmed that Paul in 1 Cor.
11 and Eph. 5 has not advanced very far beyond the Old
Testament appraisal and position of women,[148] except that
in Eph. 5 the relationship between husband and wife--allegor-
ically related to the bond between Christ and church--has received a religious deepening, spiritualization and durabili-
ty.[149]

     The analogy between marriage and the paradigmatic
relation between Christ and his church--an analogy that underlies the admonition to married couples in Eph. 5--originates
in a particular kind of rabbinic exposition of Gen. 2:21ff.:
a typological transference of the relationship Adam-Eve to
the relationship Adam-Israel.   This means that Israel comes
from Adam[150] and thus Eve is equated with Israel.[151]   Gen.
2:24 is quoted in Eph. 5:31f.[152] and the typology Adam-Israel
is transferred to the relationship Christ-church,[153] in which
Christ is understood as eschatological Adam[154] and the
church as the "new Israel."[155]   Paul's analogical methodology
implies an uncritical, biblicistic understanding of Gen. 2:21ff.
The parallel between Christ-church on the one hand and man-
wife on the other is only possible if the Yahwistic narrative
of the creation of woman from man is misunderstood as literal history.   It is also this narrative so understood which
explains the demand--based on the place of the church in
relation to Christ--that woman be unconditionally submissive
to man.   As probably no other Pauline passage, it is exactly
because of Eph. 5--and indeed on the basis of this analogy--
that Paul's understanding of the structure of marriage and

the subordination of women was accepted as dogma and is considered even today as divine decree. [156] Regardless of the fact that the man does not always--and alone--possess the higher ethical and spiritual qualities[157] required for a function as "head," such a function is attributed to him simply because he is male. Such an "order" is not only absurd, it also omits needed respect for the freedom and independence of the personhood of woman. It is true that marriage as analogue of the relationship between Christ and the church can and even must be used, but only in a limited way, since in marriage--as different from the bond between Christ and church--the partners have equal worth and equal rights. Accordingly in marriage a true and deep relationship must exclude the domination of one partner over the other.

Our critical investigation of the Pauline and deutero-Pauline statements (1 Cor. 11:3ff.; 1 Tim. 2:11-14 [to which cf. 1 Cor. 14:34f.];[158] Eph. 5:22-33)--which give "proof" for the status subiectionis of women by authority of the Fathers as quoted by Gratian and in Gratian's dicta themselves, as well as in the literature of the decretists and decretalists depending on Gratian--has shown that these passages are characterized by a clear denigration of women in ontical as well as in religious-ethical terms. As we have indicated, this negative evaluation of women must be traced back to the strong dependence of Paul and the writer of the pastoral letters on the late Jewish rabbinical tradition, [159] from which the rabbinic interpretation of Genesis and other scripture was taken. [160] Just as the conception of women in the Pauline and deutero-Pauline passages--characterized as it is by rabbinic thinking--cannot claim to be binding, so also are the legal consequences unjustified which Paul (or whoever wrote the pastoral letters), [161] as well as Gratian, supported by the authority of the Fathers, have deduced for women. Such consequences are devoid of any true foundation.

Part II   DOCTRINE

Chapter 7

THE TRADITIONAL CONCEPTION OF THE PRIESTHOOD; AN ARGUMENT FOR THE EXCLUSION OF WOMEN

Doctrinal arguments to justify the exclusion of women from service in ecclesiastical office have often been criticized and thoroughly refuted, in the theological literature of recent years. [1] But several additions can be made to the refutation. Especially the analysis of the conservative understanding of church office, which opposes admission of women to ordination, needs such addition and deepening in regard to one aspect of the concept of office--that of representation [Stellvertretung]. Of course the problem cannot be treated in detail in the framework of this study--only in a preliminary fashion --but some basic reflections may throw light on the questionableness of the traditional understanding of office and representation, insofar as it is directed against the admission of women to church positions.

a.   Traditional Understanding of Ecclesiastical Office

According to the traditional Catholic concept of church office, one who possesses the presbyterial and episcopal office is understood to be the representative of Christ, as one who in his functions of office and especially in the liturgical celebration portrays and represents Christ. [2]   Although the representation concept in this crystallized juridical form is not present in the New Testament (more on pp. 123ff.), pointers in this direction developed relatively early, [3] and in the course of time it became an essential characterization of the office-holder in Catholic theology. [4]   Several encyclicals of Pius XII[5] made use of this tradition in emphasizing the representation function of the priest as well as of ecclesiastical office-holders in general.   This emphasis is expressed repeatedly, especially in his encyclical, "Concerning the Sacred Liturgy" (Mediator Dei): "The minister at the altar offering a Sacrifice in the name of all His members represents Christ, the Head of the Mystical Body" (... personam Christi utpote Capitis gerit). [6] "Only to the Apostles, and

thenceforth to those on whom their successors have placed
their hands, is granted the power of the priesthood, in virtue
of which they represent the person of Jesus Christ before
their people, acting at the same time as representatives of
their people before God" (... Iesu Christi personam sus-
tinent).[7] The ability of the priest to represent Christ in
this form goes back according to Catholic teaching, to the
infusion of grace in the priest's ordination, or more exactly,
to the imprint of the sacramental nature of ordination. Mediator Dei speaks about this too: Priests alone have "the
indelible 'character' indicating the sacred ministers' conformity to Jesus Christ the Priest."[8] Similarly, in another place,
Pius says: "The minister by reason of the sacerdotal consecration which he has received, is made like the High Priest
and possesses the power of performing actions in virtue of
Christ's very Person."[9]

Referring expressly to the encyclical, J. Pascher[10]
develops further its concept of representation--which was
also expressed by Vatican II.[11] He sees in the eucharist a
representation and realization of the historical Last Supper,
a sacred drama in which the priest has the task of "convey-
ing the person of Christ"--an expression also used in the
encyclical--"or, to speak more exactly, to portray him faith-
fully."[12] According to Pascher, it is his ordination that
gives the priest his ability to do this: "Concerning the
priestly actor, it must be said that he is set off from the
people by virtue of his elevated position at the altar and his
vestments. He portrays Christ. Even theologically, his
significance is defined by the categories of the drama in the
statement that he and he alone is, in the eucharist, the persona of Christ." (In this connection Pascher thinks of persona in its old basic meaning of "mask" or "role" in a drama.)[13] "... In order to be able to play this role in a religious drama," the priest requires "an inner similarity to
Christ impressed upon him by the sacrament of ordination."[14]

Although in this way the ability of the priest to represent Christ is understood as the consequence of the sacrament of ordination and thus as a pneumatic power, nevertheless paradoxically--but undeniably--the male sex of the priest,
a biological quality, is considered in traditional Catholic theology to be the foremost presupposition for his representing
Christ in the priesthood. It is true that this conception appears only implicitly in the encyclical Mediator Dei, and
likewise in the texts of Vatican II, but it is clear enough[15]
and has exercised a definite influence on the thinking of

various Catholic writers about office and representation. One of these writers, O. Semmelroth,[16] says that a continuation and a pictorial representation of the "redemptive encounter" between Christ and humanity takes place in the church. This encounter is realized in the church by the fact

> that her ordained office-holders represent Christ in virtue of the indelible character of Orders and in the fact that the Christian community brings to further completion Mary's conception and compassion by hearing the word of the teaching and governing offices and by participating in the sacrifice of the priestly office.[17]

In accordance with this pattern, Semmelroth sees in the sacrifice of the eucharist a sacramental reflection of that "'rite of heavenly sacrifice' in which the sacrifice of Christ and the participating sacrifice of Mary on Calvary has eternal validity before the Father."[18] Even more clearly the exercise of ecclesiastical office is characterized as a male role and the function of the congregation as female. Thus Semmelroth comments:

> What Paul writes in the fifth chapter of Ephesians about the relation of husband to wife is to a high degree valid for the relation between the priest and the congregation, for the latter is a relationship which like that of marriage--yet even more realistically-- reflects the relationship between Christ and Mary.[19]

Other writers[20] have a similar point of view about ecclesiastical office and its relation to the Christian community. It is a point of view restricted by categories of sexual polarity, which has of course the obvious result that women are completely denied capability for church office. It is argued, for example, that Christ, the bridegroom and head of the church--the life-giving principle for the church, in fact--could not be represented by a woman, who is subject to man and as a passively receiving being could not be called (like him) the "head." This viewpoint is not seldom the main argument for the exclusion of women from Orders. Thus E. Krebs remarks: "As father, spouse and bridegroom Christ stands vis-à-vis his church.... But being father and bridegroom is the role of the male. So there is in the priesthood a mystical relationship to maleness, by which we can clearly see that Christ has entrusted this masculine office to the male."[21] M. Schmaus also perceives an inner

causal connection between the male sex of the priest and
representation of Christ, thus justifying the reservation of
the office to males:

> Thus [as in the case of Christ] the fact that the priest
> is a man is in itself a natural indication of his com-
> mission to go out into the world and proclaim the Gos-
> pel of the Kingdom of God, to give the sacraments
> and so to confer divine life in a creativity effected by
> the power of Christ. The place of women is rather
> to receive life and to take care of it. 22

Even in recent publications a similar reasoning is used to
deny women admission to service in church office. 23

b. A Critique

Apart from an obvious denigration of women--they
are allegedly not fit to represent Christ, the head, because
they are inferior, etc.--the traditional but also modern viewpoint about representation, on the basis of which women are
denied access to ecclesiastical office, implies an understanding of office incompatible with biblical statements about church
and office.   Thus while church office in the Pauline conception of church as "body of Christ" exists as an organ and a
function among other various functions within the body (cf.,
for instance, Rom. 12:4-8 and 1 Cor. 12:27ff.), incorporated
in the total organism of the body, office and the bearers of
office are placed over against congregation and church in the
traditional understanding.   Office and bearers of office seem
to be separated out from the unity of the body and associated
with Christ as "head" and "bridegroom" of the church (cf.
Eph. 5:23ff.).   Also in accordance with this pattern, New
Testament statements about church as "body" and "bride of
Christ," which in themselves reveal the relationship of the
exalted Lord to the church in its totality, are erroneously
referred in traditional ecclesiology to the relationship between church officials and the lay congregation. 24   This is
clear in Semmelroth (as well as in other theologians25), who
says:

> When tradition as well as Holy Scripture calls the
> church the bride of the Lord, the church here--strict-
> ly speaking--means the congregation in contrast to
> ecclesiastical office.   For in Catholic understanding,
> office is an exact representation of Christ, the bride-

> groom. So strictly speaking it must be 'bracketed
> out' of the church, insofar as the church is the bride.
> Similarly, in the statement that the church is the body
> of Christ, insofar as a reality is meant which is
> placed vis-à-vis Christ, the head, once again we have
> a bracketing out of the priesthood. For the priest-
> hood is just that--the visible portrayal of the head of
> the church. [26]

Of course Semmelroth preserves the distinction between Christ
and the priest, but Wintersig seems not to do even that: "In
a particular way vis-à-vis the church and the soul, to be
Christ, the bridegroom, in sacred love and gracious procrea-
tion--that is the essence and vocation of the holy priestly
order, which stands in contrast to the rank and file of the
faithful. "[27]

Undoubtedly, an illegitimate transfer of the marriage
admonition section in Eph. 5:22-33 to the relationship office-
congregation, together with an unbiblical and superficial concept of representation, has made a considerable contribution
to the formation of this understanding of church office. True,
according to Eph. 5 marriage is a reflection of the covenant
between Christ and the church, in which the position of the
husband is compared with that of Christ and the position of
the wife, with that of the church. [28] As an analogy to this,
and on the basis of the representation theory, traditional
theology sees the bishop as the bridegroom of the local
church. Realization of this fact appears in the giving of a
ring to the bishop in the ritual of his consecration as bishop.
The ring symbol indicates that the bishop as representative
of Christ is being married to the local church. [29] This
spiritual marriage was considered so real that from it far-
reaching consequences for church law were drawn, in thorough analogy to physical marriage[30]--consequences which are
in part still influential today. The relationship of the pastor
to the congregation is still expressed as spiritual marriage--
in dependence on Eph. 5;[31] the attitude that the husband is
expected to take toward his wife, according to Eph. 5, is
accepted as the standard and norm for the relation of the
priest toward the congregation. [32]

Thus office and representation are understood to mean
taking the position of Christ as head and life-giving bridegroom of the church--opposite the church--and so to carry
forward his work. Capability to do this, as we have noted
(pp. 118ff.) is linked to two presuppositions: male sex and

ordination. The more important of the two--for the purpose of representing Christ--is male sex, according to traditional doctrinal belief and operative church law (even today valid ordination is in the first place dependent upon this condition), and the result is that the objective of the office-bearer considered as representative is to portray and to imitate Christ in his earthly existence, as man. [33] Outward, biological likeness to the historical Jesus--from which a spiritual likeness and similarity of nature is too quickly concluded--thus becomes the main requirement for official representation, [34] always of course with the presupposition of sacramental ordination, which in traditional teaching perfects through grace an ability to represent Christ that is thought to be natural to male sex. At the same time this ordination sets a constitutive boundary between clergy and laity. [35] In the Decree on the Ministry and Life of Priests (Presbyterorum Ordinis) of Vatican II, this action of the sacrament is described in the following way: "The sacerdotal office of priests is conferred by that special sacrament through which priests, by the anointing of the Holy Spirit, are marked with a special character and are so configured to Christ the Priest that they can act in the person of Christ the Head. "[36] This is especially true for the consecration of bishops as the "fullness of the sacrament of orders, "[37] according to the teachings of Vatican II. By virtue of his consecration the bishop becomes immediately the "ambassador" of Christ and even more, the "image of Christ:"[38]

> From tradition ... it is clear that, by means of the laying-on of hands and the words of consecration, the grace of the Holy Spirit is so conferred, and the sacred character so impressed, that the bishops in an eminent and visible way undertake Christ's own role as Teacher, Shepherd and High Priest, and that they act in his person. [39]

Understood in this way, representation comes critically close to an identification of the bishop with Christ, as is evident in the consequences drawn from this point of view for the relationship of church members to the bishop: "The faithful, " says the Constitution on the Church, "must cling to their bishop, as the church does to Christ, and Jesus Christ to the Father, so that everything may harmonize in unity. "[40] For, "He who hears them [the bishops], hears Christ, while he who rejects them, rejects Christ and Him who sent Christ. "[41] Priests "must respect in him [the bishop] the authority of Christ, the chief Shepherd" and they

owe him for this reason love and obedience. [42]   Of course
admonitions that bishops and priests must carry out their office in the spirit of Christ are not lacking, [43] but one certainly gets the impression from the passages quoted that the
office-bearer as man and simply because of his ordination is
already brought so close to Christ--or even put in his place
--that he may to a certain extent lay claim to all the rights
of the one he represents.   Furthermore, this tendency is
strengthened by the application of the concept "father" to the
bishop and priest--a concept receiving approval in the texts
of Vatican II.   Here is another consequence of the traditional
idea of representation[44]: the office-bearer is seen as representative of God, the Father, and his office is considered as
a paternal function. [45]   The duty of obedience on the part of
the laity is the exact counterpart to the characterization of
the office-bearer as "father. "[46]

There are two distinct causes for this traditional understanding of representation.   The first results from the
human need to bring the transcendent down into the immanent
and look at it, to make that which is hidden in God available
for men. [47]   Actually, what we have here is an obvious religious desire to escape from the effort to find the transcendent
God, who is placed above every ecclesiastical institution and
can therefore never fully coincide with it.

The second cause for the traditional understanding of
representation undoubtedly lies in the intention to bestow as
much dignity as possible upon the office-bearer--placing him
above any human critique--in contrast to those under him. [48]

The words of Jesus, as recorded in Mt. 23:2-12, are
directed against both of these mistaken attitudes.   He sharply
condemns the custom of the Pharisees--which he specifically
foresees as constituting a possible danger for his disciples--
to have themselves called "Master, " "Father, " "Leader" and
to arrogate this role to themselves in relationship to the
people.   Jesus insists that there is only one Father, only
one Master and Leader and he rejects as illegitimate any
kind of assumption of these predicates by any human being.
This weakens and refutes the viewpoint still represented in
the church today, that the "vertical-authoritative" elements
must be emphatically manifested in the church and must not
be "leveled off into the horizontal, " for, it is held, the fulfillment of faith is dependent upon them. [49]   Jesus' words,
"You are all brothers" (Mt. 23:8), means that the one God
and "Father in heaven" (cf. Mt. 23:9) will not be witnessed

to in this world except by one who stands on equal footing
with his fellow-men, does not exalt himself above them, and
is ready to serve them unpretentiously. (Cf. Mt. 23:11f.;
and especially Mt. 5:14-16.)

In contrast to the attempt rashly to place the office-
bearer on the side of Christ and thus to identify him with
Christ as over against the church--on whatever grounds the
attempt is made--it must be emphatically stated that only
one is "head," "Lord," "bridegroom" of the church, the
Christ raised to the right hand of God. (Cf. Eph. 4:4ff.;
Eph. 5:23b.) He is Lord and head of the church not because
he appeared in his historical existence as a male--such an
idea betrays an unspiritual way of thinking--but rather because he is the God who became a human being, [50] who
through his suffering and death won the church for himself
and adopted it as his own "body." (Cf. Eph. 2:13ff.; Eph.
5:25f., 29; Acts 20:28.) "All life and growth, the whole
'building up' of the body," comes from him alone, the only
head, [51] through the power of the spirit. [52] "From him the
whole body is joined and knit together by every joint with
which it is supplied, when each part is working properly, and
thus makes for bodily growth ..." (Eph. 4:16). The different
offices of ministry in the church are spiritual gifts of grace
(charisma) of the exalted Lord, which he has established for
the building up of the church: "'Ascended on high ... he
gave gifts to men....' And his gifts were that some should
be apostles, some prophets, some evangelists, some pastors
and teachers, for the equipment of the saints, for the work
of the ministry, for building up the body of Christ" (Eph.
4:8, 11f.). [53] Those bearers of high office who have the
gift of leadership (1 Cor. 12:28; Rom. 12:8; 1 Thess. 5:12)
do not relinquish membership in the church any more than
do those members who have other gifts and tasks. They
continue to be members and never take the place of the head,
over against the "body." They are, to a certain extent,
organs through whom--together with those who have other
gifts[54]--the exalted Christ wants to lead and build his church,
to make it a "holy priesthood"[55] (1 Peter 2:5, 9). Thus
they stand vis-à-vis Christ in the position of servants, as
many passages in the New Testament emphasize. (E.g.,
Rom. 12:4f.; 1 Cor. 3:5ff, 4:1, 1 Peter 4:10f.; 2 Cor. 6:
3ff.) There is no other form of representation in the New
Testament than that of service and obedience toward Christ;
representation never means to take the place of Christ as
the head of the church--that is apparent from the very dissimilarity between head and member--or to play his role

vis-à-vis the church, or even to be the imaged portrayal of
the man Jesus. [56] The idea of such an imaged portrayal
clearly betrays both an inability to think theologically, and
the unspirituality and sexism of the traditional understanding
of church office.

It may not be inappropriate in this connection to point
out that sex is irrelevant for representation even according
to the concept applicable in the sphere of church law.   The
abstraction from the concrete person to be represented has
developed in this sphere to such an extent that the principle
applies even to marriage, in which the sex of the partner obviously plays a decisive role: a partner who cannot be present for the ceremony is not directed to obtain a proxy of his
or her own sex. [57] This example illustrates clearly what is
involved in deputyship: a personal-spiritual act in the name
of the one represented, [58] not a pictorial representation of
the one represented.   The will of the one who has himself
represented is the only determinant of the action of his deputy. [59] As spiritual and personal act, representation in New
Testament understanding--as different as it is in other ways
from the juridical institution of deputyship[60]--is free from
any linkage to sex.   Fitness for official representation is
grounded according to the witness of the New Testament on
the endowment of men with grace for the task of administration and on the charisma of leadership or pastoral ministry--
which is of course activated only by giving oneself in faith
to Christ and by an inner bond of the office-bearer with him.
It is true that the validity of official functions is independent
of the inner attitude of the office-bearer, but a ministry of
representation in the fullest sense is not possible without an
existential act of faith, [61] which is true for every Christian
and not only for church officials.   The New Testament is
referring specifically to oneness with Christ, when it talks
about representation or witnessing for Christ in an official
capacity.   The classic passage often adduced is 2 Cor. 5:20,
without however considering the context (vv. 14ff.), which
precisely illustrates how divine grace is a prerequisite for
representation:

> The love of Christ controls us, because we are con-
> vinced that one has died for all; therefore all have
> died.   And he died for all, that those who live might
> no longer live for themselves but for him who for
> their sake died and was raised.... Therefore if any
> one is in Christ, he is a new creation; the old has
> passed away, behold the new has come.   All this is

from God, who through Christ reconciled us to himself and gave us the ministry of reconciliation; that is, God was in Christ reconciling the world to himself, not counting their trespasses against them, and entrusting to us the message of reconciliation. So we are ambassadors for Christ (ὑπερ Χριστοῦ), [62] God making his appeal through us. We beseech you on behalf of Christ, be reconciled to God.

The inner connection between God's redeeming action for the apostle and the apostle's ministry for Christ, which is so clear in this passage, is rightly characterized by J. E. Belser as follows: "... God has given to them [i.e., the apostles] the ministry of reconciliation, after they had themselves already experienced reconciliation, so that what they have to proclaim is not a strange mystery but a happy one which had become their own."[63]

The words of Jesus to the seventy disciples whom he sent out, "He who hears you, hears me and he who rejects you, rejects me ..." (Lk. 10:16)--often misused by being taken from their context and absolutized--are a promise whose effectiveness is likewise linked to the oneness of the disciples with their Lord as indispensable presupposition. The disciples stand under the command of their Lord: "Go your way; behold I send you out as lambs in the midst of wolves"[64] (Lk. 10:3). To the disciples who return after fulfilling their mission, who express their joy that the demons were subject to them in the name of the Lord, Jesus replies that the only ground for joy is the fact that they are forever united with God: "... Rejoice that your names are written in heaven" (Lk. 10:20). Chosen by God, freely accepted by men: this is what counts in the fruitful activity of those who work for the kingdom of God in particular office and commission. Office--or ordination--in and for itself by no means brings about the identity of the human word with the word of Christ referred to in Lk. 10:16, though this idea is expressed in the Constitution on the Church of Vatican II.[65] The message of the New Testament recognizes that among the officebearers there may be shepherds not worthy of the name, who act like "thieves and robbers" to those entrusted to them (Jn. 10:1), or who do their tasks only because they are forced to do them and who are motivated by lust for gain and power. (Cf. 1 Peter 5:2f.) The promise of Jesus about the fruitfulness of his word cannot be true of them.

That only an attachment to Jesus bestows fitness and

worthiness to a ministry of representation is shown with particular clarity in the calling of Simon Peter to the pastoral ministry (Jn. 21:15-17). Jesus directs the question to Peter three times, whether he loves him, whether he loves him more than the others. Jesus makes the transfer of the pastoral function [Hirtensorge] to Peter dependent only on love to him. For Jesus is and remains the only true pastor [Hirt] (Jn. 10:11ff.), the "first and chief shepherd" ($\dot{\alpha}\rho\chi\iota\pi o\iota\mu\dot{\eta}\nu$; cf. 1 Peter 5:4), the sheep belong to him alone and the fact that he gives the apostle the "responsibility for their feeding" does not mean that he gives up "his rights of ownership of them."[66] Thus only those who are one--by means of faith and love--with the one true shepherd are able to "feed" his "sheep" in the right sense and thus act as his representative to them. The office-bearer receives the power necessary to his task only by means of unconditional devotion to Christ and faith in him. In accordance with the New Testament message, the apostle is so fundamentally and exclusively directed to this preparation through the power of the Spirit (Acts 1:8) that beside it there can be no reliance on, and building on, the power of his own nature or of his own sex. (Cf. 2 Cor. 3:5f.; 10:3ff; 1 Cor. 2:4f.; Col. 1:28f.) Indeed the apostle understands himself before Christ exactly as one who of himself is "weak" (cf. 2 Cor. 12:9f.;1 Cor. 2:3; 4: 10)--a self-understanding that obviously stands in opposition to the normal idea of the nature of the male.[67] He knows, however, that in confessing his own weakness he is strong (2 Cor. 12:10) because this attitude expects everything from God and "the power of God is made perfect in weakness" (2 Cor. 12:9). To become strong one must rely on "the grace that is in Christ Jesus" (2 Tim. 2:1; cf. 2 Cor. 4:7ff.) as alone exclusively and unconditionally effective.

But as long as church teaching and canon law, misunderstanding the fact that God in his freedom can bestow the charisma that belongs to ecclesiastical office on women just as well as on men, declare that the male sex of the ordinand is the indispensable presupposition for valid ordination and thus for the priestly vocation, support will doubtless be given to an unspiritual and unbiblical conception of ministry and the practice of ministry. This is all the more obvious as the position of women in secular society develops into that of full equality, and thus the exclusion of women from church positions is no longer accepted as in the early Christian times as an unchallenged matter of course. Instead of basing capacity for ministry on the power and spirit of God, the priest is more likely--in accordance with the one-sided male

structure of office--to expect to have this capacity because
of his masculinity, and thus to attribute to his sex an essential significance in the representation of Christ. Thus he
runs the danger of largely missing the servanthood structure
of his office, since he often takes over the role of the master, which is always accorded him as a male in our society
and which actually rests on the suppression of women. He
takes no account of the fact that this role is totally opposed
to the attitude of Jesus. 68 (Cf. Lk. 22:25ff.) The extent
to which genuine Christian understanding of the ministerial
office and representation is impeded by the patriarchate--and
the mistaken attitudes necessarily linked with it--is graphical-
ly evident in the following statement, which is by no means
unique and which clearly characterizes the unequal evaluation
of the sexes in the Catholic Church: The Church has,

> it is true, feminine and motherly traits but it is not
> women's business. Its founder is the eternal God and
> the most perfect Man, Jesus Christ. He did not found
> his church on volatile women but on the twelve male
> apostles. Women are excluded from the church regi-
> ment [!] and St. Paul writes: 'Women must keep
> silent in church' (1 Cor. 14:34). The divine power
> to forgive sins, to celebrate the mass and to mediate
> grace rests on the masculine shoulders of the apostles,
> the pope, the bishops, the priests. The church is
> founded on the hard, indestructible and storm-tossed
> rock--and men [males] are like rocks. Therefore the
> church is from the beginning and for all time men's
> business.... 69

If only to cleanse the conception of the ministry from this
kind of unspiritual elements, it is necessary that admission
to the priesthood be opened to women and in this way for the
first time church office receive its full human dimension.

With this presupposition, the witness to Christ required
of office-holders can be fulfilled in a more pure and perfect
form. 70 Then in such a renewal of official structure, it will
be seen that representation of Christ is not the result of
(male) sex but rather of an inner transformation of human
beings into the likeness of Christ through the power of the
Spirit (cf. 2 Cor. 3:18), as the Galatians passage, 3:27f. ,
testifies validly, once and for all: "As many of you as were
baptized into Christ have put on Christ. There is neither
Jew nor Greek, there is neither slave nor free, there is
neither male nor female; for you are all one in Christ Jesus."

Only when the office-bearer on the basis of his inner attachment to and union with Christ becomes transparent for him--
in which case the office-bearer's sex has become irrelevant--
is the word of Christ a reality: "He who hears you hears
me" (Lk. 10:16). Yet even in regard to such a witness,
based not on sex but on the power of Christ, the following
words of H. Gollwitzer are worthy of consideration:

> His representation--i.e., Christ's representation for
> God--goes far beyond ours, precedes it, overtakes it,
> exceeds it, completes it and fulfills it.... He is
> present to those who are absent to us. He does not
> abandon those whom we abandon. His loving is greater
> than ours. Hope in his representation is the hope of
> our representation. [71]

Chapter 8

EQUAL RIGHTS FOR WOMEN
IN THE CHURCH TODAY;
A Requirement of Justice and the Condition
for Their Full Development and Cooperation

We may conclude as the result of our investigation
that the legal sources which support canon 968 § 1 (and the
canons that are connected with it in content) imply a distinct
concept of the essential and ethical inferiority of women; that
the biblical passages--concerning the subordinate position of
women--which in part lie at the basis of these sources have
been shown by historical-critical exegesis to be conditioned
by the times and thus not convincing; that, further, the argument resulting from the traditional understanding of office
and representation--that women must be excluded from them
--carries no weight. But, if these are our conclusions, we
cannot rest content with them. For an objective treatment
of the problem before us requires a consideration of the fact
that this exclusion of women is not an item of merely theoretical significance but is a rule of law which considerably
limits the freedom of women and therefore prevents the development of their person, to the detriment of church and
society.

Of course one often hears the objection that by their
very nature women do not show the aptitude requisite to
church office and that consequently one cannot speak of de-
priving them of any freedom. Such an apriori affirmation,
grounded in no facts of experience, is based on a dated and
narrow conception of the nature of women, which, as the
history of the women's movement shows, has repeatedly
blocked the advance of women vocationally. [1] Among other
implications, it is insinuated here that a woman is not qualified for public activity; a private and more passive role in
society is more fitting for her; she does not have the capacity to direct and to lead, because she lacks the necessary
objectivity and decisiveness; and her original place has always been the "hearth," not the altar. [2] In accordance with
this kind of alleged feminine nature, woman is appointed a

limited sphere of activity, which of course leaves no room
for ecclesiastical position. Enlisting the principle of natural
law, "to each his own," one finds justification in this way
for such an attitude toward woman. [3] But it is obvious that
use of this principle in the question before us must result,
as in other social problems--e.g., in the question of slavery
and in regard to blacks[4]--in arbitrary regulation contrary to
justice. Certainly the nature of woman does not permit the
kind of definition described above. It is recognized today,
on the basis of sociological and ethnological research, that
the differing male and female behavior patterns, which have
been attributed to intrinsic and unchangeable characteristics,
are dependent upon social and cultural conditioning and therefore changes may come about in the course of history:[5] In
the past, especially, the traditional picture of woman was
derived from her narrow sphere of activity (in the house, in
the family), then anchored in the psychological and even in
the metaphysical, and finally proclaimed as immutable feminine nature. [6] (If women sometimes confirmed this conception of their nature, [7] that is in no way a proof of the cor-
rectness of the conception, for as manipulated, unfree persons, women were and are very often not in the position to
speak about themselves in an independent and competent manner. [8])

Thus, since according to the conclusions of modern
sociological-anthropological research a description of the nature of womanhood, which would integrate all the individual
distinguishing features of her sex, is impossible, a delimitation of the sphere of freedom belonging to woman is not prac-
ticable. This is true because "when one sex is dominant,
no absolute sexual difference can be determined"[9]; perhaps
it never can be, since that which binds the sexes together--
their humanness--always outweighs that which separates
them. [10] Whenever such a delimitation of the sphere of freedom belonging to woman is undertaken, as in the case of exclusion from the church ministry, it arbitrarily violates the
freedom and independence of her person--a serious injustice.
Such an action shows clearly that despite all contrary asseve-
ration, woman is not yet considered as a person equivalent
to man and thus the derogatory opinion of woman--as it appeared in blatant form in the sources discussed in earlier
chapters--continues. [11] The concept of "differentness" of
woman, used to try to justify the deprivation of freedom, is
employed as a cloak for the persisting denigration of woman.[12]
The worth of a person is recognized and respected when he or
she is granted full freedom, e.g., in the basic human right

of vocational choice, or in the opportunity for free personal development. [13] Only so can one take into account the truth established in the creation, that human beings are created free, that they are characterized by knowledge of themselves and by self-possession, that they have the capability for self-determination. [14] This truth of creation is just as true for woman as for man. Because of her independent and self-responsible personhood, she has the same possibility and necessity as a man to "define" herself, to limit herself within the dimensions of full freedom, [15] to plan ahead for herself what vocation or life situation she wishes to choose. The same worth of person demands the same possibilities and conditions for the accomplishment of freedom, and as long as these are not forthcoming, necessary respect for the worth and freedom of her person is lacking and she is not yet released from the status subiectionis.

But, looking more deeply, the claim of woman that the freedom of her person must be recognized also and exactly in the sphere of the church cannot be waived or revoked, because the will of God is that he should be unconditionally acknowledged by men and women in his sovereign freedom and power of dominion. As Lord and head of the church, Christ (God) bestows his manifold gifts and powers for the up-building of his body in an absolute freedom beyond the calculation of human beings; he whose spirit "apportions to each one individually as he will" (1 Cor. 12:11) is free and powerful to give to women as well as to men the special charisma for the ministry, along with other charisma. [16] Respect for this sovereign freedom and dominion of Christ (or God) demands that in the official church care will be taken, in obedience to its head and Lord, to provide for the full unfolding of the various charisma given by God for the upbuilding of the church. To hinder such unfolding would be disloyal to God's gifts of grace and therefore certainly culpable. [17] Ecclesiastical legality should thus be so formulated that women and men are granted a full and equal sphere of freedom, so that they may follow the call and claims of God, whatever these may be. So long as the official church in teaching and in legal regulations sets forth as normative the contention that God calls no woman to ministerial service, obstacles are autocratically placed against the working of the Spirit in the church. [18]

Therefore if today Catholic women in increasing numbers are offended by this behavior on the part of responsible office-bearers in the church and by the disrespect for women

which it expresses, and if these Catholic women speak out for
equal positions with men, this is not in the last analysis a
struggle for rights for rights' sake--not "the registration of
a claim of human beings by human beings"--but rather a
"testimony to the claim of God, " and his rights, on human
beings. [19] Before anything else, equal rights present the presupposition that women can freely answer the claim of God
and his call to them in its humanly unpredictable form and
variety. [20] Understood in this way, equal rights make possible the service of God in the sphere of the church and become at the same time the opportunity for the unfolding of
the personhood of women.

Of course women who are awakened to a consciousness
of their worth as persons (and with them every group dis-
criminated against) are summoned and obliged to lay claim to
those inherent rights which are signs of their worth as persons[21] and which should open to them possibilities for service
and for assumption of responsibilities in the church. But
exactly because of their disadvantaged position they are not
able by themselves alone to advocate this concern and to
bring it to successful conclusion. Thus justice and love require of those who have come to church offices and so to
more influential position in the church on the basis of male
sex--falsely considered as "higher"--that they help emancipate
women from their oppressed situation and from the stunted
humanity that has resulted from it. In such a way these
leaders could assist women to receive at last the respect and
the opportunities for development within the church that are
due them. [22] There is, to be sure, only small evidence of
the requisites for such assistance and the inner willingness
to help. Yet certain changes are fortunately coming about in
the viewpoint of the official church concerning equal rights
for women in the secular realm: long resisted in the church,
this development is finally recognized as genuine progress in
the history of mankind and ecclesiastical officials come forward to encourage it. [23] But only a beginning has been made,
and hesitantly, in comprehending that a fundamental reform
in the evaluation of women and in the position of women in
the church is needed before the church can legitimately and
credibly advocate a more humane treatment of women and a
more worthy position for women in the secular world. [24] The
persistent resistance of a majority of church officials to an
equal place for women in the ecclesiastical sphere is doubtless a result of the men's "clubby" and antifeminist education by which many clerics have been profoundly conditioned
so that they are simply not able to accept women as equal

partners and to appreciate even faintly the values to be gained
by admission of women to ministry in the church. How little
they accept women as fellow human beings is shown by the
fact that the clergy by and large are not shocked by the disadvantaged position of women in the church. They apparently
think that the subordination of women accords with their nature, whereas an equalization of woman with man, which from
pride of sex and struggle for ascendency they resist, would
be abnormal. It would be hard to persuade them that woman
in her present situation lacks anything at all, not to speak of
any injustice being done to her.

Although on the one hand woman has become a grievous
victim of this kind of behavior on the part of clergy and men
in general, it is also true on the other hand that woman must
share the blame for this abuse and for her own situation.
Out of convenience and insincerity[25] she has often acquiesced
in her lowly and unworthy position and accepted an extensive
paralysis of her self-respect as a human being, instead of
taking on herself--a course requiring sacrifice and therefore
avoided--to set limits to masculine sovereignty pretensions
and thus assist men to be more humane.

It is not reasonable to expect, on the basis of the in-
terdependent circumstances mentioned, that the official church
alone can bring about removal of the far-reaching disturb-
ances in relations between the sexes, with which the church
today is especially burdened. Rather, a fundamental readiness for the emancipation of women and for the formation of
life-styles involving partnership of men and women must be
developed. Of course the resolute will to overcome in this
way the anti-feminist tradition in the church must be respected
and adopted by ecclesiastical authorities,[26] so that they themselves may be willing to integrate women into all areas of
church life and ministry.

The renewal of the church--i.e., the maturation of
its members into vital and convinced Christians, who only as
such are able to dismantle structures and relationships in
the church that are unworthy of human beings and thus to set
an example to society--cannot be successful without the liberation of women as autonomous human beings conscious of
their responsibilities, and without their active participation
in the official ministry of the church.

CHAPTER NOTES

INTRODUCTION

1. Cf. W. Seibel and L. A. Dorn, Tagebuch des Konzils. Die Arbeit der zweiten Session (Nuremberg, 1964), pp. 92f., 104; L. A. Dorn and G. Denzler, Tagebuch des Konzils. Die Arbeit der dritten Session (Nuremberg, 1965), pp. 256f., 262, 278; G. Heinzelmann, Die getrennten Schwestern. Frauen nach dem Konzil (hereafter cited as Schwestern) (Zürich, 1967), pp. 71-82.

2. Most of the contributions were collected in the brochure edited by G. Heinzelmann, entitled, Wir schweigen nicht länger! Frauen äussern sich zum II. Vatikanischen Konzil (Zürich, 1964).

3. This fact is obvious not only from the increasing number of publications concerning this theme (see n. 8, below; also chapter 7, n. 1), but also from the fact that various synods since Vatican II have taken up the question of woman's place in the church. In the fifth session of the Dutch Pastoral Council the majority supported the integration of women into all forms of ecclesiastical service, including that of the priesthood. (See Herder Correspondence, vol. 7, no. 3 (March, 1970): 83f. and vol. 7, no. 5: 137ff.) The themes of the General Synod of dioceses of West Germany include a consideration of the question. (Kirchliches Amtsblatt für die Diözese Münster 102, 1969, 126.) The need for reform of the position of women in the church was also the subject of several interventions in the second regular Bishops' Synod in Rome in the fall of 1971: Cardinal Flahiff (Winnipeg) proposed for the first time the admission of women to the priestly office as well as to church office in general. In the name of the Canadian Bishop's Conference he recommended the creation of a mixed commission, which would thoroughly examine the question. (Cf. L'Osservatore Romano, weekly ed. in English [October 28, 1971]: 5.) Archbishop Carter (Kingston, Jamaica) supported his intervention, noting that earlier "cultural, not theological grounds against the ordination of women as priests are no longer valid" (op. cit., German ed., no. 5.11.1971, p. 4). Cf. also chapter 8, n. 24.

4. Cf. n. 3, above, and chapter 8, n. 24.

5. See the documentation: "Women's Place in the Ministry of Non-Catholic Christian Churches," in Concilium, vol. 34 (New York, 1968): 163-177.

6. Among other references see E. Krebs, Katholische

Lebenswerte, vol. V/2, 1st and 2nd ed., (Paderborn, 1925), p. 478; J. Pohle and M. Gierens, Lehrbuch der Dogmatik, 9th ed., vol. 3 (Paderborn, 1937), p. 581; F. Diekamp and K. Jüssen, Katholische Dogmatik, vol. 3 11th and 12th ed. (Münster, 1954). pp. 372f.; M. Premm, Katholische Glaubenskunde, vol. 3/2 (Vienna, 1955), p. 240; L. Ott, Grundriss der katholischen Dogmatik, 5th ed. (Freiburg, 1961), p. 548. Cf. also chapter 7, n. 21 and n. 23, the latter containing a listing of other authors who represent this position.

7. H. van der Meer, Priestertum der Frau? Eine theologie-geschichtliche Untersuchung (Freiburg, Basel, Vienna, 1969), (cited here and hereafter from the English translation by Arlene and Leonard Swidler Women Priests in the Catholic Church? [Philadelphia, 1973], pp. 104f.) rightly points out that the burden of proof for the contention that women are on principle and permanently excluded from the priesthood rests upon those who defend this contention.

8. Besides the study by H. Van der Meer noted in n. 7, the following literature should be especially mentioned: V. E. Hannon, The Question of Women and the Priesthood; Can Women Be Admitted to Holy Orders? (London, 1967); R. J. A. van Eyden, "Die Frau im Kirchenamt," in Wort und Wahrheit 22 (1967): 350-362; M. Daly, The Church and the Second Sex (New York, 1968); see also chapter 7, n. 1, where there is a further listing of literature.

9. A thorough treatment of the problem from the viewpoint of legal history has not yet appeared; the following studies offer either a simple summary survey of the historical development of the position of women in the church, or they deal with a very limited period of time: R. Metz, "Recherches sur le statut de la femme en droit canonique: bilan historique et perspectives d'avenir," in L'Année canonique 12 (1968): 85-113; also by R. Metz, "Le statut de la femme en droit canonique médiéval," in Recueils de la Société Jean Bodin XII/2 (Brussels, 1962) (hereafter cited as "Statut"): 59-113; and his "Recherches sur la condition de la femme selon Gratien," in Studia Gratiana XII (1967): 377-396; F. Gillman, "Weibliche Kleriker nach dem Urteil der Frühscholastik," in Archiv für katholisches Kirchenrecht 93 (1913): 239-253.

10. Cf. the literature given in n. 8, above.

PART I [preliminary]

1. Cf. U. Stutz, Der Geist des Codex juris canonici. Kirchenrechtliche Abhandlungen, ed. by U. Stutz, no. 92/93 (Stuttgart, 1918), pp. 51f., 163f., 177; J. B. Sägmüller, Lehrbuch des katholischen Kirchenrechts, vol. 1, 4th ed. (Freiburg, 1925),

p. 267; see also the Code of Canon Law, canon 6, which governs the relationship of current law to old law and in n. 2, 3 and 4 prescribes that the canons of the Code should be interpreted in the sense of the old law according to specified presuppositions. Codex Juris Canonici Pii X Pontificis Maximi iussu digestus, Benedicti Papae XV auctoritate promulgatus, praefatione, fontium annotatione et indice analytico-alphabetico ab Emmo. Petro Card. Gasparri auctus, Typis Polyglottis Vaticanis, 1948, hereafter cited as Code.

2. Cf. Stutz, op. cit., pp. 161, 164.

3. Ibid., p. 163.

4. "Sacram ordinationem valide recipit solus vir baptizatus...." In the language of the Code, the expressions ordinare, ordo, ordinatio, and sacra ordinatio are used for all stages of consecration, including those for the bishop and for the first tonsure, except where in the nature of the case or from the context it is obvious that another usage is intended. Cf. the Code, canon 950.

5. As leader of the work of the so-called commission of codification, Gasparri played a normative role in the genesis of the Code. On this see Stutz, pp. 10f.; K. Mörsdorf, Lehrbuch des Kirchenrechts auf Grund des Codex Juris Canonici, 11th ed., vol. I (Munich-Paderborn-Vienna, 1964), p. 30.

6. As fontes from the Corpus the following are given: C. 1, q. 1, cc. 52, 60; Extra 3, 43, cc. 1, 3 (Code, p. 322, n. 4). Further evidence, not taken from the Corpus Iuris Canonici, has to do with the characteristics of ordinands which are required for the permitted ordinations.

7. The canon says nothing about the question whether the exclusion of women from ordination is based, according to the lawgiver, on divine or on human law (ius mere ecclesiasticum). But if we consider the fact that the theologians had for a long time assumed in general a ius divinum in this question (cf. Van der Meer, op. cit., pp. 5f., 9), and that the Code itself repeatedly uses this concept (cf. J. A. Fassbender, Das göttliche Recht im Codex Iuris Canonici, unpub. dissert., Catholic Theological Faculty [Bonn, 1947], p. 232), it is noteworthy that no declaration of divine law is made in this canon. To be sure, according to Fassbender, p. 118, there are in the Code many legal statements, which, in the view of the lawgiver, must be ascribed to natural law or to revelation, but which nevertheless contain no formal references to these. But in the case we are considering, the lack of formal reference to divine law could, in my opinion, be traced back to the fact that we have no record of a definitive position taken by the magisterium extraordinarium on the question at issue.

8. Unfortunately the otherwise very noteworthy study by F. Gillmann, "Weiblicher Kleriker nach dem Urteil der Frühscholastiker," (see Introduction, n. 9), does not deal with this aspect of

legal evidence. A complete survey of the question requires consideration of the evaluation of women which lies at the basis of the texts.

CHAPTER 1

1. F. Heyer, in Staatslexikon of the Görres-Gesellschaft, 5th ed., ed. by H. Sacher, vol. I (1926), col. 1545, prefers the term "Dekretbuch."

2. Evidence for this title exists in the majority of handwritten mss. of the Decretum and in the early decretists, and probably comes from Gratian himself. See on this question F. Heyer, "Der Titel der Kanonensammlung Gratians," in Zeitschrift der Savigny-Stiftung für Rechtsgeschichte (hereafter cited as ZRG), Kan. Abt. 2 (Weimar, 1912): 336-342; also by F. Heyer, "Namen und Titel des gratianischen Dekretes," in Archiv für katholisches Kirchenrecht (hereafter cited as AkKR), 94 (1914): 501-517. The title refers to the purpose of the work, "to resolve the many inconsistencies found in the earlier collections" (J. F. v. Schulte, Die Geschichte der Quellen und Literatur des canonischen Rechts von Gratian bis auf die Gegenwart, vol. 1 (Stuttgart, 1875), p. 60), and in doing so "to bring uniformity to ecclesiastical law" (Sägmüller, op. cit., p. 235).

3. A. M. Stickler, Historia juris canonici latini (Turin, 1950), vol. 1, pp. 201f.; Sägmüller, vol. 1, pp. 233ff.

4. Stickler, op. cit., vol. 1, p. 204; H. E. Feine, Kirchliche Rechtsgeschichte. Die katholische Kirche, 4th ed. (Cologne, 1964), p. 276.

5. Schulte, vol. 1, p. 67.

6. "Nunc a summo incipientes, et usque ad ultimum gradum descendentes, qualiter quisque eorum debeat ordinari, sanctorum auctoritatibus ostendamus," Corpus Iuris Canonici, ed. by A. Friedberg, 2 vols. (reprint, Graz, 1955), vol. 1, col. 76 (hereafter cited as Corpus, ed. Friedberg).

7. The chapters treated more fully on pp. 23ff., which are concerned with the deaconess, contain no law in force during Gratian's time.

8. The distinctio makes no use of the scholastic method otherwise so normal with Gratian, according to which contradictory authorities are placed over against each other in dialectical fashion, with a final harmonization which Gratian seeks to base on specific principles. Cf. Schulte, vol. 1, pp. 60f. and Stickler, vol. 1, pp. 208-210.

9. "Vasa sacrata et uestimenta altaris mulieres Deo dedicatae contingere, et incensum circa altaria deferre prohibentur," Corpus, ed. Friedberg, vol. 1, cols. 85f.

10. "Unde Sother Papa Episcopis Italiae," Corpus, ed. Friedberg, vol. 1, col. 86.

11. "Sacratas Deo feminas uel monachas sacra uasa uel sacratas pallas penes uos contingere, et incensum circa altaria deferre, perlatum est ad apostolicam sedem: que omnia uituperatione et reprehensione plena esse, nulli recte sapientum dubium est. Quapropter huius sanctae sedis auctoritate hec omnia uobis resecare funditus, quanto citius poteritis, censemus. Et ne pestis hec latius diuulgetur, per omnes prouincias abstergi citissime mandamus," Corpus, ed. Friedberg, vol. 1, col. 86.

12. Corpus, ed. Friedberg, vol. 1, col. 86, n. 324, with reference to P. Hinschius, ed., Decretales Pseudo-Isidorianae et Capitula Angilramni (reprint, Aalen, 1963), p. 124 (hereafter cited as Decretales).

13. Cf. Sägmüller, vol. 1, p. 225: it was customary "for many centuries to attribute the collection, thought to be genuine, to Isidore of Seville, and materials were taken from it without hesitation, as Gratian also did." See also Feine, op. cit., pp. 276f. Concerning Isidore of Seville (560-636) see K. Baus, art. "Isidor," in Lexikon für Theologie und Kirche, ed. by J. Hofer and K. Rahner, 2nd ed. (hereafter cited as LThK) (Freiburg, 1957-1965), cols. 786f.

14. Van der Meer, op. cit., pp. 91ff.

15. Van der Meer's critique (pp. 91, 100) is directed against the study by Santiago Giner Sempere, "La mujer y la potestad de orden; incapacidad de la mujer," in Revista Española de derecho canónico 9 (1954), pp. 841-869, in which forgeries are not distinguished from authentic sources, according to Van der Meer; as a result the impression is given that there is an abundance of traditional evidence against admitting women to holy orders.

16. Decretales, p. 124.

17. Corpus, ed. Friedberg, vol. 1, col. 86, n. 324.

18. L. Duchesne (ed.), Le Liber Pontificalis (hereafter cited as Lib. pont.) (Paris, 1886), vol. 1, p. 135.

19. Lib. pont., vol. 1, p. 227: "Hic Bonifatius constituit ut nulla mulier aut monacha pallam sacratam contingere aut lavare aut incensum ponere in ecclesia nisi minister" (one section of the ms. has, correctly, "... contingeret aut lavaret," etc.); on this see p. 229, n. 11: "On sait que les femmes, même les diaconesses, étaient rigoureusement exclues du ministère de l'autel (Gélase, ep.

ad episcopos Lucaniae, c. 26); quant aux fonctions dont il est ici question, ce sont celles des bas clercs, des ostiaires ou des sacristains. La seconde épître apocryphes de Clément à Jacques (Migne, Patrologia Graeca (hereafter cited as PG), pt. 1, p. 483) les décrit longuement, supposant toujours qu'elles sont remplies par des clercs. "

20. Lib. pont., vol. 1, p. 135, n. 3.

21. Cf. A. Stuiber, art. "Liber pontificalis, " in LThK, vol. 6, col. 1016f.; G. Chr. Hansen, art. "Liber pontificalis, " in Die Religion in Geschichte und Gegenwart, 3rd ed. (hereafter cited as RGG) (Tübingen, 1957-1962), vol. 4, col. 343f.

22. Concerning this and other functions of the widow and the deaconess in the early church, see A. Kalsbach, Die altkirchliche Einrichtung der Diakonissen bis zu ihrem Erlöschen (Freiburg, 1926), pp. 45, 57f., 65; J. Funk, "Klerikale Frauen?" in Österreichisches Archiv für Kirchenrecht (hereafter cited as OAKR), 14 (1963): 274ff.; K. H. Schäfer, Die Kanonissenstifter im deutschen Mittelalter (Amsterdam, 1965), pp. 32, 58f.; L. Zscharnack, Der Dienst der Frau in den ersten Jahrhunderten der christlichen Kirche (Göttingen, 1902), pp. 130ff.

23. Of course one finds a similar, blunt rejection of feminine participation in liturgy in authentic texts, as for instance in a decretal of Pope Gelasius I to the bishops of Lucania in A. D. 494, which reads as follows: "Nihilo minus impatienter audivimus, tantum divinarum rerum subiisse despectum, ut foeminae sacris altaribus ministrare ferantur et cuncta, quae non nisi virorum famulatui deputata sunt, sexum, cui non competit, exhibere, " J. D. Mansi, Sacrorum consiliorum nova et amplissima collectio (Paris, 1901ff.), vol. 8.44, cap. 26. Accordingly the liturgical ministry of women is considered to be disrespectful of divine, holy "things. "

24. 2 Cor. 11:2b.

25. "... ait enim apostolus: Despondi vos uni viro virginem castam exhibere Christo. Illa est enim virgo aeclesia, sponsa unius viri Christi, quae nullo se patitur errore vel inhonesta reprehensione vitiari, ut per totum mundum una nobis sit unius castae communionis integritas, " Hinschius, Decretales, p. 124.

26. Cf. on this P. Browe, Beiträge zur Sexualethik des Mittelalters (Breslau, 1932), pp. 1-35; R. Kottje, Studien zum Einfluss des Alten Testamentes auf Recht und Liturgie des frühen Mittelalters (Bonn, 1964), pp. 69-83.

27. Chapter 41 is taken from the second epistle of Sixtus I; the first part of the excerpt from the letter comes from the Vita Sixti I, c. 2 (Lib. pont., vol. 1, p. 128). Cf. Corpus, ed. Friedberg, vol. 1, col. 1304, n. 451, with reference to Hinschius, Decretales, p. 108. Chapter 42 is an excerpt from the first

epistle of Stephan I and has its source in the Vita Stephani I, c. 3 (Lib. pont., vol. 1, p. 154). Cf. Corpus, ed. Friedberg, vol. 1, col. 1305, n. 465, with reference to Hinschius, p. 183.

28. "Sacra vasa non nisi a sacratis contrectentur hominibus, " on c. 41; Corpus, ed. Friedberg, vol. 1, col. 1304. "Non nisi a sacratis hominibus vestimenta sacra ferentur, " on c. 42; Corpus, ed. Friedberg, vol. 1, col. 1305.

29. "In sancta apostolica sede statutum est, ut sacra vasa non ab aliis, quam a sacratis Dominoque dicatis contrectentur hominibus. Ne pro talibus presumptionibus iratus Dominus plagam inponat populo suo, et hi etiam, qui non peccaverunt, pereant, quia perit iustus sepissime pro inpio, " Corpus, ed. Friedberg, vol. 1, cols. 1304f.

30. This critical edition of the Decretum was produced by the so-called Correctores Romani commission, established by Pius V in 1566 and consisting of many doctors and cardinals. It appeared in 1582 and was declared to be authentic and the only official edition by the constitution of Gregory XIII, "Cum pro munere" (from 1580). Cf. Schulte, vol. 1, pp. 72f.; Sägmüller, vol. 1, pp. 238f.

31. "Indignum enim valde est, ut sacra Domini vasa, quaecunque sint, humanis usibus serviant, aut ab aliis, quam a Domino famulantibus eique dicatis tractentur viris, " Corpus, ed. Friedberg, vol. 1, col. 1304, n. c. to c. 41.

32. Cf. Mittellateinisches Glossar, ed. by E. Habel, 2nd ed. (Paderborn, 1959), col. 178; Du Cange, Glossarium mediae et infimae latinitatis, (reprint, Graz, 1954), vol. 4, pp. 224-226.

33. "Vestimenta ecclesia ... nec ab aliis debent contingi aut offerri, nisi a sacratis hominibus, " Corpus, ed. Friedberg, vol. 1, p. 1305.

34. It is not clear from the relevant chapters what kind of consecration is required, but presumably a clerical, though not necessarily a priestly. For according to dist. 23, cc. 31 and 32, for instance, the acolyte status and the sub-diaconate are prerequisite to the liturgical functions mentioned.

35. The over-emphasis on ordination to the detriment of the sacrament of baptism is probably based on an excessive sacralization of the cult, which is characteristic of these chapters, and on the taboo of consecrated objects. This over-emphasis has today considerable influence in the liturgical area: cf. the critical comment on the Third Instruction concerning the orderly carrying out of the Constitution on the Liturgy (from November 5, 1970): "Ist die Liturgiereform für Rom beendet?" in Herder-Korrespondenz 24, 1970, pp. 557-559; see also n. 37, below.

36. On the basis of source materials, Browe, op. cit., p. 3, remarks: "From this point of view one realizes not only that women are kept from touching holy objects like chalice, altar, etc. --since this prohibition applied though not so insistently also to lay people in general--but also that the reason given was sometimes women's weakness and uncleanness" (see also pp. 64f.). One can see how strong were the influences of Old Testament regulations, among other things, on synodal resolutions, if one reads, for instance, the following canons of the diocesan synod of Auxerre, France, in 585 or 578: c. 36 ("No woman may receive the holy eucharist with bare hands"); c. 37 ("Also she may not touch the pall"); c. 42 ("Every woman must have her dominicale at communion"). C. J. v. Hefele, Conciliengeschichte, 2nd ed. (Freiburg, 1873-1890), vol. 3, pp. 45f. (According to Duchesne, Christian Worship, Its Origin and Evolution, 5th ed. [London, 1956], p. 224, the so-called dominicale is a linen cloth with which the hand is to be covered.) The influences of Old Testament cleanliness regulations in Gratian's Decretum are apparent in the following declarations, although it is true that they do not deal with the question we are considering at the moment: dist. 2 de cons. cc. 21, 23, § 2; dist. 23, c. 33; C. 33, q. 4, cc. 2-11. Gratian separates himself from these viewpoints to the extent of agreeing with many authorities (dist. 5, pr. § 2; Corpus, ed. Friedberg, vol. 1, col. 7) that menstruating women may not be denied the right to go to church and to receive the holy communion. Also after the birth of a child a woman may not be forbidden to enter a church, although nothing is said in this connection about receiving the sacrament at this time. Yet regulation dist. 5, c. 4, which is considered binding by Gratian, still presupposes the rite of purification, as the summary of c. 4 shows: "Antequam puer ablactetur, vel mater purificetur, ad eius concubitum vir non accedat," Corpus, ed. Friedberg, vol. 1, col. 8. See also J. Freisen, Geschichte des canonischen Eherechts bis zum Verfall der Glossenliteratur, 2nd ed. (Paderborn, 1893), pp. 849ff.

37. These chapters support the Code, canon 1306, § 1, which requires that chalices and patens, as well as purificators, palls and corporals, may be touched, before their washing, only by clerics or by those who are responsible for them. See the Code, p. 445, n. 1. According to canon 1306, § 2, which should also be mentioned in this connection, the first washing of purificators, etc., may be done only by clergy in higher orders. However the Motu proprio "Pastorale munus" of Pope Paul VI, November 30, 1963, takes account of the prescriptive law which has been in effect for a long time, when in its n. 28 it gives local bishops the right to permit clergy of lower rank, (male) lay persons and also devout women, to perform the first washing of palls, corporals and purificators. ("Permittendi clericis minoribus, religiosis laicis, necnon piis mulieribus ut pallas, corporalia et purificatoria prima quoque ablutione extergere possint," Acta Apostolicae Sedis, Commentarium officiale, Typis Polyglottis Vaticanis (1909ff.) (hereafter cited as AAS): 56, 1964, 10.) It is instructive to notice in this regulation the special mention of women--in itself superfluous--along with

laity: this reflects the former legal situation, which did not allow
women such practice.

38. "Pervenit ad notitiam nostram, quod quidam presbiteri
in tantum parvipendant divina misteria, ut laico aut feminae sacrum
corpus Domini tradant ad deferendum infirmis, et quibus prohibetur,
ne sacrarium ingrediantur, nec ad altare appropinquent, illis sancta
sanctorum conmittuntur. Quod quam sit horribile quamque detesta-
bile, omnium religiosorum animadvertit prudentia. Igitur interdicit
per omnia sinodus, ne talis temeraria presumptio ulterius fiat; sed
omnimodis presbiter per semetipsum infirmum communicet. Quod
si aliter fecerit, gradus sui periculo subiacebit," Corpus, ed. Friedberg, vol. 1, cols. 1323f.

39. See C. J. von Hefele-H. Leclercq, Histoire des conciles
d'après les documents originaux (Paris, 1907-) (hereafter cited as
Hefele-Leclercq), vol. 3/1, p. 261.

40. Cf. Hefele-Leclercq, vol. 3/1, p. 264.

41. Cf. Friedberg, Corpus, vol. 1, cols. XLVff., LIVff.

42. Cf. Friedberg, Corpus, vol. 1, col. 1323, n. 369.

43. Ibid.

44. The relevant canon of the Synod of Rouen reads:
"Dictum est nobis quod quidam presbyteri celebrata missa dectrec-
tantes ipsi sumere divina mysteria quae consecrarunt, calicem
domini mulierculis quae ad missas offerunt tradant vel quibusdam
laicis qui dijudicare corpus domini nesciunt, ... quod quantum sit
omni ecclesiasticae religioni contrarium pietas fidelium novit: unde
omnibus presbyteris interdicimus ut nullus in posterum hoc facere
praesumat, sed ipse cum reverentia sumat et diacono aut subdiacono
qui ministri sunt altaris colligenda tradat ... nulli autem laico aut
foeminae eucharistiam in manibus ponat, sed tantum in os eius.
... Si quis haec transgressus fuerit, quia deum omnipotentem con-
temnit et quantum in ipso est inhonorat, ab altari removeatur,"
H. Th. Bruns, ed., Canones Apostolorum et Conciliorum saeculorum
(reprint, Turin, 1959), vol. 2, pp. 268f.

45. This prohibition--in its application to women--was first
promulgated by the Synod of Laodicea (between A.D. 347 and 381)
in canon 44: "Women are not permitted to enter the chancel" (cf.
Hefele-Leclercq, vol. 1/2, p. 1020). The canon was repeated by
many later synods. Cf. Van der Meer, op. cit., p. 94.

46. So for instance in dist. 23, c. 29: "Mulier, quamvis
docta et sancta, viros in conventu docere non presumat. Laicus
autem presentibus clericis [nisi ipsis rogantibus] docere non audeat,"
Corpus, ed. Friedberg, vol. 1, col. 86 (also see n. 44, above).
We should further note the capitulary of Bishop Theodulf of Orléans
(750 or 760 to 821), in chapter 6 of which it is stated: "Feminae,

missam sacerdote celebrante, nequaquam ad altare accedant, sed locis suis stent, et ibi sacerdos earum oblationes Deo oblaturus accipiat. Memores enim esse debent feminae infirmitatis suae, et sexus imbecillitatis: et idcirco sancta quaelibet in ministerio ecclesiae contingere pertimescant. Quae etiam laici viri pertimescere debent, ne Ozae poenam subeant, qui dum arcam Domini extraordinarie contingere voluit, Domino percutiente interiit," Mansi, vol. 13, p. 996.

47.   Cf. the documents cited above, n. 36 and n. 46.

48.   On this see p. 66.

49.   Cf. pp. 53, 55.

50.   Such an unfavorable and lowly position for women did not always exist in this respect: according to the Testamentum Domini, the older sections of which may go back to the second or third century, deaconesses are duty bound to take the Holy Communion to sick women.   There is evidence that Monophysite deaconesses likewise had the right to distribute Communion.   In the West it seems that deaconesses, specifically sanctimonials, as late as the ninth century, carried out this duty, but the official church objected strongly. See Schäfer, Kanonissenstifter, pp. 32, 59f. ; Kalsbach, pp. 45, 57.

51.   Cf. the Code, p. 283, n. 4.   The canon reads as follows: "Minister ordinarius sacrae communionis est solus sacerdos (§ 1).   Extraordinarius est diaconus, de Ordinarii loci vel parochi licentia, gravi de causa concedenda, quae in casu necessitatis legitime praesumitur" (§ 2).   Concerning the inhuman consequences which the regulation entailed for women, see Heinzelmann, Schwestern, pp. 67f.

52.   On the basis of rescripts from the Congregation of Sacraments (from November 28, 1967 and from February 14, 1968) the Conference of Bishops in Germany received a three-year authorization to permit (male) laypersons (viri probati) to distribute the Holy Communion under certain conditions.   (Similar authorization was granted for other areas.)   The permission, according to this (temporary) ruling, could be extended to Mothers Superior of convents, if the local church official should be absent for several days.   See Kirchliches Amtsblatt für die Diözese Münster, vol. 102 (1968): 37f.

53.   On the basis of a general Instruction (Fidei custos) released by the Congregation of Sacraments on April 30, 1969, which concerns extraordinary distribution of Communion, lay women as well as nuns may be in principle empowered to distribute Communion, under certain conditions.   (Texts of the Liturgical Commission of the German Conference of Bishops, for the plenary meeting of the Conference of Bishops, February, 1970, pp. 44-47.)   But according to the order of succession prescribed in No. 3 of the In-

struction, by which the choice is made for estraordinary distributors, lay women are listed in last place. According to No. 5 of the Instruction, they are to be used only in emergencies, when a more suitable person cannot be found--which can only mean a man or at least a nun! (". . . Mulier spectatae pietatis, in casibus necessitatis seligatur, quoties scilicet alia persona idonea inveniri nequeat," Ibid., p. 46.) By rescript from the Congregation of Sacraments dated November 13, 1969, the request of the German Bishops' Conference was granted for a three-year period, whereby the general rule (Fidei custos) would apply in their area (cf. Kirchliches Amtsblatt für die Diözese Münster, vol. 103 [1970]: 51f.). Women are put in a somewhat inferior position over against men, since the regulations of the Bishops' Conference--actually more positive in comparison to the Roman Instruction--directs male laypersons to wear a cassock and surplice or an alb during the distribution of the sacrament, but women should wear "decent, civilian clothing as unshowy as possible" (Ibid., p. 51). From this rule one will draw the conclusion that women's work in the church, if permitted at all, must retain an unofficial character.

54. "Mulier, quamvis docta et sancta, viros in conventu docere non presumat. Laicus autem presentibus clericis (nisi ipsis rogantibus) docere non audeat," Corpus, ed. Friedberg, vol. 1, col. 86.

55. "Mulier, quamvis docta et sancta, baptizare aliquos vel viros docere in conventu, non presumat," Corpus, ed. Friedberg, vol. 1, col. 1367.

56. Gratian assigns dist. 23, c. 29, to the fourth Council of Carthage, dist. 4, de cons., c. 20, to the fifth.

57. Dist. 23, c. 29 is put together from cc. 36 and 37 of the collection; dist. 4 de cons., c. 20 from cc. 37 and 41. Friedberg, Corpus, vol. 1, col. 86, n. 344 and vol. 1, col. 1367, n. 242.

58. The Hispana, traditional material from the old Spanish church, contains canons of councils and papal decretals. It belongs to the most important legal collections of the first Christian millenium and was erroneously attributed to Isidore of Seville since the ninth century. See A. M. Stickler, "Hispana collectio" in LThK, vol. 5, col. 390; Sägmüller, vol. 1, p. 212.

59. Cf. F. Maassen, Geschichte der Quellen und der Literatur des canonischen Rechts im Abendlande (reprint, Graz, 1956), vol. 1, pp. 382f; Hefele-Leclercq, vol. 2/2, pp. 102ff. The critical edition of the Statuta, upon which I base the following discussion, was prepared by Ch. Munier (Les Statuta Ecclesiae Antiqua, édition-études critiques, Bibliothèque de l'institut de droit canonique de l'université de Strasbourg, 5, Paris, 1960.)

60. Cf. Sägmüller, vol. 1, p. 224; Duchesne, Christian Worship, p. 350, n. 2.

61. See Munier, Statuta, p. 70. Gratian took a rather large number of canons from the Statuta. Cf. Friedberg, Corpus, vol. 1, col. XXI.

62. Cf. Munier, op. cit., pp. 70, 101; Duchesne, op. cit. p. 350, n. 2: "It [the Statuta] is still quoted by many under the latter title [Fourth Council of Carthage], and what is more serious, pronounced as an authority for African ecclesiastical usages in the fourth century. "

63. Cf. ed. Friedberg, Corpus, vol. 1, col. 1367, n. a on dist. 4 de cons., c. 20.

64. The brothers Ballerini, who were famous for their critical-historical and canonical research, were the first to reject, about the middle of the 18th century, the assigning of the Statuta to a council of Carthage, and instead recognized its origin in southern Gaul. Munier, Statuta, pp. 24f., 101.

65. Cf. Hefele-Leclercq, vol. 2/1, pp. 102ff.

66. Cf. Maassen, op. cit., vol. 1, pp. 387ff.; Munier, Statuta, pp. 24, 101, 209.

67. Munier, Statuta, pp. 209ff. H. Lentze, OAKR 12, 1961, p. 174, and G. May, ZRG Kan. Abt. 48, 1962, pp. 381ff., find Munier's conclusions about authorship convincing. The anonymity of the author is the result of a desire to give the collection the authority of tradition, since it was intended for the purpose of reform; cf. Munier, p. 242. Concerning the person of the author, see also Th. Payr, "Gennadius" in LThK, vol. 4, col. 677f.

68. Munier, op. cit., p. 242.

69. Especially the chapter, "Les sources des Statuta Ecclesiae Antiqua, " in Munier, op. cit., pp. 105-185.

70. Cf. Munier, Statuta, pp. 127f.

71. Cf. H. Rahner, "Apostolische Konstitutionen, " LThK, vol. 1, col. 759; J. Quasten, "Kirchenordnungen, " LThK, vol. 6, col. 239.

72. Munier, op. cit., pp. 137f.

73. See J. A. Jungmann, "Didaskalia, " LThK, vol. 3, col. 371f.; Rahner, op. cit.: "the first six books [of the Apostolic Constitutions] are an extension of the Syriac Didascalia [about the year 250] to conform to conditions of the later period. "

74. For instance cc. 27 and 68, Munier, op. cit., pp. 84, 91. According to Munier, pp. 202f., 238, Gennadius felt an obliga-

tion to the ascetic ideals of a monasticism characterized by Oriental ways of thinking.

75. A. Sleumer, Kirchenlateinisches Wörterbuch 2nd ed. (Limburg, 1926), p. 241, says that the word conventus can have the general meaning of congregational assembly as well as the specific meaning of monastic community.

76. Even in our times this concept is used in order to give divine sanction to the disorder brought about in sex relationships by power-seeking actions. E.g., G. Concetti, "La donna e il sacerdozio," in L'Osservatore Romano, Nov. 1965, quoted by Heinzelmann, Schwestern (see Introduction, n. 1), pp. 89-101, esp. 99. Some (male) writers readily admit that the assumed superiority of men over women, exactly because it is unjust, is supported by these and similar spurious means. See, for example, B. J. Leclercq, Familie im Umbruch. Ehe und Familie im Strukturwandel unserer Gesellschaft, (Lucerne, 1965), p. 61: "Woman was considered capable of doing whatever man wanted her to do, but she was considered incapable of doing whatever man did not want her to do"); p. 63: "The main virtue of woman in marriage was to be subject to her husband." See also Metz, "Statut," p. 65, who comments as follows on the attempt to establish and justify the exclusion of women from liturgical functions: "l'imagination de l'homme est féconde, quand la défense de ses intérêts est en jeu."

77. The church widow of early Christian times, to whom this rule against teaching is directed, was called the "altar of God" because she regularly received the gifts of the congregation for her livelihood. See H. Achelis and J. Flemming, Die syrische Didaskalia (Leipzig, 1904), p. 274. When C. Bamberg, "Die Aufgabe der Frau in der Liturgie," in Anima 19 (1964): 312, uses the designation "altar of God" to describe the "true nature of women" and in this way argues against the admission of women to the office of the priesthood, she has made an irresponsible use of this concept, separating it fully from its historical background and "mystifying" it immoderately--just as women's veil (1 Cor. 11:5ff.), in actuality a sign of her inferiority (see chapter 6, p. 112), is glorified and mystified into a symbol of the "sponsa Christi."

78. Apostolic Constitutions, Bk. III. VI (Ante-Nicene Fathers, vol. 7, pp. 427f.). The prohibition against teaching in the Didascalia is very little different from that of the Constitutions. See on this Didascalia et Constitutiones Apostolorum, ed. by F. X. Funk (hereafter cited as Did. et Const. Ap.) (Paderborn, 1905), vol. 1, p. 190.

79. Concerning the dependence of these Pauline passages on rabbinical ways of thinking and methods of scriptural exegesis, see chapter 6, pp. 110ff., 114ff.

80. Cf., for instance, Concetti, op. cit.; F. X. Remberger, "Priestertum der Frau?" in Theologie der Gegenwart 9 (1966): 133;

also by Remberger, writing against the viewpoint of Van der Meer, "Priestertum der Frau?" in Theologie der Gegenwart 13 (1970): 93f., 98f.

81. Achelis and Flemming, op. cit., pp. 76f. (emphasis added). The author of the Apostolic Constitutions expresses himself similarly if somewhat more cautiously: "When she [the widow] is asked anything by anyone, let her not easily answer, excepting questions concerning the faith ... remitting those that desire to be instructed in the doctrines of godliness to the governors. Let her only answer so as may tend to the subversion of the error of polytheism, and let her demonstrate the assertion concerning the monarchy of God. But of the remaining doctrines let her not answer anything rashly, lest by saying anything unlearnedly she should make the word to be blasphemed.... For unbelievers, when they hear the doctrine concerning Christ not explained as it ought to be, but defectively, and especially that concerning his incarnation or his passion, will rather reject it with scorn, and laugh at it as false, than praise God for it," Ante-Nicene Fathers, vol. 7, p. 427.

82. Cf. Achelis and Flemming, pp. 266f.

83. On this see J. Jeremias, Jerusalem zur Zeit Jesu, 3rd ed. (Göttingen, 1962), pp. 395-413; J. Leipoldt and W. Grundmann, eds., Umwelt des Urchristentums (Berlin, 1965), vol. 1, pp. 173-178.

84. See Jeremias, op. cit., p. 413; J. Leipoldt, Die Frau in der antiken Welt und im Urchristentum (Leipzig, 1954), pp. 117-145.

85. Cf. Metz, "Statut," pp. 63ff; Van der Meer, op. cit., pp. 39ff.

86. "Statut," pp. 62f.; Van der Meer, pp. 10-15. The fact that according to Jewish-rabbinical regulation women were not permitted openly to teach in the synagogue (cf. n. 88, below) creates in itself an essential reason for preventing the sending out of women. The apostles repeatedly report that they themselves actively proclaim the Gospel in the synagogues. Cf. Acts 9:20; 13:14ff.; 14:1; 17:1f.

87. E.g., by Concetti, pp. 89f.; similarly, Remberger, in Theologie der Gegenwart (1966), pp. 133f., and in Theologie der Gegenwart 13 (1970): pp. 93f., 98.

88. Cf. the proof-texts from the Talmud and Midrash cited by Strack-Billerbeck, Kommentar zum Neuen Testament aus Talmud und Midrasch (Munich, 1922-1928), vol. 3, pp. 467-469, on 1 Cor. 14:34f. For instance, TMeg 4:11 [226]: "... A woman must not come to the pulpit to read publicly;" Meg 23a Bar: "... Women come in order to hear."

89. Cf. Munier, Statuta, p. 137, which points specifically
to the dependence of the teaching prohibition of the Constitutions on
1 Cor. 14:34: "Les Constitutions apostoliques citent, à l'appui de
cette interdiction ... 1 Cor. 14:34--'Mulieribus ut in ecclesia
doceant non permittimus.'" On the connection between the Didascalia
--and also with it the Constitutions--and 1 Timothy, see E. Schwartz,
"Über die pseudoapostolischen Kirchenordnungen," in Gesammelte
Schriften (Berlin, 1963), vol. 5, p. 193: "The Didascalia is basically nothing but an amplification of 1 Timothy."

90. Statuta, p. 138.

91. P. Hinschius, Das Kirchenrecht der Katholiken und Pro-
testanten in Deutschland (Berlin, 1869-1893) (hereafter cited as
Kirchenrecht), vol. 4, p. 29, n. 4, assumes that the prohibition in
the Statuta applies also to cases of emergency. Presumably, since
it is mentioned in the same connection, this assumption also applies
to the Constitutions. So also W. Plöchl, Geschichte des Kirchenrechts, 2nd ed. (Vienna, 1960-1962), vol. 1, p. 210.

92. Cf. Zscharnack, op. cit., p. 93. The relevant epistola
decretalis of Pope Urban is given by Gratian in chapter 4 of C. 30,
q. 3. ("Super quibus consuluit nos tua dilectio, hoc videtur nobis
ex sentencia respondendum, ut et baptismus sit, si instante necessitate femina puerum in nomine Trinitatis baptizaverit..." Corpus,
ed. Friedberg, vol. 1, col. 1101.)

93. Apostolic Constitutions, Bk. III. IX (Ante-Nicene Fathers,
vol. 7, p. 429). Cf. Did. et Const. Ap., ed. F. X. Funk, vol. 1.
pp. 199-201. The Didascalia contains the same regulation (ibid.,
198-200) but in a shorter and milder formulation. Cf. the notes of
the editor on Did. III. 9. 1 and Const. Ap. III. 9. 1.

94. Modern exegesis has rightly emphasized that this biblical
passage expresses the disorder which comes into sexual relations
as the result of sin, rather than any ligitimation of the authority of
men over women, cf. chapter 6, p. 109f.

95. This certainly does not diminish the value of Mary's
vocation in the slightest, which seems to be in fact the meaning of
the Didascalia and the Constitutions.

96. Cf. Achelis and Flemming, op. cit., pp. 279f.

97. Ibid., pp. 276, 281.

98. Ibid., pp. 276, 280f., 269.

99. Ibid., p. 280; Kalsbach, op. cit., pp. 29, 25.

100. Achelis and Flemming, pp. 281f.

101. Cf. Kalsbach, p. 28: "In the Didascalia the work of

the ministerium is taken from the widow and given independent status in the office of the deaconess." See also Kalsbach, p. 29.

102. Cf. Did. III. 12, 2.3, in Did. et Const. Ap., ed. Funk, vol. 1, pp. 208-210; Achelis and Flemming, pp. 281, 290. Kalsbach, p. 27, points out that, although the characterizations of deacon and deaconess are the same in the Didascalia, as far as baptizing is concerned the deaconess is rated below the deacon.

103. Cf. Kalsbach, p. 28ff. He gives a more exact characterization of the widow and the office of the deaconess in the Constitutions in comparison with the Didascalia. The baptismal duty of the deaconess in the Constitutions corresponds with that of the Didascalia, anointment of the female body before baptism.

104. "Viduae vel sanctimoniales, quae ad ministerium baptizandarum mulierum eliguntur, tam instructae sint ad id officium, ut possint aperto et sano sermone docere imperitas et rusticanas mulieres, tempore quo baptizandae sunt, qualiter baptizatoris ad interrogata respondeant, et qualiter, accepto baptismate, vivant," Munier, Statuta, pp. 99f.

105. Cf. Munier, op. cit., p. 136. Cf. with this the presentation on p. 27.

106. Munier, op. cit., p. 136.

107. Cf. Const. Ap. VIII. 25, 2 (VIII. 24, 2 contains the same arrangement for the virgin concerning the omission of laying on of hands), Did. et. Const. Ap., ed. Funk, vol. 1, p. 529; see on this Kalsbach, pp. 28f. The widow of the Didascalia, on the contrary, still belongs to the clergy, according to Achelis and Flemming, op. cit., pp. 278, 280f., and possesses an office, to be sure a very modest one. Nevertheless Kalsbach says, p. 22, that her position "in relation to the clergy is just as clearly delimited as to the laity." See also Funk's comments, Did. et. Const. Ap., vol. 1, p. 197, in the notation to Const. Ap. III. 8, 1 ("Vidua cum in illa scriptura [Didascalia] eadem esse videatur ac diaconissa, in hac [Const. Ap.] diaconissae subicitur. Didascalia porro viduae manus impositionem attribuit, quam Constitutor non agnoscit").

108. Cf. Munier, Statuta, p. 137.

109. Concerning dist. 4 de cons., c. 20 (baptismal prohibition) Gratian remarks, "Nisi necessitate cogente," Corpus, ed. Friedberg, vol. 1, col. 1367. The limitation of the baptismal prohibition is already evident (according to Plöchl, Geschichte, vol. 1, p. 210) in Isidore of Seville.

110. "Concionari in ecclesia vetantur laici omnes, etsi religiosi."

111. Code, p. 458, n. 4.

112. "Foveatur sacra Verbi Dei celebratio ... maxime in locis quae sacerdote carent: quo in casu celebrationem diaconus vel alius ab Episcopo delegatus dirigat," AAS 56, 1964, p. 109.

113. Cf. the Constitution on the Sacred Liturgy of Vatican II, Walter M. Abbott, The Documents of Vatican II, Herder & Herder (New York, 1966), p. 137.

114. Cf. M. Daly, (see Introduction, n. 8), p. 140; also Frau und Beruf (March-April, 1967): 7, 32.

115. On this see Heinzelmann, Schwestern, p. 5: "In this respect the large number of attempts of male auditors" to give women the opportunity to speak, "which had the assistance of several cardinals, was without success." As a sign of the slowly changing attitudes toward women, it is thus important to notice that in the second regular Bishops' Synod, January, 1971, a woman spoke for the first time to the Synod--she was Barbara Ward, professor of political economy and member of the Papal Commission on Justice and Peace. (Katholische Nachrichten-Agentur, no. 45, 3, November, 1971, p. 3.)

116. In 1965 the Consilium ad exsequendam Constitutionem de sacra Liturgia gave a negative answer to the modest question whether an appropriately prepared woman could take over the lector's office in a mass for women alone: the office of lector, it was answered, is a liturgical duty, which is conferred upon men only. For this reason the Epistle is to be read by the celebrant in the case mentioned. Notitiae, pub. by the Consilium ad exsequendam Constitutionem de Sacra Liturgia, 1, 1965, pp. 139f., n. 41 and n. 42.

117. The "General Introduction to the Roman Missal" (Institutio generalis Missalis Romani), ch. 3, art. 66, which was released in 1969, gives permission to the Bishop's Conference to allow women to read the lessons preceding that of the Gospel, while remaining outside the chancel, in case no man qualified for the duty of lector is present. ("Conferentia Episcopalis permittere potest ut, quando vir aptus ad exercendum munus lectoris non adsit, mulier idonea, extra presbyterium consistens, lectiones quae precedunt Evangelium proferat," Missale Romanum, Typis Polyglottis Vaticanus, 1970, p. 45.) The discrimination against woman contained in this regulation cannot be overlooked: she is admitted to the function of lector only in emergency, and the chancel is taboo for her. (Cf. the critical annotations about this by E. J. Lengeling, "Die neue Ordnung der Eucharistiefeier. Allgemeine Einführung in das römische Messbuch...," Introduction and Commentary, in Lebendiger Gottesdienst, ed. by H. Rennings, no. 17/18 [Münster, 1970], p. 259.) Some progress, though not a great deal, was made by the "Third Instruction concerning the orderly implementation of the Constitution on the Liturgy," of November 5, 1970: it declares in no. 7a, that the Bishops' Conference may decide where the woman is to stand for the reading. ("Mulieribus autem licet secundum normas de his

rebus latas: a. lectiones proferre, Evangelio excepto ... Conferentiae Episcopales pressius determinare possunt locum congruum, e quo verbum Dei mulieres in coetu liturgico annuntient," AAS 62 [1970], p. 700.)

118. "Si tamen adsit sacerdos, diacono praeferatur, diaconus subdiacono, clericus laico et vir feminae, nisi pudoris gratia deceat feminam potius quam virum baptizare, vel nisi femina noverit melius formam et modum baptizandi," canon 742, §2. An exception to the rule preferring men as minister baptismi is thus permitted in only two cases: when propriety suggests that a woman baptize, or when the woman is better informed about the form and manner required for proper baptism.

119. Kirchenrecht, vol. 4, p. 29, with no. 4.

120. The date of the Synod is disputed. Hefele-Leclercq, vol. 1/2, p. 995, put it between 343 (Synod of Sardica) and 381 (Synod of Constantinople) and forego a more exact dating. On this see F. X. Funk, Kirchengeschichtliche Abhandlungen und Untersuchungen (Paderborn, 1899), p. 369: "As far as one can see from internal evidence, it is more likely to be the end rather than the beginning of this period of time." Cf. also B. Kötting, "Laodiceia" in LThK, vol. 6, col. 794.

121. On this cf. p. 14, with n. 58, above.

122. The wording of which is as follows: "Περὶ τοῦ, μὴ δεῖν τὰς λεγομένας πρεσβύτιδας, ἤτοι προκαθημένας, ἐν τῇ Ἐκκλησίᾳ καθίστασθαι," Hefele-Leclercq, vol. 1/2, p. 1003; translated (in Hefele, vol. 1, 756): "That the so-called presbytiden or Mothers Superior should not be appointed in the church."

123. "Mulieres que apud Grecos presbiterae appellantur, apud nos autem viduae, seniores, univirae et matricuriae appellantur, in ecclesia tamquam ordinatas constitui non debere," Corpus, ed. Friedberg, vol. 1, col. 122.

124. Ibid.

125. Schulte, Geschichte, vol. 1, p. 69.

126. Hefele, (see n. 36, above), vol. 1, p. 757.

127. Adversus Haereses 79, 3.4 (PG 42, cc. 743ff.).

128. But according to Epiphanius, the presbytiden are not, as Hefele interprets, the oldest among the deaconesses but rather the oldest among the widows. ("Illud vero diligenter observandum est, solum diaconissarum officium ad ecclesiasticum ordinem necessarium fuisse; ac viduas quidem nominatim expressas, et inter illas, quae anus essent presbytidas vocatas, nunquam presbyteridas aut sacerdotissas esse factas," PG, 42, c. 746.) See also Kalsbach,

p. 52, on this passage. It is clear from the context that Epiphanius is not speaking of an office of director of presbytiden in relation to deaconesses but only of the ministry of deaconesses (or of widows) to women, for instance in baptism. Presumably the widow of the Testamentum Domini (see Kalsbach, pp. 41-45) had certain authority as director of the deaconesses.

129. Hefele, vol. 1, p. 757.

130. Ibid., vol. 1, pp. 757f.

131. E.g., according to Hefele, vol. 1, p. 758, the first Synod of Orange (A.D. 441) in canon 26 ("Diaconae omnimodis non ordinandae; si quae iam sunt, benedictioni quae populo impenditur, capita submittant"); the Synod of Epaon (A.D. 517) in canon 21 ("Viduarum consecrationem, quas diaconas vocitant, ab omni regione nostra penitus abrogamus, sola eis poenitentiae benedictione, si converti ambiumt, imponenda"); the second Synod of Orléans (A.D. 533) in canon 18 ("Placuit etiam, ut nulli postmodum foeminae diaconalis benedictio pro conditionis huius fragilitate credatur"). Cf. also Kalsbach, pp. 86f.

132. Hefele (see the previous note) names Zonaras and Balsamon, famous canonists of the Orthodox Church of the 12th century, as representatives of this conception. Kalsbach, p. 53, expressly follows Balsamon in the interpretation of the canon. ("It is hardly likely that the canon directs itself against a simple honoring of age by granting seats of honor in the church. Balsamon read the canon more correctly, when he combined the ἐν ἐκκλησίᾳ with προκαθημένας instead of with καθίστασθαι--a prohibition against giving elder women disciplinary authority over other women.")

133. On this cf. p. 10, with n. 32, above.

134. Cf. their note on v. "Mulieres," Corpus, ed. Friedberg, vol. 1, col. 122.

135. Cf. Hefele, vol. 1, p. 759.

136. Cf., e.g., canon 30 (prohibition of community bathing of clerics and male lay persons with women); canon 52 (prohibition of weddings during periods of fast); canon 53 (prohibition of dancing at weddings); canon 54 (prohibition of clerics' watching plays at weddings or at banquets). Cf. Hefele, vol. 1, pp. 768ff.

137. B. Kötting, "Laodiceia," LThK, vol. 6, col. 794.

138. On this cf. n. 45, above.

139. "Diaconissam non debere ante annos quadraginta ordinari statuimus, et hoc cum diligenti probatione. Si vero susceperit ordinationem, et quantocumque tempore observaverit ministerium,

et postea se nuptiis tradiderit, iniuriam faciens gratiae Dei, hec
anathema sit cum eo, qui in illius nuptiis convenerit," Corpus, ed.
Friedberg, vol. 1, col. 1055.

140. "Quod vero voventes matrimonia contrahere non possunt...," Corpus, ed. Friedberg, vol. 1, col. 1047.

141. The Concilium Trullanum (A. D. 691-692) repeats this
regulation in canon 14; cf. Hefele-Leclercq, vol. 3/1, p. 565. The
regulation provided for a certain amount of easing of the law of the
emperor Theodosius the Great, which was issued in 390, on the
basis of 1 Tim. 5:9, and which had set the minimum age for admission of women to the diaconate at 60. See Hefele-Leclercq,
vol. 2/2, p. 803; Kalsbach, p. 63. Explaining the age determination of forty years in canon 15 of Chalcedon, Balsamon, following
Zonaras, gives the following basis for it, which clearly documents
a conception of the inferiority of women: "Cum mulieres aut capi
fraudibus, aut sponte ad deteriora labi facillimum sit, idcirco
minorem quadraginta annis diaconissam eligi, huius canonis sanc-
tione vetitum est," PG 137, cc. 442f.

142. Cf. p. 8, above.

143. That is to say, he talks about these two in the other
chapters of quaestio 1 in C. 27, in so far as the chapters refer
to women.

144. Bruns (see n. 44, above) vol. 1, p. 29, with n. 14;
cf. also canon 14 of the Trullian Synod (Bruns, vol. 1, p. 42),
where the concept χειροτονεῖσθαι is used for the deaconess consecration as well as for the presbyterate consecration and that of
the deacon.

145. Cf. the Latin form of the formula in J. A. Assemani,
Codex liturgicus XI (Rome, 1763), 115, and an excerpt from it in
M. Blastares, Syntagma alphabeticum lit. Γ c. XI (PG 144, c.
1173). Both are printed in Kalsbach, pp. 69ff.

146. Cf. Kalsbach, p. 71.

147. Cf. Did. et Const. Ap., ed. Funk, vol. 1, pp. 522ff.

148. "Here Domine, qui non repellis mulieres, consecrantes
seipsas et volentes, ut decet, ministrare sanctis domibus tuis, sed
eas in ordine ministrorum recipis, largire gratiam S. tui Spiritus,
et huic ancillae tuae, quae vult seipsam tibi consecrare, ministerii-
que diaconici gratiam adimplere ut largitus es Phoebae ministerii tui
gratiam, quam vocasti ad opus huius administrationis...," Codex
liturgicus XI 115, quoted from Kalsbach, pp. 70f.

149. Cf. Kalsbach, p. 109. ("The χειροτονία of the deaconess with its ceremonies is in form parallel to that of the deacon.

All consecration formulas, from those of the Apost. Const. and the
Testamentum to those of the Monophysites and the Nestorians and
that handed down by Matthaeus Blastares, bear witness to this fact.")
See also J. Funk, "Klerikale Frauen?" in ÖAKR 14 (1963): 278,
280; J. Daniélou, "Le ministère des femmes dan l'Eglise ancienne, "
in La Maison-Dieu 61 (1960): 95.

150. Thus A. Ludwig, "Weibliche Kleriker in der altchristlichen und frühmittelalterlichen Kirche, " in Theologisch-praktische
Monatschrift 20 (1910): 548-557, 609-617; 21 (1911): 141-149.
Long before Ludwig: J. Morinus, Commentarius de sacris ecclesiae
ordinationibus (Antwerp, 1695), P. III. ex. X.f. 143ff. Kalsbach,
p. 109. (However in his opinion the widow-deaconess stands between
the clergy of lower and those of higher gradation of consecration.)
Also Plöchl (see n. 91), vol. 1, p. 69; Daniélou (n. 157), p. 86.

151. E.g., Schäfer, Kanonissenstifter (see n. 28, above),
pp. 48-50; and his "Kanonissen und Diakonissen" in Römische
Quartalschrift für christliche Altertumskunde und für Kirchengeschichte 24 (1910): 67f.; J. Funk, op. cit., p. 278 (p. 289 in reference to the consecration of the Roman deaconess). The sacramental character of the deaconess consecration is not excluded by
these authors, and likewise not by Ch. R. Meyer, "Ordained Women
in the Early Church," in The Catholic Citizen 53 (1967): 118. ("To
push the argument against the sacramentality of the ordination of
deaconesses too far would be in fact to deny the sacramentality of
the ordination of deacons.") Zscharnack, op. cit., pp. 113, 117,
149, speaks of the clerical character of the deaconess office, without further differentiation.

152. Thus Pohle and Gierens (see Introduction, n. 6, above),
vol. 3, p. 582. ("Although deaconesses were blessed by ecclesiastical ceremony and among the Greeks even by the laying on of hands
[see Const. Apost. VIII, 19sq.], this was no consecration...." It
seems "hasty" to conclude, he thinks, "that the consecration of deaconesses was formerly assigned to the ordines minores ... or even
to the ordines maiores.") Similarly Premm (see Introduction, n. 6,
above), vol. 3/2, p. 242; Th. Specht, Lehrbuch der Dogmatik, 2nd
ed. (Regensburg, 1912), vol. 2, p. 397; J. Brinktrine, Die Lehre
von den heiligen Sakramenten der katholischen Kirche (Paderborn,
1962), vol. 2, p. 196; E. Friedberg, Lehrbuch des katholischen
und evangelischen Kirchenrechts, 6th ed. (Leipzig, 1909), p. 165,
n. 2; G. Phillips, Kirchenrecht, 3rd ed. (Regensburg, 1855), vol. 1,
pp. 449f. Some of the writers mentioned (e.g., Pohle, Specht,
Brinktine, Friedberg, Phillips) derive their contentions from 1 Cor.
14:34f. and 1 Tim. 2:11ff. and in this way their judgment of the
sources about the deaconess and her ordination is not free from
bias. Others (e.g., Premm) depend on canon 11 of the Council of
Nicea, which they interpret to mean that the deaconess received no
imposition of hands and consequently she was numbered among the
laity. But there is a difference of opinion about the meaning of the
canon in question: cf. Kalsbach, pp. 46ff.; another meaning is
possible, according to J. Funk, op. cit., p. 227, Morinus (see

n. 150), f. 148, Daniélou, op. cit., p. 86, and others. But in any
case the laying of hands on the deaconess is specifically provided
for by later councils: cf. canon 15 of the Council of Chalcedon and
canon 14 of the Trullian Synod. Therefore Morinus, f. 143sq.,
rightly opposes the viewpoint of those theologians who dispute any
ordination (capability) of women: "Si aliquis tam austerus et tetricus
fuerit, ut nihil quod ad ordinationem Ecclesiasticam spectet, mulieribus concedi posse contendat, facile antiquissima multorum secu-
lorum traditione revincetur, eiusque tetricitas retundetur."

153. Thus Pohle and Gierens, loc. cit., p. 582; Premm,
vol. 3/2, p. 242; Brinktine, loc. cit., p. 196. Friedberg, loc.
cit., p. 165, n. 2, speaks, but without justification from source materials, only of an activity of the deaconess in the care of the sick
and the poor. (In opposition to this, Zscharnack, p. 137, says:
"The heart of her office has certainly never been and never became
the care of the sick.") None of the writers mentioned refers to the
authorization to distribute the Holy Communion that the deaconess
had in some geographical areas.

154. Concerning the lesser authorization of deaconesses in
baptizing, in contrast to that of the deacons, see p. 19, with n.
102, above. A liturgical neglect of the deaconess is likewise found
in Const. Ap. VIII. 28, 4-6 (Did. et Const. Ap., ed. Funk, vol. 1,
pp. 530f.). Note also the Nestorian "Ordo chirotoniae mulierum
diaconissarum" (in H. Denzinger, Ritus Orientalium Coptorum Syro-
rum et Armenorum in administrandis sacramentis [Würzburg, 1863/
64, reprint, Graz, 1961], vol. 2, p. 261), to which a marginal note
remarks: "Ad altare autem [diaconissa] non accedit, quoniam mulier
est," Denzinger, vol. 1, p. 123.

155. On this cf. the preceding note, 154, and also n. 36
and n. 46, above. Canon 18 of the Synod of Orleans (A.D. 533)
decrees: "Placuit etiam, ut nulli postmodum foeminae diaconalis
benedictio pro conditionis huius fragilitate credatur," Mansi (see n.
23), vol. 8. 835.

156. Cf. Kalsbach, p. 66, who in this context (p. 66, n. 5,
and p. 68) points out that the Chalcedonian decree is more strict
about the marriage of the deaconess than about that of the God-consecrated virgin, as the Chalcedonian canon 16 shows.

157. Cf. Kalsbach, p. 65, concerning the Byzantine deaconess. ("The evidence is overwhelming in its characterization of
the deaconess as appointed by the church and of her task, mainly
baptismal assistance, as ecclesiastical service; and also in indicating
her accountability to ecclesiastical officials.") Cf. also J. Funk,
op. cit., p. 276.

158. About this see Kalsbach, pp. 29f., 45, 57f.; also his
article "Diakonisse," in Reallexikon für Antike und Christentum,
Th. Klauser, ed. (Stuttgart, 1950ff.) (hereafter cited as RAC), vol.

3, col. 919ff.; Schäfer, Kanonissenstifter, pp. 32, 58f.; Zscharnack, pp. 137-139. Deaconesses, or widows and sanctimonials--as the case might be--carried out similar functions in particular areas of the Western Church but they soon became an object of strife. Cf. Schäfer, op. cit., pp. 32, 59f.; J. Funk, op. cit., pp. 279ff.; Heinzelmann, Schwestern, p. 55.

159. See E. Herman, "Balsamon," in Dictionnaire de Droit Canonique, R. Naz, ed. (Paris, 1935-1965) (hereafter cited as DDC), vol. 2, cols. 76-83.

160. "Olim aliquando ordines diaconissarum canonibus cogniti fuere, habebantque ipsae gradum ad altare. Menstruorum autem inquinatio ministerium earum a divino et sancto altari expulit. In sanctissima autem Ecclesia sedis Constantinopolitanorum diaconissae deliguntur, unam quidem communicationem non habentes ad altare, in multis autem habentes conventum, et muliebrem coetum ecclesiastice dirigentes," Responsa ad interrogationes Marci (Interr. 35), PG 138, c. 987. Similarly M. Blastares (Greek canonist in the first half of the 14th century), Syntagma Alphabeticum Γ cap. XI, PG 144, c. 1174. ("Quale autem ministerium diaconissae tunc temporibus in clero implebant, omnibus fere hodie ignotum est. Sunt qui dicunt, quod mulieribus baptizandis ministrabant.... Dicunt autem alii, quod ad sanctum altare ingredi iis permissum erat, et diaconorum officia prope illos exsequi. Verum prohibuerunt postea Patres eas illuc ascendere, et illo ministerio defungi, propter involuntarium catameniorum fluxum. ")

161. Cf. Schäfer, Kanonissenstifter, p. 58; Kalsbach, pp. 57, 68 ("Balsamon understands the correct relationship, when he sees the lay deaconess as ordinary, the nun deaconess as extraordinary").

162. Cf. Schäfer, op. cit., pp. 55ff.; Zscharnack, pp. 153f., 156 ("Early Christianity and the ancient church were both willing to legitimize the service of women and to use them ... for the upbuilding of the church; then heresy, hierarchy and monasticism became the evil enemies which choked the seed").

163. "Quae in praesenti canone tractantur, omnino exolevere. Diaconissa enim hodie non ordinatur, etiamsi quaedam ascetriae abusive diaconissae dicantur. Est enim canon, qui statuit mulieres in sacrum tribunal non debere ingredi. Quae ergo ad sanctum altare accedere non potest, quomodo diaconatus officium exercebit?" in Canones SS. Apostolorum, Conciliorum commentaria (in canon 15 Conc. Chalced.), PG 137, c. 442.

164. Cf. Corpus, ed. Friedberg, vol. 1, col. 637 with n. 397; Corpus Iuris Civilis, ed. by P. Krueger, Th. Mommsen, R. Schoell (Berlin, 1904-1906), vol. 3, col. 609.

165. Cf. Kalsbach, p. 66 with n. 4.

166. Cf. Corpus, ed. Friedberg, vol. 1, col. 1057, n. 403;
Juliani epitome latina Novellarum Justiniani, ed. by G. Haenel
(Leipzig, 1873), pp. 162f.

167. According to Kalsbach, p. 67, female ascetics (ascetriae) are women who live in a more free community form than
cloistered nuns.

168. See Kalsbach, p. 65; J. Funk, op. cit., pp. 276f.;
Heinzelmann, Schwestern, pp. 63f.

169. Cf. v. Schulte (see note 2, above), vol. 1, pp. 61f.;
Stickler (see note 3, above), vol. 1, p. 210.

170. Von Schulte, op. cit., vol. 1, p. 70, maintains that
while it is true that the dicta Gratiani had no legal authority, they
did have significant doctrinal authority, in so far as they were not
in specific cases disapproved by the schools. He says that Gratian's
statements are "a very important witness, even a definitive witness,
to the conceptions of his time." Cf. also Stickler, vol. 1, p. 212.

171. "Mulieres autem non solum ad sacerdotium, sed nec
etiam ad diaconatum provehi possunt...," Corpus, ed. Friedberg,
vol. 1, col. 750.

172. See pp. 28ff.

173. According to J. Funk, op. cit., p. 280, these are the
decretals of Benedict VIII (1012-1024), J. P. Migne, Patrologiae
cursus completus, series latina (Paris, 1878-1890) (hereafter PL)
139, c. 1621; of John XIX (1024-1032), PL 78, c. 1056; and of Leo
IX (1049-1054), PL 143, c. 602.

174. See Schäfer, Kanonissenstifter, p. 50 with n. 1.

175. Thus Schäfer, op. cit., p. 50 and J. Funk, p. 280.

176. Schäfer, op. cit., pp. 49f.

177. J. Funk, pp. 279f.; Kalsbach, pp. 85ff.; Schäfer, op.
cit., pp. 56ff.; Zscharnack, p. 122.

178. Cf. Kalsbach, pp. 72, 99; Schäfer, op. cit., p. 57,
Heinzelmann, Schwestern, pp. 55, 66f.

179. Cf. Kalsbach, pp. 65, 110; Schäfer, op. cit., p. 57,
n. 1.

180. Concerning this source--epistola 8 of Bishop Otto of
Vercelli (died A.D. 960)--see Kalsbach, pp. 92f.

181. According to Kalsbach, op. cit., pp. 80ff., 110ff.,

the prevailing form of the feminine diaconate in the West (that is, in Rome, but not in Gaul) was somewhat different from that of the Orient: the Roman (Italian) deaconess was simply 'God-consecrated' and not (as the Oriental and the Gaulic deaconess) the holder of an office. See also Kalsbach, "Diakonisse," in RAC, vol. 3, col. 926. Here Kalsbach disputes the point of view of Schäfer, Kanonissenstifter, pp. 47f., 50, n. 1, according to which the Western deaconess was also holder of office.

182. Cf. the discussion on pp. 54f., and 56f.

183. That could also be concluded by the manner in which Gratian arranges and uses canon 15 of the Council of Chalcedon (C. 27, q. 1, c. 35), which refers to the deaconess. See p. 23 above.

184. As first of the decretists, Rufinus--and then in dependence on him the subsequent decretists--specifically disputes the sacramentality of the deaconess consecration. On this cf. p. 51.

185. See pp. 50f. with n. 68.

186. While as already mentioned (see Part I [preliminary], n. 8, above) Gillman ignores this aspect of the question, R. Metz rightly devotes a large section of his study, "Le statut de la femme en droit canonique médiéval," (see Introduction, n. 9, above), to the question of the evaluation of women (see the section, "Les fondements du statut de la femme," pp. 61-82). Van der Meer also (pp. 99-103) makes a thorough study of this problem and urges (p. 7) an investigation of the time-conditioned prohibitions relating to women.

187. See also Metz, "Statut", pp. 73ff.; and his "Recherches" (see Introduction, n. 9, above), pp. 379-396.

188. Corpus, ed. Friedberg, vol. 1, col. 750f.

189. According to Friedberg, ibid., col. 484, n. 37, this is a section from a Pseudo-Isidorian letter. Cf. Hinschius, Decretales, p. 162.

190. "Mulieres autem non solum ad sacerdotium, sed nec etiam ad diaconatum provehi possunt, unde nec sacerdotes accusare, nec in eos testificari valent," Corpus, ed. Friedberg, vol. 1, col. 750.

191. Gratian often uses this method; concerning this as well as concerning the significance of Roman law for the evaluation and position of women in the church, see the discussion on pp. 39 and 43ff.

192. Friedberg, Corpus, vol. 1, col. 750, n. 3, cites as source from Roman law Dig. 50, 17, 2, to which Gratian presumably

refers. ("Feminae ab omnibus officiis civilibus vel publicis remotae sunt et ideo nec iudices esse possunt nec magistratum gerere nec postulare nec pro alio intervenire nec procuratores existere," Corpus Iuris Civilis, vol. 1, col. 868.) The cases of exception to the general complainant prohibition for women--which Roman law sets up as exceptions--are given by Gratian as cc. 1-4 in C. 15, q. 3. It is apparent from his dictum, p.c. 4 (ibid.), § 2, that the canonical law follows Roman legal regulations in both normal and exceptional cases.

193. "His ita respondetur: In veteri lege multa permittebantur, que hodie perfectione gratiae abolita sunt. Cum enim mulieribus permitteretur populum iudicare, hodie pro peccato, quod mulier induxit, ab Apostolo eis indicitur verecundari, viro subditas esse, in signum subiectionis velatum caput habere. Que ergo his omnibus viro subiecta ostenditur, cui pro alio postulare non conceditur, ad accusationem admittenda non videtur," Corpus, ed. Friedberg, vol. 1, cols. 750f.

194. The patristic texts which Gratian uses as cc. 11-20 in C. 33, q. 5, exhibit in part a similar point of view. Cf. p. 38.

195. On this cf. chapter 6, p. 112f.

196. See Corpus, ed. Friedberg, vol. 1, col. 1144, n. 155. Since the early Middle Ages, the oldest Latin commentary on the Pauline letters (called "Ambrosiaster," a characterization also used for the author of the commentary; cf. W. Mundle, Die Exegese der paulinischen Briefe im Kommentar des Ambrosiaster [Marburg, 1919], p. 8, n. 1) was mistakenly attributed to Ambrose, until proven spurious by Erasmus of Rotterdam. Throughout the Middle Ages the assumption that Ambrose was the author was so dominant that it silenced all evidence to the contrary. Cf. O. Bardenhewer, Geschichte der altkirchlichen Literatur (Freiburg, 1902-1932), vol. 3, p. 520. Yet Gratian remarks, probably following Peter Lombard (Sentences, IV. 35, ed. PP. Colleg. S. Bonaventurae, Ad Claras Aquas (1916), vol 2, p. 959): "Sed illud Ambrosii a falsatoribus dicitur insertum" (dict. p. c. 18 in C. 32, q. 7), Corpus, ed. Friedberg, vol. 1, col. 1145. However this recognition of the possibility that the Ambrose text is spurious disappears from the following text.

197. The commentary of Ambrosiaster on 1 Cor. 7:10f., which Gratian presents in shortened form as ch. 17 (Corpus, ed. Friedberg, vol. 1, col. 1144), reads in full as follows: "'Uxorem a viro non discedere; quod si discesserit, manere innuptam.' Hoc Apostoli consilium est, ut si discesserit propter malam conversationem viri, iam innupta maneat. 'Aut viro suo reconciliari.' Quod si continere se, inquit, non potest, quia pugnare non vult contra carnem, viro reconcilietur; non enim permittitur mulieri, ut nubat, si virum suum causa fornicationis dimiserit, aut apostasiae.... Si tamen apostataverit vir, aut usum quaerat uxoris invertere, nec

alii potest nubere mulier, nec reverti ad illum. 'Et virum uxorem non dimittere.' Subauditur autem, excepta fornicationis causa. Et ideo non subiecit (Apostolus) dicens, sicut de muliere; quod si discesserit, manere sic; quia viro licet ducere uxorem, si dimiserit uxorem peccantem, quia non ita lege constringitur vir, sicut mulier; caput enim mulieris vir est," PL 17, c. 230. The manner of argumentation is quite characteristic; the alleged superiority of men is pleaded in order to legitimize, legally, greater marital liberties for men! O. Heggelbacher, Vom römischen zum christlichen Recht. Juristische Elemente in den Schriften des sog. Abrosiaster (Freiburg/Switzerland, 1959), pp. 127f., remarks that the viewpoint of Ambrosiaster has been influenced by Roman law, but he has to admit (p. 127, n. 1) that church discipline, too, in many areas grants men certain privileges in marriage. For example, the penitential discipline of Asia Minor recognized only the unfaithfulness of women as adultery and punished it with fifteen years of penitence, but the same infraction committed by men was punished only by the seven-year penitence set up for extra-marital sexual relations. Concerning the influence of Ambrosiaster's position on church discipline, see also B. Kurtscheid, Die christliche Ehe (Religiöse Quellenschriften, ed. by J. Walterscheid, no. 54) (Düsseldorf, 1928), p. 20.

198. "Quidam vero, sentenciam Ambrosii servare cupientes, non de qualibet fornicatione illud arbitrantur intelligi, ut ob quamlibet fornicationem vir licite dimittat uxorem, et vivente dimissa aliam ducat, sed de incestuosa tantum fornicatione intelligitur...." Gratian corrects this interpretation in the following way: "Sed quia nulla auctoritate permittitur, ut vivente uxore alia superducatur, intelligitur illud Ambrosii in supradicto fornicationis genere: non tamen, quod vivente dimissa aliam ducere possit, sed post mortem fornicariae vel fornicarii ... ille, qui a fornicatione mundus est, vir sive mulier aliis copulari possunt; adulteri autem, si supervixerint, nullo modo aliis copulari poterunt," dict. p. c. 18 in C. 32 q. 7, ed. Friedberg, Corpus vol. 1, col. 1145. Ch. Munier, Les sources patristiques du droit de l'Eglise du VIIIe au XIIIe siècle (Mulhouse, 1957), p. 188, points out that this method of changing the meaning of a text in order to save the authority of the author was often used by the compilers of the Middle Ages, which show their great dependence on authority.

199. "Hic si quis contendat, non magis viro, quam mulieri licitum esse, si vir alicuius eodem modo fornicetur, sciat, virum ab Ambrosio appellatum non sexu, sed animi virtute; mulierem quoque nominatam sentiat non sexu corporis, sed mollicie mentis, Corpus, ed. Friedberg, vol. 1, col. 1145.

200. Cf. K. E. Georges, Ausführliches lateinisch-deutsches Handwörterbuch, 11th ed. (Basel, 1962), vol. 2, pp. 985f.

201. Corpus, ed. Friedberg, vol. 1, col. 1145.

202. Patristic statements are the main medium through

which Gratian received (cf. p. 33f.) the deprecatory conception of wom-
en and the over-rating of men which is already present in the Old
Testament (cf., e.g., Ecc. 7:25-28; Ecclesiasticus 19:2; Jer. 49:
22; also see chapter 6, pp. 101f.). In the Fathers we often come
across the conception of the female sex as essentially base, weak
in character and wicked. (Cf. K. Thraede, "Frau," in RAC, vol.
8, 1970, cols. 257ff.) This conception may be traced not only to
Jewish sources but also to gnostic-dualistic and neoplatonic sources.
(Thraede, cols. 242f.) A result of this manner of thinking is that
the Fathers characterize a woman, who, surprisingly enough, exhibits faith and virtue, as "vir" (man). Thus Ambrose, Expositio
evangelii secundum Lucam X 161: "dicit ei Iesus: mulier quae
non credit mulier est et adhuc corporei sexus appellatione signatur;
nam quae credit occurrit in virum perfectum ... carens iam nomine
saeculi, corporis sexu, Corpus Scriptorum Ecclesiasticorum Latinorum, editum consilio et impensis academiae litterarum Caesareae
Vindobonensis (Vienna, 1866ff.) (hereafter cited as CSEL), 32, 4,
p. 517; Hieronymus, Commentariorum in epistolam ad Ephesios,
lib. III cap. V: "quandiu mulier partui servit et liberis, hanc habet ad
virum differentiam, quam corpus ad animam. Sin autem Christo
magis volverit servire quam saeculo, mulier esse cessabit, et
dicetur vir," PL 26, c. 567; Berengaudus, Expositio in Apocalypsin,
ad cap. 12, 5: "Femineus quippe sexus fragilis est: femina igitur
quae fortitudine animi assumpta diabolum vincit, atque per bona
opera Deo placere studet, non incongrue vir vocatur; quia quamvis
corpore sit femina, virtute tamen animi viris bonis coaequatur,"
PL 17, c. 960, ad opera S. Ambrosii appendix. Cf. also the primary sources given by Van der Meer, op. cit. (see Introduction,
n. 7, above), pp. 78ff.

203. See W. Plöchl, Das Eherecht des Magisters Gratianus
(Wiener staats- und rechtswissenschaftliche Studien, ed. by H. Kel-
sen, vol. 24 (Leipzig, 1935) (hereafter cited as Eherecht), pp. 37-
43.

204. M. Weber, Ehefrau und Mutter in der Rechtsentwicklung,
(Tübingen, 1907), p. 181, refers to this fact and to its negative consequences for the personal development of women. Investigating the
influence of Christianity on the legal situation of women, she notes
that, "Christianity trained men to control their sexual drives, which
certainly raised the position of women a great deal, both within and
without, and in very definite forms. But on the other hand, the
new teaching allowed for the principle of patriarchalism: actual and
legal subordination of women as spouse and mother, just as it was
found in the Orient, its principles unchanged and even strengthened
in many aspects, so that it became a reactionary force in the area
of feminine freedom.... Because those conceptions of the nature of
marriage and the position of women, conditioned as they were by
the circumstances of that age, were considered to be the will of
God, they hardened into dogma and as such became normative for
the whole Christian culture into modern times. Such facts account
for the delay of progress in women's rights and the development of
their personalities."

205. Corpus, ed. Friedberg, vol. 1, col. 1254.

206. That is proved, for instance, by the 11th-century wedding ritual of the diocese of Salsbury, which was widely used. Here is the vow made by the bride: "I N., take you N., to be my wedded husband, to have and to hold from this day forward, in good fortune and in bad fortune, in wealth and in poverty, in sickness and in health, to be modest and obedient in bed and at table, until we are parted by death" (quoted from J. Freisen, Das Eheschliessungsrecht in Spanien, Grossbritannien und Irland und Skandinavien in geschichtlicher Entwicklung mit Abdruck vieler alter Urkunden dargestellt (Paderborn, 1919), vol. 2, p. 75). Gratian too sees the supremacy of man as preventing an actual equalization in marriage relationship. See on this the discussion on pp. 43f. Noteworthy also in this connection is the discussion by J. A. Brundage, "The Crusader's Wife: a Canonistic Quandary," in Studia Gratiana 12 (1967), pp. 427-441. According to Brundage, it is true that Gratian insisted that a husband was dependent upon his wife's approval, if he wanted to embark on a Crusade. But at the beginning of the 13th century two decretals of Innocent III changed the existing law to allow a man to go on a Crusade without the approval of his wife (pp. 434f.). On the contrary, a man was not by any means required to respect a vow of his wife to take part in a Crusade, even if he had already given his permission; although not in itself allowed, he could in fact retract his permission. (Brundage, p. 432, n. 17.)

207. Cf. the auctoritates patrum, which Gratian cites in support of his theory in C. 33, q. 5. More exact explanation of this appears on pp. 33ff.; see also chapter 6, pp. 110ff.

208. Cf. Metz, "Recherches" (see Introduction, n. 9), pp. 381f.; also chapter 6, pp. 114ff. But besides the harmony of the married couple, the obligation of the wife to be subordinate to her husband is also stressed by Paul in Eph. 5. This subordination likewise results from the concept of 'body'--a fact not sufficiently noted, it seems to me, by Metz.

209. See on this chapter 6, pp. 111f., 114.

210. "Quia vero in ceteris vir est caput mulieris, et mulier corpus viri, ita vota abstinentiae viro permittente mulier potest promittere, ut tamen eodem prohibente repromissa non valeat inplere, et hoc, ut diximus, propter condicionem servitutis, qua viro in omnibus debet subesse," Corpus, ed. Friedberg., vol. 1, col. 1254.

211. There is more on pp. 33ff., about these auctoritates patrum.

212. "Evidentissime itaque apparet, ita virum esse caput mulieris, ut nulla vota abstinentiae vel religiosae conversationis liceat sibi sine eius licentia Deo offerre; etiamsi viro permittente repromissa fuerint, non licet ei votum opere conplere, cum vir

volverit revocare permissum, " Corpus, ed. Friedberg, vol. 1, col.
1256.

213. Cf. Num. 30:11-15 (especially v. 14: "Any vow and
any sworn duty to fast can be validated or invalidated by her husband"). Also see p. 36.

214. Cf. Gen. 20:3; Ex. 20:17; 21:22; 2 Sam. 11:26; see
also chapter 6, pp. 101f.

215. Especially in regard to the sacrament of penance, the
dependence of women on men is very often experienced as basically
unacceptable and discriminatory: in no secular area of such a private nature is there such a great dependency. For instance, a
woman is free to consult with and be treated by women physicians
and psychotherapists. This possibility of choice is generally experienced by women as truly beneficial: not otherwise would she
experience and appreciate such a freedom in the sphere of religion.
Cf. on this problem Heinzelmann, Schwestern, pp. 27f.

216. "Statut, " p. 74.

217. Cf. Metz, "Recherches, " p. 379 ("Cette condition
[d'infériorité] se traduisait par une série d'incapacités auxquelles la
femme était soumise, tout particulièrement dans les fonctions du
culte public"); see also Metz, "Statut, " pp. 97ff., 108.

218. The opinion of Schulte, Geschichte, vol. 1, p. 70--
"Gratian's statements represent a very important, even definitive
witness to the outlook of his age"--applies also in this specific
point.

219. Cf. Munier, Sources patristiques (see n. 198), p. 167.

220. Ibid., pp. 159f.

221. Ibid., p. 184: "Pour l'interprétation des Ecritures la
science des saints docteurs et les lumières de l'Esprit Saint, qui
les assiste les recommandent de préférence à tous les autres com-
mentateurs, fussent-ils même souverains pontifes"; cf. also dist.
20 princ. § 1.

222. Patristic scriptural proofs for the subordination, a
characteristic biblical understanding not overcome even today, will
be investigated more exactly in chapter 6.

223. "Hec imago Dei est in homine, ut unus factus sit, ex
quo ceteri oriantur, habens inperium Dei, quasi vicarius eius, quia
unius Dei habet imaginem, ideoque mulier non est facta ad Dei
imaginem. Sic etenim dicit: 'Et fecit Deus hominem; ad imaginem
Dei fecit illum.' Hinc etiam Apostolus: 'Vir quidem,' ait, 'non
debet velare caput, quia imago et gloria Dei est; mulier ideo velat,

quia non est gloria aut imago Dei,'" Corpus, ed. Friedberg, vol.
1, col. 1254; the Editio Romana adds after "ut unus factus sit,"
"quasi Dominus," in note a to c. 13.

224.   "Mulier debet velare caput, quia non est imago Dei.
Sed ut ostendatur subiecta ... hoc signum debet habere...," Corpus,
ed. Friedberg, vol. 1, col. 1255.

225.   Friedberg, Corpus, vol. 1, col. 1254, n. 130, remarks on c. 13 only: "non sunt Augustini"; a corresponding assertion for c. 19 is lacking.

226.   Concerning the mistaken attribution of the Ambrosiaster
commentary to Ambrose during the Middle Ages, see n. 196, above;
concerning the mistaken attribution of the "Quaestiones" to Augustine,
cf. A. Souter's prolegomena to the edition of the "Quaestiones" in
CSEL 50, p. VII.

227.   A. Souter, A Study of Ambrosiaster (Cambridge, 1905),
proved the identity of the author by means of linguistic investigations.   Cf. also Mundle (see note 196), pp. 13f. and Bardenhewer
(see note 196), vol. 3, p. 524.   On the basis of studies in legal
history, O. Heggelbacher (see note 197), confirms Souter's conclusions.   Cf. the rescension of P. Mikat, ZRG Kan. Abt. 48 (1962):
362.

228.   See Mundle, op. cit., pp. 9-13 and H. J. Vogel's
prolegomena to the edition of the Ambrosiaster commentary in
CSEL 81/1, pp. IX-XVII.

229.   Cf. Heggelbacher, p. 4; so too Mundle, p. 14.   Concerning Ambrosiaster's origin and manner of thinking, Mundle thinks
he was "a Roman of the highest order" (p. 13).

230.   While Paul in 1 Cor. 11:7 characterizes woman as the
"reflected glory of man," Ambrosiaster draws a sharper conclusion
from the words of the apostle: "mulier ideo velat" (cf. vss. 6 and
10) "quia non est gloria aut imago Dei."

231.   "Nec illud otiosum est, quod non de eadem terra, de
qua plasmatus est Adam, sed de ipsius Adae costa facta sit mulier
....   Ideo non duo a principio facti vir et mulier, neque duo viri,
neque duae mulieres; sed primum vir, deinde mulier ex eo...,"
Corpus, ed. Friedberg, vol. 1, col. 1256.

232.   See chapter 6, pp. 111f.

233.   "Cum caput mulieris vir sit, caput autem viri Christus,
quecumque uxor non subicitur viro, hoc est capiti suo, eiusdem
criminis rea est, cuius et vir, si non subiciatur capiti suo...,"
Corpus, ed. Friedberg, vol. 1, col. 1255.

234.   "Verbum autem Domini blasphematur, vel cum con-

tempnitur Dei prima sentencia, et pro nichilo ducitur, vel cum
Christi infamatur evangelium, dum contra legem fidemque naturae
ea, que Christiana est, et ex lege Dei subiecta, viro inperare desiderat, cum gentiles etiam feminae viris suis serviant communi lege
naturae," Corpus, ed. Friedberg, vol. 1, col. 1255.

235. "Est ordo naturalis in hominibus, ut feminae serviant
viris, et filii parentibus, quia in illis hec iustitia est, ut maiori
serviat minor," Corpus, ed. Friedberg, vol. 1, col. 1254.

236. "Statut," p. 72; also cf. Metz, "Recherches," pp.
383f.

237. Cf. F. Flückiger, Geschichte des Naturrechts (Zurich,
1954), vol. 1, pp. 175, 465f.

238. Ibid., pp. 174, 465.

239. "... haec iustitia est, ut infirmior ratio serviat forti-
ori. Haec igitur in dominationibus et servitutibus clara iustitia est,
ut qui excellunt ratione, excellant dominatione," Sancti Aureli Augustini quaestionum in heptateuchum libri VII, CSEL 28/2, p. 80.
On the question of the deviation of Gratian's text from the original,
see the Notatio correctorum to c. 12, Corpus, ed. Friedberg, vol.
1, col. 1253.

240. "... si imaginem dei homo in dominatione habet, et
mulieri datur, ut et ipsa imago dei sit, quod absurdum est, quo
modo enim potest de muliere dici, quia imago dei est, quam constat
dominio viri subiectam et nullam auctoritatem habere? nec docere
enim potest nec testis esse neque fidem dicere nec iudicare: quanto
magis imperare!" Pseudo-Augustini quaestiones Veteris et Novi
Testamenti, CSEL 50, p. 83.

241. As ch. 17 in C. 33, q. 5. (Corpus, ed. Friedberg,
vol. 1, col. 1255; in ibid., n. 176, Friedberg still ascribed the
text to Augustine.) The introductory half-sentence ("quomodo enim
..."), which indicates the causal connection between the status
subiectionis of woman and her not-in-the-image-of-God situation,
is lacking in Gratian.

242. The prohibition is especially concerned with matters
relating to wills. Cf. p. 42. Also in Jewish rabbinical law women
were not competent to act as witnesses. Cf. Jeremias (see n. 83),
p. 412.

243. Cf. the regulation of Roman law (cited in n. 192) Dig.
50, 17, 2; also see pp. 41f.

244. Cf. Heggelbacher (see n. 197), pp. 46ff., concerning
the positive attitude of Ambrosiaster to Roman law.

245. Cf. Heggelbacher, op. cit., p. 48 with n. 1 and n. 2.

Ambrosiaster's crude denigration of women is however minimized
rather than criticized by Heggelbacher (pp. 32-36). The recension
of P. Mikat (ZRG Kan. Abt. 48, 1962, pp. 367f.) uncovers this
failure of Heggelbacher. He refers to Heggelbacher's sentence,
"Since women were obviously full members of the Christian community from the first and since Christianity by preserving the subordination of wife to husband has brought about the equalization of the
sexes ..." (pp. 32f.). On the contrary, Mikat says, we see no
"equalization" when we look at the position of women in marriage,
in the family, in the church and in public life, even after the victory
of Christianity in the ancient world, and Heggelbacher's evidences
from Ambrosiaster's writings do not in any way justify such a conclusion. In fact Heggelbacher is guilty of a mistaken interpretation
when he affirms (p. 35) that according to Ambrosiaster the position
of women is different from that of men. Actually what Ambrosiaster
clearly says (p. 35, n. 3) is that their position is a lesser one:
"mulier autem quia persona inferior est, condicionis causa, non
naturae, viro subiecta, timere (autem) eum iubetur" (Comm. Eph.
5, 33); "... gradu maior est vir, quia ex eo est femina" (Q. 24).
A similar minimizing and extenuating interpretation of the statements of Ambrosiaster about women (e.g., that they are not the
image of God) is given by L. Voelkl ("Vom römischen zum christlichen Recht," in Römische Quartalschrift für christliche Altertumskunde und Kirchengeschichte 60 [1965]: 126): "This negation of
women does not imply any denigration of the female sex; it only intends to say that women do not actively participate in God's creative work, and that in their maternal readiness they reply only [!]
with a Yes to the call of God. This evaluation of the nature of
women coincides with the Roman legal understanding of the position
of women, in regard to their legal competence in public affairs."

    246. The preconceived opinion of the psychic inferiority of
women was supported by "scientific" results, in order to justify
in this way the exclusion of women from higher education and especially from study in the university. Th. L. W. von Bischoff
(Das Studium und die Ausübung der Medizin durch Frauen [Munich,
1872]) concludes from the different shape of the female skull and
the smaller weight of the female brain that they possess only small
capability in mental endeavor and therefore are not able to undertake university studies. Also P. Möbius built his theory of the
"weak-mindedness" of women on the "results" of investigations of
brain anatomy (Über den physiologischen Schwachsinn des Weibes
[Halle, 1900]). It was because of the objections and prejudices of
this and similar kind against the intellectual development of women
that women were not officially admitted to the universities of Germany until the beginning of this century (in Baden in 1901, in Prus-
sia in 1908). (See the Handbuch der Frauenbewegung, ed. by H.
Lange and G. Bäumer [Berlin, 1901], vol. 1, pp. 72ff., 95f.) According to a questionnaire answered by university professors and
docents in 1953-1955 concerning their attitude towards women students, belief in the intellectual inferiority of women was at that
time by no means overcome. See H. Anger, Probleme der deutschen

Universität. Bericht über eine Erhebung unter Professoren und Dozenten (Tübingen, 1960). The verdict given here (pp. 473-494)--e.g., that in women "pure intellectual ability" is smaller or less often present, that "abstract thinking" or "any thinking at all" is less possible for them, that they have less "inventive faculty," etc. --even if there were any empirical support, completely overlooks the fact that the centuries-old exclusion of women from intellectual nurture has postponed their intellectual and personal development.

247. A classic parallel is the denigration of blacks because of cultural backwardness and lack of education. See W. T. Reich, "Kämpferische Gewaltlosigkeit. Ethische Probleme des Kampfes um die Gleichberechtigung in den USA," in Orientierung 32 (1968): 226-228.

248. "Adam per Evam deceptus est, et non Eva per Adam. Quem vocavit ad culpam mulier, iustum est, ut eam in gubernationem assumat, ne iterum feminea facilitate labatur," Corpus, ed. Friedberg, vol. 1, col. 1255.

249. This chapter has been referred to already, p. 34, in showing that the subjugation of woman under man, besides its source in her alleged principal offense in original sin, is also derived from her supposed not-in-the-image-of-God status.

250. The Editio Romana still presupposes the authorship of Ambrose. Cf. the Notatio Correctorum to c. 19 (Corpus, ed. Friedberg, vol. 1, col. 1256; it attributes to Augustine the remaining pseudo-patristic chapters [13, 17]). Even Friedberg still seems to presuppose the authorship of Ambrose for c. 19; at any rate he raises no objection at this point. Corpus, vol. 1, col. 1255, n. 188.

251. "Mulier debet velare caput, quia non est imago Dei. Sed ut ostendatur subiecta, et quia prevaricatio per illam inchoata est, hoc signum debet habere, in ecclesia propter reverentiam episcopalem non habeat caput liberum, sed velamine tectum, non habeat potestatem loquendi, quia episcopus personam habet Christi. Quasi ergo ante iudicem Christum, ita ante episcopum sit, quia vicarius Domini est, propter peccatum originale debet subiecta videri," Corpus, ed. Friedberg, vol. 1, cols. 1255f.

252. See H. Fitting, Die Anfänge der Rechtsschule zu Bologna (Berlin-Leipzig, 1888), pp. 1 f., 100f.; R. Sohm, Institutionen. Geschichte und System des römischen Privatrechts, rev. by L. Mitteis, ed. by L. Wenger, 17th ed. (Munich, 1923), pp. 140ff.

253. Cf. v. Schulte, Geschichte, vol. 1, p. 98; J. Gaudemet, "Das römische Recht in Gratians Dekret," in ÖAKR 12 (1961): 182; H. E. Feine, "Vom Fortleben des römischen Rechts in der Kirche," in ZRG Kan. Abt. 42 (1956): 1, 14, et passim.

254. Cf. Sohm-Mitteis-Wenger, op. cit., pp. 143f.; Feine,

op. cit., pp. 1ff. et passim; also by Feine, Rechtsgeschichte (see
n. 3, above), pp. 65-134.

255. Cf. Gaudemet, op. cit., pp. 188ff. Different legal
historians, who have studied the use of Roman law in the Decretum
on the basis of early, handwritten materials, have reached the conclusion "that Roman law was used increasingly step by step in the
Decretum, and that this happened during the earliest period of its
composition" (Gaudemet, p. 179). The incipient rejection of Roman
law, Gaudemet maintains, was seen to be untenable in the long run,
after the great triumph of Roman law--as proved by the history of
the progressive formulation of the Decretum (pp. 188f.). The
canonists understood "how to place the superior juridical technique,
available to them in the burgeoning school at Bologna, in the service of church law" (p. 182).

256. "Constitutiones vero principum ecclesiasticis constitu-
tionibus non preminent, sed obsecuntur," Corpus, ed. Friedberg,
vol. 1, col. 19. The self-sufficiency and independence which Gregory
VII had won for spiritual and particularly for papal power, as over
against secular, found in this sentence authoritative statement as
well as theoretical and legal support. Cf. v. Schulte, Geschichte,
vol. 1, pp. 93ff.

257. "Ubi autem [constitutiones principum] evangelicis atque
canonicis decretis non obviaverint, omni reverentia dignae habeantur,"
Corpus, ed. Friedberg, vol. 1, col. 20. This principle is repeated
and used concretely in the dictum Gratiani, p.c. 4 in C. 15, q. 3
(Corpus, vol. 1, col. 752), almost word for word with specific reference to dist. 10 ("circa huius operis initium").

258. Cf., e.g., the summaries at cc. 9, 12 and 13: "Leges
imperatorum custodiri oporet;" "Serventur ab omnibus Romanorum
principum leges"; "Romana lex nullius temeritate debet corrumpi,"
Corpus, ed. Friedberg, vol. 1, cols. 21f.

259. Cf. Gaudemet, op. cit., pp. 177f.; v. Schulte, Geschichte, vol. 1, p. 93.

260. According to Thraede (see n. 202, above), cols. 216
and 246, no direct conclusions about the position of women in Roman
society can be drawn from the regulations of Roman law, since
Roman law because of its conservative character was burdened with
"inconsistencies between legal ideal and reality." But whatever may
have been the relation between the legal situation of women and their
societal situation in the Roman empire, it was the conception of
women in Roman law which was decisive for the place of women
in church law, rather than the possibly more progressive situation
of women in Roman society (Thraede, cols. 246, 265f.).

CHAPTER 2

1. Cf. Sohm-Mitteis-Wenger, op. cit., pp. 500f.; Weber (see chapter 1, n. 204), pp. 158ff.

2. H. Krüger in Gleichberechtigungsgesetz. Kommentar, by H. Krüger, E. Breetzke, K. Nowack (Munich, 1958), p. 45.

3. Cf. Sohm-Mitteis-Wenger, pp. 500f., 510; Weber, p. 161; M. Kaser, Das römische Privatrecht, section 1 (Munich, 1955), p. 70 ("The wife ... lives ... in the family of the husband 'filiae loco' "). Krüger rightly emphasizes, op. cit., p. 45: "Only a family law so contrary to nature as the Roman could succeed in making the father the power-holder--although the relation to children is naturally determined by their need to be taken care of--and to leave the mother under the husband, along with her (agnate) children as if she were one of them.

4. See on this Sohm-Mitteis-Wenger, pp. 504f.; E. Heilfron, Römisches Recht (Rechtsgeschichte und System des Privatrechts) als Grundlage des heutigen Rechts, 7th ed. (Mannheim, 1920), p. 515; Weber, p. 161.

5. "The manus mariti ... is a form of authority by the master of the house over those who belong to the house, a counterpart of the patria potestas," Sohm-Mitteis-Wenger, p. 510.

6. In principle the right of punishment also includes the authority to kill the wife, e.g., in case of adultery. Cf. Sohm-Mitteis-Wenger, pp. 510, 531; F. Schulz, Prinzipien des römischen Rechts (Berlin, 1954), p. 113; Kaser, Privatrecht I, p. 52f. Weber, p. 161, points to the power of the husband to sell his wife into slavery, which, it is true, was considered as a crime against the sacred, since about the second century B.C. See also Schulz, p. 131.

7. Cf. Sohm-Mitteis-Wenger, pp. 510, 531; Weber, p. 161. It was furthermore the duty of the censor to avenge the misuse of family authority. See Kaser, Privatrecht I, p. 53. But according to Schulz, p. 114, magistrates did not make great use of their power of coercion.

8. Cf. Sohm-Mitteis-Wenger, pp. 510, 512; Schulz, pp. 113f.; Weber, p. 162.

9. Sohm-Mitteis-Wenger, p. 508; Weber, p. 165; Kaser, Privatrecht I, pp. 239f.; Thraede, cols. 211f.

10. According to the law of the Twelve Tables, the posession (usus) of manus over the wife (within a year after marriage) could be prevented by the so-called trinoctium, that is, the annual

absence of the wife for three nights. Cf. Weber, pp. 164f.; Sohm-
Mitteis-Wenger, p. 506; Kaser, Privatrecht I, pp. 68f.

11. Cf. Sohm-Mitteis-Wenger, p. 508; Schulz, p. 131;
Weber, pp. 165, 195; Heilfron, p. 516.

12. Sohm-Mitteis-Wenger, p. 512.

13. Cf. Weber, p. 169; Heilfron, pp. 517f.; Sohm-Mitteis-
Wenger, pp. 511f.

14. According to Schulz, p. 132, such violation is "never
adultery, even in the law of the empire." Weber, p. 175, remarks
about the marriage laws of Caesar Augustus (lex Iulia de adulteriis,
18 B.C.): The laws are regulated "only against the wife and those
guilty with her, while unfaithfulness of the husband remained unpunished, except in the case of the stuprum, i.e., the seduction of
a reputable free female citizen." Cf. also Th. Mommsen, Römisches Strafrecht (reprint, Graz, 1955), pp. 638f.: "The free
Roman wife is obliged by moral law to have no sexual relationship
before her marriage and afterward only with her husband But the
husband is subject to similar moral law only in so far as injury to
the chastity of a virgin or the wife of someone else makes him a
partner in guilt." Concerning the Roman concept of adultery and
the different penalties for it, in the case of men and women, see
H. Bennecke, Die strafrechtliche Lehre vom Ehebruch in ihrer his-
torisch-dogmatischen Entwicklung (Aalen, 1971), pp. 2-33.

15. Cf. Weber, p. 188. (Even so only one who is "guilty
with a married woman" is called an adulterer.) See also Bennecke,
pp. 22-24; Kaser, Privatrecht I, p. 73; Heilfron, p. 529.

16. Cf. Sohm-Mitteis-Wenger, pp. 513f.; Weber, pp. 194f.;
Schulz, p. 100; Heilfron, p. 516.

17. According to Th. Mommsen, Römisches Staatsrecht,
3rd ed. (reprint, Graz, 1952), vol. 3, p. 9, women were always
granted citizenship in Roman theory; the lack of political rights did
not exclude them from citizenship. Nevertheless he says (p. 201):
"Giving an individual a first name ... is in the highest sense the
distinctive feature of a citizen, since a slave or a woman does not
legally have a first name but only a male citizen as he puts on the
clothing of a man...." Similarly (ibid., n. 4): "Ancient sepulchral
inscriptions teach us that for the full name of a woman, the sex and
the family to which she belongs are sufficient. Of course a woman
always had a first name too."

18. Cf. Heilfron, p. 111.

19. Corpus Iuris Civilis, I, 868. ("Feminae ab omnibus
efficiis civilibus vel publicis remotae sunt et ideo nec iudices esse
possunt nec magistratum gerere nec postulare nec pro alio intervenire
nec procuratores existere.") Dig. 50, 17, 2.

20. Cf. Mommsen, Staatsrecht, vol. 1, p. 493. It is clear from the classification of the three factors named, which all lead to official incompetence, that the female sex in Roman law is considered to be inferior. This is proved by the attributes and characterizations of women which are repeatedly alleged in connection with the legal limitations (or rather the causes of such limitations): "infirmitas sexus" Dig. 22, 6, 9 pr.; Dig. 49, 14, 18 pr.) and "imbecillitas sexus" (Dig. 16, 1, 2, 2, and in other places), the meaning of which is not weakness of the body but weakness of the mental power of women. The latter meaning refers especially to lack of "judgment and experience" (=infirmitas), of "will power and power of judgment" (=imbecillitas). Cf. H. Heumann and E. Seckel, Handlexikon zu den Quellen des römischen Rechts, 10th ed. (Graz, 1958), pp. 246, 265. See also Metz, "Statut," p. 78, n. 3, who notes that women are labeled as inferior in these and other characterizations in Roman law.

21. Cf. Schulz, p. 141.

22. Cf. Heilfron, p. 111; M. Kaser, Das römische Zivilprozessrecht (Rechtsgeschichte des Altertums, part 3, vol. 4) (Munich, 1966), p. 150; Schulz, p. 141. A very characteristic though not entirely convincing explanation of the basis and causation of this standard rule of the praetor is given in Dig. 3, 1, 1, 5: "ratio quidem prohibendi, ne contra pudicitiam sexui congruentem alienis causis se immisceant, ne virilibus officiis fungantur mulieres: origo vero introducta est a Carfania improbissima femina, quae inverecunde postulans et magistratum inquietans causam dedit edicto." Corpus Iuris Civilis, vol. 1, col. 35.

23. Cf. Schulz, p. 141 with n. 127.

24. Mommsen, Strafrecht, p. 369.

25. Cf. Heilfron, p. 111; Schulz, p. 142.

26. Cf. Heilfron, p. 552; Kaser, Privatrecht, vol. 2, p. 163; Weber, p. 193.

27. Cf. Kaser, Privatrecht, vol. 1, p. 575.

28. Heilfron, p. 111.

29. See similar evidence in n. 20, above.

30. "Testes autem adhiberi possunt ii, cum quibus testamenti factio est, sed neque mulier neque impubes neque servus neque mutus neque surdus neque furiosus nec cui bonis interdictum est nec is, quem leges iubent improbum intestabilemque esse, possunt in numero testium adhiberi," Inst. 2, 10, 6; Corpus Iuris Civilis, vol. 1, col. 17.

31. Cf. Heilfron, pp. 144f.; Sohm-Mitteis-Wenger, pp. 539f.; Kaser, Privatrecht, vol. 1, p. 75.

32. "Tutores constituuntur tam masculis, quam feminis: sed masculis quidem impuberibus dumtaxat propter aetatis infirmitatem, feminis autem tam impuberibus, quam puberibus, et propter sexus infirmitatem, et propter forensium rerum ignorantiam," Ulp. tit. 11, §1; quoted from Sohm-Mitteis-Wenger, p. 540. The tutela mulierum serves as protection of the guardian's own interest as the woman's closest heir. Cf. Heilfron, p. 144. Actually in some situations it was possible to circumvent the agnate tutel arrangement, which was very disadvantageous for women (ibid., p. 145).

33. Cf. Heilfron, p. 145; Kaser, Privatrecht, vol. 1, p. 313.

34. Cf. Heilfron, p. 145; Schulz, pp. 141f.; Kaser, Privatrecht, vol. 1, p. 313; Sohm-Mitteis-Wenger, p. 539.

35. Cf. Schulz, p. 142; Sohm-Mitteis-Wenger, p. 540.

36. Cf. Heilfron, pp. 111, 149; Kaser, Privatrecht, vol. 2, p. 81.

37. Cf. Weber, pp. 194f.; Kaser, Privatrecht, vol. 2, p. 80f.

38. Schulz, p. 141; cf. also Thraede, col. 216.

39. "Crimen lenocinii contrahunt, qui deprehensam in adulterio uxorem in matrimonio detinuerunt, non qui suspectam habuerunt adulteram," Cod. 9, 9, 2; Corpus Iuris Civilis, vol. 2, col. 374. In reference to the question raised (in C. 32, q. 1) it is concluded from this regulation of Corpus Iuris Civilis: "Si ergo, ut ex his auctoritatibus colligitur, adulteram retinere nulli permittitur, multo minus in coniugium duci licebit cuius pudicitiae nulla spes habetur," Dictum p.c. in C. 32, q. 1; Corpus, ed. Friedberg, vol. 1, col. 1118.

40. "Hoc in mulieribus non obtinet. Non enim eis permittitur maritos suos adulterii reos facere. Unde in libro, et tit. eodem, idem Imp. (Cod. 9, 9, 1): 'Publico iudicio non habere mulieres adulterii accusationem, quamvis de matrimonio violato queri velint, lex Julia declarat, que cum masculis iure mariti accusandi facultatem detulisset, non idem feminis privilegium detulit,'" Corpus ed. Friedberg, vol. 1, col. 1118. The Glossa Ordinaria (ad v. "accusationem") qualifies the statement of Gratian by affirming that women may accuse their husbands of adultery according to church law as well as secular law. Of course, it is said, a husband has a privileged right of complaint according to secular law: "Vir enim iure mariti, scilicet sine inscriptione, sine metu calumniae, intra XL dies utiles mulierem de adulterio accusat ... quod non facit mulier.

Alias vir et mulier ad paria iudicantur...." Furthermore, according to the gloss, secular law has been changed by the ecclesiastical to the extent that only the ecclesiastical punishment for adultery is still in effect. It is true that ad v. "privilegium" the gloss indicates that there is no clear agreement about the complainant rights of women in cases of adultery. (Cf. Corpus Juris Canonici in tres partes distinctum, flossis diversorum illustratum, Gregorii Papae XIII. iussu editum, editio novissima, Lyon, 1671 [hereafter cited as Corpus], vol. 1, cols. 1596f.) See also Freisen (see chapter 1, n. 36), pp. 841, 843ff.

41. Plöchl also, Eherecht, p. 104, confirms that there has been an influence from Roman legal conceptions on Gratian at this point. These conceptions picture man as the head of woman.

42. "Debet enim inter coniuges fides servari et sacramentum, que cum defuerint, non coniuges, sed adulteri appellantur," Corpus, ed. Friedberg, vol. 1, col. 1118.

43. To be sure, we gather from c. 23 in C. 32, q. 5 (cf. also C. 32, q. 5, cc. 19 and 20) that church law, in contrast to the secular, grants to women as well as to men the right of complaint because of adultery, and that there is equality of punishment. (In the dictum we have treated Gratian does not mention c. 23, although such a reference would have been obvious.) But even c. 23 leaves no doubt that despite this equalization in law there was no equalization of husband and wife in practice. The Glossa Ordinaria ad v. "Christiana" (in agreement with the content of the chapter) states the reasons as follows: "Probatur in hoc c[apitulo] quod uxor potest aeque accusare virum suum, sicut econverso: sed non solet hoc ita frequenter accidere, triplici de causa, scilicet pro verecundia, item pro timore, item quia vir cautius peccat, nec sic de facili deprehenditur," Corpus, ed. Friedberg, vol. 1, col. 1631. Not least important of the causes for the disadvantageous and humiliating situation of wives described here is the obligation of subordination according to classic canon law, as also their disadvantaged position in the secular realm.

44. The reference is to canon 7 of the first Council of Toledo (A.D. 400), which Gratian gives as c. 10 in C. 33, q. 2. Cf. Hefele (see chapter 1, n. 36) vol. 2, p. 78.

45. "Clericis autem conceditur, si uxores eorum peccaverint, sine mortis acerbitate habere eas in custodia, et ad ieiunia eas cogere, non tamen usque ad necem affligere," Dict. p.c. 9 in C. 33, q. 2; Corpus, ed. Friedberg, vol. 1, col. 1154.

46. According to Freisen (see chapter 1, n. 36), p. 842, ecclesiastical litigation is "secular litigation to which the church has made modificatious."

47. In dictum p.c. 4 in C. 15, q. 3 (Corpus, ed. Friedberg,

vol. 1, col. 752) Gratian expressly declares that according to canon law no one has the right of complaint who does not have that right in secular law. Gratian extends this rule, which goes back to Pseudo-Isidore (cf. C. 3, q. 5, c. 11: see Friedberg, Corpus, vol. 1, col. 517, n. 101) by making it into a positive formulation: anyone is competent to act as complainant who has such competence in secular law, if no contrary canons provide otherwise. Cf. on this E. Jacobi, "Der Prozess im Decretum Gratiani und bei den ältesten Dekretisten," in ZRG Kan Abt. 3 (1913): 252f.

48. The ecclesiastical legal sources that Gratian appeals to here (a regulation of the Council of Carthage in 419) repeat the Roman legal explanations concerning the witness. Cf. Gaudemet (see chapter 1, n. 253), p. 186.

49. In this connection the statement of Ambrosiaster (C. 33, q. 5, c. 17; cf. p. 36f.), which was also influenced by Roman law, should be remembered, to the effect that a woman cannot be a witness. The regulation of canon 20 of the Synod of Compiègne, A.D. 757 (c. 3 in C. 33, q. 1, in Gratian) proves that this Roman viewpoint influenced ecclesiastical marital law: "Si quis accepit uxorem, et habuit eam aliquo tempore, et ipsa femina dicit, quod numquam coisset cum ea, et ille vir dicit, quod sic fecit, in veritate viri consistat, quia vir est caput mulieris," Corpus, ed. Friedberg, vol. 1, col. 1150.

50. Cf. Jacobi, op. cit., p. 258, n. 3: "By iudices Gratian is also thinking of advocates, a fact which is explained by the common identification of iudices and advocati in Italy." See also Jacobi, p. 245, with n. 4.

51. "Hermafroditus an ad testamentum adhiberi possit, qualitas sexus incalescentis ostendit," C. 4, q. 2/3, § 22; Corpus, ed. Friedberg, vol. 1, col. 540.

52. The dictum Gratiani C. 15, q. 3 princ. (Corpus, ed. Friedberg, vol. 1, pp. 750f.), which treats of the exclusion of women from church offices (diaconate and presbyterate), offers a clear example of the mixing up of (deutero-) Pauline quotations with Roman legal regulations for women. Cf. pp. 28ff.

CHAPTER 3

1. Cf. v. Schulte, Geschichte, (see chapter 1, n. 2), vol. 1, p. 95; Feine (see chapter 1, n. 4), pp. 276f.

2. Cf. v. Schulte, Geschichte, vol. 1, pp. 94f.; Wasserschleben-Schulte, "Kanonen-und Dekretalensammlungen," in Realencyklopädie für protestantische Theologie und Kirche (hereafter cited

as RE), 3rd ed. (Leipzig, 1986-1913), vol. 10, pp. 11f.; Sägmüller (see Part I [preliminary], n. 1), vol. 1, pp. 237f.; Feine, pp. 276f.; Stickler (see chapter 1, n. 3), vol. 1, pp. 201f., 211f.

3. See v. Schulte, Geschichte, vol. 1, p. 68; Feine, pp. 276f.

4. Sägmüller, vol. 1, p. 235; cf. v. Schulte, Geschichte, vol. 1, p. 60.

5. Cf. v. Schulte, Geschichte, vol. 1, p. 67f.; Feine, p. 277; Stickler, vol. 1, p. 211.

6. Cf. v. Schulte, Geschichte, vol. 1, p. 67; Plöchl Geschichte, (see chapter 1, n. 91), vol. 2, p. 470; Stickler, vol. 1, p. 211.

7. Cf. v. Schulte, Geschichte, vol. 1, p. 95; Sägmüller, vol. 1, p. 237; Feine, p. 277; Stickler, vol. 1, pp. 201f., 219.

8. Cf. Feine, p. 279; v. Schulte, Geschichte, vol. 1, pp. 67, 212. According to Plöchl, Geschichte, vol. 2, p. 499, Gratian's collection spread from the new school of church law in Bologna to the schools in Pavia, Paris, Toulouse and Valencia.

9. Schulte, Geschichte, vol. 1, pp. 68f.; cf. Sägmüller, vol. 1, pp. 238f.; Stickler, vol. 1, pp. 210ff.; Feine, p. 277. In his preface to the Code (op. cit., p. XXIII), Cardinal Gasparri points to the private character of Gratian's collection.

10. Cf. v. Schulte, Geschichte, vol. 1, p. 68; Stickler, vol. 1, p. 211.

11. Cf. Sägmüller, vol. 1, p. 238; Ph. Schneider, Die Lehre von den Kirchenrechtsquellen, 2nd ed. (Regensburg, 1892), p. 124.

12. Cf. Plöchl, Geschichte, vol. 1, vol. 2, p. 486; Feine, p. 293.

13. Cf. W. Holtzmann's investigation, "Die Benutzung Gratians in der päpstlichen Kanzlei im 12. Jahrhundert," Studia Gratiana, vol. 1 (1953), pp. 325ff., esp. pp. 345-349. See also Wasserschleben-Schulte, op. cit., p. 11: The authority of the Decretum "had to be increased and strengthened all the more because the popes themselves used it and cited it in their decretals."

14. Cf. Plöchl, Geschichte, vol. 2, p. 473.

15. Cf. Artonne, "L'influence du Décret de Gratien sur les statuts synodaux," Studia Gratiana, vol. 2 (1954), pp. 645ff.

16. Cf. Feine, p. 277; Freisen (see chapter 1, n. 36), p. 10; v. Schulte, Geschichte, vol. 1, p. 68.

17. Cf. A. M. Koeniger, Grundriss einer Geschichte des katholischen Kirchenrechts (Cologne, 1919), p. 39; see also v. Schulte, Geschichte, vol. 1, p. 86.

18. Schulte, Geschichte, vol. 1, p. 70; cf. Plöchl, Geschichte, vol. 2, p. 473.

19. Cf. v. Schulte, Geschichte, vol. 1, p. 68, p. 94 with n. 8; Feine, p. 277; Plöchl, Geschichte, vol. 2, p. 473; Stickler, vol. 1, p. 211.

20. Cf. v. Schulte, Geschichte, vol. 1, pp. 94ff.; Feine, p. 277; G. Le Bras, "Les écritures dans le Décret de Gratien," in ZRG Kan. Abt. 27 (1938), p. 80 ("Le décret est une justification de l'oeuvre, de l'autorité de l'Eglise et le plus solide point d'appui du système des décrétales").

21. Cf. Sägmüller, vol. 1, p. 225; E. Seckel, "Pseudoisidor," in RE, vol. 16, pp. 267, 284; R. Grand, "Nouvelles remarques sur l'origine du Pseudo-Isidore, source du Décret de Gratien," Studia Gratiana, vol. 3 (1955), pp. 3, 5.

22. Cf. Freisen, p. 7; Feine, p. 277; Seckel, op. cit., p. 292.

23. Concerning the work and worth of the Correctores Romani, see v. Schulte, Geschichte, vol. 1, pp. 72ff. Freisen, p. 12, remarks that "the Correctores did not consistently carry out their plan to establish a critically satisfactory text" and thus did not accomplish their purpose (p. 11).

24. Cf. Seckel, pp. 292f.; v. Schulte, Geschichte, vol. 1, p. 73.

25. Cf. Seckel, pp. 292f.; v. Schulte, Geschichte, vol. 1, p. 73 with n. 34; Sägmüller, vol. 1, p. 225; H. Fuhrmann, "Pseudoisidor," in LThK, vol. 8, cols. 864-866.

26. Cf. pp. 33f. Munier, Sources patristique (see chapter 1, n. 198), p. 167, remarks: "Les textes des Pères ... ont servi directement à l'élaboration du droit classique. La doctrine canonique proposée par le Maître de Bologne se fonde simultanement sur les canons patristiques et sur les décisions émanant des organismes législatifs; Gratien continue de recourir aux témoignages patristiques pour fixer les règles de la législation." Similarly also Freisen, pp. 6f. Of course the auctoritas patrum is repressed by the decretists in favor of papal authority. Cf. Munier in the precis of his work just quoted: Revue de Droit Canonique (hereafter cited as RDC) 4 (Strassburg, 1954): 191f. (Note there also a reference to

the fact that the theoretical basis for this repression of the auctoritas patrum had already been given in dist. 20.)

27.   As one can see from the Code Fontes IX (Tabellae), cols. 13 sqq., many of the texts of Gratian's Decretum which we have discussed have influenced (or as we have often pointed out, stamped their impression on) the canon law operative today:

dist. 23, c. 25 and dist. 1 de cons. c. 41-43---can. 1306 § 1, Code	
dist. 4 de cons. c. 20---	can. 1342 § 2, Code
dist. 2 de cons. c. 29---	can. 845 § 1, Code
C. 33, q. 5, c. 11---	can. 1312 § 2, Code
C. 33, q. 5, c. 19---	can. 1262 § 2, Code

Besides Munier (see the previous note), R. Metz also points out the strong influence of the Church Fathers, especially Augustine, on the Code law through the medium of the Decretum Gratiani.   See his "Saint Augustine et le Code de Droit Canonique de 1917," in RDC 4 (1954): 405ff.

28.   On this see Metz, "Statut," (see Introduction, n. 9), pp. 97-108.

29.   Thus v. Schulte, Geschichte, vol. 1, p. 212; cf. also Stickler, vol. 1, pp. 201f., 211.

30.   Cf. Feine, p. 279. For the teaching method used in the Bologna school, see v. Schulte, Geschichte, vol. 1, p. 212ff. According to Schulte a greater significance for canon law appears in those writings which by the way included everything "which had usually been presented orally." (Ibid., vol. 1, pp. 215f.)

31.   The glosses are prior in time to the Summas and the apparatus.   So v. Schulte, vol. 1, p. 216; J. Junker, "Summen und Glossen. Beiträge zur Literaturgeschichte des kanonischen Rechts im zwölften Jahrhundert," in ZRG Kan. Abt. 14 (1925): 386, 403ff. See also St. Kuttner, Repertorium des Kanonistik (1140-1234), vol. 1, (Vatican City, 1937), pp. 3ff., 124.

32.   Cf. v. Schulte, Geschichte, vol. 1, pp. 215ff.; Feine, p. 279.

33.   Cf. v. Schulte, Geschichte, vol. 1, p. 95 with n. 11.

34.   Freisen, p. VI; cf. F. Thaner, ed.: Roland Bandinelli, Die Summa magistri Rolandi, nachmals Papstes Alexander III (Innsbruck 1824; reprint, Aalen, 1962), p. IV.

35.   J. F. v. Schulte, ed.: Paucapalea, Summa über das Decretum Gratiani, (reprint, Aalen, 1965), p. III; Thaner, p. IVf. ("The formation of canon law took place in the reciprocal feed-back between school and papacy.") Similarly, Freisen, p. VI.

36.   Thaner, p. IV.

37. Cf. Kuttner, op. cit., p. 126; A. van Hove, Prolegomena ad Codicem Juris Canonici (Commentarium Lovaniense in Codicem Juris Canonici), 2nd ed., (Mechlin-Rome, 1945), vol. 1/1, pp. 433f.

38. Kuttner, pp. 126f.

39. Cf. v. Schulte, Geschichte, vol. 1, p. 113; Kuttner, p. 126.

40. "... presbyteram suam, i.e. uxorem, quam in minoribus ordinibus constitutus habuit.... Vel presbyteras intelligimus conversas ecclesiae, quae et matricuriae appellantur, quia gerunt curas, quas matres gerere solent; vestimenta namque abluunt, pavem conficiunt et coquinatum praeparant," Paucapalea, Summa, ed. Schulte, p. 26.

41. See the discussion on pp. 21f.

42. See chapter 1, n. 36.

43. Etymologiarum libri XI, 1 (PL 82, c. 414); cf. Schulte, ed., (see n. 35, above), p. 11, n. 4. According to Browe (see chapter 1, n. 26), p. 2, Isidore took the idea from J. Solinus' third-century Collectanea rerum memorabilium (recogn. Mommsen, Berlin, 1864), p. 17, which is in large measure dependent on Plinius' Natural History and Mela's Chorography. (Cf. the article, "Julius Solinus," in Pauly's Realencyclopädie der classischen Altertumswissenschaft [Stuttgart, 1918], vol. 10/1, cols. 823-838.) Rufinus of Bologna follows Solinus immediately and explicitly. (See n. 84, below.)

44. "Nam solum mulier menstruale animal est, cuius contactu sanguinis fruges non germinant, acescunt musta, moriuntur herbae, amittunt arbores fructus, ferrum rubigo corrumpit, nigrescunt aera; si canes inde ederint in rabiem efferuntur," on dist. 5 pr. §2 v. "item mulier que menstrua patitur," ed. Schulte p. 11.

45. "Sed in poenitentiali Theodori contra legitur, ut si mulier ante praefinitum tempus praesumpserit ecclesiam intrare, tot dies in pane et aqua poeniteat, quot ecclesia carere debuerat," Paucapalea, Summa, ed. Schulte, p. 11. Schulte refers (ibid., n. 9) to the regulations of Theodore which Paucapalea probably has in mind. Theod. poen. I, 14, § 17sq. (in F. W. H. Wasserschleben, Die Bussordnungen der abendländischen Kirche (Halle, 1851; reprint, Graz, 1958), p. 199): "Mulieres autem menstruo tempore non intrent in ecclesiam neque communicent, nec sanctimoniales nec laicae. Si praesumant, tribus ebdomadis jejunent" (§ 17). "Similiter poeniteant, quae intrant ecclesiam ante mundum sanguinem post partum, i.e. XL dies" (§ 18).

46. "Beatus Greg. illam dicit in hoc non peccare, quae

gratias actura humiliter ecclesiam ingreditur. Theodorus vero de ea dicit, quae non causa orationis sed alia qualibet necessitate ducta temere ingreditur," Schulte, ed., p. 11.

47. Despite his generally progressive and humane attitude on the subject--for the time in which he lived--Gregory the Great calls menstruation vitium: "... que [mulieres] naturae suae vitio infirmantur," Corpus, ed. Friedberg, vol. 1, col. 8, Palea § 1.

48. Paucapalea, Summa, ed. Schulte, p. 11.

49. Ibid., pp. 133f.; see also the discussion on pp. 31f.

50. "Ita quod nec docere potest, nec testis esse, nec fidem dare, nec iudicare," Schulte, ed., p. 134.

51. Cf. Kuttner, op. cit., p. 128, with reference to Thaner, p. xxxiii (see also p. xli).

52. "Antiquitus diaconissas i.e. evangeliorum lectrices in ecclesiis ordinari moris fuisse, dubium non est, quarum nulla ante quadragesimum annum ordinari debebat, nec post ordinationem matrimonium eis contrahere ullomodo licebat," ed. Thaner, p. 121.

53. Only the Monophysite deaconess, as far as I could determine. Cf. Kalsbach (see chapter 1, n. 22), p. 58; J. Funk (see chapter 1, n. 22), p. 278. But the Monophysite deaconess had other functions as well.

54. Kalsbach, p. 94.

55. Freisen, p. 700.

56. So Kalsbach, pp. 88f., 112. While Kalsbach sees in the diaconissa and the abbatissa two completely different and independent offices, Schäfer (Kanonistenstifter [see chapter 1, n. 22], pp. 51ff. and his "Kanonissen und Diakonissen" [see chapter 1, n. 151], p. 58ff.) assumes the identity of the canonical abbess (=director of canonesses, not to be confused with the monastic abbess) and the deaconess, implying a development of the deaconess to the canonical abbess, in whose office the deaconess office continues to exist. According to this suggestion, the title deaconess was "gradually suppressed by the subsequently more common name of abbess, a result of the victorious spread of monasticism in the east and in the west," Kanonissenstifter, p. 55. Nevertheless, Schäfer (ibid., p. 58) expressly emphasizes that "the functions of the diaconate in the early church" extended quite far "beyond the direction of the (God-consecrated) women."

57. Cf. F. Diekamp-K. Jüssen, Katholische Dogmatik, 12th ed. (Münster, 1954), vol. 3, p. 373. See also Van der Meer (see Introduction, n. 7), p. 87, who (with a reference to Schäfer, "Kan-

onissen und Diakonissen," p. 60 with n. 1) refers to the fact that
Carthusian nuns still receive stole and maniple in the consecration
of virgins, although they are permitted to sing only the Epistle; the
stole, however, indicates that they formerly sang the Gospel also.
(When the bishop says to them, at the time of the maniple investi-
ture, "Act manly!," the absurd idea is suggested that actions like
the reading of the Gospel and the Epistle are in themselves beyond
the nature of women and really should be reserved for men, who
are thus "complete human beings.")

58. This will be considered in the treatment of the statements of the later decretists about the deaconess.

59. "Mulieres autem eiusdem ordinis [sacerdotii] nec sunt
nec esse possunt," on C. 15, q. 3 princ., ed. Thaner, p. 33.

60. "Dicimus ergo mulieris vocem nullatenus admittendam
in accusatione vel testificatione, nisi in crimine simoniae vel
haereseos vel laesae maiestatis sive in causa matrimonii," ed.
Thaner, p. 34.

61. On C. 33, q. 5, c. 11: "In hoc capitulo ostenditur, quod
si uxor abstinentiam cibi vel potus vel indumentorum vel alicuius
alterius excepto quam carnalis debiti ex consensu viri voverit, illo
in contrarium iubente votum observare non debet. Hic sensus atque
decretum praesentibus capitulis manifeste probatur; debet enim mulier viro scilicet capiti suo semper subesse, quod his quinque capitulis manifeste docetur," ed. Thaner, p. 199.

62. "Uxores nullomodo occidendas superius assignavit,
verumtamen absque mortis periculo poenitentiae custodiae manci-
pandae sunt," ed. Thaner, p. 191.

63. Cf. H. Singer, ed.: Rufinus of Bologna, Summa decretorum des Magister Rufinus (reprint, Aalen, 1963), pp. cxvi-cxvii;
Kuttner, op. cit., p. 132.

64. Cf. Singer, pp. lxxx, lxxxvi; Kuttner, p. 132.

65. "Satis mirandum ducimus, quomodo concilium diaconissas
post annos XL statuat ordinandas, cum Ambrosius dicat diaconas
ordinari esse contra auctoritatem. Ait enim, in epistol. (I.) ad
Timotheum super illum locum 'Mulieres similiter pudicas' etc.:
'Occasione horum verborum Catafrige dicunt diaconas debere ordinari, quod est contra auctoritatem,'" ed. Singer, p. 437.

66. Cf. Singer, p. 437, n. f. According to J. Schmid,
"Glossen," in LThK, vol. 4, cols. 968ff., the Glossa Ordinaria to
the New Testament was written by Anselm of Leon at the beginning
of the 12th century. Its usage was wide-spread in the 12th and
13th centuries, which explains its name.

67. That is to say, the Glossa Ordinaria to the Bible depends

mainly on the works of the Church Fathers; it is to a large extent only an extract from their exegesis. Cf. Schmid, loc. cit., cols. 968ff.; A. Kleinhans, "Exegesis," in LThK, vol. 3, col. 1284.

68. Cf. Singer, p. 437, n. f. Ambrosiaster's commentary on 1 Tim. 3:11 reads as follows: '"Mulieres similiter pudicas,' etc. (cf. 1 Tim 3:11). Quia sanctum praecipit creari episcopum, adaeque et diaconum, non utique disparem vult esse plebem.... Ideoque etiam mulieres, quae inferiores videntur, sine crimine vult esse, ut munda sit Ecclesia Dei. Sed Cataphrygae erroris occasionem captantes, propter quod post diaconos mulieres alloquitur, etiam ipsas diaconas ordinari debere vana praesumptione defendunt, cum sciant apostolos septem diaconos elegisse. Numquid nulla mulier tunc idonea inventa est, cum inter undecim apostolos sanctas mulieres fuisse legamus? Sed ut haeretici animum suum verbis, non sensu legis astruere videantur, Apostoli verbis contra sensum nituntur Apostoli; et cum ille mulierem in Ecclesiae in silentio esse debere praecipiat, illi e contra etiam auctoritatem in Ecclesia vindicent ministerii," PL 17, c. 496f.

69. Cf. chapter 1, n. 196.

70. "Sed aliud est eas ordinari sacramento tenus ad altaris officium, sicut ordinantur diacones: quod quidem prohibetur; aliud ad aliquod aliud ecclesie ministerium: quod hic permittitur. Hodie tamen huiusmodi diaconisse in ecclesia non inveniuntur, sed forte loco earum abbatisse ordinantur," ed. Singer, p. 437.

71. Cf. Kalsbach, pp. 69ff. 109; J. Funk (see chapter 1, n. 22), p. 278.

72. Because of the indicated characteristics of ordination, several writers come to a conclusion opposite to that of Rufinus. Cf. chapter 1, p. 24, with n. 151.

73. Cf. Kalsbach, p. 11.

74. So too M. Meinertz, Die Pastoralbriefe des heiligen Paulus (Die Heilige Schrift des Neuen Testaments, vol. 7), 4th ed. (Bonn, 1931), p. 46.

75. Kalsbach, p. 11 (who refers in n. 2, p. 11, to Belser, Meinertz, Wohlenberg); cf. Schäfer, Kanonissenstifter, p. 65. The most recent exegesis comes to the same conclusion: cf. G. Holtz, Die Pastoralbriefe (Theologischer Handkommentar zum Neuen Testament, vol. 13) (Berlin, 1965), p. 85.

76. "Deacons must likewise be honorable, not double-tongued, not addicted to much wine, not greedy for gain."

77. Cf. n. 68, above: "... mulieres, quae inferiores videntur." Note there also the reference to Paul's command of

silence for women (1 Cor. 14:34f.). Of course Ambrosiaster overlooks the fact that Paul himself permitted women helpers in his
missionary activity, who could not have been on principle excluded
from the ministry of the word. (Cf. Rom. 16:1, 3, 12; 1 Cor. 16:
19, among other references.) So too Holtz, op. cit., p. 73, who
also (p. 72, with n. 88) points to the fact that grave doubts have
been raised--from the standpoint of textual criticism--in regard to
1 Cor. 14:34-36. See also chapter 6, n. 158.

78. Cf. Kalsbach, pp. 89, 94.

79. Cf. Kalsbach, pp. 90f; Schäfer, "Kanonissen und Diakonissen," p. 57; J. Funk, pp. 281f. According to the Code, consecration of abbesses is rated as simply benediction, i. e., as a
sacramental. Cf. H. Hanstein, Ordensrecht (Paderborn, 1953), p.
244; J. Baucher, "Abbesses," in DDC, vol. 1, cols. 65f., where
it is specifically emphasized that the benedictio of the abbatissa con-
fers no special authority in comparison to the consecration of abbots, which according to canon 625 of the Code gives authority to
confer minor orders and public blessing.

80. "In secundo capitulo (= C. 20, q. 1, c. 13) dicitur de
diaconissa, que ante annum XL. non debet velari, i. e. ordinari ut
infra Cs. XXVII, q. I c. Diaconissam (c. 23), " ed. Singer, p.
382.

81. "Sanctimoniales ante annum quadragesimum non uelentur, "
Corpus, ed. Friedberg, vol. 1, col. 846.

82. "Nisi infirmetur; tunc enim etiam per puerum, si magna
necessitas ingruerit, poterit communicare infirmum, " ed. Singer,
p. 554; on this question Rufinus refers specifically to Burchard.
Cf. Singer, p. 554 with n. h.

83. Cf. n. 43, above. According to Singer, p. cxxiv, the
work of Solinus given there belonged "to the 'school authors' who
were used in the Middle Ages for instruction in geography and natural science. "

84. "Adeo autem execrabilis et immundus est sanguis ille,
sicut ait Iulius Solinus in libro de mirabilibus mundi, ut eius contactu fruges non germinent, arescant arbusta, moriantur herbe,
amittant arbores fetus, nigrescant era, si canes inde ederint in
rabiem efferantur. " Sexual intercourse during menstruation could
cause abortions: "Non autem solum propter immunditiam sanguinis
a menstruata arcenda est voluptas, sed etiam ne vitiosus fetus ex
illo coitu nascatur..., " ed. Singer, p. 16; in Singer, p. 17, more
precise statements are made about this and additional very strange
viewpoints of medical "science" of the time. Cf. also the statements of Paucapalea, p. 48.

85. "Illud de enixa vero muliere hodie evacuatum est propter

ecclesie contrariam consuetudinem et maxime propter illud ex peni-
tentiali Theodori...," ed. Singer, p. 16 with n. a; cf. p. 48, with
n. 45, above.

86. On C. 33, q. 5, c. 17: "Mulierem (etc.) nec testis
esse in causis criminalibus; nam in civilibus potest esse testis,
preterquam in testamento," ed. Singer, pp. 506f.

87. On C. 4, q. 2/3: "Item queritur in secunda, quomodo
generaliter sit verum quod quicunque prohibetur ab accusatione,
prohibeatur et ab accusationis testificatione, cum mulieres secundum
leges accusare non possint, tamen possint esse testes, ut infra Cs.
XV. q. III. De crimine quod publicorum (c. 1). Sed femine in
causis utique civilibus possunt esse testes, in criminalibus autem,
in quibus solis instituitur accusatio, testes esse non valent, ut infra
Cs. XXXIII. q. ult. cap. ult. (17). Si quis autem velit contendere
quod in criminibus etiam mulierum testimonium accipietur, respond-
eatur quia, etsi secundum legem forte in secularibus criminibus
admitterentur, secundum canones tamen in ecclesiasticis criminibus
nunquam mulierum testimonium accipietur," ed. Singer, p. 274.
Yet Rufinus allows women complainant rights in case of adultery,
though they are clearly not as favorable as those granted to men.
Rufinus (ed. Singer, p. 491), following C. 32, q. 5, c. 23: "Hic
evidenter docetur quia mulieres possunt accusare viros de adulterio,
sed non facile, scil. de suspitione, et sine metu calumnie, quemadmodum viri possunt...," ed. Singer, p. 491.

88. Cf. Kuttner, op. cit., p. 135; von Hove (see n. 37,
above), vol. 1/1, p. 434.

89. "Antiquitus ordinabantur in ecclesiis diaconisse, i. e.
evangeliorum lectrices, que quia modo non sunt in ecclesia, forsitan
dicemus eas abbatissas et iste ante quadragesimum annum ordinari
non debent," Ms. Bamberg Patr. 118 (B. III. 21), fol. 225rb, quoted
from F. Gillmann, "Weibliche Kleriker nach dem Urteil der Frühscholastik," in AkKR (see chapter 1, n. 2), 93 (1913): 244, n. 3;
this passage is lacking in the Schulte edition of Stephan's Summa,
which is likewise the case in some of the following statements by
Stephan on the question before us.

90. See p. 49.

91. See p. 53.

92. "In primitiva ecclesia permittebatur quibusdam sancti-
monialibus legere evangelium, que diaconisse vocabantur, quod
hodie non fit," Ms. cit., fol. 199va, quoted from Gillmann, op.
cit., p. 244, n. 4.

93. See Schäfer, Kanonissenstifter, pp. 55, 60, 272f.;
Zscharnack (see chapter 1, n. 22), pp. 153ff.

94. Similarly, Kalsbach, pp. 88f.

95. "Idem posset dicere de quolibet inferiori ordine. Set de hoc dicit, quia forte videtur, quoniam antiquitus fiebant diaconisse, qui ordo hodie in ecclesia non est," Ms. cit. fol. 206vb, quoted from Gillmann, p. 244, n. 5.

96. Cf. ed. Schulte, p. 272; see n. 82, above.

97. "Pallas vero et vela que in sanctuario sordidata fuerint ... diaconi cum humilibus ministris intra sanctuarium, et velamina dominicae mensae abluant, ne forte pulvis dominici corporis male decidat," Corpus, ed. Friedberg, vol. 1, col. 1304. The chapter is taken from epistola II of Pseudo-Clemens, which in part existed before the Pseudo-Isidore collection (cf. Friedberg 1.c., n. 404), and supports canon 1306, § 2, the Code (p. 445, n. 2). See chapter 1, n. 37.

98. On dist. 1 de cons. c. 40, § 1: "His hodie generali consuetudine derogatum est. Forte autem non dicetur inconveniens, sie haec religiosis feminis lavanda mandentur, sicut in ecclesia Mediolanensi veglonissae, i.e. quaedam religiosae mulieres oblatas praeparant ad sacrificium altaris.... Et huiusmodi veglonissae ecclesiae suppellectilem lavant, laceratum reconsuunt, oblatas ut diximus in usum sacrificii praeparant," ed. Schulte, p. 267.

99. The Summa was completed after 1171; cf. Kuttner, p. 145; van Hove, vol. 1/1, pp. 434f.

100. So Kuttner, p. 145 (who refers in n. 1, p. 145, to Maasen, Schulte, Singer, Gillmann). Joannes Faventinus himself acknowledges this in his preface. Cf. Singer, p. xlvi, with n. 4.

101. Cf. Gillmann (see n. 89, above), p. 245 with n. 3 (Gillmann is dependent on Ms. München lat. 3873 fol. 81vb); see pp. 54f.

102. Cf. Gillmann, pp. 245f.; see pp. 50f.

103. "Est vellum ordinationis, quod XL. anno dabatur diaconissis," Ms. cit., fol. 95va, quoted by Gillmann, p. 246, with n. 2. The same view is expressed in a gloss which, as Gillmann (p. 345, n. 1) notes, is added by a later hand in the margin of the Bamberg ms. of Stephan's Summa on dict. Grat. p.c. 10 in C. 20, q.1 ad v. "velamen": "Multa sunt velamina, sicut invenire poteris in diversis huius libri capitulis. Est enim velamen conversionis.... Est et velamen consecracionis.... Est et velamen ordinacionis, quod modo obsolevit, quod inponebatur diaconissis et non nisi post XL annos...."

104. So Schäfer, Kanonissen und Diakonissen, pp. 62, 64 (with sources). There is no mention of veil presentation to the deaconess in the consecration formulary of the Apostolic Constitutions (VIII, 20), and also none in the formulary recorded by J. A.

Assemani (Cod. liturg. XI, Rome, 1763, 115)--although there it is presupposed that the ordinand is wearing a veil: the stole is placed under the veil. It is true that the presentation of the veil is specifically mentioned in the consecration ritual recorded by M. Blastares, Syntagma alphabeticum lit. Γ, c. XI (PG 144, c. 1175), yet the presentation of the veil is not the core of the ordination ritual but rather the laying on of hands during the consecration prayer.

105. Cf. Singer, p. xlvif. ; Kuttner, p. 145.

106. Cf. van Hove, vol. 1/1, pp. 436f. ; Kuttner, p. 169. (It can be assumed that the Frenchman Stephan of Tournay, educated in Bologna, stimulated Decretum studies in France.) Ibid., p. 169, with n. 5 and p. 135.

107. On the basis of his investigations, T. P. McLaughlin, ed., The Summa Parisiensis on the Decretum Gratiani (Toronto, 1952), p. xxxiff., places the origin of the Summa as early as about 1160--in contrast to previous researchers: Schulte (1160's or 1170's), Gillmann and Kuttner (about 1170).

108. So McLaughlin, pp. xxvif. Against Schulte and Kuttner (who refers to Schulte), McLaughlin disputes the dependence of the Summa Parisiensis on Rufinus. Ibid., pp. xxviif., xxxiii.

109. "[Mulieres] non debent ordinari ut clerici, " ed. McLaughlin, p. 32; see also the discussion on pp. 21f.

110. "Hic innuitur quod modo non sunt diaconissae sicut in primitiva ecclesia, " ed. McLaughlin, p. 175.

111. "Vel convertam quae vivit de beneficio ecclesiae, vel quae fuit uxor eius qui est presbyter, " ed. cit., p. 32.

112. On dict. Grat. p. c. 24 in dist. 23 ad v. "Vasa": "... Et licet audias mulierem consecrari non intelligas quod propterea liceat mulieribus vasa vel vestimenta contingere; intellige circa altare ornando eis esse permissum alibi. Propter necessitatem vestimentorum, i. e. abluendum vel suendum, licet, " ed. cit., p. 24. Stephan of Tournay writes in similar fashion (see p. 55).

113. On dist. 23, c. 29, ad v. "Mulier": "De muliere dixerat (scil. Gratianus) quod non debet offerre incensum circa altare, etc., et ea occasione aliud removendum removet, ne scilicet doceat viros, nam mulieres potest abbatissa, " ed. cit., p. 24f. ; also on C. 33, q. 5, c. 17 v. "Mulierem constat, nec docere potest": "Mulieri non licet viros in conventu [orig.: convento] docere. Nec est contra quod sanctimonialis mulieres docere potest, " ed. cit., p. 255.

114. "Magister epilogat quod dictum est quia vota abstinentiae ante permissa, potest vir cassare si voluerit. Secus autem

ostenditur in voto continentiae, quia [si] semel ex consensu viri continentiam voverit, deinceps ad servitutem praeteritam eam revocare non potest. In hoc etenim non ad imparia judicantur, licet in aliis operibus vir caput sit mulieris," ed. cit. , p. 254.

115. Ad v. "nec testis esse": "Videtur huic decreto obviare: 'Ex eo enim quod prohibet Lex Julia de adulteris mulierem damnatam testari, potest ostendi mulierem non damnatam testem exsistere posse.' Sed in testamentis mulier testis exsistere non potest, quoniam in testamentis septem testes desiderantur, puberes, masculi, cives Romani. Viri etiam testes vocantur ubi testes exsistant. Mulier testamentum scire non potest, veluti solutionem factam esse potest mulier astruere non debet" (the last sentence is corrupt), ed. cit. , p. 255 with n. 46.

116. "In aliis vero contractibus veluti in emptione, venditione, locatione, conductione, mulier testis esse potest, licet a civilibus officiis ob sexus fragilitatem sint exemptae," ed. cit. , p. 255.

117. Cf. p. 29.

118. Cf. H. W. Hertzberg, "Debora und Deboralied," in RGG, vol. 2, cols. 52f.

119. On C. 33, q. 5, c. 17 ad v. "nec iudicare"; "nec contra quod in veteri testamento mulieres iudicasse leguntur. Miracula etenim veteris testamenti magis sunt admiranda quam in exemplum humanae actionis trahenda," ed. cit. , p. 255.

120. Cf. Kuttner, p. 180 (who refers to Gillmann, "Die Heimat und die Entstehungszeit der Summa Monacensis," in AkKR 102 (1922): 25-27); van Hove, vol. 1/1, p. 437.

121. Cf. on this Gillmann, "Weibliche Kleriker," p. 245, with n. 1; see also p. 56, with n. 103, above.

122. "Velamen ordinis quondam dabatur diaconissis, que nunc non sunt in ecclesia, set non ante XL. annum," Ms. München, lat. 16084, fol. 25ra; quoted from Gillmann, "Weibliche Kleriker," p. 245 with n. 1.

123. (Manus inpositio) "consecratoria religionis soli episcopo conpetit et est sacramentum et certis temporibus fieri debet.... Cum sit sacramentum, regulariter non iteratur," Ms. cit. , fol. 7vb; quoted from Gillmann, "Weibliche Kleriker," p. 245, n. 2; also by Gillmann, "Die Siebenzahl der Sakramente bei den Glossatoren des Gratianischen Dekrets," in Der Katholik 89 (1909), p. 190, n. 1.

124. Cf. the discussion on p. 51. Concerning Rufinus's concept of sacraments, see also Gillmann, "Die Siebenzahl der Sakramente," pp. 184ff.

125. Cf. Kuttner, Repertorium, p. 151. (Here the Summa is considered the work of the Bologna school; but see Kuttner, "Ré-flexions sur les Brocards des Glossateurs," in Mélanges Joseph de Ghellinck II (Gembloux, 1951), pp. 783-787.) The text of the sources from the Summa has been graciously made available to me by my teacher, Prof. Dr. P. J. Kessler, who is engaged in the prepara-tion of the edition of Sicardus's Summa.

126. Cf. Kuttner, op. cit., p. 151; van Hove vol. 1/1, p. 435.

127. Kuttner, p. 151; cf. v. Schulte, Geschichte, vol. 1, p. 144.

128. "Qui sacerdotes esse non possunt, sacerdotes accusare non possunt nec in eos testificari," Ms. München lat. 4555, fol. 46r.

129. "Mulier caput velare debet duplici ex causa: propter peccatum originale et propter reverentiam episcopalem; non habet potestatem loquendi coram episcopo. Item docere non potest et similia," Ms. cit., fol. 46r.

130. One gathers from another, liturgical work by Sicardus, the so-called Mitrale, that he, like Rufinus, agrees with the views of Solinus (see n. 84, above) about the impurity and harmfulness of menstruation blood. Sicardus gives a remarkable justification for the regulation of Lev. 12:1ff., which he considers equally binding in the New Covenant (the regulation makes women unclean and unable to enter the temple for 40 days after the birth of a son and 80 days after the birth of a daughter): "Duo fuere in lege praecepta, quorum alterum ad parientem, alterum pertinebat ad partum. Ad parientem, ut si mulier masculum pareret, XLta diebus ab ingressu templi ve-luti immunda cessaret: quia puerperium in immunditia conceptum dicitur XLta diebus informe; at si feminam, spatium temporis dupli-caret: sanguis enim menstruus, qui partum comitatur, usque adeo censetur immundus, ut eius tactu, sicut Solimus ait, fruges arescant et herbae moriantur. Sed quare tempus pro femina duplicatur? Solutio: quia dupla est feminei germinis maledictio; habuit enim maledictionem Adae, et insuper, 'In dolore paries,' vel quia, sicut ait peritia physicorum, feminae in conceptu manent informes duplo tempore masculorum, Mitrale V c. 11, PL 213, 242. It is true that in his Summa (on dist. 5) Sicardus--in agreement with the viewpoint of Gregory the Great (dist. 5, c. 2)--remarks as follows: "In lege autem continetur de muliere enixa menstruata, quod arcea-tur ab ingressu templi, hodie vero ex humilitate intrans non argui-tur," Ms. cit., fol. 3r; yet the limitation "ex humilitate intrans" remains characteristic of his attitude toward this question!

131. "Reverentia [utensilium] consistit in faciendo et non faciendo.... In non faciendo.... Item non nisi a sacris hominibus utensilia contractentur nec etiam a monialibus contractentur, ut

d. XXIII (Ms.: XLII) Sacratas (c. 25)," Ms. cit., fol. 74r. Thus
Sicardus agrees here with this Pseudo-Isidorian decretal. A conception of respect which ignores essentials in favor of superficiali-
ties also lies at the basis of the passage about the proper attitude
toward the sacrament of the altar (on dist. 2 de cons.): "tractandi
reverentia hec est, ut sacerdotes vel quicumque nitidi, nitide faciant
hostias, factas conservent, ut nichil habeant inpuritatis. Similiter
in vino et aqua, ut B[urch.] 1. I 'Panis,'" Ms. cit., fol. 76r.
Such an "impurity" arises, in the judgment of the times, when wom-
en touch the host. In the passage from Burchard (V 29, PL 140,
c. 758) to which Sicardus refers, besides clergy only boys may
therefore take charge of the (unconsecrated) hosts. Cf. also Rather
of Verona (890-974): "nulla femina ad altare accedat, nec calicem
Domini tangat. Corporale mundissimum sit," PL 136, c. 559.

132. In its context the following passage must be understood
in that sense: "Quid si iudeus vel gentilis ordines et dignitatis ac-
ceperit consecrationem? R[espondent] quidam, quod esset episcopus.
E contra quod si mulier consecraretur. Item quod foris est, quomodo ordinabitur? Item nonne si servus daret sentenciam, retracta-
retur?," Ms. cit., fol. 12r.

133. "Est preterea in coniugio quoddam vestigium trinitatis.
Est enim vir principium, unde mulier; et uterque principium, unde
proles," Ms. cit., fol. 60v.

134. "Vir est principium mulieris et finis, sicut Deus est
principium et finis totius creaturae," Summa Theologiae I, q. 93,
a. 4 and 1.

135. This attitude of submissiveness is demanded from wom-
en in all spheres, except, apparently, that of marriage intimacy:
(on C. 35): "pares sunt coniuges in continentia.... In ceteris vero
vir est caput uxoris; unde vir sine consensu uxoris potest votum
abstinentie facere, non autem uxor sine viro. Immo si, cum erat
in capitulo, fecerit, post acceptus vir, si voluerit, inmutabit. Deni-
que si abnuit quod prius annuerat, ut calamus vento sic cedat femina
uiro," Ms. cit., fol. 70r.

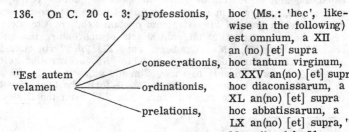

136. On C. 20 q. 3: professionis, hoc (Ms.: 'hec', likewise in the following)
est omnium, a XII
an(no) [et] supra

consecrationis, hoc tantum virginum,
a XXV an(no) [et] supra

"Est autem
velamen ordinationis, hoc diaconissarum, a
XL an(no) [et] supra

prelationis, hoc abbatissarum, a
LX an(no) [et] supra,"
Ms. cit., fol. 51r.

But that is, as far as I know, the only place where Sicardus mentions the deaconess.

137. Cf. Gillmann, "Die Siebenzahl der Sakramente," (see n. 123, above), p. 199, n. 2.

138. Cf. Kuttner, p. 149; van Hove, vol. 1/1, p. 435.

139. According to v. Schulte, Geschichte, vol. 1, p. 141, Simon repeatedly refers to Joannes Faventius and considers his work to be the perfect summa.

140. "Et est velum ordinationis, quod olim dabatur diaconissis quadragenariis...," Bs. pag. 71a, Rs. fol. 66r/v; quoted from J. Juncker, "Die Summa des Simon von Bisignano und seine Glossen," in ZRG Kan. Abt. (see chapter 1, n. 2) 15 (1926): 474; Gillmann's Weibliche Kleriker does not deal with Simon's statement on C. 20, q. 1, c. 13.

141. On dist. 32, c. 19 ("Mulieres, quae apud Graecos presbiterae appellantur, ... in ecclesia tanquam ordinatas constitui non debere") ad v. "tanquam ordinatas constitui": "ut scilicet tanquam prebendam stipendium ecclesie habeat. Alias autem elemosina ei fieri potest. Vel constitui non debet abbatissa vel inter sacras virgines consecrari," Ms. Bamberg Can. 38 (D. II. 20), fol. 5ra; quoted from Gillmann, op. cit., p. 245, n. 2.

142. Cf. Juncker, op. cit., p. 479; also see Juncker, Summen und Glossen, in ZRG. Kan. Abt. 14 (1925), p. 474.

143. Ad v. "virginem": "Virginem esse abbatissam convenit, quia ecclesiam virginem prefigurat. Episcopus autem Christum significat, unde non requiritur in eo virg[i]nitas corporis. Nam et Christus duas legitur habuisse uxores ... s.," Ph. fol. 162ra; quoted from Juncker, Die Summa des Simon, p. 474.

144. On dist. 26, c. 2, ad v. "sicut femina": "Qu[eritur] quare corrupta non possit in abbatissam promoveri, quemadmodum et corrumpens etiam miles per fornicationem in episcopum possit promoveri. Respon[sio]: Formam Christi gerit episcopus, formam ecclesie abbatissa figurat. Christus esse quodammodo divisit: primo copulando sibi ecclesiam de iudeis in apostolis, deinde per apostolos in gentibus, que quidem senper una fuit et unica. Unde apostolus: despondi enim vos uni viro virginem castam exhibere Christo. Hinc ergo habes, quod non est mirum, si iste promoveatur, illa autem non. Secundum Si," Ms. Bamberg, can. 17, fol. 77rb; quoted from Juncker, Die Summa des Simon, p. 471. As Juncker (loc. cit., pp. 471ff.) has been able to show, Simon's glosses on C. 20, q. 1, c. 12--quoted in the previous footnote--form the basis for this text (which carries the symbol "secundum Si") from the Distinctiones Bambergenses.

145. See the discussion on p. 121.

146. Cf. Van der Meer (see Introduction, n. 7), pp. 128ff;

R. A. van Eyden, "Die Frau im Kirchenamt. Plädoyer für die Revision einer traditionellen Haltung," in Wort und Wahrheit 22 (1967): 355.

147. As will be shown in chapter 6, p. 115, Eph. 5 is a marriage exhortation marked by the patriarchal conceptual level of the author; no conclusions about clerical office can be drawn from it.

148. Cf. Van der Meer, pp. 132f.; v. Eyden, op. cit., p. 355. The insignia of the bishop, the ring, which the abbess also wears, has no biblical basis.

149. "I betrothed you to one husband, in order to bring you as a pure virgin to Christ."

150. So too Van der Meer, p. 133.

151. Cf. van Hove, vol. 1/1, p. 436; v. Schulte, Geschichte, vol. 1, p. 161 (not before 1187). The Summa has not yet been edited, but through mediation of my teacher, Prof. Dr. P. J. Kessler, Prof. A. M. Stickler has graciously placed at my disposal a microfilm of Mss. München lat. 10247 and Vatican lat. 2280. In this way it was possible for me to take into account several texts not used by Gillmann in "Weibliche Kleriker," pp. 246-249.

152. Cf. v. Schulte, Geschichte, vol. 1, pp. 163ff.; Kuttner, pp. 157f.; van Hove, vol. 1/1, pp. 435f.

153. "Set quomodo dicit Calcedonense concilium diaconissas debere ordinari, cum Ambrosius, qui precessit, dicat hoc esse contra auctoritatem super illum locum apostoli in prima epistola ad Timotheum: 'Mulieres similiter oportet esse pudicas' etc. Ait enim occasione horum verborum: Catafrige dicunt diaconissas debere ordinari, quod est contra auctoritatem," Ms. München lat. 10247, fol. 229ra.

154. "Set ordinabantur diaconisse, i.e. eligebantur et quadam sollempnitate constituebantur ad aliquod officium, quod conpetit diaconis. Forte cantabant et dicebant evangelium in matutinis et orationem et tale officium et talis prelatio dicebatur diaconatus," Ms. cit., l. c.

155. "Tale officium nunc explent abbatissas in quibusdam locis nec modo tales diaconisse apud nos inveniuntur, nisi quis dicat abbatissas esse loco earum et de tali ordinatione loquitur concilium Calcedonense, Ambrosius loquitur de ordinatione ad ordines," Ms. cit., l. c.

156. Thus on C. 20, q. 1, c. 13 ad v. "ut non velentur": "Velo ordinationis, i.e. non ordinentur, ut sint diaconisse. Solebant enim olim quedam monace ordinari in diaconissas, non quoad ordinem

set quoad quoddam ministerium, ut in matutino in lectionibus annun-
cient evangelium vel aliud consimile. Set modo hoc non fit, set sine
speciali institutione adhuc quedam monace in quibusdam locis in matutino anuntia[n]t evangelium," Ms. Vatikan lat. 2280, fol. 233 rb;
similarly on C. 11, q. 1, c. 38 ad v. "diaconissam": "Olim sic
dicebantur quedam monache a quodam officio. Forte modo non sunt,
nomen tamen adhuc retinetur, unde et quelibet monacha dicitur qu-
andoque diaconissa," Ms. Vat., fol. 170 vb. By the diaconissa of
c. 30 in C. 27, q. 1 Huguccio likewise understands any God-dedicated woman or nun: "pro qualibet devota vel monacha intelligitur
[diaconissa]," Ms. Vat., fol. 258rb. Huguccio, like his predecessors, relates ch. 13 in C. 20, q. 1, which concerns veiling of dedicated virgins, to the deaconess and therefore mistakenly equates the
subject of this chapter with that of canon 15 of Chalcedon: "Velum
ordinationis est, quod olim dabatur diaconissis XL. anno, ut infra
ead. Sanctimoniales (c. 13) et XXVII. q. 1 Diaconissam (C. 23)...,"
Ms. Vat., fol. 233rb.

157. "Alii dicunt, quod olim mulier ordinabatur usque ad
diaconatum, postea fuit prohibitum tempore Ambrosii, postea iterum
ordinabantur tempore huius concilii, nunc non ordinantur. Set prima
expositio prevalet," Ms. München 10247, fol. 229ra.

158. "Set dico, quod mulier ordinem accipere non potest.
Quid inpedit? Constitutio ecclesie et sexus, i. e. constitutio ecclesie
facta propter sexum. Si ergo de facto ordinetur femina, non accipit
ordinem, unde prohibetur exercere officia ordinum, ut di. XXIII.
Sacratas (c. 25)," Ms. cit., 1. c.

159. On C. 27, q. 1, c. 23 ad v. "ordinari": "Quid si
est ermafroditus? Distinguitur circa ordinem recipiendum sicut
circa testimonium faciendum in testamento, ut IIII. q. III. Item
ermafroditus (c. 3 § 22). Si ergo magis calet in feminam quam in
virum, non recipit ordinem, si secontra, recipere potest, set non
debet [Ms.: deberet] ordinari propter deformitatem et menstruosita-
tem, arg. di. XXXVI. Illiteratos (c. 1), et di. XLVIIII. c. ult.
Quid si equaliter calet in utrumque? Non recipit ordinem," Ms.
cit., l. c. Huguccio expresses the same point of view to C. 4,
q. 2 and 3, c. 3 22 ad v. "sexus incalescentis": "... Si quidem
habet barbam et semper vult exercere virilia et non feminea et
semper vult conversare cum viris et non cum feminis, signum est,
quod virilis sexus in eo prevalet et tunc potest esse testis, ubi mulier non admittitur, scil. in testamento et in ultimis voluntatibus,
tunc etiam ordinari potest. Si vero caret barba et semper vult
esse cum feminis et exercere feminea opera, iudicium est, quod
femininus [Ms.: feminini] sextus in eo prevalet, et tunc non
admittitur ad testimonium, ubi femina non admittitur, scil. in
testamento, set nec tunc ordinari potest, quia femina ordinem non
recipit," Ms. Vat. 2280, fol. 140va. For example, Huguccio includes in virilia opera (officia) touching the consecrated vessels
and cloths during the church services. For that reason women,
even nuns, he says, are to be excluded from such duties. Thus

on dist. 1 de cons. c. 41: "... nec etiam illis [scil. monialibus sacratis et deo dicatis] licet contractare vel contingere set intelligo ministrando quod est officium virorum ut d. XXIII Sacratas (c. 25). De hoc enim ibi reprehenduntur quia virilia officia exercebant, alias licet eis illa [scil. sacra vasa et vestimenta] tangere et honeste contractare, Ms. Vat., fol. 331va. It is quite clear from Huguccio's discussion of dist. 23 that these and other so-called virilia officia and also the feminea opera have nothing to do with essential male and female functions but are simply the kind of discussion he gives the following justification for the prohibition of women's preaching and teaching in a gathering of men: "no [tandum] quod ideo prohibentur mulieres docere viros, ne putarent se debere preferri," Ms. München 10247, fol. 25rb.

160. Even in modern canonical literature, for instance, the question whether a hermaphrodite can be consecrated is solved in exactly the same fashion used by Huguccio (and thus by Roman law). Cf. H. Jone, Gesetzbuch der lateinischen Kirche, 2nd ed. (Paderborn, 1952), vol. 2, p. 191; A. Lanza, "De requisita sexus virilis certa determinatione et distinctione ad ordines," in Apollinaris 19 (1946):49-66. Phillips (see chapter 1, n. 152), vol. 1, p. 451, expresses the most extreme consequence of this principle, that only man is fit for ordination: "Male sex is so important for ordination that whenever a person belongs to the male sex and is baptized" (characteristically, being baptized is put in second place!), "he is fit for ordination under any circumstances except his own clearly expressed will, so that a male child, a sleeping or even an insane man is preferred in this respect to the most saintly women."

161. "Tribus de causis dicitur vir ymago dei et non femina, primo: quia sicut deus unus est et ab illo omnia, sic et unus homo factus fuit a principio ex quo sunt ceteri et ita in hoc habet similitudinem cum deo ut sicut omnia ex illo uno sic ex uno homine omnes alii...; secundo: quia sicut de latere christi in morte dormientis in cruce origo ecclesie fluxit scilicet sanguis et aqua quibus significantur ecclesie sacramenta per que ecclesia subsistit et habet originem et efficitur sponsa christi, sic de latere ade dormientis in paradiso fo[r]mata est sibi sponsa quia inde sumpta est costa, de qua formata ets eva; tertio: quia sicut christus preest ecclesie et eam gubernat ita vir preest uxori et eam regit et gubernat, et his tribus de causis dicitur homo esse ymago dei et non femina, et ideo ipse ad modum femine non debet habere signum subiectionis, set libertatis et prelationis. --Quarto vero modo tam vir quam femina dicitur esse ymago dei, unde illud 'faciamus hominem' id est 'faciamus eum nostre ymaginis et nostre similitudinis' id est essentie divine capacem per rationem, per intellectum, per memoriam, per ingenium et hoc dicitur tam de femina quam de viro," Ms. München 10247, fol. 266rb.

162. "Item tribus de causis dicitur vir gloria dei et non femina; primo quia potentior et gloriosior apparuit deus in creatione viri quam femine, nam precipue per hominem manifestata est

gloria dei cum eum fecerit per se et de limo terre contra naturam,
set femina facta est de homine; secundo quia homo factus est a deo
nullo mediante quod non est de femina; tertio quia deum glorificat
principaliter, id est nullo medio, set femina mediante viro, quia
vir ipsam feminam docet et instruit ad glorificandum deum," Ms.
München, fol. 266rb. Similarly, later on, concerning c. 13 (ibid.)
ad v. "vir non debet velare": "dum orat, id est signum subiectionis habere quasi non sit liber ad deum id est quasi non subsit ei
nullo medio," Ms. cit., l.c. Huguccio's statement that only man
is "gloria dei" is taken over verbatim by Guido of Baysio in his
Rosarium (fol. 373v) on C. 33, q. 5, c. 13 ad v. "mulier non est
gloria dei" (cf. p. 68) and also by Aegidius Bellamera in his commentary on Gratian's Decretum (Remissorius III, fol. 89r).

163.   The position taken by Concetti against the priesthood
of women (see Heinzelmann, Schwestern [see Introduction n. 1],
pp. 89-101) implies very consistently an understanding and evaluation of women which is strikingly similar to that of Huguccio.   He
affirms, p. 99, that in accordance with the order of creation,
primacy belongs to man; Christ has therefore not granted the
priesthood to women, "in order to respect the order of creation
and the plan of salvation, both of which require the dominance of
the male: of the old Adam and the new Christ." "The role of
mediator" belongs "in accordance with the will of God and of
Christ to man because of his superior position and because of his
natural capabilities to represent Christ, the highest mediator, in
concrete forms of expression." It is true that at one point, characteristically, there is a difference in the argumentation: while
Huguccio unhesitatingly presents his conviction of the inferiority of
women--the viewpoint of his times agreed with him--Concetti, taking account of the different outlook of modern times, affirms that
this "dominance" of man does not impair "the equality and worth
of the sexes," since "different functions" are allotted to men and
to women. Since the ground has been cut from under the idea of
women's inferiority, the attempt is made by using such threadbare
arguments to conceal and minimize the legal situation of women,
which is still disadvantageous despite the continuing emphasis today
on equality of the sexes.

164.   Cf. v. Schulte, Geschichte, vol. 1, pp. 167ff.

165.   Cf. Kuttner, Kanonistische Schuldlehre von Gratian
bis auf die Dekretalen Gregors IX.   (Vatican City, 1935), p. X;
Kuttner, Repertorium, p. 158.

166.   Schulte, Geschichte, vol. 1, p. 168.

167.   Kuttner, Schuldlehre, p. XIII.   The Poenitentiale was
written, according to Kuttner, between 1207 and 1215; according to
Gillmann, "Wiebliche Kleriker," p. 250, n. 1, it was not completed before 1208.

168.   According to v. Schulte, Geschichte, vol. 1, p. 210,

Robert uses and quotes from Huguccio and Joannes Faventinus, among others.

169. "... De substantia ordinis sunt sexus, baptismus, prima tonsura, ceterorum ordinum [funcamentum], potestas ordinantis et eius intentio et forte intentio ordinati et verba...," Ms. Bamberg Patr. 132 [Q. VI. 42], fol. 13v, quoted from Gillmann, "Weibliche Kleriker," p. 250, n. 1.

170. "... Sexus este de substantia ordinis, quia mulieres benedicuntur, non ordinantur, licet inveniatur, quod aliquando fuerunt diaconisse. Set in alio sensu dicebantur diaconisse quam hodie diaconus. Nunquam enim habuit femina illud officium, quod modo habet diaconus..., Ms. cit., l.c., quoted from Gillmann, p. 250, n. 1.

171. See Kuttner, Repertorium, p. 93; van Hove, vol. 1/1, p. 431.

172. Cf. v. Schulte, Geschichte, vol. 1, pp. 173f.; van Hove, ibid.

173. So v. Schulte, Geschichte, vol. 1, p. 175.

174. See Kuttner, Repertorium, p. 103; van Hove, vol. 1/1, pp. 431f.

175. The edition containing the Glossa Ordinaria and used in the following discussion: Corpus Iuris Canonici in tres partes distinctum; glossis diversorum illustratum, Gregorii Papae XIII. iussu editum, Lugduni, 1671.

176. Ad v. "ordinari": "Videtur obviare huic Ambro[sius] qui praecessit hoc Concilium. Ait enim super illum locum Apostoli in I. epistola ad Tim. 'Mulieres similiter oportet esse pudicas': Ocassione horum verborum Cataphrygae dicunt diaconissam debere ordinari, quod est contra auctoritatem," Corpus, ed. cit., vol. 1, col. 149b.

177. "Respon[deo], quod mulieres non recipiunt characterem [ordinis] impediente sexu et constitutione Ecclesiae," Corpus, ed. cit., l.c.; cf. also on C. 15, q. 3 princ. v. "Tertio": "per mulieris testimonium non potest Clericus convinci de crimine, tum quia mulier non est, nec potest esse eiusdem ordinis," Corpus, ed. cit., vol. 1, col. 1073; C. 33 q. 5 C. 17 v. "nec testis": "... nec contra Clericos in causa criminali [potest mulier esse testis], quia non potest esse, quod ipsi sunt," Corpus, ed. cit., vol. 1, col. 1827.

178. "... Unde nec officium ordinum exercere possunt, 23. dist. c. Sacratas (c. 25); nec ordinabatur haec: sed fundabatur super eam forte aliqua benedictio, ex qua consequebatur aliquod officium speciale, forte legendi homilias vel Evangelium ad Matuti-

nas, quod non licebat alii, Corpus, ed. cit. , vol. 1, col. 1496.
Joannes speaks similarly in other places about the deaconess office,
as on C. 20, q. 1, c. 13 ad v. "non velentur": "Velo ordinationis, ut sit Diaconissa, non ad ordinem, sed ad quoddam ministerium Evangelicum in matutinis lectionibus nuntiandis," Corpus, ed.
cit. , vol. 1, col. 1122; on dict. Grat. p. c. 10 in C. 20 q. 1 ad
v. "velamen": "... Velum ordinationis, quod olim imponebatur
Diaconissis in 40. anno, ut infra ea[dem] c. Sanctimoniales (c.
13, " Corpus, ed. cit. , vol. 1, col. 1221.

179. Ad v. "docere non praesumat": "Hoc enim est
sacerdotale officium, ut (C.) 16, q. 1, c. adiicimus (c. 19).
Idem plenius habes (C.) 33, q. 5, c. mulierem (c. 17)," Corpus,
ed. cit. , vol. 1, col. 115. On C. 16, q. 1, c. 19 ad v. "sacerdotes" Joannes, it is true, declares that a woman may preach if
she has permission of the priest: "Vel per licentiam Sacerdotum....
Similiter Laici praedicant et mulieres de licentia Sacerdotis, ut
supra dist. 23 c. mulier in fine," Corpus, ed. cit. , vol. 1, cols.
1097f. However Joannes misunderstands the authority alleged in
dist. 23, c. 29: it maintains on the contrary an express prohibition against teaching by women. Added is a prohibition against
teaching by a layman, which is however limited: the male lay person, but not a woman, may teach when requested by the clergy.
(Cf. p. 13.)

180. Ad v. "mulier" he refers to C. 33, q. 5, c. 17--i.e.,
to the statement of Ambrosiaster, who says that women are excluded from all public functions. Reference is also made to the
prohibition of teaching in dist. 23, c. 29. Permission to baptize
in cases of necessity is supported (following dict. p. c. 20 in dist.
4 de cons.) by the decretal of Urban I in C. 30, q. 4, c. 4
(Corpus, ed. cit. , vol. 1, col. 1983).

181. In dist. 2 de cons. c. 29 ad v. "peruenit": "Quidam
fatui Sacerdotes per Laicos, vel mulieres corpus Domini mittebant
infirmis: quod prohibetur hic, ne fiat: sed ipsimet porrigant, qui
si contra fecerint, deponantur"; ad v. "per semetipsum": "vel per
Diaconum, si necesse est ... vel per Laicum catholicum, " Corpus,
ed. cit. , vol. 1, cols. 1924f.

182. On C. 4 q. 2/3 c. 3 § 22 (Hermaphroditus): "Quaesi-
tum fuit, utrum hermaphroditus, id est qui habet sexum maris et
foeminae, possit esse testis in testamento? et respondetur, quod
si magis appetit ea, quae viri sunt, potest: alias non ... "; ad v.
"ad testimonium": "Scilicet in testamento, ubi mulier non potest
esse testis secundum legem, ut Instit. de testam. § testes [I. 2,
10, 6; Corpus Iuris Civilis, vol. 1, col. 17]; in iudicio autem esse
non potest, (C.) 15 q. 3 c. de crimine (c. 1). Sed quid si in omnibus est parilitas? Item numquid talis potest ordinari? ... Ioan.
Sed certe in omnibus his respici debet sexus, qui magis incalescit
... Hug. ," Corpus, ed. cit. , vol. 1, col. 773. The symbol "Hug."
indicates that the application of this principle of Roman law to
canon law, especially to the law of ordination, goes back to Huguccio.

183. On C. 33, q. 5, c. 17 ad v. "auctoritatem": "Virilia. enim officia mulieribus sunt adempta, C. 3, q. 7, c. infamis § tria (p. c. 1); Dig. ad Vell. l. 2 (D. 16,1,1,2)" (Corpus, ed. cit., vol. 1, col. 1827). On C. 15, q. 3 princ. ad v. "legibus": "Dig. de reg. iur. l. [si] foeminae" ("Feminae ab omnibus officiis civilibus vel publicis remotae sunt...," D. 50,17,2; Corpus Iuris Civilis, vol. 1, col. 868), Corpus, ed. cit., vol. 1, col. 1073.

184. See n. 182, above.

185. On C. 15, q. 3 princ. ad v. "mulieres": "Foemina de iure non potest esse iudex, ut (C.) 33, q. 5 cap. Mulierem (c. 17) et (C.) 3, q. 7, §tria (p. c. 1), Dig. de reg. iur. l. foeminae (D. 50,17,2), nisi ei princeps scienter deleget causam, ut (C.) 2, q. 5, c. Mennam (c. 7) et (C.) 23, q. 4, c. Si quos (c. 47), (C.) 12, q. 2 c. Cum deuotissimam (c. 8). Vel nisi ex praescripta consuetudine hoc habeat, ut extra de arb. c. Dilecti (Extra 1,43,4). Item nec docere potest, ut 23. d. c. Mulier (c. 29)," Corpus, ed. cit., vol. 1, col. 1073.

186. On C. 33, q. 5, c. 17 ad v. "nec testis": "In causa criminali, nisi in illis casibus in quibus infames admittuntur, nec in testamento, Instit. de test. § testes (I. 2,10,6), nec contra Clericos in causa criminali, quia non potest esse, quod ipsi sunt, supra (C.) 2 quaest. 7 c. Ipsi Apostoli (c. 38), nec etiam contra Laicos, ut not(atur) (C.) 15, q. 3 c. De crimine (c. 1)," Corpus, ed. cit., vol. 1, col. 1827.

187. On C. 15, q. 3, c. 2 § "Non est permissum": "Mulier non potest quemquam in iudicio publico accusare, nisi suam, vel suorum prosequatur iniuriam," Corpus, ed. cit., vol. 1, col. 1074.

188. On dist. 56, c. 5 ad v. "quod suum est": "Mulieres enim ad hoc natura genuit, ut partus ederent ... et pudor est foeminis nuptiarum praemia non habere," Corpus, ed. cit., vol. 1, col. 293. The gloss takes over fully the conception in Roman law of the nature and vocation of woman. Cf. C. 6, 40, 2 ("Cum enim mulieres ad hoc natura progenuit, ut partus ederent, et maxime eis cupiditas in hoc constituta est...," Corpus Iuris Civilis, vol. 2, col. 271); Dig. 21, 1, 14 ("Maximum enim ac praecipuum munus feminarum est accipere ac tueri conceptum" Corpus Iuris Civilis, vol. 2, col. 271). Chapter 5 in dist. 56 mentioned above, which is taken from the epistola of Hieronymous ad Pammachium (cf. Friedberg, Corpus, vol. 1, col. 221, n. 45), expresses clearly the understanding of the procreation process in antiquity and in the Middle Ages: the vulva of women is equated with the earth, which receives the seed: "sic genus humanum recipit terra, id est vulva, quod suum est et receptum confovet, confotum corporat, corporatum in membra distinguit...," ed. Freidberg, Corpus, vol. 1, col. 221.

189. Joannes, like Gratian, is strictly limited by a narrow

concept of the doctrine of the Fathers about the derivation of woman from man and about woman as the originator of sin. This is
obvious from the gloss to the patristic texts in cc. 11-20 in C.
33, q. 5; on c. 12 (ibid.) ad v. "est ordo naturalis" Joannes remarks: "id est a nativitate et ortu proveniens, nam foemina de
corpore viri est," Corpus, ed. cit., vol. 1, col. 1825; on c. 13
ad v. "ut unus": "id est, imago Dei dicitur ipse homo, quia sicut
aqua profluxit ex latere Domini, sic etiam Eua ex latere Adae,"
ed. cit., l.c.; on c. 13 ad v. "mulier": "... Deus non gloriatur
per ipsam, sicut per virum, nam per eam prima praevaricatio
est inducta," ed. cit., l.c.; on c. 19 ad v. [peccatum] "originale":
"quod originem habuit ab ipsa quoad homines," Corpus, ed. cit.,
vol. 1, col. 1827.

190. On C. 33, q. 5, c. 4 ad v. "hunc": "... vir dupli-
cem habet servitutem in uxore, unam quoad debitum reddendum,
aliam quoad ministerium sibi exhibendum," Corpus, ed. cit., vol.
1, col. 1821; also cf. the gloss on c. 12 (ibid.) ad v. "ut serviant": "Hoc adeo verum est, quod patronus consentiendo libertae,
ut contrahat, amittat in ea operas, cum in officio viri debeat
esse," Corpus, ed. cit., vol. 1, col. 1825.

191. On C. 7, q. 1, c. 39 ad v. "iudicari": "Judicare
potest maritus uxorem, corrigendo eam ... sed non verberando
eam ... sed temperate potest eam castigare, quia est de familia
sua ... sicut dominus seruum ... et etiam mercenarium suum,"
Corpus, ed. cit., vol. 1, col. 836; also cf. the gloss on C. 27,
q. 1, c. 26 ad v. "receperint": "Uxores viris, et filii parentibus
et servi dominis subditi sunt, unde ab illis coerceri et secundum
ius debent corripi, ne in causam anathematis incidant," Corpus,
ed. cit., vol. 1, col. 1497; C. 33, q. 5, c. 14 ad v. "ut pene
famulas": "non tamen quod immoderate verberentur," ed. cit.,
vol. 1, col. 1825. The gloss on C. 33, q. 2, c. 10 ad v. "Placuit" concerns the clerics' right to punish their wives: "Dicitur
hic quod si uxores clericorum peccaverint, eas non occidant, sed
eas custodiant, ne de caetero habeant licentiam peccandi, mace-
rando eas verberibus et fame, sed non usque ad mortem." With
reference to C. 7, q. 1, c. 39, the gloss ad v. "potestatem" expressly grants also to male lay persons the right to punish their
wives (Corpus, ed. cit., vol. 1, col. 1656).

192. On C. 27, q. 1, c. 23 ad v. "ordinari" (in fine),
Corpus, ed. cit., vol. 1, col. 1496. Concetti, p. 94, quotes only
the negative position of Joannes Teutonicus on the problem of ordaining women, without mentioning the opposite opinion in any way.
He also ignores Joannes' prejudicial thinking about the female sex,
which makes it in his opinion unfit for consecration. In other passages also Concetti is careless about "traditional proofs," which he
gathers together without noting their time-conditionedness or investigating their validity.

193. One viewpoint is especially ignored by the argument of
Joannes, which represents the opinion of the time, although it is

also ignored by the opposing position. This is the viewpoint that an ordination is meaningful and finally also valid only when the ordinand has the charisma required to carry out his office. The narrower view results from the fact that the sacramental character of ordination--corresponding to scholastic thinking--is excessively and one-sidedly emphasized, while the spiritual quality of the ordinand is largely overlooked.

194. Representatives of the traditional ecclesiastical doctrine involve themselves in contradictions when they claim that both baptism and male sex are required for ordination. For example, G. Phillips (see chapter 1, n. 152) gives the following justification for these two requirements, appealing to texts of the Corpus Iuris Canonici that we have already discussed: "First, concerning the necessity of baptism for the reception of ordination, it is the gateway and the foundation for all other sacraments.... One must first be born through baptism in order to be able to act and in order to be able himself to give birth" (vol. 1, pp. 444f.). But then Phillips suddenly forgets this fundamental importance of baptism for ordination, when he seeks to justify the requirement of male sex and in connection with it the unfitness of women for ordination: "But even the strongest faith of a baptized woman is never strong enough to empower her to receive ordination.... In accordance with divine command woman is subject to man and not called to authority. Adam was created before Eve, but Eve sinned before Adam, and therefore she is rightly subject to his sovereign authority.... Christ is the bridegroom of the church and like him the priesthood is mysteriously wedded to the church. Only men can procreate [!], only priests can create priests. Therefore a woman cannot ascend to even the lowest steps of authority; she may not receive the royal distinctive marks of the priesthood ..." (vol. 1, pp. 446f.). Apart from the inconsistency and the completely perverted understanding of ecclesiastical office ("sovereign authority"!), it is clear from such language that the conception of women as unfit for ordination because of their sex implies an opinion of women as inferior human beings--in fact is identical with such an opinion.

195. Cf. Plöchl (see chapter 1, n. 91), vol. 2, p. 510; Kuttner, Repertorium, p. 87.

196. Kuttner, ibid.; v. Schulte, Geschichte, vol. 2, p. 188.

197. "Adde: tu dic quod [mulier] ordinari non potest ut supra dictum est, et est ratio, quia ordo est perfectorum membrorum ecclesiae, cum detur ad collationem gratiae in altero. Mulier autem non est perfectum membrum ecclesiae sed vir" (Rosarium, fol. 329r; the edition I have used [Lyon, 1549] adds as "Additio": "adde quod mulier non est imago Dei sed vir"; among evidences given are Gen. 1; Wisdom 2 (23); 1 Cor. 11; C. 33, q. 5, cc. 13 and 19).

198. On C. 33, q. 5, c. 13 ad v. "gloria" (Rosarium,

fol. 373v), Guido takes over, word for word, the statements of Huguccio (pp. 63f. with n. 162).

199. "Preterea mulier fuit causa effectiva damnationis quia fuit principium prevaricationis [Text: privatonis] et Adam per ipsam deceptus est, (C.) 33, q. 5 Adam (c. 18) et c. seq., et ideo non potuit esse [causa] effectiva salutis cum ordines sint effectus gratie in altero et sic salutis," Rosarium, fol. 329r.

200. "Sed causa materialis salutis potuit esse mulier, imo materialiter cum de viro sumpta fuerit quia de costa Ade fuit facta mulier, (C.) 33, q. 5 Nec illud (c. 20); debuit esse virgo Maria [causa] salutis, et hoc est verum quod sexus muliebris fuit causa materialis salutis nostrae scilicet beata virgo de qua materialiter Christus salus nostra processit...," Rosarium, fol. 329r. In referring to Guido, Aegidius Bellamera, on C. 27, q. 1, c. 23 ad v. "characterem," simply copies Guido's justification for the unfitness of women for ordination (Remissorius III, fol. 28r).

201. "... dic quod non appellatur hec presbytera, eo quod esset ordinata: nam si mulier ordinaretur, non reciperet characterem impediente sexu et constitutione ecclesie, quamvis quidam contradicunt, prout no[tatur] (C.) 27, q. 1 Diaconissam (c. 23). Sed idcirco hec appellatur, quia est ordinati socia," Rosarium, fol. 43r.

202. On C. 11, q. 1, c. 38 ad v. "diaconissam": "de qua loquitur (C.) 27, q. 1 diaconissam (c. 23), ibi Jo[annes] exponit i.e. abbatissam vel diaconissa olim dicebatur mulier que ministrabat sacerdoti, de qua loquitur lex ... hodie non est in sancta ecclesia," Rosarium, fol. 205v.

CHAPTER 4

1. Cf. Sägmüller (see Part I [preliminary], n. 1), vol. 1, pp. 239f.; Feine (see chapter 1, n. 4), p. 283.

2. Cf. Sägmüller, vol. 1, p. 240; Feine, p. 284. The Quinque Compilationes Antiquae (ed. by Friedberg, Leipzig, 1882) contain no material on our subject which is not also in the decretals of Gregory IX.

3. Cf. Sägmüller, vol. 1, p. 242; Feine, p. 287.

4. Cf. Sägmüller, vol. 1, p. 243; Feine, p. 287; Stickler (see chapter 1, n. 3), vol. 1, pp. 245ff. The critical editions of the Corpus Iuris Canonici by J. H. Böhmer (1747), E. L. Richter (1839) and E. Friedberg (1879-1881) reconstruct the original text of the decretals as far as possible by restoring the "partes decisae." (Cf. Sägmüller, vol. 1, p. 243.)

5. Sägmüller, ibid.; cf. also Feine, p. 287; Stickler, vol.
1, pp. 247ff.

6. Cf. Feine, pp. 287f.; Stickler, vol. 1, pp. 247f.

7. The following contain no further important texts on the
subject before us: the collections of decretals which appeared after
the Gregorian collection and which like the latter belong to the
Corpus Iuris Canonici--i.e., the so-called Liber Sextus of Boniface
VIII, the Constitutiones of Clement V and the Extravagantes of John
XXII (which in contrast to the compilations named have a purely
private character) and the Extravagantes Communes.

8. The text of the decretal reads as follows: "Nova quaedam nuper, de quibus miramur non modicum, nostris sunt auribus
intimata, quod abbatissae videlicet, in Burgensi et in Palentinensi
dioecesibus constitutae, moniales proprias benedicunt, ipsarum
quoque confessiones in criminibus audiunt, et legentes evangelium
praesumunt publice praedicare. Quum igitur id absonum sit pari-
ter et absurdum, [nec a nobis aliquatenus sustinendum] discretioni
vestrae per apostolica scripta mandamus, quatenus, ne id de cetero
fiat, auctoritate curetis apostolica firmiter inhibere, quia, licet
beatissima virgo Maria dignior et excellentior fuerit Apostolis universis, non tamen illi, sed istis Dominus claves regni coelorum
commisit," Corpus, ed. Friedberg, vol. 1, col. 886f.

9. The protest of the Pope can only refer to a blessing
used in official-liturgical form, as, for instance, in the consecration of virgins. Against that, a claim is also made in a capitulary
of Charlemagne (from 789): "Auditum est aliquas abbatissas contra
morem sanactae Dei ecclesiae benedictionem [Text: benedictionis]
cum manus impositione et signaculo sanctae crucis super capita
virorum dare necnon et velare virgines cum benedictione sacerdo-
tali. Quod omnino vobis, sanctissimi patres, in vestris parrochiis
interdicendum esse scitote," MGH Capit. I 60.

10. Confession of sins, as a statement of conscience before the abbess, was a regulation for nuns in many monastic rules
and thus was not unusual in actual practice. (See B. Poschmann,
Die abendländische Kirchenbusse im frühen Mittelalter [Breslau,
1930], p. 72; P. Browe, "Die Kommunionvorbereitung im Mittelalter," in Zeitschrift für katholische Theologie [hereafter cited as
ZkTh] 56 [1932]:399f.) Now the Pope bases the prohibition of this
and other functions named on the contention that Mary did not possess the potestas clavium, which in the Middle Ages was understood to mean mainly the power of binding and loosing acquired by
ordination. (Cf. L. Hödl, Die Geschichte der scholastischen
Literatur und der Schlüsselgewalt, Part 1 [Münster, 1960], pp.
381ff.) Therefore it must be presumed that the reference here is
not only to such a devotional confession, but to a kind that makes
confession before a priest--and the resultant absolution--dispens-
able. M. Bernard, Speculum virginum. Geistigkeit und Seelenle-
ben der Frau im Hochmittelalter (Cologne, 1955), pp. 115f., is

apparently correct in seeing in the prohibition the outcome of de-
veloping theological reflection about the sacrament of penance and
thus regards it as a preventive measure against the extensive
practice of confession to lay persons.

11.　See L. Hödl, "Schlüsselgewalt," in LThK vol. 9,
and n. 10, above.

12.　E. g. , by Concetti (quoted in Heinzelmann, Schwestern),
pp. 89f.

13.　Adversus haereses, 1.3, t. 2 (PG 42, c. 743); cf.
Concetti, p. 91 with n. 3.

14.　Cf. Van der Meer (see Introduction, n. 7), pp. 151f.
with n. 171.

15.　Marie, l'Eglise et le Sacerdoce II. Etude théologique
(Paris, 1953), pp. 38f. ("On n'a jamais produit qu'une seule
raison: Marie n'était pas capable du sacrament de l'ordre:
'propter femineum sexum.' ")

16.　Van der Meer, p. 152.

17.　Cf. the Dogmatic Constitution on the Church, chapter
8, 63-65 (AAS 57, 1965, 64f.; Abbott, Documents of Vatican II,
pp. 92f.).

18.　So Semmelroth, for instance, Maria oder Christus?
Christus als Ziel der Marienverehrung (Frankfurt, 1954), p. 131:
Mary is, "to speak exactly, not simply the image of the church....
Mary is rather the image of the church insofar as the latter--as
'Laós,' as lay community receiving and offering together--encount-
ers Christ, who through the office meets with his people." (Cf.
also ibid. , p. 145.) Similarly, Laurentin, "Marie et l'Eglise dans
l'oeuvre salvifique," in Marie et l'Eglise II (1952), p. 55: Mary
is called type of the church but not of the church in its hierarchical functions. Contrariwise, M. J. Scheeben, Die Mysterien des
Christentums, 2nd ed. (Freiburg, 1951), pp. 449f. , saw in Mary
exactly the type of the "official" church, of its authority in ordination and jurisdiction. According to Scheeben, the grace-giving
motherhood of the church, patterned after and based on the spiritual motherhood of Mary, receives full development and expression
in the so-called office-priesthood of the church. Of course the
viewpoint of Scheeben did not remain undisputed: see on this and
on Scheeben's Mariology in general Cl. Dillenschneider, Maria im
Heilsplan der Neuschöpfung (Colmar-Freiburg, 1960), pp. 271ff.;
also, Die heilsgeschichtliche Stellvertretung der Menschheit durch
Maria, ed. by C. Feckes (Paderborn, 1954), pp. 308-322, 360-
367.

19.　See pp. 120ff. , for further (critical) discussion about
the traditional understanding of church office.

20. So Semmelroth, op. cit., pp. 130f. His identification of this church with Laós (see n. 18, above) excludes the office holders from the "people of God." Opposing this view is the concept of church and office in Lumen Gentium of Vatican II, which is certainly a sign of progress in so far as all members of the church, and thus also the office holders, belong to the "people of God."

21. Cf. A. M. Ritter and G. Leich, Wer ist die Kirche? Amt und Gemeinde im Neuen Testament, in der Kirchengeschichte und heute (Göttingen, 1968), p. 68.

22. Cf. K. H. Schelke, Jüngerschaft und Apostelamt. Eine biblische Auslegung des priesterlichen Dienstes (Freiburg, 1957), pp. 125-132; Ritter and Leich, p. 60.

23. According to the prevailing opinion of theologians and canonists, abbesses, including those of the Middle Ages, possess, in fact, no jurisdictional power; the authority of their office is characterized as simple potestas dominativa. (Cf. J. Baucher, "Abbesses," in DDC, vol. 1, pp. 67ff.; Pie de Langogne, "Abbesses," in Dictionnaire de théologie catholique [Paris, 1920ff.] [hereafter cited as DThC], vol. 1, pp. 18ff.). This point of view is critically investigated by Van der Meer, pp. 115-128, who (like other writers, e.g., Metz, "Statut," p. 99; cf. also Schäfer, Kanonissenstifter, pp. 140ff., 152) comes to the conclusion that historical facts refute the presupposition that the abbess' authority is only a quasi-jurisdiction or potestas dominativa. Van der Meer says that only on the basis of this presupposition--that the abbess as woman cannot possess jurisdictional authority--could one deny that she has such authority--a position, however, that cannot withstand an unbiased view of the facts. (My own position on this question cannot be given within the framework of this study.) In an investigation worth noting in this connection, Th. J. Bowe, Religious Superioresses. A Historical Synopsis and Commentary (Washington, D.C., 1946), pp. 27-30, presents the work of a number of writers, from the 15th to the 19th centuries, who affirm that a woman may have jurisdictional power in the church by means of special authorization by the Pope.

24. "Dilecta in Christo filia abbatissa de Bubrigen." (According to Friedberg, Corpus, vol. 2, col. 201, n. 4, the original form was Quedlinburg) "transmissa nobis petitione monstravit, quod, quum ipsa plerumque canonicas suas et clericos suae iurisdictioni subiectos propter inobedientias et culpas eorum officio beneficioque suspendat iidem confisi ex eo, quod eadem abbatissa excommunicare eos non potest, suspensionem huiusmodi non observant, propter quod ipsorum excessus remanent incorrecti. Quocirca discretioni tuae mandamus, quatenus dictas canonicas et clericos, ut abbatissae praefatae obedientam et reverentiam debitam impendentes, eius salubria monita et mandata observent, monitione praemissa ecclesiastica censura appellatione remota compellas," Corpus, ed. Friedberg, vol. 2, col. 201.

25. Cf. Friedberg, <u>Corpus</u>, vol. 2, col. 201, n. 2 and n. 3.

26. The so-called cannonesses formed a community that did not live according to strict monastic rule; they were not bound by ceremonial vow, having the right to reenter the world freely, and they retained their own property and foundation benefices. Foundation clergy (<u>canonici</u>), who were commissioned with pastoral care and divine services in the foundation churches, were also attached to the foundations which usually were established in the neighborhood of already existing parish churches. Cf. Schäfer, <u>Kanonissenstifter</u>, pp. 11ff. <u>et passim</u>.

27. Cf. Schäfer, <u>ibid</u>., p. 143.

28. <u>Ibid</u>., pp. 142f.

29. The canons had to promise obedience, according to Schäfer, p. 103, not only to the abbess but also to the bishop and the foundation chapter.

30. Cf. Schäfer, <u>Kanonissenstifter</u>, pp. 143f; and his "Kanonissen und Diakonissen," p. 54.

31. In the canonist and dogmatic theology of the Middle Ages, the power of excommunication was understood as manifestation of the power of the keys. See Hödl (see n. 10, above), pp. 184, 382.

32. So too Bowe (see n. 23, above), p. 24 ("In view of the fact that in using the words 'ecclesiastical censure' the pope at the same time restricted to the abbot the right to invoke this penalty, he appeared to regard the act of suspension as something distinct from this penalty").

33. Cf. Mörsdorf (see Part I [preliminary], n. 5), vol. 3, p. 395.

34. Perhaps we may use for this the term "provisional suspension" (see Mörsdorf, vol. 2, p. 116, and vol. 3, p. 354). See also the interpretation of the decretal by the decretalists, p. 89 with n. 121 of chapter 4 and p. 93 with n. 142 of chapter 4.

35. "De monialibus tua a nobis fraternitas requisivit, per quem eis sit beneficium absolutionis impendendum, si vel in se invicem vel conversos vel conversas suas, aut clericos etiam, in suis monasteriis servientes, manus iniecerint temere violentas. Super hoc igitur tuae consultationi taliter respondemus, ut auctoritate nostra per episcopum, in cuius dioecesi earum monasteria fuerint, absolvantur," <u>Corpus</u>, ed. Friedberg, vol. 2, col. 903.

36. According to Schäfer, <u>Kanonissenstifter</u>, p. 154, abbesses "since the 13th century at the latest used their own seals

for confirmation of foundation documents." The authentication of
solemn decisions of the whole chapter, since the second half of the
12th century, according to Schäfer, p. 161, took place in German
foundations "under the great seal (sigillum maius ecclesiae N. N.)
of the church in question," along with the seal of the abbess, who
earlier was often alone responsible for the seal (ibid. , n. 7).

37. Cf. Corpus, ed. Friedberg, vol. 2, col. 841.

38. Cf. Friedberg, Corpus, vol. 2, col. 445, n. 4.

39. See C. 3, q. 7, c. 2 (2), Corpus, ed. Friedberg, vol.
1, col. 525.

40. The decisive excerpt of the decretal reads: "Quia vero
praefatum monasterium ad ius et proprietatem apostolicae sedis per
privilegium praedecessoris nostri" (in the previous section of the
decretal two of his predecessors are named) "pertinere monstratur,
ne ius ecclesiae Romanae remaneat indefensum, eandem abbatissam procuratricem ipsius duximus statuendam, ut, quum
adversus Romanae ecclesiae possessiones et iura non nisi cen-
tenaria currat praescriptio, ipsa super hoc et aliis vice nostra
procuret quae coram te in iudicio fuerint procuranda," Corpus, ed.
Friedberg, vol. 2, col. 445f.

41. Cf. Friedberg, Corpus, vol. 2, col. 231, n. 3.

42. An order that cared for the sick. Cf. K. Hofmann,
"Hospitaliter," in LThK, vol. 5, col. 492f.

43. Cf. Corpus, ed. Friedberg, vol. 2, col. 231. The
decretal's section on discipline is summarized by Raymond of
Pennaforte as follows: "In mulierem singularem tanquam in arbi-
tratricem compromitti non potest; secus si mulier habet alias
iurisdictionem de iure communi vel consuetudine. Nam tunc etiam
super rebus temporalibus ecclesiae potest in eam valide compromitti" ibid.

44. "Testes autem considerantur conditione, natura et vita.
Conditione, si liber, non servus.... Natura, si vir, non femina,"
Corpus, ed. Friedberg, vol. 2, col. 914.

45. "Nam varium et mutabile testimonium semper femina
producit" (ibid. ; according to Friedberg, n. 41, this concept is
taken from Vergil, Aen. IV, 569, where the reading is: "varium
et mutabile semper femina...").

46. The rubric attributes the chapter to a council of Mainz,
contrary to Friedberg, Corpus, vol. 2, col. 454, n. 1 (canon 4 of
the Synod of Nantes, A.D. 895); according to Hefele (see chapter
1, n. 36), vol. 3, p. 104, it is from canon 3 of the A. D. 658
Synod of Nantes, which reads as follows: "not even mother, sister
or aunt may stay in the house with the priest, since there have

been cases of terrible incest. Also no woman may serve at the altar. "

47. Note especially canon 44 of the Synod of Laodicea (between A.D. 347 and 381), which forbids women access to the altar, and which is repeated by many later synods. Cf. chapter 1, n. 45.

48. "Sed secundum auctoritatem canonum modis omnibus prohibendum quoque est, ut nulla femina ad altare praesumat accedere, aut presbytero ministrare, aut infra cancellos stare sive sedere," Corpus, ed. Friedberg, vol. 2, col. 454. The part of a sentence omitted by Raymond of Pennaforte (cf. p. 70), which must be added, reads as follows: "sed secundum auctoritatem canonum modis omnibus"; it is clearly the connecting term between the two textual excerpts of the decretal, not only in form but also in content.

49. This is also the sense in which Van der Meer, pp. 96f., understands the canon. However he does not take into account the omitted sentence fragment (see n. 48, above) and thus he overlooks the inner connection already present in the text between the two prohibitions--which are in themselves dissimilar--and so his comments remain conjecture. W. Hellinger, "Die Pfarrvisitation nach Regino von Prüm (part 2)," in ZRG Kan. Abt. 49 (1963), pp. 98f., also interprets the prohibition as a measure to protect celibacy. In this connection reference should also be made to C. 18, q. 2, c. 25 (= cc. 26 and 27 of the Concilium Lateranense II, A.D. 1139), since this chapter shows a construction very similar to X 3.2.1: certain women in orders (presumably canonisses) are forbidden to have their own guest rooms or private quarters where under pretext of hospitality they might receive male guests, contrary to good morals. Immediately after this statement, the following regulation for the liturgical Divine Office is added: "Simili modo prohibemus, nec sanctimoniales simul cum canonicis et monachis in ecclesia in uno choro conveniant ad psallendum," Corpus, ed. Friedberg, vol. 1, col. 836.

50. Cf. X 1.17.15 (Corpus, ed. cit., vol. 2, col. 140), according to which it is merely prohibited that the illegitimate son of a priest serve him as acolyte.

51. Cf. Code, p. 273, n. 3. The first of the sources cited there is X 3.2.1.

52. "Minister Missae inserviens ne sit mulier, nisi, deficiente viro, iusta de causa, eaque lege ut mulier ex longinquo respondeat nec ullo pacto ad altare accedat." An offence against this regulation was for a long time considered a mortal sin. Cf. A. Arndt, "Darf eine Frau zur heiligen Messe ministriren?" in AkKR 81 (1901): 163 ("Whoever would disobey this prohibition of the church would not be free from mortal sin, as all writers confirm who mention it. 'Therefore Laymann says rightly,' declares

St. Alphons, 'that the priest should rather celebrate without an
acolyte than that he should permit a woman to approach the altar.' ")
Similarly, Jone, Gesetzbuch (see chapter 3, n. 160), vol. 2, p. 70.

53. The text reads: "... Jusqu'où peut aller le munus
liturgicum des femmes, dont le baptême leur donne droit et devoir
(Const. art. 14), ce sera à étudier de près; mais, que dans
l'organisation actuelle de la liturgie, les femmes n'aient pas à
remplir un ministerium autour de l'autel, cela est certain. Car le
ministerium dépend de la volonté de l'Eglise, et l'Eglise catholique
n'a, en fait, jamais confié le ministerium liturgique à des femmes.
--En conséquence, toute innovation arbitraire en ce domaine sera
considérée comme une infraction grave à la discipline ecclésiastique
et devra être éliminée avec fermeté," La Documentation catholique,
Paris, 1er mai 1966, 807; quoted from Heinzelmann, Schwestern,
pp. 19f., n. 18.

54. AAS 56 (1964), p. 104; Abbott, Documents of Vatican
II, pp. 156f.

55. "Iuxta liturgicas normas in Ecclesia traditas, vetantur
mulieres (puellae, nuptae, religiosae), ne in ecclesiis quidem,
domibus, conventibus, collegiis, institutis muliebribus, ad altare
sacerdoti inservire," AAS 62, 1970, p. 700.

56. Herder Korrespondenz, 24, 1970, p. 559.

57. AAS 57, 1965, p. 38; Abbott, op. cit., p. 58.

58. Cf. Plöchl, Geschichte, vol. 2, p. 517; Feine, p. 290;
van Hove, vol. 1/1, p. 472.

59. Kuttner, Schuldlehre (see chapter 3, n. 165), pp. xiiif.;
Feine, p. 290.

60. Cf. Kuttner, Repertorium, p. 445 (the Summa was not
completed before 1227); likewise, van Hove, vol. 1/1, p. 513.

61. 'Notandum, quod foemina non potest recipere characterem alicuius ordinis clericalis. Ambr[osius] super illum locum
Apostoli in prima epistola ad Tim[otheum] 'Mulieres similiter
oportet esse pudicas' ait occassione horum verborum: Cathafrigae
dicunt diaconissam debere ordinari, quod est veritati contrarium,
quia mulieres characterem non recipiunt, impediente sexu et
constitutione Ecclesiae. Unde nec possunt praedicare etiam Abbatissae, nec benedicere, nec excommunicare, nec absolvere, nec
poenitentias dare, nec iudicare, nec officium aliquorum ordinum
exercere, quantumcumque sint doctae, sanctae vel religiosae, dist.
23 mulier (c. 29) et sacratas (c. 25), (C.) 33 qu. 5 mulierem (c.
17), ext[ra] de sent[entia] excom[municationis] de monialibus (X
5.39.33), licet enim beatissima Virgo Maria dignior et excellentior
fuerit Apostolis universis, non tamen illi, sed istis Dominus claves
regni coelorum conmisit, ext[ra] de poen[itentiis] et remiss[ionibus]

nova (X 5. 38. 10). Quidam tamen mentiuntur adhuc cum Cathafrigis foeminam recipere characterem, etiam diaconalem et presbyteralem, inducunt pro se (C.) 27, q. 1 diaconissam (c. 23) et si quis rapuerit (c. 30) in fi[ne], in illis expresse videtur probari de ordine diaconali, de ordine presbyterali probant per 32. dist. presbyter (c. 18), sed illa capitual 'diaconissam' et 'si quis rapuerit' vocant diaconissam illam, super quam forte fundebatur aliqua benedictio, ratione cuius consequebatur aliquod speciale officium, forte legendi homeliam in matutinis, vel aliud, quod non licebat aliis monialibus; in illo autem capitulo 'presbyter' appellatur presbytera, quia erat uxor presbyteri, vel etiam vidua, vel matricuria, id est, de rebus ecclesiae curam habens ad instar matrisfamilias...," Summa, p. 316f. Gillmann, "Wiebliche Kleriker," p. 252, n. 1, remarks that Vincent of Beauvais in his Speculum historiale (1254) 1. VII, c. 70, treats the subject in question by a word-for-word excerpt from Raymond's Summa; also that Johannes of Freiburg in his Summa confessorum (1280-1298) 1. III, t. 23, q. 1, takes the whole title "De impedimento sexus" literally from Raymond--with explicit reference to him--making only a few additions himself.

62. Ad v. "praedicare," William of Rennes, from whom (according to Schulte, vol. 2, p. 240, n. 7, and Gillmann, p. 252) the glosses have come in the edition of Raymond's Summa (Rome, 1603) that I have used, observes that the preaching prohibition applies to the public proclamation in the church or in a synod but not to the teaching and admonition of nuns within the cloister. He rejects public preaching (Summa, p. 316) by referring to what Augustine says--"mulier semel docuit, et totum mundum subvertit" --in which the negative consequences of the Yahwistic narrative of the Fall on the evaluation of women in the church become obvious.

63. Ad v. "excommunicare," William, referring to the decretal Dilecta (X 1. 33. 12) and the teaching of some canonists, does allow the abbess the right to suspend from office and benefice the clerics under her, and this means a certain amount of jurisdictional authority ("habent enim, ut dicunt, iurisdictionem talem qualem"), Summa, p. 316.

64. The exercise of the function of judge in spiritual matters (de spiritualibus causis) is in principle denied to women, according to William (ad v. "iudicare," ibid.), but not in secular affairs, when and where prescriptive law permits it. (As verification William offers X 1. 43. 4.)

65. See n. 8, above.

66. Ad v. "homiliam," William remarks that besides the homily, deaconesses may have recited the oration in matins, but now this is done by all nuns because of the lack of clerics. But, he says, the deaconesses about whom the chapter "Diaconissam" is speaking (C. 27, q. 1, c. 23) do not exist any longer; their installation in the offices mentioned (reading the homily, etc.) may have been called "ordination" but not a conferring of a (consecra-

tion) character or ecclesiastical orders ("... quarum ordinatio vo-
cabatur institutio ad praedicta officia, non collatio alicuius charac-
teris, aut ordinis ecclesiastici," Summa, p. 317). William follows
Huguccio completely (see p. 62) in the question whether and under
what circumstances a hermaphrodite may be ordained (ad v. "mentiuntur," Summa, p. 316).

67. Cf. v. Schulte, vol. 2, p. 90; van Hove 1/1, p. 476.

68. "... nec premissis obstat quod legitur (C.) 27, q. 1
dyaconissam (c. 23) et c. si quis rapuerit (c. 30), iura enim illa
loquuntur de dyaconissis non que ordinem dyaconalem habeant sed
que inter alias moniales prerogativam aliquam obtinebant forte
circa omelias in matutinis legendas...," Summa, fol. 30 v.

69. Cf. v. Schulte, vol. 2, p. 93; van Hove 1/1, p. 477.

70. Ad v. "benedicunt": "quod non possunt, (C.) 33, q. 5
mulierem (c. 17), nec velant, (C.) 20, q. 2 statuimus (c. 3) nec
absoluunt, infra de sen[tentia] exc[ommunicationis] de monialibus
(X 5.39.33), nec docent, 23. dist. mulier (c. 29), nec iudicant,
(C.) 33, q. 5 mulierem (c. 17)," Apparatus, fol. 544v.

71. Ad v. "episcopum": "haec enim muliebri sexui non
conveniunt, supra de pe[nitentiis] et remiss[ionibus] nova (X 5.38.10),"
Apparatus, fol. 551v.

72. On X 5.38.10 ad v. "publice": "in matutino autem
possunt legere, (C.) 27 (Text: 38) q. 1 diaconis[sam] (c. 23),"
Apparatus, fol. 544v.

73. "... Laici autem bene possunt dicere psalmos, qui
dicuntur in horis, sed non in modum officii ... moniales autem
literatae dicunt officia, quia et ipsae possunt dici accipere aliquem
ordinem in benedictione, unde etiam aliquae inter eas sunt diaconissae, (C.) 27, q. 1 diaconissam (c. 23), qui ordo licet suffi-
ciat ad officia dicenda, non tamen [est de] septem ordinibus
ecclesiae," Apparatus, fol. 453r.

74. Similarly also on X 2.30.4 ad v. "procuratricem" (in
reference to the competence of the abbess to act as deputy in a
lawsuit): "Dig. de procur[atoribus] (1.) foeminas (dist. 3.3.41)
contra, sed hoc est speciale in mulieribus constitutis in dignitate
... vel ex quo est abbatissa, potest esse procuratrix in rebus
monasterii ... vel hoc fuit de speciali gratia quod alias non licet,"
Apparatus, fol. 347r.

75. Ad v. "suspendat": "No[tandum] hic quod Abbatissa
potest suspendere clericos suos ab officio et beneficio. Et hoc est
ea ratione, quia ex consuetudine iurisdictionem habet ordinariam,
inf[ra] de arbit[ris] dilecti (X 1.43.4), alias enim est contra ius
commune ... excommunicare autem non possunt, ut hic, nec abso-
luere, inf[ra] de senten[tia] ex[communicationis] de monialibus

(X 5. 39. 33), rationem invenies infra de poe[nitentiis] et re[missioni-
bus] nova (X 5. 38. 10), " Apparatus, fol. 158v/159r.

76. Cf. van Hove, vol. 1/1, p. 474. But according to v.
Schulte, vol. 2, p. 115 and van Hove, vol. 1/1, p. 473, the author was writing up to the very end of his life (1263).

77. Cf. v. Schulte, vol. 2, p. 115.

78. Ad v. "Evangelium": "In matutinis forte poterant legere Euangelium, unde etiam diaconissae appellantur, (C.) 27
[Text: 17] q. 1, c. diaconissam (c. 23), " Corpus, Lyon, 1671, II
1869.

79. Ad v. "praedicare": "Mulier enim nec praedicare,
nec docere potest, quia hoc officium extraneum est a mulieribus,
nec sacra vasa contingere ... nec possunt velare moniales ... nec
absolvere eas ... nec iudicare, nisi forte aliqua nobilis hoc habeat
ex consuetudine ... nec arbitrium in se suscipere ... nec procuratrix esse potest in iudicio ... nec advocare potest in iudicio ... et
generaliter viri officium mulieribus est interdictum, " Corpus, ed.
cit. , vol. 2, col. 1869f.

80. "Sic ergo mulier habet iurisdictionem, infra de
arbit[ris] c. dilecti (X 1. 43. 4). Sed contra videtur, quod mulier
iudicare non potest, (C.) 33, q. 5 c. mulierem (c. 17), nec
ciuilibus fungitur officiis, C(od.) de procur[atoribus] l. alienam
(2. 12. 18). Dig. de reg[ulis] iur[is] l. 2 (50. 17. 2). Dicas, quod
Abbatissa habet iurisdictionem talem qualem, non ita plenam, sicut vir habet. Dicas ergo, quod potest suspendere ab officio et
beneficio monachas suas et clericos suae iurisdictioni subiectos,
secundum quod hic satis innuitur, sie inobedientes fuerint: habet
enim administrationem temporalium et spiritualium.... Item ratione suae administrationis post suam confirmationem potest con-
ferre Ecclesias et beneficia et instituere clericos in Ecclesiis sui
monasterii ... sicut abbates.... Sicut enim abbas de consensu
capituli repraesentat ... eodem modo abbatissa. Excommunicare
autem non potest vel absolvere, infra de sen[tentia] excomm[uni-
cationis] c. de monialibus (X 5. 39. 33). Et potest dici quod nec
ab officio potest suspendere, nec interdicere, quia et hoc pertinet
ad claves ... et non dicit hic Papa, quod possit, quia non sexui
foemineo, sed virili traditae sunt claves regni coelorum: licet
enim beatissima virgo Maria excellentior sit Apostolis universis,
non tamen illi, sed iliis tradidit claves regni coelorum, infra de
poen[itentiis] et re[missionibus] c. nova (X 5. 38. 10), nec potest
velare moniales, (C.) 20, q. 2 c. statuimus (c. 3). Praeterea
mulier non debet habere talem potestatem, quia non est facta ad
imaginem Dei, sed vir, qui est imago et gloria Dei; et mulier debet subesse viro et quasi famula viri esse, cum vir caput sit mulieris, non e converso, (C.) 33, q. 5 c. haec imago (c. 13) et cum
caput (c. 15), " Corpus, ed. cit. , vol. 2, col. 431f.

81. There seems to be here a contradiction to previous

statements according to which, on the basis of the content of the decretal, the abbess is granted authority to suspend from office and benefice. But apparently the power of suspension referred to above should be understood as the consequence of the abbess' administrative authority, potestas dominativa, which allows her a certain right of punishing those under her, whereas here on the contrary reference is made to the right of censuring, which only higher ecclesiastical authority possesses. (Cf. p. 74.)

82. The edition (col. 432) has the following marginal reading ad v. "imaginem": 'Qualiter intelligatur, quod mulier non sit facta ad imaginem Dei, tradit B. Thom[as] I, p. q. 93 [Text: 5] art. 4 ad 1. argum[entum]." Allusion is made to the following statement of Thomas: "In relation to that with which the meaning of an image principally has to do--that is, in relation to spiritual nature--the image of God is in man and also in woman.... In relation to something secondary, it is true that the image of God is in man in a way not found in woman. For man is origin and goal of woman, just as God is origin and goal of the whole creation. Therefore the Apostle adds to the words, 'Man is the image and reflection of God but woman is the glory of man,' the reason for this (1 Cor. 11:8f.): 'For the man does not come from the woman but the woman from man. Neither was man created for woman but woman for man.'"

83. Ad v. "per Episcopum": "Impedit enim sexus muliebris, ne Abbatissa possit absolvere moniales, sicut hic patet, nec confessionem earum audire, nec eas benedicere, vel Evangelium legere, quia sexui foemineo claves Eccl[esiae] commissae non fuerunt," Corpus, ed cit., vol. 2, col. 1905.

84. Cf. p. 76; also gloss on X 5.40.10 ad v. "non foemina": "Hoc intellige in criminali, in quo casu mulier testis esse non potest secundum canones, (C.) 33, q. 5, c. mulierem (c. 17); sed in civilibus et matrimonialibus bene ferunt testmonium.... Item in testamentis mulier non admittitur," Corpus, ed. cit., vol. 2, col. 1936.

85. On X 5.40.10 ad v. "varium": "Quid levius fumo? flamen; quid flamine? ventus; quid vento? mulier; quid muliere? nihil," ibid.

86. "Sic (C.) 33, q. 5, c. cum caput (c. 15), unde sibi potius creditur quam uxori" (two references are given for this: X 4.2.6 and C. 33, q. 1, c. 3; Corpus, ed. cit., vol. 2, col. 1455).

87. Cf. v. Schulte, vol. 2, p. 127; Plöchl, vol. 2, p. 520.

88. Cf. van Hove, vol. 1/1, p. 476.

89. "Sed et praeter regulas supradictas requiritur sexus: nec enim mulieri, sed homini sunt ordines conferendi, sicut dicit

Ambrosius ad Timotheum, super illo verbo 'Mulieres similiter
pudicas' etc. quia nec tonsurari debent ... nec mulieris coma
amputanda est, 30. dist. quaecunque mulier (c. 2), nec potest
postestatem clavium exercere, arg[umentum] infra de ma[ioritate]
et obe[dientia] dilecta [Text: dilectae] (X 1.33.12) et expressum
supra de poen[itentiis] nova quaedam (X 5.38.10), nec etiam ad
altare servire debet, infra de coha[bitatione] cle[ricorum] et mulie-
[rum] c. 1 ad fi[nem] (X 3.2.1), 23. dist. mulier [Text: mulieri]
(c. 29) et c. sacratas (c. 25), de consec. dist. 1 in sancta (c. 41),
(C.) 33, q. 5 mulierem (c. 17), potest tamen euangelium dicere
ad matutinum, (C.) 27, q. 1 diaconissam (c. 23), quamuis quidam
exponunt ibi diaconissam id est abbatissam, ordinari id est velari;
nec obstat 32. dist. presbyter (c. 18), quia ibi appellatur presbytera quasi presbyteralis, non quod esset ordinata, sed ordinati socia, unde in sequenti cap[itulo] ibi vocantur tales foemine seniores
uniuirae vel matricurie, id est maternam [Text: maternae] curam
ecclesie habentes, sicut dicuntur matresfamilias," Summa Aurea,
co. 188.

90.   Authority used for this is dist. 30, c. 2 (= canon 17
of the Synod of Gangra/Asia Minor, between A.D. 325 and 370):
"Quecumque mulier, religioni iudicans conuenire, comam sibi
amputauerit, quam Deus ad velamen eius et ad memoriam subiectionis illi dedit, tanquam resolvens ius subiectionis, anathema sit,"
Corpus, ed. Friedberg, vol. 1, col. 107. The stipulation is clearly influenced by the Pauline passage 1 Cor. 11:5ff. --and therefore
by rabbinical viewpoints, which in this way have had influence on
ecclesiastical legislation.

91.   Hostiensis also in another place (Summa Aurea, col.
173)--following many of his predecessors--understands the ordination of the deaconess as bestowing the so-called "velum ordinationis, quod olim dabatur diaconissis in 40. anno."

92.   According to v. Schulte, vol. 2, p. 125, he worked on
the book to the very end of his life, A.D. 1271); cf. v. Hove,
vol. 1/1, 1. 479.

93.   "Subaudi, in missarum sollenniis, in matutinis enim
ipsum forte legere possunt, unde et diaconisse appellantur, (C.)
27, q. 1 diaconissam (c. 23)"; ad v. "publice": "quasi dicat si
priuatim in capitulo solis monialibus suis regulam exponeret, vel
ad instructionem morum aliqua exempla bona vel alia simplicia
verba proponeret, hoc non reprobaretur," Commentaria V, fol.
101r.

94.   "Et haec est quarta abusio ... mulier enim nec praedicare, nec docere debet, nec etiam sacra vasa contingere, 23. dist.
sacratas (c. 25) et c. mulier (c. 29), (C.) 33, q. 5 mulierem (c.
17), quia nec etiam masculi laici hoc possunt officium exercere";
ad v. "id absonum sit": "imo haec quae praemissa sunt et quae
officia virilia censentur a quibus mulieres regulariter sunt excluse,
ut patet Dig. de reg[ulis] iur[is] 1. 2 (50.17.2) ... unde nec

possunt etiam proprias moniales velare ... nec absolvere ... nec
iudicare, nec arbitrium suscipere, nisi forte aliqua nobilis hoc
habeat ex successione vel consuetudine ... sed nec possunt instituere vel suspendere... ," Commentaria V, 1. c.

95. While Bernard of Botone is of the opinion that the abbess by reason of her administrative authority can appoint clerics
and suspend them from office and benefice (cf. pp. 81f., above),
Hostiensis grants her only the right to grant benefices and to with-
draw them (on X 1.33.12 ad v. "suae iurisdictioni": "... potest
et beneficium concedere ...""; ad v. "excommunicare": "nec suspendere, licet de facto posset prebendas suas subtrahere, quamvis
alii dicant, quod suspendere potest ..."; Commentaria I, fol. 173v.

96. "Sic ergo mulier habet iurisdictionem ut hic et infra
de arbi[tris] dilecti (X 1.43.4). Sed contra: quia mulier iudicare
non potest, (C.) 33, q. 5 mulierem (c. 17) ... nec virilibus fungi
officiis, Dig. de reg[ulis] iur[is] 1. 2 (50.17.2). Sol[utio]: quod
dicunt contraria, regulariter obtinet. Fallit in mulieribus nobili-
bus.... Fallit hoc et in muliere praelata eadem ratione, ut hic,
talis tamen non habet plenam spiritualem iurisdictionem, quia nec
potest confessiones audire vel absolvere, nec alia, quae ad claves
ecclesiae pertinent, exercere, quantumcunque magna et nobilis
habeatur. Et est ratio, quia licet beatissima virgo excellentior
sit apostolis universis, non tamen illi, sed istis volvit filius suus
tradere claves suas, infra de poniten[tiis] nova quaedam (X 5.38.10).
Nec est facta mulier ad imaginem et similitudinem Dei, sicut vir,
unde et est quasi famula viri, cum vir [sit] caput sit mulieris,
(C.) 33, q. 5 haec imago (c. 13) et c. cum caput (c. 15) secundum
B. Sed et propter pudorem foemineum non debet se virorum coetui
immiscere, C[od.] de his qui ve[niam] aeta[tis] impe[traverunt] 1.
2 § foeminas (2.44.2).... Ideo nec potest moniales velare, nec
excommunicare, ut dictum est ... potest tamen habere administrationem spiritualium et temporalium, ut hic ... potest et beneficium
concedere, ex quo hanc administrationem habet.... Tenentur etiam
subiecti sui eidem obedientiam et reverentiam exhibere et ipsius
monita et mandata salubria adimplere... ," Commentaria I, fol.
173 r/v.

97. "Nihil dicit de sententia suspensionis, numquid ergo
ipsam tenentur servare? sic secundum quosdam, quia ipsa suspen-
dit.... Verum est de facto, sed in alio loco istius literae non
dicit, quod de iure hoc facere possit, non autem quod fit, sed quod
fieri debeat, spectandum est.... Et ideo quicquid dicant alii, tu
dicas, quod ad minus ab officio suspendere non potest; quia hoc
quasi clavium est, et nomine censurae ecclesiasticae continetur,
quod quia ipsam abbatissa exercere non potest, iudicibus ad quos
recurrat committitur, ut sequitur. Cum enim excommunicare,
suspendere et interdicere connexa sint, sive ab eodem et ad idem
inventa, cui ratione defectus iurisdictionis denegatur unum, et reliquum est denegandum.... Maxime, quia ex quo mulieribus talia
generaliter prohibentur ... semper sunt prohibita, nisi inveniantur
expresse concessa, sed non invenies expressum in iure, quod

mulier possit de iure suspendere, ergo non debes ex opinione capitanea hoc supplere...," Commentaria I, fol. 173v.

98. Ad v. "compellas": "q[uasi] d[icat] ad abbatissam pertinent monitio, mandatum, sed non coercitio," Commentaria I, l. c.

99. "In multis iuris nostri articulis deterior est condicio feminarum quam masculorum," Corpus Iuris Civilis I, 7.

100. "Est enim deterior conditio feminarum quam virorum in multis.... Primo, quia mulier non potest iudicare ... nisi princeps hoc ei committat.... Vel nisi consuetudo hoc ei concordat.... Secundo quia non potest in se arbitrium suscipere.... Tertio quia non potest docere, publice predicare, confessiones audire, nec alia, que ad claves pertinent exercere, infra de pe[nitentiis] nova quedam (X 5.38.10). Quarto quia non potest ordines suscipere, 23. di. sacratas (c. 25). Sed contra (C.) 27, q. 1 diaconissam (c. 23). Sol[utio]: improprie loquitur. Vel dicitur fieri diaconissa non, quod ordinetur ad modum diaconi, nec characterem recipiat, sed ut evangelium in matutino valeat recitare, non in apparatu vel solenniter, sed simpliciter in modum lectionis. Quinto quia non potest postulare.... Octavo quia non potest accusare.... Nono quia non potest adoptare.... Quartodecimo est conditio mulieris deterior in testamenti testificatione.... Quintodecimo in procuratione, quia non potest procuratoris officium exercere ... nisi forsan a principe constituatur.... Decimooctavo in viri subiectione, et capitis velatione, et in similtudine ad Dei imaginem formatione, (C.) 33, q. 5 haec imago (c. 13) et c. cum caput (c. 15) et c. mulierem (c. 17)," Commentaria I, fol. 204v.

101. "Est autem melior [conditio feminarum] ... quia licet eis ius ignorare ... sed in casibus tantum in iure expressis...," Commentaria I, l. c.

102. On X 5.3.40 ad v. "excusare": "... moniales vero non solum per ignorantiam, sed etiam per simplicitatem, nam permissum est mulieribus ignorare iura," Commentaria V, fol. 25v. Similarly on X 2.22.10 ad v. "Tantum venditio": "... sexu muliebri parcendum erat propter fragilitatem ... et potissime, quando agitur de apicibus iuris," Commentaria II, fol. 118r. Quite clearly a mental [geistige] weakness and frailty is meant. Of course Hostiensis shares the universally held view of the physical weakness and inferiority of woman. For instance, on X 4.2.4 (v. "complesset") he presents the following reason, among others, for the earlier female puberty: "... naturaliter debilior est sexus muliebris, unde communiter minus vivit: quia et minus habet caloris naturalis, ideo quanto citius finitur, tanto citius naturaliter perfici debet.... Plat[o] vero dixit, quod hoc ideo est, quia citius crescit mala herba quam bona, sed et dici potest, quod facilius est mulieri pati quam homini agere, unde et semper mulier est parata, non idem in homine...," Commentaria IV, fol. 11r.

103. On this see van Hove, vol. 1/1, p. 495f.; v. Schulte, vol. 2, p. 274 (there is no indication of the date of composition; which is also true for A. Lambert, "Bellemère," in DDC, vol. 2, pp. 296f.--according to Lambert, Bellamera died in A.D. 1407).

104. On X 1.43.4: "Sexto queritur et prosequamur casus, in quibus mulieris conditio est deterior.... Desimussextus est, quia non potest docere publice, vel praedicare, seu confessiones audire, nec alia quae ad claves ecclesiae pertinent, exercere ... vel sacramenta tractare.... Decimusseptimus est, quia non potest ordines suscipere" (as evidence for this, dist. 23, 25, is given, as in Hostiensis; Aegidius refutes--similarly to Hostiensis--the contradictory authority of C. 27, q. 1, c. 23; we have already, chapter 3, n. 200, dealt with his reasoning for the exclusion of women from Holy Orders, a crass denigration of women taken from Guido of Baysio). "Tricesimus primus est, in viri subiectione, capitis velatione, dei similitudine et ad dei imaginem formatione, C. 33, q. 5 haec imago (c. 13) et cum caput (c. 15) ... atque ingressu sacrarii, dum divina celebrantur et altaris appropinquatione ... et sic intelligitur lex, quae dicit in multis iuris articulis foeminarum conditio est deterior," Praelectione III, fol. 141v/142r.

105. "Sed quare sunt mulieres remotae ab officiis civilibus et publicis? Ratio est, quia sunt fragiles et minus discretae regulariter.... Item in iudicatura specialis ratio est, quia iudex debet esse constans et non flexibilis ... modo mulier est varia et fragilis ... item quia non est prudens, nec erudita, sicut debet esse iudex per se," Praelectiones III, fol. 141r. The right of adoption is denied to women for the following reason: "Ratio rationis, quia patria potestas est quid bonum, dignum et sacrum ... modo foeminae non habent dignitatem a se, sed a viro," ibid., fol. 141v.

106. "Réflexions sur la condition canonique de la femme, d'après l'oeuvre de Gilles Bellemère (1337-1407)," in Bulletin des facultés catholiques de Lyon, 76e année, new series no. 16 (1954): 9f.

107. "Et est ratio, quia mala herba cito crescit," Praelectiones III, fol. 142v. This comparison is presumably taken from Hostiensis (cf. n. 102, above) as well as the explanation added: "alia ratio, quia naturale est, quod quanto quodcunque ens citius ad finem tendit, citius perficiatur, ut apparet in musca," ibid.

108. "Ratio differentiae est propter fragilitatem, inbecillitatem, ac minorem constantiam naturalem et discretionem mulieris," Praelectiones III, fol. 142v/143r.

109. E.g., M. Schmaus, Katholische Dogmatik, 6th ed. (Munich, 1964), vol. 4/1, p. 754: "The limitation of ordination to men ... does not mean any disregard for or denigration of women in the church. It is only an expression of the dissimilarity of man and woman.... A woman remains empowered for and obligated to the ministry conferred by universal priesthood." (It is

not evident how the "dissimilarity of man and woman" should be
expressed in this case: of course there is no area of tasks in the
church which men do not share with women!) Remberger (see
chapter 1, no. 80), pp. 131f. and Concetti (quoted by Heinzelmann,
Schwestern [see Introduction, n. 1]), p. 99, agree with Schmaus.

110. Cf. Gillmann, "Zur Frage der Abfassungszeit der
Novelle des Johannes Andrea zu den Dekretalen Gregors IX. ," in
AkKR 104(1924):261-275; van Hove, vol. 1/1, p. 479.

111. Cf. v. Schulte, vol. 2, pp. 220f.; van Hove, vol.
1/1, p. 479.

112. On this see p. 65 with chapter 3, n. 177.

113. See p. 78 with n. 61, above.

114. On X 5.38.10: "... ultra quae constat, quod in sacramento requiritur res et signum ... sed in sexu foemineo significari non potest aliqua praeeminentia gradus, cum habeat statum
subiectionis--1 ad Timo[theum] 2: 'muliere[m] docere non permitto,
nec dominari in virum,' quia enim parilitate male fuit usa, ideo
fuit subiecta; Gen 3: 'sub viri potestate eris'--sacramenti ergo,
quod praeeminentiam habet, characterem non recipit," Novella V,
fol. 125v. Quite similarly Thomas says (S. T. , Suppl. q. 39, a. 1):
"... quia, cum sacramentum sit signum, in his quae in sacramento
aguntur requiritur non solum res, sed signum rei.... Cum igitur
in sexu foemineo non possit significari aliqua eminentia gradus, quia
mulier statum subiectionis habet; ideo non potest ordinis sacramentum suscipere," Summa theologiae, cura et studio P. Caramello,
Turin/Rome, 1948, vol. 4, p. 773.

115. See chapter 6, pp. 109ff.

116. "Clerici debent coronam portare, quod non licet mulieri...," Novella V, fol. 125v. This ridiculous objection is also
made by Phillips (see chapter 1, n. 152), vol. 1, pp. 446f: "...
she may not receive the royal sign of differentiation of priesthood--
cutting her hair would be a disgrace to her."

117. See n. 90, above.

118. On X 3.2.1 ad v. "ministrare": "cum [femina] non
sit capax ordinis," Novella III, fol. 7r.

119. Ad v. "monita": "... tenendum est igitur secundum
Hostien[sem], quod saltem ab officio suspendere non potest...,
cum enim excommunicatio, suspensio et interdictum contineantur
sub censura, uno prohibito, iure connexionis prohibentur et reliqua,
et satis est istud mulieribus non expresse permissum..., Novella
I, fol. 267v.

120. Cf. Mörsdorf (see Part I [preliminary], n. 5), vol.

2, pp. 111, 116.

121. Ad v. "ab officio suspendere": "Unde dixit Vin[centi-us], quod abbatissa proprie suspendere non potest ea suspensione, qua celebrans incurrit irregularitatem, sicut nec penitentiarius, licet posset large interdicere, scilicet capellanis, ne celebrent vel percipiant illa die portiones, et obedire tenentur, Novella I, 1. c.

122. Ad v. "imago": "sicut enim a deo procedit omnis creatura, sic et ab Adam omnis humana, et ab eo solo, sed non ab Eva sola, cum ipsa Eva processerit ab Adam, et sic ipsa non est imago Dei in creatione," Novella I, 1. c.

123. Cf. v. Schulte, vol. 2, 281; van Hove, vol. 1/1, p. 496 (neither writer gives the date of composition).

124. Commentaria V, fol. 196r; cf. p. 88 with n. 114, above.

125. "Not[a], quod deterior est conditio mulierum quam masculorum in istis...," Commentaria V, 1. c.

126. "Not[a], quod femina prohibetur ministrare altari, et etiam accedere, quod intellige, etiam si sit monialis..., non enim est capax ordinis," Commentaria III, fol. 9r.

127. "Not[a] primo, quod abbatissae clerici, canonicae et omnes de mona[sterio] obedire tenentur; potest ergo femina esse procuratrix ecclesiarum, quod intellige, sicut abbatissa, quia tunc administratio sibi conceditur ratione dignitatis, secus si simplex femina, ut 1. femina[s] Dig. de procu[ratoribus] (3.3.41), in hoc enim est deterior conditio feminarum, quia non possunt esse iudices, advocatae vel procuratrices.... Not[a] quod abbatissa habet iurisdictionem ... not[a] quod Papa mandat alteri, per censuram ecclesiasticam compellat monachos et clericos obedire abbatissae, et sic datur intelligi, quod ipsa punire non posset per sententiam censurae resistentes sibi ... certe hic non dicitur, quod teneat suspensio. Vin[centius] dicit ... (cf. p. 89 with n. 121). Istam etiam opinionem, quod non possit suspendere ab officio, tenet glo[sa] et etiam Ho[stiensis]..." (for continuation, see n. 119, above); Commentaria I, fol. 309r.

128. "No[tandum] ... quod privilegium concessum monachis, ut possint absolvi per abbatem, si invicem se percusserint, non habet locum in monialibus, ut ipsas possit absolvere abatissa, propter incapacitatem clavium femineo sexui non concessarum ... absolvet ergo episcopus," Commentaria V, fol. 217r.

129. On X 5.1.13: "not[a], quod abbatissa benedicitur, sicut et abbas..., non est tamen eiusdem effectus benedictio abbatissae, cuius est benedictio abbatis. Abbas enim benedictus monachos benedicit ... et minores ordines confert ... quae non facit abbatissa, cum sit actus virilis, de maio[ritate] et obe[dientia] c.

dilecta (X 1.33.12), de poeni[tentiis] et remissio[nibus] c. nova
(X 5.38.10)," Commentaria V, fol. 7r. Current law (the Code,
canon 964, n. 1) also provides that regular abbots who are priests,
after receiving consecration as abbots, may bestow tonsure and
minor orders on those of their subjects having at least simple
vows. (Cf. Mörsdorf, vol. 2, p. 96.)

130. Cf. v. Schulte, vol. 2, l. 293; van Hove, vol. 1/1,
p. 497. (There is no indication when it appeared.)

131. Commentaria VII, fol. 111r; see p. 88.

132. "Dic quod hoc officium ab eis [mulieribus] est extraneum...," Commentaria VII, l. c.

133. "Gl[osa] concludit, mulierem habere aliqualem iurisdictionem, licet non ita plenam, sicut masculi, ita quod a beneficiis potest suspendere monachas, ut hic dicitur. Tu dic, licet
doc[tores] non dicant, muliere ut singularis et privata considerata,
non potest iudicare, nec muneribus fungi virorum, sed ratione
dignitatis sic: quia non ipsa, sed dignitas hoc agere dicitur, ut
hic... Et hoc vult dicere gl[osa] dum dicit: Et habet administrationem temporalium et spiritualium, quare ratione administrationis,
quam gerit, hoc possit..., Commentaria II, fol. 89r.

134. "Per praedicta dicit gl[osa] quod non potest excommunicare ipsa abbatissa, nec absolvere, quia non ita plenam habet
potestatem, sicut masculus. Sed revocat in dubium, an possit suspendere ab officio, quia planum quod sic.... In contrarium facit,
quia suspendere ab officio dependet ex potestate clavium ... que
potestas non cadit in mulierem.... Potestas enim clavium non
mulieri, sed Petro tradita est. Licet enim beatissima virgo Maria
excellentior sit omnibus Apostolis, non tamen sibi, sed Apostolis
fuerunt traditae claves regni celorum, de peni[tentiis] et remi[ssioni-
bus] nova quedam (X 5.38.10). Item non debet postestatem clavium
habere, quia non est facta ad imaginem Dei, sed vir solus, qui est
gloria et imago Dei. Item mulier debet subesse viro et quasi famula esse viri, non econverso, (C.) 33, q. 5 haec imago (c. 13).
Per praedicta infert, quod neque ab officio suspendere, neque excommunicare ... possit ... sed isto casu ad superiorem est re-
currendum, ut hic dicit tex[tus], quia habebit hoc observari facere;
quod ab officio non suspendat, tenent doc[tores] et patet ratione
quia excommunicare non potest, ut supra dictum est, ergo nec
suspendere ab officio. Consequentia procedit a pari, cum utrunque
concernat claves.... Abb[as] dicit, quod suspensionem officii, qua
non servata suspensus incurrat irregularitatem, foemina facere non
potest, sed bene potest quandam suspensionem facti inducere, ut
prohibere, ne aliquibus diebus celebrent, aut quotidianas distribu-
tiones non percipiant, sic et potest a beneficiis et prebendis suspendere.... Et hoc etiam hic tenet Host[iensis] scilicet quod non
possit suspendere, quia appelatione censurae conprehenditur excommunicatio et suspensio.... Uno ergo prohibito, et reliquum censetur prohibitum. Item sufficit quod non apparet permissum...,"
Commentaria II, l. c.

135. "Hoc ideo, quia abbatissa ratione sexus incapax est
potestatis absoluendi, cum sit incapax potestatis clavium ... per
quod sequitur quod confessiones non audit neque eas [moniales]
benedicit, nec evangelium legit," Commentaria VII, fol. 127v.

136. Cf. van Hove, vol. 1/1, p. 497; v. Schulte, vol. 2,
p. 312. (There is no indication of the time of writing.)

137. Cf. v. Schulte, vol. 2, pp. 312ff.

138. "No[ta] primo ex tex[tu] quod licet abbatissa possit
habere iurisdictionem fori contentiosi, ut in c. dilecta de exces[si-
bus] prela[torum] (X 5. 31. 14) et idem in alia muliere de iure
speciali, ut in c. dilecti de arbi[tris] (X 1. 43. 4) et quod ibi no[ta-
tur] et (C.) 12, q. 2 cum devotissimam (c. 8), iurisdictionem tamen fori penitentialis habere non potest. Et est ratio diversitatis,
quia iurisdictio fori penitentialis procedit ex potestate clavium et
ordinum quorum mulier totaliter est incapax, adeo quod si de
facto mulier ordinatur non recipit characterem secundum commu-
nem opionem quod etiam tenet glo[sa] in c. diaconissa[m] (C.) 27,
q. 1 [Text: 2] (c. 23)," Lectura V, fol. 110r. The edition I used
(Venice, 1504) indicates, in a footnote supplementing the prohibition of hearing confessions, that according to the opinion of Guido
of Baysio male sex is required for reprimanding another person,
because a woman cannot be allowed to do this kind of thing "propter
eius inconstantiam et varietatem."

139. The prohibition of public preaching leads Nicolaus,
as Hostiensis and others, to the supplementary remark that, however, the abbess is permitted to give private admonitions to her
nuns: "... potest ergo in secreto monere moniales dando bona
exempla et explanando sacram scripturam," Lectura V, l. c.

140. "Tertio nota ibi absonum et absurdum, quia ad impu-
gnationem alicuius sententiae sive actus sufficit probare absurdita-
tem quae sequitur, valet ergo argumentum ab absurdo," Lectura V,
l. c.

141. "No[ta] quod femina non est tante fidei sicut masculus, unde potest optime adduci iste ... quia in casibus in quibus
femina admittitur non facit tantam fidem sicut masculus, et ideo
si duo sunt viri ex una parte et duae mulieres pro contraria parte,
praeferendum est testimonium virorum; nam dicitur mulier non a
sexu sed a molliti[a]e mentis, ita et vir non a sexu sed a con-
stantia et virtute animi...," Lectura V, fol. 134r.

142. "No[ta] primo ex ista glos[a] quod abbatissa est capax collationis beneficiorum, potest ergo habere ius conferendi et
instituendi; ista enim sunt iurisdictionis spiritualis et non ordinis.
--Secundo no[ta], quod ea quae dependent a potestate clavium non
cadunt in mulierem etiam alias habentem iurisdictionem spiritualem,
unde abbatissa non potest absolvere moniales a peccatis earum ut
in c. nova de pe[nitentiis] et re[missionibus] (X 5. 38. 10) nec

excommunicare ut hic. Ex quo not[a] quod non habens ordinem non potest excommunicare, licet sit persona religiosa.... Idem dicit gl[osa] in suspensione ab officio et in potestate interdicendi ab ingressu ecclesiae et divinis officiis, et hanc opinionem sequuntur communiter hic doc[tores] dicentes quod licet abbatissa possit suspendere a beneficio, subtrahere prebendas et lato modo interdicere et suspendere ab ordine, ut puta precipiendo subiectis ne celebrent donec satisfecerint, tamen stricte et proprie interdicere vel suspendere ab ordine non potest ea scilicet suspensione et interdictione que inducit irregularitatem in contrarium facientibus; hoc probatur ex eo quia excommunicatio, suspensio et interdictum continentur appellatione censurae ecclesiasticae.... Cui ergo interdicitur ratione incapacitatis unum, videntur interdicta reliqua, cum omnia dependent ab ordine, Lectura I, fol. 128r/v.

CHAPTER 5

1. The relevant passage of the gloss (on C. 27, q. 5, c. 23, ad v. "ordinari") does not tell us which decretists or theologians are referred to; also the literature of the decretists and decretalists used provides no indication.

CHAPTER 6

1. See Munier, Sources patristiques (see chapter 1, n. 198), pp. 205ff.; R. Metz, "Saint Augustin et le Code de droit canonique de 1917," in RDC 4 (1954):405-419.

2. See pp. 46f. with chapter 3, n. 27.

3. See pp. 34f. Against the possible objection that the statements of Ambrosiaster have nothing to do with the teachings of genuine Church Fathers and that therefore no weight should be given to his idea that women are by nature not made in the image of God, it must be pointed out that the influence of Ambrosiaster on church doctrine and law can hardly be overestimated, since his writings were associated with those of Ambrose and Augustine over the centuries. Besides, the God-likeness of woman is a highly debated truth, in part denied, among the genuine Church Fathers. (Cf. Van der Meer [see Introduction, n. 7], pp. 61f. and E. Schüssler, Der vergessene Partner. Grundlagen, Tatsachen und Möglichkeiten der beruflichen Mitarbeit der Frau in der Heilssorge der Kirche [Düsseldorf, 1964], p. 72.) Also according to Thomas, woman is in one sense not the image of God. (See chapter 4, n. 82.) This point of view is likewise found in contemporary theologians: e.g., H. Doms, "Zweigeschlechtlichkeit und Ehe," in Mysterium Salutis. Grundriss heilsgeschichtlicher Dogmatik, vol.

2, ed. by J. Feiner and M. Löhrer (Einsiedeln, 1967), pp. 730f.,
734f.; also by Doms, "Ehe als Mitte zwischen ihrem Urbild and
ihrem Nachbild," in Ehe im Umbruch, ed. by A. Beckel (Münster,
1969), pp. 241, 243.

    4. "... Sic etenim dicit [sc. scriptura]: Et fecit Deus
hominem; ad imaginem Dei fecit illum." Ambrosiaster omits Gen.
1:27b--"male and female he created them"--this part of the verse
would have made his argument quite impossible.

    5. Cf. W. Gesenius, Hebräisches und aramäisches Hand-
wörterbuch über das Alte Testament, 17th ed. (Leipzig, 1921), p.
10; L. Köhler-W. Baumgartner, Lexicon in Veteris Testamenti
libros (Leiden, 1953), p. 12: "אָדָם is collective and means mankind, people" (may be combined with plural and singular); "later
and isolated, אָדָם may mean a single person.... In Gen. 2:5-5:5
there is a mixture of the collective אָדָם = man and n(omen)
m(asculini) Adam. Thus we have הָאָדָם, e.g., in Gen. 2:7,8,19
and 4:1--the (type) man = Adam; but אָדָם in Gen. 5:1a = mankind."
Cf. also F. Stier, "Adam" in Handbuch theologischer Grundbegriffe,
ed. by H. Fries (Munich, 1962-1963), vol. 1, p. 13.

    6. Cf. P. Heinisch, Das Buch Genesis (Bonn, 1930), p.
101; O. Procksch, Die Genesis (Kommentar zum Alten Testament,
ed. by E. Sellin (Leipzig, 1924), vol. 1, pp. 449f.; G. von Rad,
Genesis, a Commentary (Philadelphia, 1961), p. 55; W. H. Schmidt,
Die Schöpfungsgeschichte der Priesterschrift, 2nd ed. (Neukirchen-
Vluyn, 1967), pp. 144f. (references to further literature are found
on his p. 145, n. 1).

    7. Cf. Procksch, p. 450; von Rad, pp. 46f.; W. Eichrodt,
Theologie des Alten Testaments, part 2/3, 5th ed. (Göttingen,
1964), p. 81; O. Loretz, Schöpfung und Mythos. Mensch und Welt
nach den Anfangskapiteln der Genesis (Stuttgart, 1968), p. 87; W.
Trilling, Am Anfang schuf Gott ... Eine Einführung in den
Schöpfungsbericht der Bibel, 2nd ed. (Leipzig, 1964), p. 68; H.
Wildberger, "Das Abbild Gottes" (Gen. 1:26-30) I, in Theo-
logische Zeitschrift 21 (Basel, 1965):249.

    8. Boehmer, "Wieviel Menschen sind am letzten Tage des
Hexaemerons geschaffen worden?" in Zeitschrift für die alttestamentliche Wissenschaft (Berlin, 1881ff.) (hereafter cited as ZAW)
34 (1914):34. F. Schwally, "Die biblischen Schöpfungsberichte,"
in Archiv für Religionswissenschaft (hereafter cited as ARW) 9
(1906), pp. 172-175, sees in v. 27 the idea that Gen. 1 originally
had to do with an androgynous mythos--an idea that P. Winter,
recently, shares (ZAW 68 [1956], pp. 78f.; 70 [1958], pp. 260f.).
In v. 27b Schwally wants to replace אֹתָם by אֹתוֹ. Against this,
see Eichrodt, part 2, p. 81 with n. 35, and von Rad, p. 58
("The plural in v. 27 ['he created them'] is intentionally contrasted
with the singular ['him'] and prevents one from assuming the creation of an originally androgynous man").

9. Translated: "Blessed art thou, Yahweh, our God, King of eternity, who has not made me a woman!"

10. I. e., let them have dominion ... (Gen. 1:26).

11. Boehmer (see n. 8, above), p. 33.

12. Cf. Schmidt, p. 145, n. 1.

13. Agreeing with this opinion rejected by Schmidt are, for instance, H. Gunkel, Genesis, 6th ed. (reprint of 3rd ed.) (Göttingen, 1964), pp. 112f.; likewise Heinisch, p. 101 and P. Morant, Die Anfänge der Menschheit. Eine Auslegung der ersten 11 Genesiskapitel (Lucerne, 1960), p. 61. Boehmer, p. 33, rightly remarks about this interpretation: "It seems that unconsciously and unintentionally the Paradise narrative of Gen. 2f. --where apparently a human pair, and otherwise no human beings, are presented--has become a model for the understanding of 1:26-30 and thus has suggestively influenced the exposition of this passage. Conceivably enough--when the whole weight of century-old, even millenia-old tradition has hindered objective research...."

14. Schmidt, p. 145.

15. Schmidt, p. 145, n. 1, refers to numerous parallels, including Gen. 8:6,5; 6:6f.; 7:23.

16 The appropriate parallel may be found in "light," Gen. 1:3-4 (Schmidt, p. 145, n. 1).

17. Schmidt, ibid.

18. Schmidt, p. 146, n. 1, gives numerous illustrations of this--for instance, the Levitical cleanliness regulations that differentiate between men and women.

19. Schmidt, pp. 145f.; cf. also Cl. Westermann, Genesis (Neukirchen-Vluyn, 1966ff.), p. 221.

20. Like many other commentators, Schmidt sees in the dominion status of mankind a consequence of the Godlikeness of men (p. 142); see also n. 23, below.

21. Schmidt, pp. 146f. with n. 1 (p. 147).

22. J. Jervell, Imago Dei. Gen. 1:26f. im Spätjudentum, in der Gnosis und in den paulinischen Briefen (Göttingen, 1960), pp. 94, 110, demonstrates that in late Judaism the idea arose that the procreation charge (Gen. 1:28) was given to the man alone; the man would diminish his Godlikeness if he did not procreate. Cf. also J. B. Schaller, Gen. 1:2 im antiken Judentum, unpub. dissert. (Göttingen, 1961), p. 156 ("It is occasionally admitted that the command of Gen. 1:28 is intended for woman too [cf. Billerbeck,

vol. 2, pp. 372f.], but this has not been a generally accepted point of view. Actually, reference of this command to the man alone corresponds to Israelite marital law"). Of course it remains a question whether the rabbinical interpretation really corresponds with the content of the statement of Gen. 1:28. But since the Old Testament regarded reproduction as the exclusive province of the male, the rabbinic exposition of Gen. 1:28 is not completely impossible. Cf. Gen. 9:1,7 ("God blessed Noah and his sons and said to them: 'Be fruitful and multiply, and fill the earth.... And you, be fruitful and multiply, bring forth abundantly on the earth and have dominion over it.'" The similar charge--to that of Gen. 1:28--is here directed exclusively to men.

      23. Cf. F. Horst, Gottes Recht. Gesammelte Studien zum Recht im Alten Testament (Munich, 1961), pp. 226, 239; E. Schlink, Gottes Ebenbild als Gesetz und Evangelium. Der alte und der neue Mensch (Munich, 1942), p. 71; similarly, Loretz, p. 93 ("Godlikeness is ... the presupposition of the dominion status of men"); also see Westermann, p. 213.

      24. Perhaps a confirmation of this is to be found in Gen. 5:1b, 2: "On the day when God created man [adam], he made him according to the image of God. Male and female he created them and gave them the name 'man' [adam], on the day he created them." Here the concept "adam" is expressly applied to woman also, but with it also the Godlikeness characterizing adam. Cf. H. Renckens, Urgeschichte und Heilsgeschichte. Israels Schau in die Vergangenheit nach Gen. 1-3 (Mainz, 1959), pp. 96f., on the passage: "... Man is image of God because he is a human being..."; see also Stier, p. 13. On the contrary, Boehmer, p. 34, thinks that for text-critical reasons--he refers to a variant reading of the LXX and certain commentaries, which he fails to identify--and for objective reasons, "their name" (שְׁמָם) in Gen. 5:2b should be read as "his name" (שְׁמוֹ). Other commentators, however, keep the reading שְׁמָם (their name) of the Hebrew original text throughout. E.g., J. Skinner, A Critical and Exegetical Commentary on Genesis (International Critical Commentary), 2nd ed. (Edinburgh, 1930), p. 130; likewise La Sainte Bible 1/1 (La Genèse, traduite et commentée par A. Clamer) (Paris, 1953), p. 166 ("l'appellation enfin d'Adam des deux représentants d' l'humanité ... ").

      25. Cf. A. S. Kapelrud, "Mensch (im AT)," in RGG, vol. 4, p. 862; L. Köhler, Theologie des Alten Testaments, 4th ed. (Tübingen, 1966), p. 53.

      26. The following literature deals with this problem in detail: N. Peters, Die Frau im Alten Testament (Düsseldorf, 1926); G. Beer, Die soziale und religiöse Stellung der Frau im israelitischen Altertum (Tübingen, 1919); J. Döller, Das Weib im Alten Testament (Münster, 1920); Th. Engert, Ehe- und Familienrecht der Hebräer (Munich, 1905); M. Löhr, Die Stellung des Weibes zu Jahwe-Religion und -Kult (Leipzig, 1908).

27. Cf. M. Noth, Geschichte Israels, 6th ed. (Göttingen, 1966), pp. 104, 133.

28. Cf. W. Plautz, "Zur Frage des Mutterrechts im Alten Testament," in: Zeitschrift für die alttestamentliche Wissenschaft (hereafter cited as ZAW), new series 33 (1962):10 with n. 3. Plautz shows that "most of the indications of former matriarchy," which some thought could be found among the Israelites (e.g., name giving through the mother, separate living quarters for wives--Gen. 2:24), "do not hold up under investigation and can be equally well explained by other phenomena." Only a particular type of marriage and the (relatively exalted) position of the queen mother in Judah may go back to the influence of an older (Canaanite?) culture on the patriarchal society of the Israelites. (Pp. 29f.)

29. Cf. Ex. 20:17; J. Leipoldt, Die Frau in der antiken Welt und im Urchristentum (Leipzig, 1954), p. 103; Beer, pp. 6f.

30. Cf. Gen. 20:3; 2 Sam. 11:26; correspondingly the married woman is "be'ula" (past participle of ba'al = to rule, possess; cf. Gen. 20:3; Dt. 22:22; Is. 54:1), which is translated in the LXX and in Paul (Rom. 7:2) by ὑπανδρος--subordinate to the authority of man. Cf. W. Bauer, Griechisch-deutsches Wörterbuch zu den Schriften des Neuen Testaments, 5th ed. (Berlin, 1958), col. 1657.

31. Cf., e.g., Gen. 4:17f.; Gen. 5:3ff.; 10; 11:10-26.

32. Plautz, op. cit., p. 26, notes that the phrase jld lo--"she bore him" children, e.g., in Gen. 30:4f., 17, 19--"is usual in describing birth in marriages which are strongly patriarchal." In Wisdom 7:1f. the Old Testament idea of the reproductive process develops into a theory in which Greek influence may have been effective: "In the womb I was formed into flesh, in ten months by the seeds of man my blood congealed...." On this cf. E. Lesky, "Die Zeugungs- und Vererbungslehren der Antike und ihr Nachwirken," in: Abhandlungen der Akademie der Wissenschaften und der Literatur (Geistes- und sozialwissenschaftliche Klasse), 1950, no. 19, pp. 1227-1425.

33. Cf. Gen. 29:31-55; 30:1-24; 35:17; Ps. 127:3-5.

34. Ex. 23:17; 34:23; Dt. 16:16; cf. Beer, pp. 34f.

35. Cf. Num. 3; 4; Lev. 1;2;3;4.--Beer, p. 38; Löhr, n. 16 on pp. 48f.; Engert (n. 26), p. 61. According to Ex. 38:8 and 1 Sam. 2:22, women had only certain services to perform at the entrance to the holy tent, but in the later (post-exilic) time even that possibility no longer existed for women. Cf. Beer, p. 39.

36. Cf. Ex. 15:20f.; Judges 4:4ff.; 5; 2 Kings 22:14ff. See H. Rusche, Töchter des Glaubens (Mainz, 1959).

37. Beer, pp. 37f.; cf. Köhler, op. cit., p. 53. From
the fact that there is no feminine form in the Old Testament for
the characteristics "pious" (חָסִיד), "righteous" (צַדִּיק) and "saintly"
(קָדוֹשׁ) (cf. Leipoldt, p. 72), we may conclude that no active, responsible role was allowed for women in the Yahwist religion.
The same conclusion may be drawn from the fact that the "I" who
is the official person praying in the Psalms is a man. (A few
characteristic examples: "Blessed is the man who does not walk
in the counsel of the ungodly ... but his delight is in the law of
the Lord ..." [Ps. 1:1f.]; "Let thy hand be over the man at thy
right side, over the son of man whom thou didst raise up for thy-
self" [Ps. 80:18]; "Blessed is everyone who fears the Lord, who
walks in his ways! You shall enjoy in truth the fruit of the labor
of your hands.... Your wife blossoms like a fruitful vine within
your house, your sons blossom like olive shoots around your table.
Thus shall the man be blessed who fears the Lord" [Ps. 128:1-4].)

38. Cf. cc. 13 and 20 in C. 33, q. 5.

39. Renckens, p. 253, is critical of a hasty reference to
the teachings of the Fathers because of their scriptural commentaries which are "often slavishly dependent on literal interpretation. "

40. Cf. c. 13 in C. 33, q. 5 ("Hec imago Dei est in
homine, ut unus factus sit, ex quo ceteri oriantur, habens imperi-
um Dei, quasi vicarius eius ... "); also c. 20, ibid. ("... Ideo
non duo a principio facti vir et mulier ... sed primum vir,
deinde mulier ex eo ... ").

41. Cf. J. Schildenberger, "Adam" in LThK, vol. 1, col.
126 (From the origin of the first woman [Eve] from Adam [2:21f.]
the equal value of woman with man, as well as the coordination
and the subordination of woman to man, is established). Similarly,
see Morant (see n. 13, above), p. 130; H. Muschalek, Urmensch-
Adam. Die Herkunft des menschlichen Leibes in naturwissen-
schaftlicher und theologischer Sicht (Berlin, 1963), p. 207. Concetti (see chapter 3, n. 163), p. 99, very clearly refers to the
order of creation as the reason for excluding women from the
priesthood: "It is true ... that in the order of creation--the Bible
says this clearly--primacy belongs to the male. " Doms argues
similarly, op. cit. (see n. 3, above), pp. 241-243.

42. Renckens, p. 208.

43. Ibid., p. 209.

44. Cf. Renckens, pp. 208f.; likewise, Th. Schwegler,
Die biblische Urgeschichte im Lichte der Forschung (Munich, 1960),
p. 25.

45. See Revue biblique, new series, 62 (1955), pp. 414-
419; cf. N. Greitemann, "Rabies theologica," in Wort und Wahrheit

16 (1961), p. 242: "The decrees of the Bible Commission from 1905-1915 and 1932" were "not annulled, it is true, but the administration of their obligatory character has been relaxed since 1955."

46 Thus Morant, pp. 128f. (See also p. 128, n. 9 [p. 211], where other exegetes, who represent the same position, are mentioned.) Also ibid., p. 145; and Muschalek, pp. 205ff., 230f.

47. Cf. Schwegler, p. 90; Muschalek, pp. 204f.

48. Schwegler, pp. 25-28, rightly notes the fateful consequences of uncritical Bible study which have already taken place in the course of church history.

49. Thus Schildenberger (n. 41, above), col. 126; Renckens, p. 200 and especially pp. 254ff.; Schwegler, p. 90; also H. Haag, "Die biblische Schöpfungsgeschichte heute," in H. Haag, A. Haas and J. Hürzeler, Evolution und Bibel (Freiburg, 1962), p. 49--referring to Schwegler, though with some reservation: "It should not be taught how she [woman] was created, but what she is: the natural partner of man, who, however, lives in a certain state of dependency on him."

50. More attention will be paid to these texts on pp. 110ff., since they are in part basic to the auctoritates patrum utilized by Gratian.

51. Cf. Renckens, p. 213.

52. Renckens, pp. 214f.

53. Thus H. W. Wolff, "Das Kerygma des Jahwisten," in Gesammelte Studien zum Alten Testament (Munich, 1964), pp. 349f. According to E. Sellin and G. Fohrer, Einleitung in das Alte Testament, 10th ed. (Heidelberg, 1965), p. 165, the only agreement on this is that J cannot be dated later than 722 B.C. There are differences of opinion about the earliest possible date. Disagreeing with Wolff, Sellin and Fohrer place the appearance of J in the decades between 850 and 800 B.C.

54. Stier, p. 15; H. Haag, "Die Themata der Sündenfall-Geschichte," in Lex tua veritas (Trier, 1961), pp. 110f.

55. Cf Haag, ibid., p. 111.

56. Cf. Stier, p. 15; F. Hesse "Paradieserzählung," in RGG, vol. 5, col. 99.

57. Haag, op. cit., pp. 109f. (It is, however, not clear, according to Haag, whether the Yahwist found the passage about the creation of women already a part of the adāmāh narrative or himself put the two together. Ibid., p. 110.) See also ibid., p. 2f.

58. Thus the Canaanites are, according to Gen. 9:18, 22, derived from a common tribal father, Ham, the son of Noah; according to Gen. 28:13f. (cf. Gen. 35:10ff.), Jacob is the tribal father of Israel and his brother, Esau, the father of the Edomites (Gen. 36:9ff.); see also the ancestral tree in Gen. 10. In this way the Yahwist explains the forgotten historical origins of particular tribes and clans. See Renckens, p. 226; Wolff (see n. 53, above), p. 360.

59. Cf. Renckens, pp. 198f.

60. Renckens, p. 199.

61. See p. 102 with n. 32, above. When in the Old Testament certain tribes are named for women and are derived from them (e.g., "Rachel" and "Leah" tribes--see S. Mowinckel in ZAW, Beih. 77 (1958), pp. 129-150), the reason may be found in the polygamous structure in the Old Testament, which is characterized, according to Plautz (n. 28, above), p. 15, by the fact that "the relationship between a woman and her own children is closer than that of the husband to all of his children." But that does not change the fact that--as Plautz says, p. 17--"all mothers and children ... are subordinate to the common spouse and father" and "their names, relationship and children's inheritance are determined by the legal superiority of the father."

62. Thus J. Scharbert (rescension of J. de Fraine, "La Bible et l'origine de l'homme"), Biblische Zeitschrift 6 (1962):309 ("The fact that the writers of biblical pre-history, as well as Paul too, recognize Adam as the only first man is of course due to the Israelite-Judaic thinking about tribal ancestors. Since woman is likewise a human being, she must also, according to this viewpoint, be derived from the Adam-human being, which, however, could then be explained only by a non-mediated intervention of God"). Renckens, p. 198, says, similarly: "It fits thoroughly into the strongly monogenetic thought structure of the Garden of Eden account ... that the first woman is formed from the first human being and thus is herself the second human being."

63. Eskimos relate that woman was created from the thumb of man (Westermann, op. cit., p. 314); other mythic examples of the derivation of woman from a part of the body (including the rib) of man are given by L. J. Seifert, Sinndeutung des Mythos. Die Trinität in den Mythen der Urvölker (Vienna, 1954), pp. 250f. and also by H. Baumann, Schöpfung und Urzeit des Menschen im Mythus der afrikanischen Völker (Berlin, 1964), pp. 128, 159, 240, 249. Baumann, pp. 239f., traces this myth cluster, especially the rib motif, to Christian-Islamic influence, although this is disputed by others. It is worth mentioning that a mythic idea often connected with the assumption of a secondary creation of woman is that she is in some way a defective being. Cf. Baumann, pp. 204, 369.

64. Thus Westermann, p. 313.

65. This perception is expressed by the so-called consanguinity formula in Gen. 2:23 ("bone from my bone and flesh from my flesh"); cf. W. Reiser, "Die Verwandtschaftsformel in Gen. 2:23," in Theologische Zeitschrift 16 (Basel, 1960): 4 ("Despite man's closeness to the animal, he is not profoundly related to the animal. Man is related only to man. That is the meaning of the consanguinity formula in the Yahwistic narrative of the creation of woman").

66. Thus Gunkel, op. cit., p. 13; similarly, von Rad, p. 68; Renckens, p. 199f. Referring to Procksch, Plautz (n. 28, above) opposes the assumption that Gen. 2:24 may reflect an original matriarchy, as Gunkel affirms (p. 13). Plautz says, p. 28: "It is not a matter of a law of custom but of a force of nature."

67. See Westermann, p. 311 ("In giving names man discovers, conditions and orders his world.... In this way a supreme autonomy of man in his circumscribed realm is brought to expression"). Similarly, Loretz (see n. 7, above), p. 115; Schmidt (see n. 6, above), p. 229, n. 1.

68. There is not yet any agreement among exegetes in the explanation of this motif. According to S. N. Kramer, "Enki and Ninhursag. A Sumerian 'Paradise' Myth," Bulletin of the American School of Oriental Research, Suppl. 1 (1945): 8f., the symbol of the rib should probably be traced to a Sumerian play on words; so too Westermann, p. 314 (in a reference to J. B. Pritchard, "Man's Predicament in Eden," in Rv. Rel. 13 (1948-1949): 15: "... in Sumerian there is established through a play upon words, a definite connection between the rib and 'the lady who makes live'"). Westermann thus has reservations about an etiological view of the rib motif, as we find it, e.g., in von Rad, pp. 82f. According to H. Baumann, Das doppelte Geschlecht. Ethnologische Studien zur Bisexualität in Ritus und Mythos (Berlin, 1955), p. 304 (see also pp. 170f. with n. 122), the narration motif--creation of woman from the rib of man--is an abbreviated expression of an underlying mythic understanding according to which woman is formed from the left (in mythical language, the female) side of the original man Adam pictured as androgynous. O. Schilling, Das Mysterium Lunae und die Erschaffung der Frau nach Gen. 2:21f. (Paderborn, 1963), uses a comparison from the history of religions to suggest that the rib is a representation of the moon and thus a fertility symbol. Schilling says that in using this symbol the biblical writer has given the moon idol into the hands of the creator God and thus the creation concept has overcome any kind of physical or mythical self-generation.

69. Gunkel, p. 13; similarly, Döller (see n. 26, above), p. 6, who however, in contrast to Gunkel, treats the passage uncritically: "A certain dependence of woman on man is already expressed in the creation account, in that she is simply there for his sake, as his helper."

70. Loretz, pp. 115f.

71. Thus von Rad, pp. 66f.; similarly, Eichrodt, vol. 2, p. 77.

72. However, many exegetes (e.g., Schmidt, p. 201--although in contradiction to p. 147, n. 1--and Westermann, pp. 316f.) succumb to the danger of idealization, in that they dispute any form of a secondary position of woman in the Yahwistic creation account. On the other hand, I. Bertinetti, Frauen im geistlichen Amt. Die theologische Problematik in evangelisch-lutherischer Sicht (Berlin, 1965), p. 88, rightly notes: "No exegetical device can obscure the fact that the second creation account presupposes a clear, if limited, priority of the male."

73. Renckens, p. 195. According to targum Jeruschalmi I, the "help" which the woman affords to Adam is exclusively sexual, as also the Aramaic translation of Gen. 2:18 suggests: "It is not right that Adam should sleep alone, I will create for him a woman, who will be as support by his side" (Schaller [see n. 22, above], p. 38); Augustine (De Genesi ad litteram I, 93, in CSEL 28/1, p. 271) similarly interprets the concept "helper" as simply the contribution of woman to the procreation of offspring ("Si autem quaeritur, ad quam rem fieri oportuit hoc adiutorium, nihil aliud probabiliter occurrit quam propter filios procreandos, sicut adiutorium semini terra est, ut virgultum ex utroque nascatur"). Contrariwise, Westermann, p. 317, maintains: "The phrase 'a helper fit for him' does not mean woman as sexual partner nor woman as helper in the field; any such delimitation destroys the sense of the passage. The personal fellowship between man and wife in the widest sense is intended...." Cf. also ibid., p. 309.

74. Cf. Renckens, pp. 203, 227f.; Haag, Schöpfungsgeschichte, p. 49; Loretz, p. 120; Westermann, p. 313.

75. Renckens, pp. 203f.; also see J. Begrich, "Die Paradieserzählung. Eine literargeschichtliche Studie," in Gesammelte Studien zum Alten Testament (Munich, 1964), p. 28.

76. So too Bertinetti, op. cit., p. 88; similarly, Loretz, pp. 28f. with n. 45 and n. 46.

77. Cf. Schwegler, pp. 19f., 86.

78. Especially in the explanation of the Bible Commission (cf. p. 103, above) concerning the historical character of the narrative of the origin of woman from man.

79. This is pointed out by Renckens, p. 205, and Boehmer (see n. 8, above), pp. 31ff., who rightly oppose any such interpretation.

80. Thus Renckens, p. 205; also see Schmidt, p. 229; similarly Bertinetti, p. 89.

81. Cf. Metz, "Statut" (see Introduction, n. 9), p 62.

82. Cf. Hesse (see n. 56, above), col. 99; so also Loretz, pp. 120, 131.

83. Haag, Schöpfungsgeschichte, pp. 45f.; see also his Sündenfall-Geschichte, p. 7.

84. See more on this in Begrich; Haag, Sündenfall-Geschichte, pp. 101ff.; also see Westermann, pp. 258, 265f.

85. Cf. Begrich, p. 29 and many other places. Also according to Haag, Sündenfall-Geschichte, pp. 5ff., the temptation story (Gen. 3:1-7), which is significant in the context of our discussion, is of independent origin; J has worked it into the "Garden of Eden theme" (which, according to Haag, should be distinguished from the so-called adāmāh theme of Gen. 2-3). Cf. also Westermann, pp. 265f.

86. Begrich, pp. 36f. This explains "the succinctness and plainness in the story of the temptation of the man"; the psychological depth of the temptation of the woman by the serpent is lacking. (Pp. 29f.) Other exegetes who are not occupied with the problem of source analysis in J too quickly find in the succinctness of the description an opinion of the narrator that woman has a special influence on man toward evil as well as toward good (cf. Begrich, p. 29). Still others construct from the narration an easier inclination to temptation and thus a moral inferiority of woman in comparison to man. So, e.g., B. K. Budde, "Die biblische Paradiesesgeschichte," in ZAW Suppl. 60 (Giessen, 1932): 46: "It [the serpent] proves its cleverness by going to the woman, who is of course considered to be the more unwise and more sensual of the two humans..."; a similar judgment is made by Heinisch, p. 120 and Procksch, (see n. 6, above), p. 31.

87. Cf. Haag, Sündenfall-Geschichte, p. 5; Renckens, p. 247; note especially F. Hvidberg, "The Canaanitic Background of Gen. 1-3," in Vetus Testamentum 10 (1960): 285-294 (ibid., p. 287: "The Canaanitic Baal appears not only in the form of a man ... but also in the form of a serpent"); also see Loretz, pp. 117, 121.

88. Hvidberg, op. cit., p. 289.

89. Cf. Siefert (see n. 63, above), pp. 272f., 286 (here the dependence of this mythic motif on the patriarchial culture is expressly indicated); cf. also F. Herrmann, "Symbolik in den Religionen der Naturvölker," in Symbolik der Religionen, ed. by F. Herrmann (Stuttgart, 1961), vol. 9, p. 132.

90. See Gen. 31:19; Judges 17:4ff.; 1 Kings 15:13; Jer. 7: 17; 44:15-19, 25. According to Beer (see n. 26, above), p. 41 with n. 2, Israelite women possessed many amulets and statues of

gods, including representations of the fertility goddess, Astarte, which were found in Palestinian excavations. Because of the danger of culture corruption and idolatry, marriages of Israelite men with Gentile women were strictly prohibited. Cf. Ex. 34:16; Ezra 9:1ff.; Neh. 13:23ff.

91. Cf. n. 86, above. The statements of the commentators named in no way fall short of those of rabbinic late Judaism, which were influential in the New Testament (cf. 1 Tim. 2:14 and 2 Cor. 11:3) and also in the writings of the Church Fathers. (Concerning rabbinic exposition of Gen. 3, see E. Brandenburger, Adam und Christus. Exegetisch-religionsgeschichtliche Untersuchung zu Röm. 5:12-21; 1 Kor. 15 [Wissenschaftliche Monographien, vol. 7] [1962], pp. 39f., 49f., 44f.).

92. Several writers have taken special notice of the negative consequence of the extensive exclusion of women from the Yahweh religion. E.g., Köhler (see n. 25, above), p. 53: "Yahweh's covenant with Israel is a covenant with men, for they represent the people.... Women have no place in this revelation and therefore in the worship of Yahweh they are a continuing danger." Cf. also W. Rudolph, Jeremia (Handbuch zum Alten Testament, ed. by O. Eissfeldt, first series, vol. 12), 3rd ed. (Tübingen, 1968), p. 55: "According to this passage [Jer. 7:16ff.], the worship of the queen of heaven [i.e., the Babylonian-Assyrian Ishtar] is first of all a matter for women, who actually come off somewhat badly in the Yahweh religion." Bertinetti also, pp. 23f., rightly points out this connection: "The lack of the possibility of regular religious activities misled women into unofficial religious practices. Thus the prevention of official cultic practices resulted commonly in the development of a kind of surrogate religion, characterized by men as superstition and idolatry. One may see here the completely natural reaction to an unwarranted exclusion of a whole section of the people from a religious practice which had become the business of the male population alone, yet this reaction could also be seen as continuance of ancient folk superstition carried out by insufficiently enlightened women." The membership of women in Christian heresies (Montanism, etc.) may be similarly explained. See Heinzelmann, Schwestern, pp. 50f.

93. Cf. Bertinetti, p. 93.

94. Cf. Renckens, p. 256; Bertinetti, p. 94; von Rad, pp. 75, 81f.; Westermann, pp. 74ff., 266f., who alludes to the etiological character of myths of the Fall outside the Bible, to which the sentences of punishment in Genesis that do not belong to the original part of the Garden of Eden story go back in the final analysis. See also Schmidt, pp. 215, 218.

95. Cf. Stier, p. 17 ("Old Israelite ears probably wanted to hear, and were supposed to hear, that field and woman are exactly the bearers of fruit upon which the Canaanite fertility cult was to bestow its prosperity").

96. In 1 Cor. 14:34 the subjection of woman is demanded, among other reasons, because of "the law." The commentators often refer to Gen. 3:16. And according to Strack-Billerbeck, vol. 3, p. 468, the Apostle must have had this passage in mind; yet one should not insist on the term law, since traditional custom was often accepted as Torah (= law). H. von Campenhausen is more cautious (Die Begründung kirchlicher Entscheidungen beim Apostel Paulus [Sitzungsberichte der Heidelberger Akademie der Wissenschaften, phil. -hist. sec., 2nd essay, 1957]), p. 24: "Paul seems to be following [(i.e., in the regulation that women must remain silent)] a practice of the Jewish synagogue which is also attested, he thinks, by ancient 'law' (14:34)..., but it is not clear what Paul is thinking about here and whether he is thinking at all about a particular passage of the Pentateuch."

97. Cf. c. 15 in C. 33, q. 5 (Jerome on Tit. 2:5): "... Verbum autem Domini blasphematur, vel cum contempnitur Dei prima sentencia et pro nichilo ducitur ... dum contra legem fidemque naturae ea, que Christiana est, et ex lege Dei subiecta, viro inperare desiderat..."; cf. also cc. 18 and 19.

98. H. Greeven, Die Frau im Urchristentum (Sonderdruck des Zentralblatts für Gynäkologie 81, 1959), p. 298; also see Renckens, p. 255 ("Instead of formulating a law, the judgment is ... a statement of fact.") Likewise, Van der Meer, p. 28 ("Nor is Gen. 3:16 a law [in the sense of 'precept'] but an existing fact"). Also see von Rad, p. 82.

99. On this see Seifert (n. 63, above), pp. 259, 262f.; Herrmann (n. 89, above), pp. 138-141; so, too, Westermann, pp. 74f.

100. Van der Meer, pp. 28f.

101. Gratian also treats this sentence as the Apostle's word, as his punctuation shows. (Cf. Friedberg, Corpus, vol. 1, col. 1254.) On the contrary, in the Quaestiones veteris et novi Testamenti (CSEL 50, 243), ed. by A. Souter, from which chap. 13 is taken, only 1 Cor. 11:7a is printed as quotation--not the sentence added by Ambrosiaster.

102. The words used there are in literal agreement with c. 13: "mulier debet velare caput, quia non est imago Dei," ed. Friedberg, Corpus, vol. 1, col. 1225.

103. Cf. Jervell (see n. 22, above), p. 308: "Paul clearly considers that only the man was created on the sixth day. Only later was the woman created...." Cf. also E. F. Scott, The Pastoral Epistles (Moffat New Testament Commentary 13) (London, 1948), p. 27.

104. See especially Jervelle, pp. 293, 295f., 311; Schaller, p. 189; J. Weiss, Der erste Korintherbrief, 10th ed. (Götting-

en, 1925), p. 270; H. D. Wendland, Die Briefe an die Korinther, 12th ed. (Göttingen, 1968), p. 91 ("Paul is doubtless using here a traditional exposition of the creation narrative, an exposition which corresponds to the actual and thorough subordination of women in cultic and legal realms dominant in the world of antiquity").

105. So Jervell, pp. 298f.; similarly, Wendland, p. 90.

106. Cf. J. Jeremias, "Adam," in Theological Dictionary of the New Testament (Grand Rapids, Mich., 1964-1969), (hereafter cited as ThD), ed. by G. Kittel, vol. 1, p. 141; also 1 Tim. 2:13 (reference to the primacy of Adam in creation as explanation of the prohibition against teaching by women) is conditioned by this principle. See J. Jeremias, Die Briefe an Timotheus und Titus (Das Neue Testament Deutsch), 8th ed. (Göttingen, 1965), p. 19; N. Brox, Die Pastoralbriefe, 4th ed. (Regensburg, 1969), pp. 134f.

107. Jervell, pp. 109ff., presents a great deal of evidence from rabbinic writings of the limitation of image-of-God status to Adam and thus to the male. In addition see Schaller, pp. 113, 152f., 172, esp. p. 189.

108. Tanch B Tazria 10, in Jervell, 1. 110 (with further references to sources); in summary Jervell, p. 111, says: "The tendency of rabbinic theology is not only to deny image-of-God status to Eve--from the standpoint of salvation history--but also to every woman" [emphasis added]. Yet there are other viewpoints in rabbinic writings which grant this status to both man and woman; the married couple is seen as humanity in the image of God. (Evidence is given by Jervell, pp. 111f.) It is true that Paul in 1 Cor. 11:3ff. is not influenced by this viewpoint, though perhaps he is in 1 Cor. 11:11f. See Jervell, pp. 311f.

109. Cf. Jervell, p. 299; Schaller, p. 189.

110. Cf. Jervell, p. 300; H. Schlier, "$\kappa\epsilon\varphi\alpha\lambda\acute{\eta}$," in ThD, vol. 3, p. 679.

111. Schaller, pp. 24, 33, points out that the LXX, which is influenced by Jewish tradition, translates the expression כְּנֶגְדּוֹ (= as his--Adam's--complement, Gen. 2:18) with $\kappa\alpha\tau'\,\alpha\grave{v}\tau\acute{o}\nu$. Also see Jervell, p. 300.

112. Jervell, 1. 301 ("A rabbinic reason for denying women the image-of-God status was precisely that they did not have the same religious duties as men"); see also ibid., p. 109. Similarly, Schaller, p. 152: according to one rabbinic tradition image-of-God status consists in circumcision, i.e., in actual membership in the people of God--thus a woman is ipso facto considered to be not image-of-God.

113. According to Schaller, pp. 188f., the series God-Adam-Eve is found in the targum translation of Gen. 1:26f. and

2:18. Since Paul in 1 Cor. 11:7 directly characterizes man as "image of God," contrary to his usual custom and without reference to Christ as mediator, it is practically certain, Schaller says, that Paul's series was also originally God-man-woman and that he simply enlarged it for christological purposes.

114. Cf. Schlier, ibid. ("κεφαλή means the one who stands above the other in the sense that he establishes the other's being"); Wendland, p. 90 ("The term 'head' means the outstanding, the superior, especially the head of a community").

115. Weiss (see n. 104, above), p. 270.

116. Cf. Wendland, p. 91.

117. See Jervell, p. 303 with n. 433, p. 114.

118. See Jervell, pp. 305ff.

119. Cf. Jervell, p. 305.

120. Jervell, p. 307, Weiss, p. 274 and H. Lietzmann (An die Korinther 1,2 [Handbuch zum Neuen Testament, vol. 9], 4th ed. [Tübingen, 1949], p. 54), who finds support in Dibelius, understand by τοὺς ἀγγέλους demons and evil spirits; see also n. 128, below.

121. M. Dibelius, Die Geisterwelt im Glauben des Paulus (Göttingen, 1909), pp. 18ff., indicates that in widespread popular belief magical power was attributed to the veil.

122. Jervell, p. 308.

123. Cf. Jervell, pp. 368f.

124. Cf. Jervell, p. 304 with n. 436; likewise Brandenburger (see n. 91, above), pp. 39f., 44f., esp. 49f. (the last containing numerous references).

125. Cf. Jervell, p. 305 with n. 442; also see Brandenburger, pp. 49f.: According to Slavonic Enoch 31, 6 and Apocalypse of Abraham 23, the devil's attack against Adam was possible only through Eve.

126. Paul here compares the Christian people to a virgin, whom he has betrothed to Christ. Christ and the congregation are placed parallel to Adam and Eve. Paul fears that as Eve succumbed to the seduction of the serpent, so the mind of the faithful may be turned away from the sincere and pure devotion to Christ. The comparison is only apt if at its base lies the idea that Eve was led by the serpent to be unfaithful to Adam. As a matter of fact, there is a well-known rabbinic tradition according to which Eve did succumb to sexual seduction by the serpent. Paul is here

dependent on this tradition. Cf. Jervell, p. 304; Brandenburger, p. 50; Strack-Billerbeck, vol. 1, p. 138.

127. Jervell, pp. 304f. and Brandenburger, p. 50, among others, point to the late Jewish tradition as basis for 1 Tim. 2:11ff. So also Brox (see n. 106, above), pp. 134f., who refers to W. Nauck, Die Herkunft des Verfassers der Pastoralbriefe, unpub. dissert. (Göttingen, 1950), pp. 96ff., according to whom 1 Tim. 2:13-15a, which underlies the prohibition of teaching in 1 Tim. 2: 12, is a short Midrash which leans closely to the rules of rabbinic exegesis. Brox, p. 133, says that the occasion for the teaching prohibition is an heretical (gnostic) practice, which gave women complete liberty to teach in open assumbly. No scholarly certainty exists about the authorship of the Pastoral letters: Catholic and some Protestant exegetes hold to their genuineness, but there is a growing inclination, including that of Catholic scholars, to think that "the assumption of genuineness makes it more difficult to explain the meaning of the letters." Brox, p. 25; see the thorough discussion of the authorship question, ibid., pp. 22-60.

128. The LXX translates "sons of God" (Gen. 6:2) with ἄγγελοι τοῦ θεοῦ; cf. the parallels in 1 Cor. 11:10: διὰ τοὺς ἀγγέλους.

129. Weiss, pp. 274f.

130. See Strack-Billerbeck, vol. 3, pp. 427-437.

131. Cf. cc. 13 and 19 in C. 33, q. 5; also see dictum Gratiani C. 15, q. 3 princ. ("in signum subiectionis velatum caput habere").

132. Jervell, p. 309. (Jervell also, p. 309, n. 459, notes that in rabbinic understanding the woman was ordered, after the Fall, to wear long hair. Cf. Strack-Billerbeck, vol. 3, p. 442.)

133. Cf. Wendland, p. 92.

134. See Lietzmann (n. 121, above), p. 55.

135. Cf. Wendland, p. 92 ("It should not be claimed that v. 11 annuls all that has been previously been said").

136. See E. Schweizer, "σάρξ," in ThD, vol. 7, p. 125; also by Schweizer, "σῶμα," in ThD, vol. 7, p. 1078.

137. This could also be inferred from the fact that Eph. 5:30--"For we are all members of his (i.e., Christ's) body"-- contains in many mss. the addition "from his flesh and from his bones," a clear reference to Gen. 2:23. In the same way E. Best, One Body in Christ. A Study in the Relationship of the Church to Christ in the Epistles of the Apostle Paul (London, 1955), p. 178,

says: "The ἐκ (i.e., from his flesh, etc.) suggests, that as Eve came from Adam so the Church comes from Christ; this reproduces the conception of Christ as the ἀρχή of the Church, its originating cause..."; cf. also S. F. B. Bedale, "The Theology of the Church," in Studies in Ephesians, ed. by F. L. Cross (London, 1956), p. 72.

138.   Cf. Renckens, p. 203; Gunkel, p. 13.

139.   Thus Schweizer, "σάρξ," in ThD, vol. 7, p. 137, 12ff.; F. Mussner, Christus, das All und die Kirche. Studien zur Theologie des Epheserbriefes (Trier, 1955), pp. 150f.: "Of course woman is not literally the 'body' or the 'self' of man, but in marriage she becomes 'one flesh' with her husband, according to Gen. 2:24, so that love of the husband for his wife meets something in her which belongs to his own (physical) essence." See also F. Foulkes, The Epistle of Paul to the Ephesians. An Introduction and Commentary (Tyndale New Testament Commentaries) (Michigan, 1963), p. 160: "Christ loves her [i.e., the church] as His body.... Even so husbands are to love their wives, as their own bodies. It would seem that Genesis 2:24 is already in mind, though it is not quoted till verse 31.... Paul ... comes closer to the terms of Genesis 2:24 when he says, 'For no man ever yet hated his own flesh....' "

140.   F. Rienecker, Der Brief des Paulus an die Epheser (Wuppertal, 1961), p. 209, understands Eph. 5:28f. exclusively in this sense, although he fails to take account of its timebound nature. ("The body has not independent will, rather its whole life-movement is regulated by the impulse that comes from the head. So it is with the relationship between Christ and his people and thus with the relationship between between man and woman.")

141.   E. Schweizer, "σῶμα," in ThD, vol. 7, p. 1064.

142.   Ibid., p. 1063; "In sexual intercourse the body of one belongs to the other."

143.   Perhaps there is an exception to this in 1 Cor. 6:15f.: "Do you not know that your bodies are members of Christ? Shall I therefore take the members of Christ and make them members of a prostitute? ... Do you not know that he who joins himself to a prostitute becomes one body with her? For it is written, 'The two shall become one' " (Gen. 2:24).

144.   According to Mussner (see n. 139), p. 148, the extent of this power-of-command is comparable to that of a master over his slaves!

145.   This expression in v. 28a and v. 29 ("flesh") has a variation in v. 28b as follows: "He who loves his wife loves himself." Here a certain identity of the married partners is implied (cf. Metz, "Recherches" [see Int., n. 9], p. 381) and the concept

"body" is almost given the significance of person. But wife is
still seen as dependent on and in relation to husband (as part of
himself ["body"] or as himself) and defined more exactly by his
person--never the reverse! The objective significance of the concept "body" or "flesh" applied without question to women fits especially well the concept σκεῦος (instrument, vessel), which, in an
exclusively sexual sense, is applied to wives in 1 Thess. 4:4 and
1 Peter 3:7--in dependence on late Jewish linguistic usage. Thus
this concept--combined with that of κτᾶσθαι--characterizes the
marriage relationship of husband to wife as that of possession, in
which the wife has only a passive role and to a certain extent is
looked upon as an object to be used. See Ch. Maurer, "σκεῦος,"
in ThD, vol. 7, pp. 361f., 365-367.

146. Cf. Bedale (see n. 137, above), p. 71.

147. M. Weber, Ehefrau und Mutter in der Rechtsentwicklung (Tübingen, 1907), p. 184, remarks aptly about this: "Thus
Paul seems to think of the unconditional subjection of the wife as
presupposition for the realization of that mystical image in marriage, and apparently for him obedience is much more indispensable than any other attitude on her part [emphasis added]. For he
demands of the husband: 'You men, love your wives ... just as
Christ has loved his church and given himself for it...,' but then
he says to the wives: 'but the wife must respect the husband.'"

148. Cf. Weber, pp. 182f. But this is not true for 1 Cor.
7 and Gal. 3:27f.

149. Weber, p. 184.

150. Cf. Schaller, pp. 184, 189. Again, the theory of
male procreation, i.e., the Jewish idea of tribal ancestors, lies
behind this point of view.

151. Cf. Schaller, p. 189.

152. "For this reason a man (ādām) shall leave his father
and mother and be joined to his wife; and the two shall become one
flesh (Gen. 2:24). This is a great mystery, and I take it to mean
Christ and the church."

153. Cf. Schaller, p. 189.

154. See Schweizer, "σῶμα," ThD, vol. 7, p. 1077.

155. Cf. Schaller, p. 102.

156. According to Mörsdorf (see Part I [preliminary], n.
5), vol. 2, p. 139, the headship of the husband in marriage (cf.
c. 1112 with cc. 93 and 98, § 4) is generally recognized in canonistic studies as a divine principle of marriage. Cf. also Doms,
Ehe als Mitte zwischen ihrem Urbild und ihrem Nachbild, pp. 241-
243.

157. E.g., Augustine in two passages quoted by Gratian suggests a higher ethical demand on men because of their supposed superiority: "... ad eos pertinet et virtute vincere, et exemplo regere feminas" (C. 32, q. 6, c. 4); "Si caput est vir, melius debet vivere vir, et precedere in omnibus bonis factis uxorem suam" (ibid., c. 5). Actually, however, the claim to dominion and power over women and to a privileged position toward them is usually derived from a simple assertion of the superiority of men.

158. Weighty text-critical considerations have been raised against the 1 Cor. 14:34f. passage. See G. Fitzer, "Das Weib schweige in der Gemeinde." Über den unpaulinischen Charakter der mulier-taceat-Verse in 1 Korinther 14 (Theologische Existenz heute, no. 110) (Munich, 1963); H. Lietzmann-W. G. Kümmel, An die Korinther I, II (Handbuch zum Neuen Testament, vol. 9), 4th ed. (Tübingen, 1949), p. 75.

159. See the rabbinic sources and parallels to these passages in Strack-Billerbeck, vol. 3; also Schaller, pp. 187-189; cf. n. 104, above.

160. Cf. v. Campenhausen (see n. 96, above), p. 42; Brox, pp. 134ff.

161. The "Pauline" prohibition of teaching by women (cf. 1 Cor. 14: 34f. and 1 Tim. 2:11ff.) already had authoritative influence on early church liturgies. Cf. W. Lock, A Critical and Exegetical Commentary on the Pastoral Epistles (International Critical Commentary, vol. 11) (Edinburgh, 1924), p. 29, which refers to the following liturgies: Canon. Hippol. §§ 81-88 ("mulier libera ne veniat veste variegata in ecclesiam ... neve omnino loquantur in ecclesia quia est domus Dei." The "justification" ["quia est domus Dei"] is very instructive on the question of the valuation of women); Test. Dom. II, 4; Apostolic Constitutions, III, 6.

CHAPTER 7

1. Besides the works of Van der Meer and v. Eyden quoted frequently in previous chapters of this book, see the following: V. E. Hannon, The Question of Women and the Priesthood. Can Women be Admitted to Holy Orders? (London, 1967); M. Daly, The Church and the Second Sex (New York, 1968); J. Peters, "Women in Church Vocation," in Concilium 34 (New York, 1968), pp. 126-138; R. J. Bunnik, Das Amt in der Kirche. Krise und Erneuerung in theologischer Sicht (Düsseldorf, 1969), pp. 140-147. In addition, the following may be mentioned from Protestant literature, which contains an abundance of material on the question of ordination of women: G. Heintze, "Das Amt der Pastorin," in Evangelische Theologie (hereafter cited as EvTh) 22 (1962): 509-535; H. D. Wendland, "Das geistliche Amt in der heutigen Kirche," in Kirche

in der Zeit 17 (1962): 81-85; H. D. Wendland, O. H. v. d. Gab-lentz and W. Stählin, "Die Frau und das geistliche Amt der Kirche," in Quatember 27 (1962-1963): 63-77; M. Barot, "Die Ordination der Frau: ein ökumenisches Problem," in Zusammen. Beiträge zur Soziologie und Theologie der Geschlechter, ed. by Ch. Bourbeck (Witten, 1965), pp. 329-337; I Bertinetti (see chap. V, n. 72); K. Klein, "Das Amt der Pastorin," in EvTh 26 (1966): 96-109.

2. On this see the standard investigation by P. E. Persson, Repraesentatio Christi. Der Amtsbegriff in der neueren römisch-katholischen Theologie (Kirche und Konfession, vol. 10) (Göttingen, 1966). (Persson does not undertake a conceptual differentiation be-tween deputyship and "repraesentatio" since he considers them to be internally connected.)

3. See J. Pascher, "Die Hierarchie in sakramentaler Sym-bolik," in Episcopus. Studien über das Bischofsamt (Regensburg, 1949), pp. 278-295, esp. pp. 290-294; M. C. Vanhengel, "Die Rolle des Priesters in der Symbolik der Sakramente," in Theologie der Gegenwart 9 (1966): pp. 137-144, esp. pp. 137-139. Cf. also the text from the Ambrosiaster commentary on 1 Cor. 11:10 (C. 33, q. 5, c. 19 in Gratian): "Mulier ... non habeat potestatem loquendi, quia episcopus personam habet Christi. Quasi ergo ante iudicem Christum, ita ante episcopum sit, quia vicarius Domini est, propter peccatum originale debet subiecta videri," Corpus, ed. Friedberg, vol. 1, col. 1255f.

4. Cf. Persson, who gives many source references; W. Kasper, "Amt und Gemeinde," in Glaube und Geschichte (Mainz, 1970), p. 396, n. 24, points out the change in meaning of the con-cept repraesentatio from the first to the second millenium, from a "more symbolic-sacramental-actualist connotation to a more juridic-static connotation."

5. For instance in the encyclicals "Mystici Corporis Christi" (AAS 35, 1943, 193-248, esp. 200, 210f., 232) and "Hu-mani generis" (AAS 42, 1950, 561-577, esp. 568).

6. AAS 39, 1947, 556, n. 93; cf. also no. 84: "The priest acts for the people only because he represents Jesus Christ, who is head of all His members and offers Himself in their stead.... The people, on the other hand, since they in no sense represent the Divine Redeemer and are not a mediator between themselves and God, can in no way possess the sacerdotal power," AAS, 553f.; English text, National Catholic Welfare Conference (Washington, D.C., 1948), p. 33.

7. Ibid., no. 40, AAS 538; Eng. text, op. cit., p. 18.

8. Ibid., no. 42, AAS 539; Eng. text, p. 19.

9. Ibid., no. 68, AAS 548; Eng. text, p. 28. Many fur-ther references to this concept are given by Persson, pp. 73ff., 115 with n. 80, 116f.

10. Pascher (see n. 3, above), pp. 278-283.

11. See p. 122; Persson, p. 12 with n. 15.

12. Pascher, p. 282.

13. Cf. ibid., p. 283.

14. Pascher, Die christliche Eucharistiefeier als dramatische Darstellung des geschichtlichen Abendmahles (Munich, 1958), p. 4; also by Pascher, Die Liturgie der Sakramente, 3rd ed. (Münster, 1962), p. 9. Similarly, Schmaus, Dogmatik 4/1, 6th ed. (1964), p. 757. It is often said that the unity between Christ and priest is expressed in the recitation of the words of consecration, when the priest says, "Hoc est corpus meum," not, "Hoc est corpus Christi." E.g., M. Premm, Katholische Glaubenskunde. Ein Lehrbuch der Dogmatik, (Vienna, 1955), vol. 3/1, p. 26; similarly, Pascher, Die Hierarchie, p. 295.

15. No. 198 (AAS 39, 1947, 592); Decree on the Ministry and Life of Priests, art. 11 (AAS 58, 1966, 1008; Eng. text in Abbott, op. cit., pp. 555f.); Dogmatic Constitution on the Church, art. 20/21 (AAS 57, 1965, 23f.; Eng. text in Abbott, pp. 39ff.)

16. According to Persson, p. 121, "the customary ways of thinking" (about office and representation) appear in Semmelroth "in extraordinarily clear and concentrated formulation."

17. Semmelroth, Maria oder Christus? (see chapter 4, n. 18), p. 131; and his Das geistliche Amt (Frankfurt, 1958), p. 208 ("The meeting of the teaching office-holders of the church with the obedient congregation is, by virtue of Christ's presence, a representation of the revelation of God in Jesus Christ to the members of the congregation who receive the revelation and thereby imitate the obedient Mary"). The author expresses a similar opinion, though somewhat more cautiously--the comparison of the congregation to Mary is abandoned--in "Demokratie in der Kirche?" in Martyria--Leiturgia--Diakonia, ed. by O. Semmelroth (Mainz, 1968), p. 406.

18. Maria oder Christus?, p. 99.

19. Ibid., p. 149.

20. E.g., Laurentin, Marie, L'Eglise et le Sacerdoce, vol. 2, pp. 74ff.: The church is said to have two aspects, it is "Jésus-Christ répandu et communiqué" and "l'épouse du Christ"; according to the first aspect, the church is masculine and is represented by men, while according to the second aspect it is essentially feminine--its prototype is Mary. Similarly, A. Wintersig, "Liturgie und Frauenseele" (Ecclesia orans. Zur Einführung in den Geist der Liturgie, ed. by I. Herwegen, vol. 17) (Frieburg, 1925), pp. 16ff.

21. Krebs, Katholische Lebenswerte 5/2, 1st and 2nd ed. (Paderborn, 1925), pp. 483f.; cf. also G. Bichlmair, Der Mann Jesus, 2nd ed. (Vienna, 1946), p. 118: "Christ is the bridegroom, the church his bride. As vicars and workers together with Christ, the apostles and their successors had to take a similar position toward the church. They were supposed to portray in allegorical form the one bridegroom of the church, and of course for this reason they had to be males." So argues Wintersig also, op. cit., p. 18.

22. Schmaus, Dogmatik 4/1, 5th ed. (1957), p. 661. In the 6th ed. (1964), pp. 753f., this point of view--which is clearly based on the Aristotelian-Thomistic concept of the procreation process (cf. Van der Meer, pp. 143ff.)--is abandoned, but it is still maintained that only men are by nature suited to public functions. Ibid., p. 753.

23. E.g., Concetti, in G. Heinzelmann, Die getrennten Schwestern (Zürich, 1967), p. 99 ("... The role of mediator" belongs, "according to the will of God and Christ, to the male because of his preeminence and his natural qualifications for portraying in concrete forms the highest Mediator, which is Christ"). See also A. Winklhofer, Kirche in den Sakramenten (Frankfurt, 1968), p. 227 ("Should he, the head, be portrayed in this concrete symbolization by a woman--contrary to the order of creation--a woman who is subject to man and not the 'head'? Church office follows the order of creation"). Remberger (see chapter 2, n. 80) pp. 134f., simply grants to women the capability to represent Christ in the so-called universal priesthood. Cf. in addition C. Bamberg, "Die Aufgabe der Frau in der Liturgie," in Anima 19 (1964): 304-317; I. F. Gorres, "Über die Weihe von Frauen zu Priesterinnen," in Der Christliche Sonntag 17(1965):197-199.

24. C. Persson, pp. 129f.

25. E.g., Krebs, Wintersig, Laurentin (cf. pp. 205f. with n. 20 and n. 21).

26. Das geistliche Amt, p. 27; and his Maria, pp. 130, 146.

27. Wintersig (see n. 20, above), p. 18. A similar form of magnification of the position of the priest is given by M. Premm, Katholische Glaubenskunde, vol. 3/2 (Vienna, 1955), p. 389: "By the ordination of the priest the ordained one is lifted out of earthly spheres and stands before us like another Christ, as mediator between God and man in all religious concerns."

28. See pp. 114f.

29. In the Pontificale Romanum (Regensburg, 1888), vol. 1, p. 84, the formula used in the presentation of the rings is as follows: "Accipe annulum, fidei scilicet signaculum: quatenus sponsam Dei, sanctam videlicet Ecclesiam, intemerata fide ornatus,

illibate custodias. " (It is true that the formula does not use the expression "sponsa episcopi, " which was well known throughout the Middle Ages.) Concerning the origin and development of the ring symbol, see V. Labhart, Zur Rechtssymbolik des Bishofsrings (Cologne, 1963).

30. See J. Trummer, "Mystisches im alten Kirchenrecht. Die geistige Ehe zwischen Bishof und Diözese," in ÖAKR 2 (1951): 62-75.

31. Ibid. , p. 66.

32. Cf. Semmelroth, Maria, p. 149.

33. In fact the factor of visibility in representation of Christ plays a decisive role in the traditional understanding of church office. Cf. Persson, pp. 22, 24 with n. 38. This visibility reaches its highest degree in the papal office: "Christ himself acts in the actions of the pope. Christ appears in each of them, in the here and now. We can hear and see Christ himself in what the pope does. Yes, the pope plays the role of Christ. One can say of him, 'Personam Christi gerit....' " The pope represents "in the visible world Christ, the Head of the church. " (Schmaus, Dogmatik, vol. 3/1, 5th ed. (1958), p. 488.)

34. Thus, clearly, Bichlmair (see n. 21, above) and Concetti (see n. 23, above); similarly, too, Schmaus, vol. 4/1 (6th ed.), p. 753: "It is reasonable that that baptized person who serves as the instrument of Christ in a special way should also share in his natural individuality. " Premm, op. cit. , pp. 242f. says: "The priest is the image of the High Priest Christ, leader of the faithful, person of authority--all of which are things belonging essentially to the masculine sphere. "

35. According to the encyclical of Pius XII, Mediator Dei, (AAS 39, 1947, 539) the boundary line drawn by the ordination of the priest between clergy and laity is just as firm as the boundary line drawn by baptism between Christians and non-Christians.

36. Decree on the Ministry and Life of Priests, art. 2 (AAS 58, 1966, 992; Eng. text, Walter Abbott, Documents of Vatican II, p. 535.

37. Dogmatic Constitution on the Church, art. 26 (AAS 57, 1965, 31); Abbott, p. 50.

38. Ibid. , art. 27 (AAS 57, 1965, 32); Abbott, p. 51.

39. Ibid. , art. 21 (AAS 57, 1965, 25); Abbott, pp. 41f.

40. Ibid. , art. 27 (AAS 57, 1965, 33); Abbott, p. 52.

41. Ibid. , art. 20 (AAS 57, 1965, 24); Abbott, p. 40.

42. Decree on the Ministry and Life of Priests, art. 7 (AAS 58, 1966, 1003); Abbott, p. 549. A similar injunction is directed to all believers in the Decree on the Bishop's Pastoral Office in the Church, art. 16 (AAS 58, 1966, 680); Abbott, pp. 407ff.

43. See Decree on the Bishop's Pastoral Office in the Church, art. 16 (AAS 58, 1966, 679ff.); Abbott, pp. 406ff.

44. Cf. Persson, pp. 90, 117.

45. Decree on the Bishop's Pastoral Office in the Church, art. 16 (AAS 58, 1966, 680); Abbott, pp. 407ff. Dogmatic Constitution on the Church, arts. 21, 28 (AAS 57, 1965, 24, 35); Abbott, pp. 40ff., pp. 52ff.

46. See Persson, pp. 101f., 117f.; F. Wulf, "Stellung und Aufgabe des Priesters in der Kirche nach dem zweiten Vatikanischen Konzil," in Geist und Leben 39 (1966), p. 48 ("In a few decades one may even judge that the image of the priest in Vatican II, especially in the decree on priests [cf. ibid., art. 9, on the relation of priests to laity], is still strongly influenced by paternalistic viewpoints").

47. Cf. Semmelroth, Das geistliche Amt, p. 41 ("The clerical office ... portrays the God whose people is the church and offers to the people a visible appearance of God, so that in meeting with him they may live as the people of God").

48. A. M. Henry, Obéissance commune et obéissance religieuse (Supplément de la Vie Spirituelle 6, 1953), p. 262, is rightly critical of such a basis for authority and obedience: "Toute théologie de l'obéissance dont l'insistance irait dans le sens d'une identification entre supérieur et autorité du Christ, resiquerait de compromettre gravement les valeurs religieuses et personnelles les plus fondamentales et les plus certaines" (quoted from A. Müller, Das Problem von Befehl und Gehorsam im Leben der Kirche. Eine pastoraltheologische Untersuchung (Einsiedeln, 1964), p. 126, n. 1). Müller likewise, pp. 125f., points to the negative consequences--for understanding obedience--of an identification of human authority with divine authority: "A doctrine of obedience should proceed from the difference, rather than from the similarity, existing between obedience to God and obedience to men." On this problem see also Kasper (see n. 4, above), p. 398; Persson, p. 50.

49. Thus W. Heinen, "Die Gestalten des Vaters und des Paternalen in der Lebengestaltung der Gesellschaft," in Jahrbuch des Instituts für christliche Sozialwissenschaften der Westfälischen Wilhelms-Universität Münster, ed. by J. Höffner and W. Heinen, (Münster, 1965), vol. 6, p. 18: "The perpetuation of the status of son or of daughter in a universal fraternization contradicts the order of reality, if the vertical (hierarchical superiority or inferiority) is leveled out into the horizontal." Similarly, F. Gamillscheg in Die Presse (Jan. 18, 1965), p. 3: "The vertical-

hierarchical-authoritative elements must work together in the
church with the horizontal-fraternal elements, in order to preserve
the cruciform pattern necessary for all Christians.... The con-
servatives, the 'Catholics on the right,' must provide for these
vertical elements" (quoted by W. Daim, Progressiver Katholizismus
(Munich, 1967), p. 124). Daim writes against this view, pp.
116ff., and also in "Rückkehr zur Brüderlichkeit," in Kirche und
Zukunft (Vienna, 1963): 11ff., where he refers to Mt. 23:8f. Daim
thinks that church office can be subsumed under the "brother" concept and can be rewritten in its terms. So, too, W. Dirks, "Über
die Stellung des Laien in der Kirche," in M. Lehner-A. Hasler,
Neues Denken in der Kirche. Standpunkte (Lucerne, 1968), pp.
207ff.

50. So, rightly, M. Daly, The Church and the Second Sex
(see Introduction, n. 8), p. 157.

51. R. Schnackenburg, Die Kirche im Neuen Testament
(Quaestiones disputatae, vol. 14) (Freiburg, 1961), pp. 151f.

52. Cf. Schnackenburg, op. cit., p. 152; H. Schürmann,
"Die geistlichen Gnadengaben," in De Ecclesia, ed. by G. Baraúna
(Freiburg-Frankfurt, 1966), vol. 1, p. 505.

53. Cf. Schnackenburg, pp. 114, 152; Ritter and Leich
(see chapter 4, n. 21), pp. 68f.; Schürmann, op. cit., p. 500.
According to this passage, there can be no separation between
charismatic and official ministries; the fundamental charismatic
structure of the church comprehends the clerical office. Cf. H.
Küng, "The Charismatic Structure of the Church," in Concilium 4,
(New York, 1965) pp. 41-61; W. Pesch, "Kirchlicher Deinst und
Neues Testament," in Zum Thema Priesteramt, ed. by Pesch,
Kötting, Dias and others (Stuttgart, 1970), pp. 14f.

54. On this see Kasper, op. cit., p. 402: "The charismatic structuring of the Christian congregation is not simply a product of the clerical office: it is not based dualistically on a polarity of office-congregation, but rather pluralistically on a fullness
of charisma."

55. Cf. Schnackenburg, pp. 25, 152; Ritter-Leich, pp. 69,
72.

56. Representatives of such an understanding of office and
deputyship have been named above, p. 206 with n. 21 and p. 209
with n. 33 and n. 34.

57. Cf. A. Kradepohl, Stellvertretung und Kanonisches
Eherecht (Kanonistische Studien und Texte, ed. by A. M. Koeniger,
vol. 17) (Bonn, 1939), pp. 100, 143.

58. Cf. Mörsdorf (see part I [preliminary], n. 5), vol. 1,
p. 230.

59. Cf. Kradepohl, op. cit., p. 7 (The voluntary action of the deputy must "conform to that of the one who empowers him.")

60. The difference is especially the result of the essential incongruity between the one to be represented (Christ) and the one who represents him, and therefore the concept representation is basically inadequate and should only be cautiously used in consideration of that fact. Cf. the discussion of Kasper, op. cit., p. 396: "The concept of representation ... contains no mystical or juridical identification with Christ but rather a differentiation. Precisely as the church, and in particular the office, completely disappears behind its mission and so makes itself insignificant, it is truly the epiphany of Christ." It seems to me that a further but similar differentiation from representation in the juridical sense consists in the fact that the office-holder does not in himself possess the competence to function as representative of Christ but rather Christ has in his grace bestowed that competence upon him.

61. See the noteworthy discussion of this in K. Rahner, Kirche und Sakramente (Quaestiones disputatae, vol. 10) (Frieburg, 1960), pp. 87-95.

62. J. E. Belser, Der zweite Brief des Apostels Paulus an die Korinther (Freiburg, 1910), p. 190, translates ὑπὲρ Χριστοῦ as "in the place of Christ" (for this he refers to Mt. 10:40; he also finds support in 2 Cor. 5:15, where ὑπέρ likewise has the meaning of "in the place of," according to Belser.) Similarly, K. Prumm, Diakonia Pneumatos. Der zweite Korintherbrief als Zugang zur apostolischen Botschaft. Auslegung und Theologie (Freiburg, 1967), vol. 1, p. 345: "... This equation of the apostle with Christ in the decisive point of the final source of the commissioning is already established by verses 18 and 19 of 2 Cor. 5. This makes it possible with Chrysostom to attribute the same objective significance to 'for Christ' of v. 20 as to 'in the place of Christ.'" Against this view, W. Bauer, Griechisch-deutsches Wörterbuch (Berlin, 1958), 5th ed. col. 1658, translates ὑπὲρ Χριστοῦ (2 Cor. 5:20) as "as Christ's helper we beseech you."

63. Belser, op. cit., p. 187. Similarly A. Schlatter, Paulus, der Bote Jesus. Eine Deutung seiner Briefe an die Korinther (Stuttgart, 1934), p. 565: "... Whoever is in Christ has God for himself. At the same time that Paul receives the divine love--since he is not living for himself--he is blessed with a ministry which, corresponding to that which had happened to him himself, consists in his being the messenger of that divine will which creates reconciliation."

64. What is clearly pointed out here is the quite different style of living and living arrangements of the disciples, in comparison to their environment, which characterized the disciples and which necessarily led to a tense and dangerous situation for them. They could endure only by an unconditional trust in their Lord. Cf. W. Grundmann, Das Evangelium nach Lukas (Theologischer

Handkommentar zum Neuen Testament, ed. by E. Fascher, vol. 3), second ed. (Berlin, 1961), p. 209.

65. Cf. Dogmatic Constitution on the Church, art. 20 (AAS 57, 1965, 24; Abbott, pp. 39f.) P. Fransen makes a more exact differentiation in "Einige dogmatische Bemerkungen über das christliche Priestertum," in Der Priester in einer säkularisierten Welt (Informationsblatt des Instituts für europäische Priesterhilfe, vol. 2, 1968, Heft 1/2), p. 46: he says that the hierarchy operates only in its sacerdotal task--particularly in the administration of the sacraments--"in persona Christi," but not in the exercise of jurisdictional authority. "The will of the hierarchy cannot be purely and simply equated with the divine will." Cf. Fransen, "(Heilige) Weihen," in Sacramentum Mundi IV (Freiburg, 1969) pp. 1281-1283. On this question see also Persson, pp. 49f.

66. R. Schnackenburg, "Episkopos und Hirtenamt. Zu Apg. 20:28," in Episcopus (Festschrift for Card. M. v. Faulhaber), p. 80.

67. See Bichlmair (see n. 21, above), p. 216: "The man who is creative, ready for action, the man who works and gets things done, is an image and reflection of the creative God, who operates and governs with omnipotence." Also ibid., pp. 7, 127.

68. Daly, op. cit., pp. 146ff., refers to a faulty development of man in a patriarchy, corresponding to a lack of development of woman's personality; L. Rinser, Unterentwickeltes Land Frau (Würzburg, 1970), pp. 23, 81f., 88, makes the same point.

69. H. Stadler, Männergespräche, 3rd ed. (Leutesdorf, 1961), p. 24. (The publication is provided with the imprimatur of the General Vicar of the diocese of Trier, Dr. Weins.) Similarly, Bichlmair, p. 11: "The Christian religion was established by a man. How should it not be a masculine affair? Twelve men were the first assistants of the man Jesus. He made men to be the pillars of the church. He called men to be priests and distributers of his sacraments. In the earliest succession men were the flag bearers of his kingdom. The first [!] places in the Catholic House of God are reserved for men." In connection with the fact that the existing patriarchal structure in the church is understood as divine directive, a higher evaluation of masculinity results, according to K. Rahner, "Der Mann in der Kirche," in Sendlung und Gnade. Beiträge zur Pastoraltheologie (Innsbruck, 1959): The male has by nature, he says, "a sensitivity for the transcendental purity of the religious" (p. 304); the "transcendental, anonymous, indirect, silent side of religion is characteristic" of the male (p. 305); the male is reticent to speak of holy things (p. 306). It is a task peculiar to the male to bring into the church peacefulness, reasonableness, trustworthiness, sense of responsibility, clarity of intention (p. 308). Somewhat the opposite qualities are attributed to femininity by Rahner; although he is at pains to call them equally legitimate expressions of humanity--a hopeless undertaking since

they are forms of human nature stunted by repression--he is obviously not able to give them equivalent evaluation. Note, for instance, his summons to a "manly Christianity." (Pp. 296ff.) It is true that the author has separated himself from this extreme viewpoint in his more recent publications: see "Die Frau in der neuen Situation der Kirche," in Theologisches Jahrbuch (Leipzig, 1966), pp. 121-133. Appealing to the earlier Rahner work, a cliché-ridden description of the nature of the sexes and its effect on the church has been written by H. Halbfas (Jugend und Kirche. Eine Diagnose [Düsseldorf, 1964], pp. 205ff.); it clearly implies a denigration of women.

70. A similar conception is represented by J. Peters (see n. 1, above), pp. 297f.: Office carried out and characterized only by men inevitably leads to a one-sided and deprived office and to the like injury to the church's transmission of grace. Thus a "humanizing of ecclesiastical office," its extension and enrichment, is definitively required and for this women must have their place in the ministry: "Together they [man and woman] must create a profile of the ministerial office and practice it together, so that it loses its one-sidedness [p. 297].... Humanity is whole only in the togetherness of man and woman and with this argument we wish to state that it is not only possible, it is also desirable, that women be admitted to the office.... The first question about the office-bearer must therefore not be, Must it be a man or can it also be a woman? but rather, How can we use the very best humanity for the transmission of divine grace?" (p. 298). On the other hand, E. Gössmann, "Die Frau als Priester?" (trans. into English, "Women as Priests?" in Concilium, vol. 34 [Eng.], 1968, pp. 115-125), does not recognize that the admission of women to the ministry can have, and will have, positive consequences for office and its structure--especially in cleaning out the patriarchal elements. She expects that the ministerial office itself without any help from women "will be renewed from within and in relation to the community;" only when that happens will it "make sense to extend the office to women" (pp. 291f.). This statement lacks a requisite objective understanding of organic development.

71. H. Gollwitzer, Von der Stellvertretung Gottes. Christlicher Glaube in der Erfahrung der Verborgenheit Gottes. Zum Gespräch mit Dorothee Sölle (Munich, 1967), pp. 147f.

CHAPTER 8

1. See J. Mörsdorf, Gestaltwandel des Frauenbildes und Frauenberufs in der Neuzeit (Munich Theological Studies, 2nd div., vol. 16) (Munich, 1958), pp. 288-290; B. Friedan, The Feminine Mystique (New York, 1963), pp. 69-79; M. Vaerting, Wahrheit und Irrtum in der Geschlechterpsychologie, 2nd ed. (Weimar, 1931), pp. 242f.; J. Leclercq (see chapter 1, n. 76), pp. 63, 66.

2. Thus Heinen (see chapter 7, n. 49), p. 22; see also p. 18 et passim. Also descriptions of the conservative picture of women, e.g., in Schüssler, (see chapter 6, n. 3), pp. 29ff., and H. Ringeling, Die Frau zwischen gestern und morgen. Der sozialtheologische Aspekt ihrer Gleichberechtigung (Hamburg, 1962), pp. 22f.

3. Thus, e.g., in Krebs (see chapter 7, n. 21), pp. 478; Schmaus, Dogmatik, vol. 4/1, 6th ed., p. 754; similarly in Premm (see chapter 7, n. 26), vol. 3/2, p. 243 ("Women are excluded from the priesthood not because they are inferior but because they are different; this difference points to the ministry of motherhood, which is a kind of hidden, unofficial priesthood").

4. Cf. A. M. Knoll, Katholische Kirche und scholastisches Naturrecht. Zur Frage der Freiheit (Vienna, 1962), pp. 24ff.; W. Daim, Die kastenlose Gesellschaft (Munich, 1960), pp. 359f.

5. The following basic investigations--already partly cited--should be noted: M. Vaerting, op. cit.; M. Mead, Male and Female (New York, 1949); S. Hunke, Am Anfang waren Mann und Frau. Vorbilder und Wandlungen der Geschlechterbeziehungen (Hamm, 1955) (e.g., p. 261: "That which we characterize as 'male' and 'female' is the product of our culture and cannot claim universal validity any more than the dogma of the polar antithesis of the sexes can do so"; or, p. 264: "One must be careful not to confuse the historical and sociological qualities of the sexes with their essential nature"); H. Schelsky, Soziologie der Sexualität (Hamburg, 1962); H. Ringeling, op. cit.; S. Farber and R. H. Wilson (eds.), The Potential of Woman. A Symposium (New York, 1963); E. E. Maccoby (ed.), The Development of Sex Differences (Stanford, 1966).

6. See Hunke, p. 251; Ringeling, pp. 15, 33. When G. v. LeFort in Die ewige Frau, 19th ed. (Munich, 1960), brings the vocation of women within the formula, "mother and servant," the traditional role of woman is crystalized into a structure of nature; W. Trillhaas remarks about this: "Here a late bourgeois ideal is misinterpreted as Christian" (quoted from L. Preller, "Die berufstätige Frau als Glied der Gesellschaft," in Die berufstätige Frau heute und morgen [Schriften der Gesellschaft für sozialen Fortschritt, vol. 17] [Berlin, 1966], p. 50).

7. So. e.g., O. Schneider, Vom Priestertum der Frau, 2nd ed. (Vienna, 1937). (A passage from her book is used by Premm, op. cit., p. 243, as evidence that in his discussion of the exclusion of women from orders it is not a question of "male theology"; but Premm ignores the fact that the "evidence" is not "what women themselves say" but a recapitulation of "male theology," which is actually the result of women's lack of independence.) See also O. Mosshammer, Priester und Frau (Freiburg, 1958).

8. J. Leclerq, op. cit., p. 61, freely admits this: "Everything that was publicly said was said by men.... Men view woman

as spiritually inferior. She was good only for house-work, in which she had to serve men.... Since men unceasingly repeated all this and since they alone did the speaking, women believed it... "; any opposition was sharply condemned. Cf. also Vaerting, op. cit., p. 14: "Women who are ruled over have the tendency in general to accept uncritically the views of men.... " (Also ibid., p. 46; Preller (see n. 6, above), pp. 44, 50.)

9. Hunke, p. 264; and also Vaerting, p. 9: "We can only approach a solution of the problem of natural sex differences when both sexes grow up in exactly the same circumstances. But that can come about only when the full realization of equal rights of the sexes becomes a fact." Vaerting, p. 11, also rightly notes that: "The otherness of women, as it predominantly appears today, is not congenital but is rather the typical otherness that differentiates the ruled from the ruler." See also Ringeling, p. 35.

10. Vaerting, p. 17, has already noted this fact: "The results of scientific investigations during the last decades have shown a preponderant similarity of the sexes and only a small dissimilarity. In all cases the similarity of the sexes was greater than the dissimilarity. A large majority of men and women showed the same qualities, with only a small minority indicating differences. Those qualities usually designated as masculine were found in almost as many women as men, while those called feminine were found in almost as many men. The differences between individuals within the same sex was much greater than that between male and female." Also ibid., p. 21; Ringeling, pp. 33ff.

11. E.g., the investigations of H. Anger, Probleme der deutschen Universität. Bericht über eine Erhebung unter Professoren und Dozenten (Tübingen, 1960), pp. 451-500, have shown numerous proofs of this; cf. also chapter 6, n. 3 and chapter 7, n. 69.

12. Vaerting, pp. 22f., makes a similar observation: "Although today the theory of the equal value of the sexes is recognized, as the result of advancing equal rights, the ancient clovenfoot of feminine inferiority very often appears in the presentations of the sex psychologists, because the male is always dominant." This statement is confirmed by an analysis of the various descriptions of feminine nature often advanced by theologians. Cf. Schüssler, pp. 77f. That the thesis "equal but different" is actually camouflage for the persisting denigration of women (Vaerting, p. 14, has already criticized this thesis) is especially clear from the fact that the legal situation of women in the church has hardly changed from what it used to be--it is still, afterward as well as before, the consequence of their derogation.

13. Cf. the encyclical Pacem in Terris of John XXIII (AAS 55, 1963, 259ff.).

14. Ibid. (AAS 55, 259); J. B. Metz, "Freiheit," in Handbuch theologischer Grundbegriffe, ed. by H. Fries, vol. 1, p. 408;

K. Rahner, "Würde und Wert des Menschen," in Schriften zur Theologie (Einsiedeln-Cologne, 1955), pp. 258f.

15. Cf. Metz, op. cit., p. 411.

16. According to biblical studies (e.g., of Gal. 1:15, Heb. 5:4ff.; Romans 12:6ff.; 1 Cor. 12:27ff.; Acts 6:3ff.), it is obvious that office presupposes God-given charisma, and thus office and charisma are not to be understood as two disparate entities independent of each other. Besides the literature indicated above (see chapter 7, n. 53), see J. Peters, "Women in Church Vocation," in Concilium 34 (New York, 1968), p. 137, and van Eyden (see chapter 3, n. 146), p. 357.

17. See the Dogmatic Constitution of the Church, art. 12 (AAS 57, 1965, 16f.; Abbott, pp. 29f.); but here, characteristically, the discussion concerns only charisma not related to the ministerial office. But H. Küng in The Church, trans. by Ray and Rosalun Ockenden (New York, 1967), p 421, says: "... This special commission, as much as the unasked and unanticipated gift of the Spirit, takes its origins from the grace of God who has freedom to call whom he wishes; the men who commission, as much as those who are commissioned, must be the willing tools of God."

18. Protestants have already clearly pointed out that such procedure is unacceptable and injurious to the church. Heintze (see chapter 7, n. 1), pp. 531ff., remarks: "We fall into the great danger of hindering the spirit of God when concern for the possible 'crossing of boundaries' by women and the possible infringement of 'masculine privileges' becomes for us stronger than gratitude for the great enrichment bestowed upon the church by the self-reliant ministry of women in partnership with men." (See also ibid., pp. 526f.) Discerning Roman Catholic theologians have also recently warned of this danger, e.g., Peters, p. 295: It is presumptuous to try to limit the spirit of God to a single sex. "Who knows whether we might not in this way partly extinguish it?" While numerous Protestant denominations have drawn the consequences consistent with this realization--admitting women to ordination--a practical implementation of such insight is still lacking in the Catholic Church.

19. Cf. F. K. Schumann, "Die Frage der Menschenrechte in der Sicht des christlichen Glaubens," in Wort und Gestalt (Witten, 1956): 374. So, too, P. Althaus, "Person und Persönalichkeit in der evangelischen Theologie," in Person und Recht (Munich, 1962), p. 14: "The right of personhood is grounded in a moral obligation that comes from God.... By insisting on this human right, man gives honor to God."

20. E. Gössmann disregards this variety of charisma, with which women as surely as men are endowed, when she asks women "to forego rising above the laity" in order to help the laity to full development. (Die Frau im Aufbruch der Kirche [Theologische

Fragen heute, ed. by M. Schmaus and E. Gössmann, vol. 5] [Munich, 1964], pp. 119f.) It is true that she tones down this contention somewhat in "Die Frau als Priester," English trans. in Concilium, "Women as Priests?," vol. 34 (1968), pp. 115-125. Apart from the fact that ministerial office is inaccurately described or at least very much misunderstood ("rising above"!), it is apparently presumed by Gössman that women cannot be endowed with the charisma requisite for office--since the same request is not made of the male laity. Van Eyden, p. 360, sucessfully refutes this standpoint when he remarks: "Why should we not strive to give women at the same time their rightful place in the lay apostolate and in ministerial office? As long as women are admitted to other areas of church life and an exception is made only in regard to the ministerial office, it is impossible to speak of any true recognition of their equality of position in the church. This reflects unfavorably on their position in the lay apostolate.... Certainly one would not draw the conclusion that all male lay persons remain such and none become priests."

21. Cf. the following statements by John XXIII in his encyclical Pacem in Terris: "The long-standing inferiority complex of certain classes because of their economic and social status, sex, or position in the State, and the corresponding superiority complex of other classes, is rapidly becoming a thing of the past. Today, on the contrary, the conviction is widespread that all men are equal in natural dignity; ... for man's awareness of his rights must inevitably lead him to the recognition of his duties. The possession of rights involves the duty of implementing those rights, for they are the expression of a man's personal dignity. And the possession of rights also involves their recognition and respect by other people." (The Encyclicals and Other Messages of John XXIII, TPS Press (Washington, D.C., 1964), pp. 337f.)

22. This opinion is also expressed in a letter to Orientierung (32, 1968, pp. 104f.) from a woman theologian (Dr. theol. W. E.) who remarks: "I turn to you because I think that support must come from the circle of priests and of men; for since we ourselves are not represented anywhere there is little we can do for ourselves. The situation here is like that in the race question. There too it is not sufficient that a white person has nothing against a black's receiving appropriate jobs, etc.; rather, he must be the one who helps blacks get what they should have."

23. This happened repeatedly in the second Vatican Council. See Dorn-Denzler, Tagebuch des Konzils (Third Session), pp. 265f.; Heinzelmann, Schwestern, pp. 71-83. The statements of the Council Fathers were brought together in the Pastoral Constitution on the Church in the Modern World, art. 9, 29 (AAS 58, 1966, 1031, 1049; Abbott, pp. 206f., 227f.)

24. It is true that in Vatican II several interventions requested, beyond improvement of the position of women in the world, also an increased possibility for employment of women in the church.

(See Heinzelmann, Schwestern, pp. 71-74, 77-79; the written intervention of Archbishop Hallinan of Atlanta is noteworthy for his ad-
vocacy of admission of women to the diaconate and to appointment
to various commissions. Ibid., pp. 78f.) But the Council texts
ignored these suggestions. The need for reform of the position of
women in the church was seen more clearly in the second regular
Bishops' Synod in Rome. While some bishops included in their reform proposals (cf. Introduction, n. 3) the admission of women to
ecclesiastical office--including that of the priesthood--such a possibility was sharply rejected by Cardinal Slipyj (Ukraine), who appealed to Scripture and church tradition (cf. L'Osservatore Romano,
English ed., November 11, 1971, p. 9). Despite express request
by the Committee for Responsible Activity of Women in the Church
(AFK), the German bishops in the Synod did not advocate integration of women into ecclesiastical office. (Aktion Information Letter
of March 12, 1971.) When Cardinal Höffner (Cologne) was asked
about his attitude toward the reform proposals of the Canadian
Bishops' Conference (see Introduction, n. 3), he expressed a narrow view of women and their claim to free opportunities for self-
development. He thus strongly rejected the Canadian proposal:
"Women's opportunities for apostleship in our church do not depend
upon whether or not they can become priests." He said he did not
see why the position of women in the church should be determined
simply by the question of the priesthood; in the modern democratic
state there are regulations which do not apply to both sexes. Besides, he said, it is not yet theologically clarified whether doctrinal questions do not prevent the ordination of women (Publik, no.
44, v. 29. 10, 1971, p. 13). In a letter of December 24, 1969,
to Cardinal Alfrink--occasioned by the approaching fifth meeting of
the Dutch Pastoral Council in January, 1970--Pope Paul VI also
declared against the admission of women to the priestly ministry.
He objected to the fact that in the outlines and issues for discussion worked out for the meeting a critique was included concerning
the thesis that only a man can become a priest (AAS 62, 1970, 67).
The Pope speaks similarly in a sermon on the occasion of the
declaration of St. Teresa of Avila as Teacher of the Church: on
the basis of an uncritical, biblicistic scriptural interpretation he
derives the exclusion of women from the "hierarchical functions of
the teaching and priestly office" from the passage 1 Cor. 14:34 ("Women should keep silence in the churches"). (AAS 62, 1970, 593.)
On the Corinthian passage see chapter 6, n. 158.

25. One can see to what degree this quality has impressed
itself on the behavior of women--and still does so--in the common
idea that insincerity is an element in women's character. E.g.,
O. Weininger, Geschlecht und Charakter (Vienna, 1903), p. 355:
"Women are not sincere in any phase of their lives." Other writers, however, see in this fact an intrinsic consequence of the repression and faulty education of women. E.g., B. L. Hutchins,
Conflicting Ideals: Two Sides of the Women Question (London,
1913), p. 30: "Girls are raised according to profoundly hypocriti-
cal ideals." Likewise M. Wollstonecraft (quoted by Germaine
Greer, The Female Eunuch [New York, 1971], p. 349). Women

will have to put forth great moral effort to refute this injurious prejudice against them.

26. The Canadian bishops have been the first to take a stand for this, in their hearing and accepting the request of the Canadian Women's Associations concerning a reform of the valuation of women and the place of women in the church. (Cf. _Osservatore Romano_, English ed., October 28, 1971, p. 5.)

BIBLIOGRAPHY OF SOURCES

Achelis, H. and J. Flemming, Die syrische Didaskalia (Texte und Untersuchungen zur Geschichte der altchristlichen Literatur, ed. by A. v. Harnack and C. Schmidt, New Series, vol. 10). Leipzig, 1904.

Acta Apostolicae Sedis, Commentarium officiale. Typis Polyglottis Vaticanis, 1909ff.

Aegidius Bellamera. Praelectiones in decretalium libros, 6 vols. Lyon, 1548-1549.

_____. Remissorius ... ad commentaria in Gratiani decreta, 3 vols. Lyon, 1550.

Antonius de Butrio. Commentaria in quinque libros decretalium, 7 vols. Venice, 1578; reprint: Turin, 1967.

Apostolic Constitutions, Ante-Nicene Fathers, vol. 7, Edinburgh, 1902.

Bruns, H. Th., ed., Canones Apostolorum et Conciliorum saeculorum IV, V, VI, VII, P. 1. 2. Berlin, 1839: reprint: Turin, 1959.

Codex Juris Canonici. Pii X Pontificis Maximi iussu digestus, Benedicti Papae XV auctoritate promulgatus, praefatione, fontium annotatione et indice analytico-alphabetico ab Emmo. Petro Card. Gasparri auctus. Typis Polyglottis Vaticanis, 1948. (Cited as Code.)

Codex Juris Canonici Fontes, cura et studio Emmi. Justiniani Card. Seredi editi, vol. 9 (Tabellae). Typis Polyglottis Vaticanis, 1939.

Die sogenannten Apostolischen Constitutionen und Canonen, trans. by F. Boxler (BKV 63). Kempton, 1874.

Corpus Juris Canonici in tres partes distinctum, glossis diversorum illustratum, Gregorii Papae XIII. iussu editum, editio novissima, Lyon, 1671. (Cited as Corpus.)

Corpus Juris Canonici, ed. by Ae. Friedberg, 2 vols. Leipzig, 1879-1881; reprint: Graz, 1955. (Cited as Corpus, ed. Friedberg.)

Corpus Juris Civilis, ed. by P. Krueger, Th. Mommsen, R. Schoell, 3 vols. Berlin, 1904-1906.

Corpus Scriptorum Ecclesiasticorum Latinorum, editum consilio et impensis academiae litterarum Caesareae Vindobonensis, Vienna, 1866ff.

Didascalia et Constitutiones Apostolorum, ed. by F. X. Funk, I-II. Paderborn, 1905. (Cited as Did. et Const. Ap.)

Duchesne, L., ed., Le Liber Pontificalis, vol. 1. Paris, 1886. (Cited as Lib. pont.)

Goffredus de Trani, Summa super titulis decretalium, Lyon, 1519; reprint: Aalen, 1968.

Guido van Baysio. Rosarium, Lyon, 1549.

Hinschius, P., ed. Decretales Pseudo-Isidorianae et Capitula Angilramni, Leipzig, 1863; reprint: Aalen, 1963. (Cited as Decretales.)

Hostiensis (Henricus de Segusio). Commentaria in quinque libros decretalium, 5 vols. Venice, 1581; reprint: Turin, 1965.

_____. Summa Aurea. Venice, 1574; reprint: Turin, 1963.

Huguccio. Summa on the Decretum Gratiani (ms.: Munich lat. 10247; Vatican lat. 2280).

Innocent IV (Sinibaldus Fliscus). Apparatus in quinque libros decretalium. Frankfurt, 1570; reprint: Frankfurt, 1968.

Johannes Andreae. Novella Commentaria in quinque libros decretalium, 5 vols. Venice, 1581; reprint: Turin, 1963.

Le Liber Pontificalis, see Duchesne.

McLaughlin, T. P., ed. The Summa Parisiensis on the Decretum Gratiani. Toronto, 1952.

Mansi, J. D. Sacrorum conciliorum nova et amplissima collectio. Florence, 1759ff.; reprint: Paris, 1901ff.

Migne, J. P. Patrologiae cursus completus, series latina, 221 vols. Paris, 1878-1890. Series graeca, 161 vols. Paris, 1857-1866.

Munier, Ch. Les Statuta Ecclesiae Antiqua (Bibliothèque de l'Institut de droit canonique de l'Université de Strasbourg), Paris, 1960. (Cited as Statuta.)

Nicolaus de Tudeschis. Lectura in decretales. Vols. 1-3, Lyon,

1534; vols. 4-5, Venice, 1504.

Paucapalea. Summa on the Decretum Gratiani, ed. by J. F. v. Schulte. Giessen, 1890; reprint: Aalen, 1965.

Petrus de Ancharano. Commentaria in quinque libros decretalium, 5 vols. Bologna, 1581.

Raymund of Pennaforte. Summa de poenitentia et matrimonio cum glossis Joannis de Friburgo. Rome, 1603.

Roland Bandinelli. The Summa of magistri Rolandi, later Pope Alexander III, ed. by F. Thaner. Innsbruck, 1874; reprint: Aalen, 1962.

Rufin of Bologna. Summa decretorum of Magister Rufinus, ed. by H. Singer. Paderborn, 1902; reprint: Aalen, 1963.

Sighard of Cremona. Summa decretorum (ms.: Munich lat. 4555).

Stephan of Doornick (Stephanus Tornacensis). The Summa on the Decretum Gratiani, ed. by J. F. v. Schulte. Giessen, 1891; reprint: Aalen, 1965.

Summa Parisiensis, The Summa Pariensis on the Decretum Gratiani, ed. by P. McLaughlin. Toronto, 1952.

INDEX

Abbess 50, 53, 54, 57, 60, 61, 65, 69, 71, 73-76, 78, 80-85, 89f, 91f, 93-96, 180, 183, 203, 211, 219
Abbot 73, 74, 81, 90, 183, 218
Achelis-Fleming 19
Acolyte 77, 90, 96, 206f
Adam 63, 68, 89, 98ff, 221ff
Adultery 30, 161, 170ff
Aegidus de Bellamera 86f
Agnate family 40, 42
Ambrose 27, 30, 34, 35, 37, 38, 51, 53, 56, 61, 62, 65, 66, 88, 95, 160, 165, 168
Ambrosiaster 27, 30, 35-38, 49, 51-53, 57, 59, 61-63, 66, 78, 83, 89, 95, 97, 98, 102, 110f, 160, 165ff, 175, 182, 183, 220
Antonius de Butrio 91f
Apostolic Constitutions 15-20, 24, 146-148, 150, 155, 185
Aquinas, Thomas 59, 88, 89, 211, 220, 241
Astarte 231
Augustine 34-37, 168, 208, 238

Balsamon, Theodor 25, 153, 157
Baptism 5, 18, 19, 20, 25, 49, 64, 66, 67, 71, 96, 141, 150, 156, 193
Belser, J. E. 126
Bernard of Botone 80-83, 87, 89, 91, 97, 213
Bible Commission 103f, 226, 229
Bishops 26, 38, 58, 60, 71, 76, 80, 121, 122, 123, 191, 241f
    Canadian Bishops 253
Boehmer, J. 98, 99, 100, 101
Burchard of Worms 12
Byzantine 24, 25, 27

Calvin, Calvinists 110
Canon law 23, 28, 39, 43, 44, 47, 54, 62, 75, 78, 82f, 84, 127
Canoness 73f, 90, 204
Canons 74
Carthusians 50
Celibacy 23, 24, 51
Censure 74, 75, 80, 89f
Chabonne, R. 87
Charisma 250, 251
Christ 63, 68, 72, 73, 115-120, 122, 124, 127, 128, 234, 236, 241, 245
Christianity 162, 167
Church, concept of 117ff, 132
Church Fathers 33ff, 57, 67, 98, 103, 107, 108, 110, 116, 178, 184, 220, 231
Church Office 117ff
Circumcision 99, 102
Claudius 42
Code of Canon Law 5, 6, 11, 13, 20-22, 77, 96, 98, 130, 137, 142, 183
    Canon 968, § 1 1, 2, 5, 6, 64
Collyridian women 21
Communion, to sick 53, 55, 66, 144f
Concordia Discordantium Canonum see Decretum
Corpus Iuris Canonici 2, 3, 5, 8, 45, 47, 94, 97, 137

Correctores Romani 22, 46
Councils, Carthage 14
    Chalcedon 23, 25, 27,
    49, 51, 53, 61, 62, 80, 95,
    96, 156, 192
    Laodicea 65
    Lateran 65
    Lyon 79
    Nicea 155
Creation 37, 99-101, 222ff

Deaconess 9, 51-54, 56, 58,
    60-62, 64, 65, 68, 69, 79,
    80, 81, 85, 88, 95, 140,
    144, 150, 152ff, 180, 192,
    208, 212
Deacons 52, 55, 154, 182
Decretalists 78ff, 97
Decretals 40, 70ff, 73, 74,
    75, 76, 77, 79, 81f, 84, 85,
    90-92, 94, 96
Decretists 47ff
Decretum 3, 7, 14, 20, 21,
    26, 28, 33, 39, 45, 46, 47,
    53, 61, 64, 65, 70, 71, 78,
    80, 81, 86, 96, 98, 138,
    141, 169, 176, 178
Diaconate 21-27, 30, 44, 49,
    50-55, 62, 73, 79, 95, 159
Didascalia 14, 16-19, 146,
    147, 149, 150, 185
Divorce 102, 107
Duchesne, L. 9

Epiphanius 21
Eucharist 12, 13, 25, 33, 49,
    118, 119
Eve 63, 68, 104, 108, 111,
    112, 233ff
Excommunication and suspension
    73-76, 78, 80, 81, 84, 85,
    89-93, 204, 208, 211, 213

Fall of man 105, 108ff
Forgeries 8, 10, 11, 139;
    see also Pseudo-Isidore
Freisin, J. 49
Friedberg, Ae. 9, 12

Gasparri, Cardinal 5
Gennadius 14
Glossa Ordinaria 13, 51, 68,
    69, 81, 83, 84, 87, 88, 91,
    93, 95, 96, 97
Goffredus de Trani 79, 80, 83,
    88
Gollwitzer, H. 129
Gratian 3, 8, 9, 10, 12, 20-
    23, 25, 27, 29-39, 43-45,
    48, 50, 53, 55-60, 63, 65,
    66, 70, 71, 78, 81, 93, 94,
    98, 102, 107, 108, 110, 111,
    113, 114, 138, 158, 159,
    164, 176
Guido de Baysio 68f
Gunkel, H. 106

Hefele-Leclerc 12, 21, 22
Henricus de Segusio see
    Hostiensus
Hermaphrodite 62, 66
Hinschius 9, 20
Holy Communion see
    Eucharist
Hospitalers 75, 76
Hostiensus 83, 84, 85f, 87,
    89f, 92, 212
Huguccio 56, 61, 62, 63, 64,
    65, 68, 78, 79, 88f, 95f,
    192, 193f

Imago dei 34-36, 38, 63, 82,
    84, 86f, 89, 97, 98, 99,
    110, 113, 166, 211, 220,
    222f
Incest 206
Isidore of Seville 46, 48, 76,
    139, 145
Israel, Israelite 101, 102,
    105, 109, 115, 223, 231
Ivo of Chartres 12

Jerome 35
Jervelle, J. 113
Jesus 16, 17, 71, 99, 107,
    122, 123, 126, 127, 128
Joannes Andrea 87f, 89f, 92
Joannes Faventinus 55, 56,
    58, 60, 95

Joannes Teutonicus 64-69, 78, 79, 88f, 93, 95, 96, 196, 197, 198
Justinian 39, 41, 42

Kalsbach, A. 49, 52
Krebs, E. 119
Küng, Hans 250

Laurentin, R. 72
Laurentius 64
Liber Pontificalis 9
Liturgy Commission 77

Manus Marriage 40, 41, 170
Marriage 23, 31, 32, 43, 115f, 119, 121, 147, 162, 163, 171, 189, 224, 236f
Mary 69, 71, 72, 73, 82, 84, 92, 96, 97, 119, 149, 201f, 240
Matricuria 79
Mediator dei 117, 118, 242
Metz, René 16, 33
Montanists 51, 52, 79
Monasticism 9, 25, 147, 180
Munier, Ch. 14, 17

Natural law 35, 36
New Testament 29, 33, 60, 64, 98, 110, 117, 125, 126, 127
Nicolaus de Tudeschis 92f
Nova Quaedam 71, 73, 76, 79, 81, 82, 84, 89, 91, 92, 96, 97
Nuns 9, 53, 54, 55, 56, 57, 59, 61, 65, 74, 80, 84, 90, 92, 95, 144

Old Testament 10, 11, 29, 33, 35, 57, 59, 89, 94, 98ff, 142, 222ff
Ordination and consecration 2, 3, 5, 7, 8, 10, 11, 20, 22, 23, 24, 26, 27, 50, 51, 62, 63, 64, 65, 67, 68, 69, 71, 73, 78, 79, 80, 82f, 88,

89-96, 117, 118, 122, 126, 127, 137, 141, 155f, 182, 186, 193, 198f, 208f, 212, 215
Original Sin 38

Pacem in terris 251
Pasher, J. 118
Patria potestas 40
Patriarchalism 101f, 104, 105f, 162, 191, 224ff, 247
Paucapalea 47, 48, 49, 53, 56
Paul, Pauline 29, 31, 32, 34, 39, 44, 60, 62, 82, 94, 103, 108, 110-116, 120, 127, 128, 193, 212, 232ff
Penance, sacrament of 164
Peter 127
Peter of Ancharano 89f
Polygamy 101f
Popes
    Alexander III 47, 49
    Boniface I 9
    Fabian 28
    Gelasisu I 140
    Gregory the Great 26, 48, 53, 180
    Gregory VII 169
    Gregory IX 47, 70, 76, 78, 91, 96
    Gregory XIII 45
    Honorius 73, 75
    Innocent III 47, 67, 70, 71, 74, 75, 96
    Innocent IV 47, 79f, 83
    Pius IV 45
    Pius V 45
    Pius XII 117, 118
    Soter 8, 9
    Urban II 17, 20, 149
Power of the Keys 71, 73, 82-85, 90, 91ff, 96, 97, 201
Presbytera 7, 21, 22, 48, 57, 69, 79, 83, 88, 95
Presbyteriate 30, 44, 79, 128f, 154
Presbytides see Presbytera
Priest and Priesthood 2, 28, 50, 57, 58, 59, 68, 71, 72, 73, 77, 118, 121-123, 127, 128, 194, 199, 215, 241,

243, 246f
Priestly creation narrative
107ff
Protestants 1f, 250
Pseudo-Isidorian decretals 8-
10, 14, 46, 62, 65, 85, 91,
94, 189

Quedlinburg, abbess of 73f
Quinque Compilationes Antiquae
70

Rahner, Karl 246f
Raymond of Pennaforte 70, 78,
79, 80, 83, 85, 88
Renckens, H. 103, 104, 106
Representation [Stellvertretung]
117-129, 239ff
Robert of Flamesbury 64
Rolandus Bandinelli 49, 50,
53, 54, 56, 64
Roman law 26, 28, 30, 33,
34, 37-44, 49, 50, 54, 57, 62,
64, 66, 67, 75, 84, 85f,
94, 95f, 159, 169, 170ff
Rufinus 50, 51, 53-56, 58, 61,
65, 66, 95, 187

Schmidt, W. H. 100, 101
Schulte, von, J. E. 92
Scripture, interpretation of
103ff
Semmelroth, O. 72, 119, 120,
121
Sexuality 248f
Sicardus 58-60, 188, 189
Simon de Bisiniano 60
Statute Ecclesia Antiqua 14,
15, 17, 19, 20, 46, 94,
145, 146
Stephan of Tournay 54-56, 65,
66
Suhard, Cardinal 103
Summa Monacensis 58, 59
Summa Parisiensis 56f
Synagogues 148
Synods
Laodices 21, 22, 48,
206
Nantes 96

Reims 12
Rouen 12, 143
Trullian 22, 154, 156

Theodore 53
Theodore of Canterbury 48

Van der Meer, Haye 8, 71,
72, 139, 206
Vatican II 1, 13, 20, 72, 78,
118, 122, 123, 125, 135,
141, 151, 203, 243, 251
Veil 58, 59, 83, 84, 88, 112,
147, 185f, 192, 234

Ward, Barbara 151
Weiss, J. 112, 113
Widows 19, 20, 140, 147,
148, 150, 152, 153, 155
Wintersig, A. 121
Women
Contempt of 9, 63, 64,
82, 86f
Derived from man 103,
105f, 107, 111, 112, 114
Evaluation of 6, 28, 32,
133
In the Bible 99ff
Inferiority of, alleged
59, 85, 87, 89, 93, 95, 97,
98, 101, 112, 130
Inherent rights 133, 135
Injustices to 130ff
Menstruation 48, 49, 53,
142, 180, 183
Ordination or consecra-
tion of 22-24, 26-28, 33;
see also Ordination and
consecration
Prohibitions against 8,
10-12, 14, 15, 20, 22, 28,
29, 32, 37, 42, 44, 46, 49,
53, 54, 57-59, 65f, 76, 80,
81, 84, 86, 91, 96, 142f,
147, 149, 151, 153, 159,
193, 196, 206, 208, 219,
235
Subjection of, subordination
of 29-33, 35, 38, 44, 49,
63, 65, 67, 90, 228

Yahwistic Creation Narrative 32,
35, 63, 64, 100-105, 107-109,
111, 114, 115, 208, 224ff